JENNIFER'S MEMOIRS

JENNIFER'S MEMOIRS

Eighty-five Years of Fun
and Functions

BETTY KENWARD

Writer and creator of the original
Jennifer's Diary in *Tatler, Queen* and
Harper's and Queen

HarperCollins*Publishers*

HarperCollins*Publishers*
77–85 Fulham Palace Road
Hammersmith, London W6 8JB

Published by HarperCollins*Publishers* 1992

1 3 5 7 9 10 8 6 4 2

A catalogue record for this book is
available from the British Library

ISBN 0 00 255113 6

Set in Linotron Galliard by
Rowland Phototypesetting Ltd
Bury St Edmunds, Suffolk

Printed in Great Britain by
HarperCollinsManufacturing Glasgow

These memoirs are written in humble gratitude
to Almighty God, in whom I have great faith
and who has given me good health, courage,
and so many loyal and true friends who have helped me
throughout my life.

Acknowledgements

My thanks for certain extracts from articles and certain photographs previously published in *Harpers & Queen* in which the copyright rests with the National Magazine Company Limited, and which are used herein by kind permission of the National Magazine Company Limited. Also thanks to the National Magazine Company for the loan of a word processor and other equipment with which to produce my 'Memoirs'.

My heartfelt thanks to Fleur Tukham and Jinny McLeod-Hatch for giving up their weekend free time to type and check copy; to Jill Sudbury for typing so efficiently, and to Fiona Macpherson for reading the manuscript. Lastly to Juliet Van Oss, for being so patient with me in putting this book together.

Contents

ONE

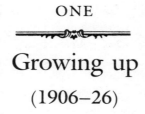

Growing up

(1906–26)

I was born on Bastille Day, 14th July 1906, in Cadogan Gardens. I was the first child of parents who desperately badly wanted a son. As my father was the eldest son of a family that went back to Cardinal Kempe, who was Archbishop of Canterbury and Lord Chancellor of England in the fifteenth century, and so far his brothers and sisters had only produced daughters, a son was all-important.

When I arrived my father accepted the fact that I was a girl and was always loving and kind to me. My mother, who was very pretty, and very immoral, had always been desperately spoilt, and because she had been determined to produce the first boy in the family, never forgave me for being a girl! She took not the slightest interest in me. She would not even choose my name, so my father called me Elizabeth, as his mother wanted a granddaughter of that name. I was never given a second name.

My mother went to Brighton to recuperate from my birth, and I was christened at Rottingdean, as she thought it a good idea that I should be christened quietly in a little country church, with none of the family present. My poor mother was really ashamed of having given birth to a daughter! I fortunately had a very good young nanny called Ethel Durand, who was devoted to me and tried to make up for my mother's lack of love for me, so my early life was quite pleasant.

One year and three weeks later, my mother gave birth to twin sons! There was the greatest rejoicing in the family, as there were as yet still no other boy cousins – and there never were! My beloved twin brothers Peter and George were the only boys born of their generation to carry on my father's family name Kemp-Welch.

Their arrival changed my life considerably. My beloved Nanny had to look after 'the twins', who were rather delicate, and a new undernurse called Mabel arrived to help with me and with general nursery duties. When we went out for walks, Nanny pushed the large double pram with the twins, and Mabel pushed my pram, and later my pushchair. But Nanny still gave me lots of love, and all her spare time.

We had grown out of Cadogan Gardens and soon moved to a house in Surrey, from which it was easy for my father to commute to his London office each day. I have little recollection of that house except the coal cellar.

The reason for this was a temporary nurse, who came to look after us while Nanny was away. The temporary said it was quite unnecessary for Mabel to come out for walks to push me when I was tired, that Mabel must stay at home and do chores in our nurseries, and that I could quite well walk beside the twins' pram. After walking until my rather fat little legs ached like mad, I asked to ride in the middle of the twins' double pram for a while, but she refused, and I was dragged on sobbing. When I arrived home, my legs ached so much, and I decided that I hated the temporary nanny, and that I would run away from her!

I remembered the very dark, rather frightening coal house. I found the door ajar, and I went in there sobbing and sat amongst the coal. I heard voices, so I stopped crying and sat very quietly. I heard my name being called over and over again. Then it was quiet. Then again the voices, my mother, the temporary, Mabel, the cook, and the parlourmaid. Still I kept quiet, though I was rather hungry! I still ached, and I was really determined not to go back to that horrid temporary nanny.

Eventually I heard my father's voice join the others. He was the only one who thought of opening the coal shed door, and when he called my name I at once answered 'Yes Daddy' and stood up. It was now about 7 p.m.; I had been missing for three hours. My father picked me up and carried me into the house triumphantly. I was black all over from the coal dust and I was at once put into a bath, happily by Mabel.

I cannot remember my mother's reaction, but I can remember my father coming up to my bedroom and sitting me on his knee and asking me to tell him why I went and hid. From then on Mabel came for walks with us and put me in my pushchair when I was tired, and she hardly ever let me out of her sight until our beloved Nanny returned. That was the first incident in my life that I remember clearly, although I was not then three years old.

From early childhood we never met or knew our cousins and were told by our mother that Daddy's side of the family were ghastly and she did not want us to have anything to do with them. The truth was that a couple of years after my parents were married, my mother was caught in bed with one of my father's brothers-in-law, and his side of the family would not have her near, or ever speak to her again. Daddy always stood by her loyally.

We lived in Surrey for a couple of years, then returned to London to a large family flat in Kensington Court, which was convenient for us children to be exercised in Kensington Gardens where in those days, to our joy, the old lady with the balloons always stood at the gate. While we were there, I started lessons in the morning with a daily governess called Miss Whelan, who later also taught the twins before they went off to their preparatory school at a very early age.

During this period of living in London I saw a lot of my father, and really got to know and love him. When I was six or seven he would take me out with him. I went racing with him, and even to a first night of a musical comedy, when my mother cried off at the last moment with a headache. It was through my father that I got to know so many well-known people by sight, which was to be invaluable to me later in life.

In 1914, when I was eight years old, my mother decided, because of the war, that we should go and share a house with a widower with one child, a daughter years younger than I was, in Warwickshire, and that Daddy should have a bachelor service flat, and his club in London, and come to Warwickshire at weekends and share the expenses.

The widower, who was a good horseman, soon became my mother's boyfriend, which of course at our age my brothers and I did not realize. The nursery-schoolroom quarters at the house in Warwickshire were away from the main part of the house, with their own staircase, and as I was told I must stay in this wing I seldom saw my mother. I had a daily governess from the village called Miss Webb, and there was a children's maid.

At first my father came down most weekends, and always took me out riding and walking and came up to my schoolroom for a card game or to play Pelmanism or draughts before bedtime. But over the years his visits became less and less frequent, and in time he of course found girlfriends in London.

My mother suddenly started going racing in Ireland quite often, and after a while she had two or three horses in training on the flat there, in spite of always saying how poor we were! Trainers then only charged two pounds ten shillings a week to train a horse!

My dear Webbie, who bicycled up from the village, knew how much
I loved riding and going out with the hounds in winter, so when the
hounds were meeting anywhere near, she always found some excuse
why she could not come to teach me that day! Off I went to the meet
on my pony, often staying out far later than I should, with a long ride
home.

No one ever checked where I was. The children's maid and the
grooms knew I had taken my pony to the meet, but no one else
enquired. My supper was brought to the schoolroom and the children's
maid saw that I went to bed. In those days I lived for the school
holidays when my brothers were home, especially the summer holidays
when we went to our grandparents.

The greatest joy in the lives of the twins and me from when we were
tiny was our annual summer visit to our step-grandfather and our
beloved maternal grandmother, General Sir George and Lady Greaves,
in South Wales. When we were very young we were put in the train
at Paddington accompanied by Nanny and Mabel, and a large hamper
for luncheon. It was in those days quite a long journey with a very
frightening long spell underground in the dark smelly Severn Tunnel.
This always terrified me and made me feel rather sick!

On arrival at Saundersfoot station in Pembrokeshire, we would find
Granny waiting for us on the platform, always in a well-cut dress or
suit, a straw hat, and, invariably, with a feather boa round her shoulders. She kissed the three of us with real love and affection, before we
all proceeded out of the station. There, waiting for us, was the head
groom, Willie Davies, in his dark blue coat with brass buttons, white
breeches, top boots, and a black top hat with a cockade, standing
beside Granny's very smart dogcart, drawn by her bay cob called Gay.
Also waiting for us was another groom with a horse-drawn waggonette
to take the rest of the party, which comprised Nanny, Mabel, and the
twins, with all the luggage.

Granny got up into her seat and took the reins, then I was lifted up
beside her, and Davies jumped up behind, and off we went at a fast
trot to Netherwood, a distance of about a mile. As we entered the high
wrought-iron gates of the tree-lined drive, and I heard the steel-rimmed
wheels of the dogcart crunch on the gravel, my heart throbbed with
excitement and joy! Here we were at last, for a few weeks of real
freedom and love.

My step-grandfather, called 'Dod', was always at the front door to
meet us. He had been a great soldier. He had a very fiery temper and

a bushy white moustache, and we were in awe of him though he always spoilt us. He had spent all his life in the army, finishing up as Lieutenant-General and Commander-in-Chief and a Member of the Council of the Government of Bombay. He received a KCMG in 1881, a KCB in 1885, and the GCB on his retirement in 1896, when he was also made a full General.

Dod's first wife died in 1880 without any children. He remained a widower until my grandmother's first husband, an army surgeon called Major William Venour (our grandfather), who was on Dod's staff in India, died. Dod and Granny were married in April 1903.

In 1896 Dod bought Netherwood. It was a pretty, rather rambling house (now a boarding school) with a distant view of the sea, lots of stables, a dairy, and outbuildings, ideal for us children for hide and seek and so on. There was a large acreage of rough shooting, and wonderful walks with superb wild flowers. As we grew older, we could ride around without going on to anyone else's property.

Dod farmed the land just to provide the house with fresh milk, cream, butter that was churned twice a week by Brace the cowman, chickens, eggs, and hams. The garden also produced masses of fruit and vegetables. All the outdoor staff were provided with milk and wood off the estate and many other 'perks', as was the custom in those days. The sea and the lovely sandy beach at Saundersfoot were about half a mile away, and down there Dod had a boathouse with a lawn all around, where his successful racing yacht *Holly*, designed by Dixon Kemp, and two other smaller boats were housed in the winter.

In the summer, with its folding chairs and tables, the boathouse made a splendid beach house for us. Nanny used to set out our picnic lunch, brought down from the house by Willie Davies. Willie always opened up the boathouse for us. As we grew older, and once Nanny had married and left us, we arranged our own picnics here, still with the help of Willie Davies, and we were then often joined by young friends who lived in the neighbourhood. We spent our summer holidays here until 1922, when Dod died.

Granny then sold Netherwood and the boathouse to her neighbour the 2nd Lord Merthyr, and she went to live in a much smaller house with no land, just above Saundersfoot village.

My childhood was not really a very happy one, and in a way a rather lonely and insecure and unreliable one. Although I was always provided with comfortable living quarters, a governess, ponies that changed, as they would be sold quite frequently by my mother at a profit, and my beloved dogs, I had little parental love. My parents, who never got divorced, both lived very separate lives until they got together again in their old age. I began to make my own friends quite young. Some of these, I realized in later life, took pity on me, and invited me to stay and have fun with their families. Sometimes I was landed on neighbours, who usually had my pony as well!!

During term time, from time to time my mother would suddenly want me out of the way and I would be sent to kind neighbours for a few days or longer. Mr and Mrs Joshua Fielden – he was Joint Master of the Warwickshire Hounds with the 19th Lord Willoughby de Broke from 1911 to 1924 – would often have me to stay at Kineton House. They had a daughter, Joan, who was a little older than I was, who also had a governess.

Lord and Lady Willoughby de Broke, who were then living at Compton Verney, were also angelic to me. I used to ride up to Compton Verney, tie my pony up to something solid, walk into the big hall and call for Lady Willoughby de Broke, who always found time to come and talk to me. I would probably have tea with her, or if it was early there were sweets, but always a welcome.

Earlier in my childhood I had been sent on several occasions to visit 'Aunt Emily', a distant old married cousin of my mother, who lived with her husband and daughter at Weybridge. I dreaded going there as it was an icy cold house, and I was made to have my bath at night, and to come downstairs at 7.45 a.m. for before-breakfast 'prayers' which were attended by all the staff. I never went to stay with Aunt Emily, or her family, when I grew up.

When I was eleven my mother wanted to get me right out of the way, as I was growing up and complicating her life. So, without any explanation, she packed me off to Granny and Dod in Wales, happily with my pony and my dogs! By now my step-grandfather was in his eighties, and Granny in her seventies. She was, like my mother, very beautiful, but since a bad attack of measles when sixteen, she was stone deaf and carried a trumpet you spoke into (there were no hearing aids then). Granny always had two Pomeranian dogs with her who barked at everyone, so warned her when anyone was approaching. They did not take too kindly to my Pekinese and Jack Russell terrier, but they settled down.

I stayed there for well over a year, with my beloved twin brothers joining me every school holiday.

By now it was the last year of the First World War. I had absolutely no lessons during that period! But Granny, being very practical, and seeing that my stay might be a long one, taught me in the afternoons to sew. She was a beautiful needlewoman. She also made me work jolly hard in the mornings! Twice a week I spent the morning with the parlourmaid, learning to clean silver – they had given up a butler soon after the outbreak of war – and learning how to lay a dinner table, how to fold napkins and so on. The other four mornings I spent in the kitchen, where the cook, who was old and unmarried but was always known as Mrs Jones, was very strict! I had to be there punctually at 8.30 a.m., having had my breakfast alone in the dining room. I was put to work really hard, then she allowed me ten minutes before luncheon to change and tidy myself for lunch in the dining room with my grandparents. I learnt to roast and to boil birds and beasts, to pluck and draw chickens and game, to clean and fillet and cook fish, to paunch, skin and cook a rabbit, to make scones and cakes, to make sauces and gravies, and even to thoroughly scrub the red tiled floor in the kitchen! I also learnt to make butter in a hand-turned churn.

All of this was to prove useful to me later in life, for even if I did not actually have to do it myself, I was able to teach a cook, who would have more respect for you if you really knew about everything from first-hand experience. I only wish I had also been made to do one morning a week with the housemaid, as I have never learnt to clean a room, so I hate housework! I was also taught by the gardener how to make wreaths. These were always made at home, for locals who had died, and in the winter greenhouse flowers were used.

During the period I spent with my grandparents in Wales, the great flu epidemic started and a record number of people died. As she could not get around herself, my grandmother would send me off on my pony to visit the families of some of the sick, often taking butter and eggs or a can of good home-made soup strapped to my saddle.

On one of these visits I was very scared. It was at the postman's house where, when I arrived, they were all in tears, the young daughter of about ten years having died that morning. The mother asked me if I would like to come and see her. Being very frightened at the idea of seeing someone dead, I said I could not leave my pony, but someone quickly came forward to hold my pony, and I was taken upstairs. It was the first time I had seen anyone dead, and I dreamt about it for weeks.

The village church was not very far away; we always walked there along a gravel path through a wood. At one period I would go and look to see if a grave was being dug and, if so, would slip away in the afternoon and attend the funeral until I was caught doing this and forbidden to go to any more funerals except with my grandmother.

When I was twelve and a half years old and the war was over, my mother decided I should go to a finishing school in Brussels! So on a cold January morning, after spending the night in London staying with two old step-sisters of my father who I met for the first time, I said goodbye to my dear father at Victoria station, and boarded the boat-train for Folkestone, accompanied by a mistress and a few other girls.

I was very sad at leaving my father, and rather frightened at the prospect of any form of school. Yet I was excited at having my own passport, and to be crossing the English Channel for the first time. We went from Folkestone to Ostend by boat, and then up to Brussels by train.

Les Tourelles, as my finishing school was called, was in Avenue Longchamp, and was run by a rather chubby, good-hearted Belgian lady called Mademoiselle Delstanche, and a quiet and very charming, well-groomed American called Miss Tungate, which proved a splendid combination. It was a comfortable house with central heating and hot and cold water in every bedroom, and plenty of bathrooms. These bedrooms were either single or double, and downstairs the rooms were just like a private house. Today Les Tourelles is a small hotel. I cannot remember our classrooms, but I am sure they were luxurious too.

We had only one hour of English subjects daily which had to cover history, literature, geography, mathematics and compositions, with no homework! We were also taught music (I had had music lessons since I was six, with little success), dressmaking, French literature, and, most important, the French language. We were taken to the opera and concerts and to classic French plays to hear French well spoken. Our art tuition included visiting endless museums and galleries.

Each week we also had a session of invaluable instruction, by the American, Miss Tungate, on deportment, hygiene, care of our hair, make-up and how to use it, how to present ourselves to the best advantage, and how to put on clothes and to wear them. To me, at twelve and a half years of age and straight from the depths of Wales, this was a new world! At first I think very little sank in, but it did in due course, and much of it came back to me in later years, for which I have always been grateful.

I was treated as a sort of freak by the other girls, as I was nearly four years younger than the youngest girl there. I was rather spoilt by the two heads, who were sure I would be homesick, and therefore a problem. They did not know my background and very strange home life! I soon got to know Mademoiselle Delstanche and Miss Tungate extremely well, and I came to respect and grow fond of them both.

My mother had decided against my coming home for the Easter holidays, as she said it would unsettle me! So I stayed, with one other girl whose parents were in the Far East. We spent three weeks being taken around Belgium sightseeing, with a week at the sea at Le Zoute, where I had my first golf lessons, and I bought my first set of golf clubs, a present from my father.

By the first of July, I had grown up a lot, and I arrived in Warwickshire wearing high heels and nail varnish, which was of course immediately forbidden.

I was very happy at Les Tourelles. My only setback came at the beginning of the third term. I had made great friends with a very nice English girl who lived with her uncle and aunt as her parents were dead. Her uncle was a Master of Hounds, so we had a lot in common over hunting and horses, and Bunty and I had asked to share a room that term.

When she arrived back, she told me very sweetly that her aunt would not let her share a room with me, as she knew of my mother, and that my mother was living with a man who was not her husband. I was very shattered, as I knew little of the facts of life. It was a sharp lesson, but it made me realize early on what a lot high standards meant in life.

At the end of the summer term, two and a half years later, when I was then just fifteen years old, I was taken ill soon after I arrived back at a different house in Warwickshire. This was one my mother and her boyfriend had moved to, one he had had built near the house my mother was building.

The doctors diagnosed that I had appendicitis, but as my mother was absolutely against all operations it was agreed I should be carefully dieted and that I might grow out of it. For years I suffered appendicitis attacks, sometimes in agony and doubled up with pain.

Owing to the diet that I was to undergo, I was not allowed to return to Brussels but was kept at home, which was an unhappy experience. By now, my brothers and I realized we had no security in our lives, and, compared with our friends, it seemed to us, very little money. I suppose this was because my mother was pretty extravagant, and my father's girlfriends very demanding!

My brothers were now at school. They were originally down for Eton, where my father and two uncles went to school, but my mother stopped them going there. As our Uncle Martin had been at Charterhouse, they were sent there. My brothers spent their holidays more and more with school friends.

To live a lonely country life in Warwickshire after my happy sojourn in Brussels was frustrating. I was made to work in the house, and still I had no tuition except useless music lessons. I spent all my spare time riding, and when possible hunting.

One morning during this period, Commander Colin Buist, who in later years I knew quite well, telephoned to ask if he could bring the Duke of York over to try a horse that my mother's boyfriend had for sale. They came to try the horse in the morning, and stayed for luncheon, at which there were just the five of us. His Royal Highness, as he was then, was so sweet and kind to me at luncheon. I cannot remember now if he bought the horse!

In June the following year, when I was nearly sixteen, my mother, who had the strangest ideas, thought I should go on the stage! I was very plain to look at, I could not act, sing or play any instrument, so what gave her this idea I will never know. In spite of my reluctance and my fear (I had a great inferiority complex), my mother was adamant, and arranged an audition for me at the Winter Garden Theatre.

I was sent to London by train with the address and name of whoever she had contacted and told to go in a taxi straight to the theatre. They seemed to expect me, and after a short while I was asked to go on the stage with full lights on. The curtain was up on an empty house, except for a few people connected with the forthcoming production, which was to be a musical.

When I got on the stage I learnt that stages were not flat, but sloped considerably towards the audience. I must have been the oddest sight that any of these dear theatre people had ever seen! They were so kind to me, patiently asking me about my acting abilities, which I said were nil, the same with my singing and dancing. At the end of this short interlude they gently said that they would let me know if there was a place for me.

Filled with mortification at this terrible episode, I took a taxi to Claridge's to lunch with my father. He was horrified to hear what I had been through, and I think he quietly hoped he did not know anyone at the audition! I went back to Warwickshire that afternoon and told my mother that I was definitely not going on the stage!

After this I decided to run away from home and to find some sort of work. I packed a few things into a suitcase and got up very early to walk to Kineton station, well over a mile away, and caught a train around 8 a.m. for London. There I took a taxi, as I had no idea of how to find my way anywhere in London. I went straight to William Street in Knightsbridge, to the home of a distant cousin of my grandmother's, called Miss Peter Green, whom I had met and liked.

She had a hat shop, which was a very unusual thing to own in those days. I got to the door, paid for my taxi, and with my suitcase walked up to her flat on the second floor, above the hat shop on the first floor, where she had once invited Granny and me to tea.

The flat had its own entrance. Happily for me she was at home. The look of amazement when she saw me was funny, and even funnier when I blurted out at once 'I have run away from home and I have come to work for you in your hat shop.' She was about forty-five years old then, and very understanding.

After a short discussion she told me I could sleep on the sofa in her sitting room that night, and that I should let my dress down, and also go out and get a packet of hairpins to put my long hair up. Like that, I could start in the workroom and showroom next day. I was not to tell the other girls that I was any relation, or how old I was.

My dear spinster cousin soon found me a bedroom in a very respectable hostel for young ladies where we could have bed and breakfast. My salary was just enough to pay for that, but with my luncheon, and fares, there was little over! I telephoned my father that evening, and told him I had run away, and where I was, and I asked him not to tell my mother as I was afraid she would come and make a row and insist on my going home. He did of course tell her as she was quite worried, but somehow he persuaded her to leave me alone.

The head milliner and the other two girls were very kind to me, and my being able to sew was a great asset, but I spent more time in the showroom than the workroom. I shall always remember the excitement of selling my first hat! Many of the clients were friends of my elderly cousin, who was a great character with a lovely sense of humour. Her rather pompous brother, Charles Green, had just been made a bishop and wrote to her, putting underneath his signature 'Bishop elect', whereupon she immediately replied and under her signature put 'Milliner established'.

In those days Peter Green kept a very firm eye on me, and if I was not spending the weekend with friends she would not leave me alone in London but would take me with her to her cottage at Fulmer, where she always entertained amusing and interesting people. Later, when she was in her fifties, she married a very dear widower with no children called Richard Morten, who owned the very pretty old Hills House in Denham, where they lived blissfully happily until he died. On being widowed Peter sold Hills House, and built a smaller one opposite which she called Dickfield House. I was always so grateful to Peter Morten for rescuing me from my mother. Years later, when she was dying of cancer, I went up and down to Denham from London, where I was working, to be with her several times a week. I was with her when she died at the age of seventy-five. She very sweetly left me a cottage, which I never had time to use and sold to a friend of Peter Morten's in the end, for about sixpence!

When I ran away from home, I refused any financial help from my father other than the dress allowance he had always given me. I was determined to be independent. After a few weeks I received a letter from him telling me he had opened an account at Harrods in my name, which he would pay. He explained that at Harrods I could buy food, clothes or a railway ticket! This was very sweet of him, but my pride would not let me use it at the time.

I worked very hard and happily in the hat shop for well over a year. I earned extra money by delivering hats after working hours, which also provided a wonderful way of learning my way around London. In the following autumn I got measles very badly, then on top of that jaundice. I was really ill, and so weak I could hardly walk.

Eventually my father took me away to Brighton to recuperate, and during that time he said he would rent a flat or house in London, if I would run it for him. This I agreed to do, so I left the hat shop and we had two good live-in maids. My father's girlfriends happily never came there, and in due course I think rather faded out!

My brothers, who were still at public school, stayed there quite frequently in the holidays, and we had our friends around us and a really happy home for the first time in our lives. My mother appeared on the scene at intervals, but never for more than a night or two. During most of the twenties I again did a lot with my father and I met many interesting people. I also somehow made a number of my own friends and was invited out, and away to stay, quite frequently.

When I was still in my teens I met Miss Barbara Cartland, who was five years older than I was, through her brother Ronald Cartland, who was then at Charterhouse with my brothers. He was a very dear young man, who had started what might have been a brilliant political career, had he not been killed in World War II. Barbara seemed absolutely fabulous to me in those days! She used to tell me of some of the romantic episodes going on in her life, usually involving a duke, or at least an earl! Her imagination used to carry her away and I lapped up every word she spoke. I have often since then wondered if I was a sort of trial run for the secretaries to whom she dictates her vastly successful novels from a chaise longue each afternoon.

In the mid-twenties, my father bought me the first of two good show hacks which I kept at Windsor with a Mr Stillwell; I went down every morning to ride out on Windsor racecourse, and to have tuition in show riding from him. I still managed to get several days' hunting in the Midlands each season with kind friends who mounted me. I watched a lot of polo at Hurlingham, which was of a very high standard in those days, as all the young officers in the cavalry regiments played polo. In spite of getting up early to ride, I went dancing nearly every night, either at the Berkeley, the Café de Paris, Ciros or the original Embassy Club, which then was very chic. I met my first serious love when I was around eighteen years of age. He was up at Cambridge, rode well, and raced fast cars. This was a very happy period in my life; and it was enjoyable running a home for my father and my brothers, whom I adored.

In the mid-twenties, my brother Peter went up to Cambridge, and the other, George, started working at Schweppes, which had originally been nearly a family firm. Having completed three years going through every department, from bottle washing, lorry driving and delivery to administration, George was given three years off to go up to Cambridge too.

The elder twin, Peter, played real tennis and rackets for Cambridge, and he also played rackets for England, twice in both America and Canada. When George went up to Cambridge, he got a blue for cricket and for soccer, and captained the Cambridge soccer eleven. I believe they were the first twins to get double blues. George later played cricket for Warwickshire, and twice went to the West Indies with the late Lord Tennyson's cricket eleven. I was so proud of them.

This very happy period of my life was not to last. By about 1925 my mother's visits to the flat were becoming more frequent. She had finally quarrelled with her boyfriend in Warwickshire, and decided to come and spend more time with us and take over! My father was never strong enough to stand up to my mother. She at once said I must have a job! My mother arranged that I, and another girl, who was more trained than I was, should start a beauty parlour in Bond Street! This was duly opened one summer and I absolutely hated it! But my mother, for whom it seemed to open up a new world and way of life, soon wanted to run it herself anyway. The following January, when I was invited to join a party of friends for a skiing holiday in Switzerland, she took over my half, and ran it successfully for many years. My original partner retired soon after my mother joined.

My grandmother wanted to present me at court when I was nearly nineteen but my mother firmly refused to let her! I always regretted this, but there was nothing I could do to persuade my mother, and even my grandmother was frightened of her!

A most exciting week for me and many of my contemporaries was the General Strike in the summer of 1926. We all immediately volunteered to do our bit. One of my brothers went to the docks at Dover as a porter, and the other one worked on a milk train from Cambridge to London. Our friends drove or conducted buses and trains. I, driving my little snub-nose two-seater Morris, joined others on Horse Guards Parade at Whitehall, where, round the clock, there were cars of all makes and sizes – including racing cars and limousines – waiting for instructions to drive someone or something to any part of the United Kingdom at a moment's notice. We slept and ate when we could. It was for us most exciting, and we all felt we were doing something worthwhile. Cars the size of my little Morris were kept to the London area, where we had some scary moments from demonstrators, especially in the suburbs.

Some of the cars would return with windscreens smashed or the body of the car battered. My car was never damaged, but I did have a cauliflower with a spanner taped to it thrown into it, just missing my head by inches. This made our week more exciting, and I know many of us, very irresponsibly, were rather sorry when the strike was over!

In the late twenties my parents and I met a very nice and kind couple who were then quite prominent in the racing world. I went to stay at their country home, and they invited me to go racing with them, and often to parties, during which time I also made friends with his daughter by his first marriage.

Then suddenly one day a bill from Goodes for china was sent to me in error, instead of to my mother. From this I learnt that the husband of this couple was having a rip-roaring affair with my mother! He had given her a flat in Mayfair, which she'd decorated at his expense, regardless of cost. The discovery of this liaison was a real shock. I found it utterly sordid and did not know how to deal with it. I did not know if my father knew, or if the lover's wife knew. So after a lot of thinking I decided to keep dead quiet about it, except to sort out the bill with Goodes!

To this day I don't think my father ever realized the situation clearly. I hope he didn't. The wife, of course, got to know and the situation was very tense for a while; then it all died down eventually, when the affair waned after several years.

I still see his very sweet daughter from time to time. We never discussed or referred to the affair. Perhaps she never knew about it.

TWO

Marriage and the start of war

(1927–40)

During the late twenties I became friends with the famous author and playwright Edgar Wallace and his family. His elder daughter Patricia was a contemporary of mine, and we were great friends. On a Saturday night I often used to go with them to the theatre, where one of his plays would be running. Then, after the theatre, we would motor down to the Wallaces' riverside home at Bourne End for the rest of the weekend. Here we might be joined for a late supper by producers, actors and actresses, and sometimes by trainers and jockeys. We would usually sit up talking until 2 or 3 a.m. Some would stay the night, others go on home. On Sundays, there would always be a large luncheon party, often with more guests, all of them interesting. Then 'Crazy', as Edgar Wallace was fondly known by many friends, would get into his small electric launch, with only two or three others, and quietly glide up and down the Thames. It was the only time I remember seeing him relax. I spent quite a few weekends there, and I always enjoyed myself.

Early in September 1929, I went to a party at the Mayfair Hotel given by Edgar Wallace and his wife 'Jim'. The party was a farewell one before the Wallaces set off the following week for three months in America, where he was to attend business meetings about producing his plays and films in America; he was also going to look for copy for his thrillers in the famous American prison Sing Sing.

I had recently decided not to marry the love of my life, whom I have already mentioned, mainly because my brothers thought he was too much of a playboy! When I told him I would not marry him he said 'Then I will never marry'. He never did marry, and sadly he was killed in the first autumn of the Second World War while on active service.

As I said goodbye to my host and hostess, I said how much I envied Pat Wallace going on this trip. Edgar Wallace quickly replied 'Come with us! I will ring your father in the morning.' Within a week I had an American visa, and I sailed with the Wallace family! They had the Royal Suite on the Cunard liner *Berengaria*, at that time Cunard's newest ship. Pat Wallace and I shared a first-class cabin, and we never had a cross word, probably thanks to her more than me! We have been friends all our lives.

Not only was there Edgar Wallace and his wife Jim, and their young daughter Penny, and his son Bryan Wallace, who, like Pat, was by his first marriage, but there were also a valet, ladies' maid, and secretaries and so on. We younger members of the party had a marvellous time joining in all the fun of the ship, and dancing late into each night.

Dear Edgar Wallace worked the whole way over to New York. At that time he was not only writing thrillers as fast as he could, but was also writing another play; he already had one running in the West End. Amazingly, too, he was also writing a daily racing column for the *Star* evening paper!

During this voyage, the great Wall Street Crash started. The Captain had all the news tapes stopped as he feared suicides among the passengers. Happily no one took this drastic step.

We stayed in two large apartments at the Marguery Hotel (no longer in existence) on Park Avenue, which was extremely comfortable with a good restaurant downstairs. The restaurant, I believe, still exists. During this period, while with the Wallaces, I met many interesting personalities from the theatrical, publishing, racing and even the criminal world. Edgar Wallace would sometimes have an ex-convict round for a talk – all made copy for his books! I remember him being away rather mysteriously for a couple of days, and we heard afterwards that he had been going round the underworld and prisons! Of course under police protection.

During that visit to New York, Pat and I were several times taken to dine out at what is now the 21 Club. In those days of Prohibition it was called Jack & Charlie's. On arrival you had to knock three times, were looked at through a small grid, and if you were recognized or had the right password were let in.

One weekend we were staying at a country club, where George Gershwin was also a guest. After dinner on the Saturday night George Gershwin sat down at the piano and played to about ten of us for a couple of hours. It was enchanting. He was a fascinating and rather shy man to meet, and played the piano as well as he composed, quite beautifully. We were all spellbound!

During my visit to New York I was at the Horse Show in Madison

Square Gardens with friends called Stewart-Richardson, an English husband and an American wife, when I was suddenly taken ill. It was one of my appendicitis attacks! I was taken back to my friends' apartment, where their doctor said I must be operated on as soon as possible. So, with the agreement of Edgar and Jim Wallace, I was taken to the Presbyterian Hospital at the Medical Centre, and operated on that evening. My mother was told only after my operation!

I was very disappointed and upset at this happening to me, as that week I was to have gone on with the Wallaces to Hollywood, which I know would have been a great experience.

In those days you were kept in hospital for two or three weeks after an operation. When I came out it was time to go home for Christmas, as I had always promised to do. So I sailed home alone, in the Cunard liner *Homeric*.

On the return voyage from America I met a couple called Mr and Mrs Guthrie Cooper. They invited me to stay for a weekend in the New Year, and invited Guthrie's cousin Peter Kenward, who was, like myself, very keen on riding and hunting. Peter was then in the 14th/ 20th Hussars, who were stationed at Hounslow, so it was easy for us to meet. I was soon taken down to meet and then to stay with his parents, who lived at Preston House, Preston Candover, which they had bought in 1927, with a big acreage which they added to considerably with very good shooting. The following winter I was often invited for shooting parties. When they bought Preston House they spent thousands on it both inside and outside. Sadly they had suffered badly from the Hatry and world financial crash of 1929–33 and eventually had to sell Preston House very cheaply to Colonel Miles Courage, complete with all its beautiful curtains and carpets, and some of their lovely furniture.

During this time I also saw a lot of Mr and Mrs Alan Butler. I had known Lois Butler, who was a Newfoundlander and daughter of Sir Robert Reid, since I was seventeen as she was a friend of Peter Green. Lois was at that time a young widow with a little daughter. She had been married to Colonel Hugh Knox-Niven, uncle of David Niven.

Through Lois, I got to know David Niven and his sister, Grizel, and his mother, Lady Comyn-Platt. Lois soon married her second husband Alan Butler, for many years Chairman of de Havilland Aircraft, a firm that he had saved financially as a very young man. Alan not only piloted his own aeroplane, but also owned one of the big yachts of the day, called *Sylvia* after his sister. It infuriated him that I would not ever fly in his aeroplane. I had a horror of flying, which I did not overcome for many years.

Alan and Lois very kindly invited me to stay with them for Cowes week two years running in the late twenties. One year we were moored next to *Elettra*, the fine yacht owned by Marchese Guglielmo Marconi, who one day invited Alan and Lois and their guests on board *Elettra*. Little did I realize then what an honour it was to meet this man who had changed the world with his discovery in 1895 that radio waves could be used for communication, and in 1901 that they could go round the world! Even in the 1920s he was full of what further generations might yet achieve through the air! My recollection of Marchese Marconi was of a dedicated man, whose eyes sparkled as he talked about long and short waves, and 'harnessing' them; that was the word he used. He was, I well remember, immaculate in yachting clothes of white flannels and navy blue blazer; I think he was fairly good looking, and he was certainly, for me, full of charm!

Lois and Alan Butler, while in no way flamboyant, did things very comfortably, and each August they rented a house at Bembridge where their son and daughter stayed with a Norland nurse and good staff. While the children enjoyed Bembridge's sandy beach with all the other children and nannies, their parents lived on board *Sylvia* so that they were near enough to spend time with their children and also for Alan to commute by air to de Havillands — Bembridge already had a small airfield at this time.

I also used to see quite a lot of Romaine Combe, a most amusing and very attractive girl, who always told me she was determined to marry well, as her cousin, then Duchess of Sutherland, had done.

Romaine had several very eligible boyfriends including Sim Feversham, the 3rd Earl of Feversham, to whom we all thought she would soon become engaged. Then suddenly she rang me one morning and said she had met Robin Castlereagh, who was now the 'love of her life'! His mother, then Marchioness of Londonderry, was one of England's greatest hostesses, famous for her Eve of the Opening of Parliament parties at Londonderry House, and a very formidable lady! In 1931 Robin Castlereagh, who became the 8th Marquess of Londonderry in 1949, and Romaine Combe were married and I went to their wedding.

I was married a year later in 1932. As a result of his parents' financial crash, Peter Kenward had had to leave the regiment early that year and start working in a branch of the Kenward & Court Brewery, of which his father, who had made a fortune in brewing, was Chairman. Peter had never been brought up to do a day's work, so it was very hard for him to start now.

My brothers both implored me not to marry Peter, partly because of his drinking, and partly because he had no idea about a serious working career, but I would not listen.

Peter and I were married in June at St Margaret's, Westminster. Ours was a large wedding – I had ten bridesmaids and two pages, and there were several hundred guests. My mother insisted on this. Although she arranged for my wedding dress to be made by a designer friend, my mother never saw it until I went up the aisle! Lois Butler helped me and came to the fittings, and helped choose the bridesmaids' dresses. Her son David was a page and her daughters Betty and Carol were bridesmaids. The reception was held at the Mayfair Hotel, and Ambrose and his band, the top dance band of the thirties, played at it – Ambrose's wedding present to me! We had a ten-day honeymoon in the New Forest, and then we went to live in the village hotel at Lydd in Kent (Peter started to work at the Kenward & Court brewery there), until we could find a house.

While we were there, David Niven, who was then in the army and on a course at Lydd, often came in to see us. We eventually rented, furnished, the very old Vine House in Lydd village with its lovely walled garden, which still stands there today. My son Jim was born at Vine House the following year. Romaine rang to congratulate me, but I also remember her saying that it was not fair my having a son first time, when it didn't matter for me whether it was a boy or girl! She had given birth to her daughter Jane, now Lady Rayne, the previous year; two years later she had a second daughter, Annabel, now Lady Annabel Goldsmith; then happily the present Marquess of Londonderry was born, in 1937.

During the thirties, when I lived quietly in Kent, and during the war, I rather lost touch with my pre-marriage friends. I did see Romaine a few times after the war at their Park Street home, then sadly she died, far too young, of cancer in 1951.

In 1934 it was decided my husband should work at the Kenward & Court brewery at Hadlow, also in Kent, and we moved to a much larger Georgian-type house that belonged to the brewery. Jim's first nanny, who came from Lydd, got married when he was eleven months old – she still keeps in touch with me – and I got another young nanny, who also eventually married, but not until Jim was nearly six years old and already had a daily governess.

In those days in Hadlow, I was lucky in having a cook, a daily housemaid, and a parlourmaid.

After I got married I always had my breakfast in bed. I had never seen my grandmother or my mother get up for breakfast, so I thought once you got married it meant breakfast in bed!

At Hadlow, because I had a good staff, I was free to help with the local Conservatives, the Women's Institute, and other aspects of village life. I also gardened a lot, and entertained in a quiet way.

I was very happy and contented living this quiet country life, my one anxiety being that my husband was drinking heavily. Peter had often got drunk before we were married. Being young and inexperienced, I imagined these lapses to be the result of the bad falls he had suffered while hunting and racing. Once he gave up racing and riding, I thought his head would get stronger. This was, alas, not the case.

Eventually, after we'd been married four to five years, I began to learn through my son's nanny, who always knew the local gossip, that he was also unfaithful!

In 1938 I could bear his drinking and his absences no longer. After one twenty-four-hour absence, when I had been unable to cancel a small dinner party for rather new neighbours, Peter appeared in the middle of dinner, very drunk, with a bottle under each arm saying 'Hello everyone, here I am with my babies.' I was shattered, as I had excused him and had said that he had had to go to London suddenly on business. The guests thought it quite funny, but I nearly died of embarrassment.

Shortly afterwards, after consulting my father and my father- and mother-in-law, I took Jim and Nanny to London, to a tiny flat in North Court, Chelsea. I took a job with *Vogue*, running their Enquiry Desk, to keep myself occupied and to pay Nanny's wages.

My year with *Vogue* was at first a great strain and very worrying. I worked in a very glamorous office, and as I had been living in the country for so long I felt absolutely out of the swing of things. Once again, my friends came to my rescue. I rang everyone I thought could help in their line, asking which were the best places to lunch, to dine, to dance, what were the best current exhibitions, where were the best places to buy old silver, porcelain, antiques and so on, and consulted the fashion department on where I should direct people for clothes. In no time I had got a very comprehensive card index, and I felt more confident. About a year back, they had inserted a little note in American *Vogue*, the gist of which was 'All readers of *Vogue* visiting London and wanting to know where to go for all the things mentioned in it should go and visit the *Vogue* office in London where they will get the best advice'. Up to then this had not been advice of a very high standard; they had fired several of my predecessors. I saw quite a lot of firing all round in my first week or two, and I wondered how long I would last! Once I had got my Enquiry Desk running, the whole job was great fun, and I learnt a lot and laughed a lot.

Miss Betty Penrose was the editor. She rather burnt the candle both ends and was not in her office very early, but she had a brilliant eye for what 'looked' good in *Vogue*. Betty Penrose was fortunate in having the most wonderfully loyal and intelligent number two called Miss Audrey Withers, who was always in early, and could deal with any situation. When Betty Penrose returned to America to edit another Condé Nast magazine, Audrey took over and made an excellent editor of *Vogue* for many years. They had a wonderful team then with Anne Scott-James and Lesley Blanche in charge of features, Madge Garland, later Lady Ashton, and Nina Leclerque, on the fashion side. They of course used all the best American, French, and English photographers and artists. The American Mr Condé Nast was still alive in those days; he came in to my office on one of his London visits about three weeks after I had started at *Vogue*. He wanted me to organize a dinner party for him as he was alone, and gave me the names of his guests. This was apparently a success, so on every visit I saw him or heard from him with some request or other. Once or twice his request was to cancel some date he had made – not always so easy! – then to arrange something else. Sadly, as he was a great character, I never saw him again after I left *Vogue*. I was always interested that Condé Nast had each issue of English *Vogue* meticulously marked up with who had been responsible for every page or article, every photograph or drawing, and how much each one had cost. This had to be sent to him personally in New York, so he had his hand right on the pulse of English *Vogue*. I sometimes volunteered to help with the marking, as it was so interesting to me too.

My one bugbear while I worked for *Vogue* was the 'knitting' page. I had been taught by my grandmother to sew, but I had never learnt to knit, and I know nothing about the art except that if you drop stitches it is a disaster. *Vogue* published a photograph of a very pretty bed jacket, and with it the details of how to make it. The snag was that there was a big fault in those directions! The knitting side of the magazine was for some reason, I never knew why, somewhere near Fleet Street, not in the Burlington Gardens office of *Vogue*. Knitters did not know this, and they used to arrive in my Enquiry Office with their half-knitted garment and expect me to put them right. They were furious when I could not help them and when I sent them on somewhere else. Some were quite abusive and difficult to get rid of politely, so you can imagine how my heart sank when I saw them coming in to my lovely office, with their brown paper parcels.

I did this from within London for several months, then, because of pressure from my dear in-laws and Peter's promise to reform, I returned to Hadlow with Jim and Nanny. I also thought that it was a better life for Jim to live in the country with his pony and dogs than in a small London flat.

However, I kept on my job with *Vogue* for some months, until war was imminent in 1939, and commuted from Tonbridge by train daily. I had decided that the strain of entertaining was too much, so cut it all out. I made a point of trying to get home in time to see Jim, before he went to bed, and I spent the weekends with him and Peter.

This was the summer war began. Peter, who had been a regular soldier in a cavalry regiment and was still on the reserve, had been called up a few weeks before war actually broke out, and was sent to the mechanized cavalry depot at Catterick. The 14th/20th Hussars were at that time in India. The cellars of our brewery made a wonderful air raid shelter, which we first used on the day that war was declared! The sirens went off in the morning of 3rd September and we all bundled down there. Happily this one proved to be a false alarm!

When war broke out Jim's nanny had married and left us, but he had a children's maid and daily governess. I had my own maids in the house, plus Peter's old nurse of eighty years, whom I had brought out of London, and four school teachers who had been evacuated with the hundreds of children who came to the village, four of whom were also billetted on me.

I spent the first afternoon of the war with my super Austrian cook and Austrian parlourmaid in Tonbridge Police Station, as all foreigners had to register at once. They were both terrified, as, being refugees from their country, and having already gone through war, they thought they might be locked up or deported. The Superintendent made no objection to them coming back with me and continuing their work. That first week we had to put up blackout curtains, which seemed an endless task.

The Women's Voluntary Service coped marvellously with the influx of evacuees. I was not a regular member of the WVS, as I never wanted to be regimented or to wear a uniform, but I was roped in to help them. I remember so well cooking many pounds of local plums in buckets to help feed the great number of children, some of whom had never eaten hot or freshly cooked food, or even used a spoon or fork. They had always eaten straight out of a tin!

Several weeks went past, then Peter came home on forty-eight hours' leave, and announced that he had rented a small furnished house in Richmond, Yorkshire, so that the army, who wanted our house, could have it. Jim and I were to move to Yorkshire right away, as Peter thought he would be there for some time, and did not like living in barracks. I didn't sleep a moment that night! I felt the bottom had fallen out of my life.

Everything in the house was to be stored in our exceptionally large, long drawing room, and that was to be firmly locked up. A few months later the army needed this room too, and when I went back to supervise the removal of the furniture to storage, and saw the devastation already done to the rest of the house, I wondered if I would ever return to live there.

Our little furnished house in Richmond looked over the River Swale, and was very cosy. I had got permission from the police to take my Austrian parlourmaid, who was only twenty, with me, and we had a splendid soldier servant, who I discovered had been an assistant chef and could cook well, so we lived very comfortably.

The drink problem with Peter was no easier, and I lived in constant fear of his doing something stupid. However, we got through the first winter of the war without anything serious happening. Peter's commanding officer and his wife, the late Colonel and Mrs Nigel Weatherall, who had a son Jim's age called William, and a faithful old nanny, were saints. So were several fellow officers who were jolly sweet and sympathetic to me about the problem, which happily never happened 'on duty'. The warm-hearted Yorkshire people who lived around were angelic to us, and I made new friends, some of whom I have to this day. Lady Jean Christie, aunt of the present Marquess of Zetland, who was then living with her parents, the 4th Marquess and Marchioness of Zetland, at nearby Aske, as her husband, Captain

Hector Christie, was a prisoner of war, was always fun and welcoming. She and I often went racing together.

One day, when Jean had a rather larger car than usual, she asked me, on our way to pick up a couple of friends from the depot, if I would drive the car there, and she would drive it home. I thought this was rather strange as the two other passengers were men, but I did as I was asked. When we got home I learnt that the car belonged to her father. She had not had a chance to ask him if she could borrow it, so she thought if we had an accident, he would be easier about it if I was driving! Happily we had no problems.

Among those stationed at Catterick Depot then was Captain 'Putty' Johnson, who became a very good Member of Parliament after the war. Putty Johnson was a bachelor and a great and rather large character who owned a couple of steeplechasers that he trained nearby. He would always drive them himself in a horsebox to various race meetings in the district. As petrol was rationed, and in very short supply, a lift to go racing was always welcome. I accepted Putty's kind invitation to sit up front in his horsebox on several occasions. One Boxing Day when going racing at Wetherby he grumbled that the horsebox was pulling badly. When we arrived at the racecourse, we realized why, as when the groom and the two horses were unloaded so were the army chef and a couple of his staff who had hitched a lift uninvited!

Going racing during the war was nearly always an experience! Getting to Windsor perhaps gave one the greatest variety. I went with a private bus party from London; I went cross country from Surrey by bus and train; there were times when I bicycled to the course, not from London; I travelled from London by train, then went on in a variety of horse-drawn vehicles, ranging from a governess-cart or hansom cab to a waggonette. In the summer I would walk out of the station to the landing stage by the edge of the river and get taken up to the course in a rowing boat or punt. On one of these journeys by punt, we met, on nearing our destination, a rather fast river steamer which rocked the punt as it went past, then swamped us with its wash. I arrived at the racecourse soaked from the waist downwards! Happily it was a hot summer's day and I soon dried.

During my period in Yorkshire I looked after Jim myself. He went to a pre-preparatory day school which enabled me to do a certain amount of voluntary war work at the cavalry depot, including going out on a mobile canteen to outlying military points. That was a pretty icy job in mid-winter! There were quite a lot of children Jim's age in the district, so he was often out when not at school, or had children at our house.

In the early spring of 1940, Peter was sent to France with the Fife and Forfar Yeomanry, another mechanized cavalry regiment, as his own regiment was still in India.

We gave up our little rented house in Richmond, and Jim and I went to live with my dear father- and mother-in-law at Tenterden in Kent. We found a small day school for Jim in the town, and I helped my mother-in-law with various war-time commitments. My father-in-law was also busy with some sort of civil defence work of which he was Chairman.

News from the war front became worse in June. The enemy were advancing across Europe and we could, at times, hear the gun fire in France quite clearly. Then came the news of Dunkirk. I knew from Peter's last letters that he might be there. Then suddenly on 22nd June 1940 – my wedding anniversary – my father-in-law came home in the middle of the morning and said that Jim and I had to leave that day! All children were to be evacuated at once from the area as things were getting so bad across the Channel, and we might be invaded at any time.

I was pretty worried at the news, as I then had no home of my own, and the last thing I wanted to do was to go and stay with my mother and father in Warwickshire, as my mother was so desperately difficult. My brother Peter and his dear wife Peggy, who had so often had Jim, Nanny and me to stay at their Hertfordshire home when things were difficult for me, had also given up their home for the war.

I suddenly thought of my bachelor uncle Brigadier Martin Kemp-Welch, who was then Commandant at Sandhurst and lived in the big Commandant's house that went with the job. After a lot of delay getting through on the telephone, I spoke to him at lunch time and asked if he could have us both. With his usual kindness he immediately said yes.

So Jim and I set off by train that afternoon. At Headcorn station we were held up outside, as troop trains with survivors from Dunkirk were stopping at the station for the men to be given cups of tea. I somehow managed to get on to the platform and talked to some of the men to learn which regiments they were from. I did not know if Peter was dead or alive, or perhaps a prisoner of war, and longed for news, but I did not gain much!

When I arrived at Waterloo station to get a train to Camberley, the evening newspaper men were all shouting out 'France has fallen'. My heart sank again that day! I eventually arrived at the Commandant's house in time for dinner. My elder twin brother Peter was stationed quite near, so my dear Uncle Martin already had my sister-in-law and her two young children and a nanny staying in the house for the time being.

My uncle was divine to me, as I felt so lost not knowing what the future could be. He told me not to worry, that Jim and I could stay there as long as I liked, and that there was also his little house near Winchester, which he eventually left to me when he died.

After about a week of suspense, I got a telephone call from Peter to say he was back and in a rest camp. He wanted Jim and me to join him as soon as he was posted. A few days later, we left the comfort of my uncle's home and went with Peter to the mechanized cavalry depot at Lulworth, where he had been posted temporarily.

No accommodation was provided for wives, so once I had driven Peter to the barracks I drove off with Jim hoping to find a hotel to stay at. We asked at every sort of inn, but without any luck. It seemed hopeless, and I felt tired and desperate. Then I had the brilliant idea of going to the vicarage of a small neighbouring village, and asking the vicar, who was most kind, for help. He gave me the name of a family, who very kindly took us in for the night. I had their young son's tiny room and his sheets, and they put their son and Jim in a caravan in the garden! Next day I managed to get accommodation in a small local hotel.

It was here that I and others heard Mr Winston Churchill make his famous speech – that we would fight them on the beaches . . . Things really looked very bad for England. We were now standing alone, and our defences were pretty weak. At the end of a week, Peter was posted back to the cavalry depot at Catterick, so we packed up and drove up from Dorset to Yorkshire in one day. Happily, kind friends I had telephoned had Jim and me to stay, and Peter went to live in barracks until we got an officer's quarter in the camp.

By now it was August, so we settled in for another winter in Yorkshire, one that happened to be one of the hardest for years! Our semi-detached army quarter was for a major, so quite spacious, and enabled us to have a spare room. It was, however, very sparsely furnished with quite awful old beds, so I went south and got out of store comfortable beds, carpets, curtains, odd pieces of furniture, electric fires, and oil stoves, and sent them up to the army quarter, which we soon made quite warm and comfortable.

On one of my trips to Kent that September I went back to our old house to see the gardener about winter planting. During our discussion in the garden we watched with great interest two British and German aeroplanes, probably a Spitfire and Messerschmitt, having a set-to overhead. The British pilot won and the German flew off. I did not try to see inside the house.

Soon we resumed a life up north much as it had been the previous winter. Jim started back at the same pre-prep school in Richmond, going daily by bus. Then Gladys Weatherall asked me if I would share a governess for Jim if she got one for her younger son William, who was going to the same pre-prep school but not progressing very well. I agreed, so long as lessons took place in our house where I could keep an eye on the teaching, as I knew that if he was at their home William would play up! That arrangement held until we left and was a great success.

My Austrian maid had left me for a good job in a factory when we had left Richmond the previous year (she later married well and has always kept in touch with me), but when I returned this time I quickly found a super replacement who had been one of the housemaids at Aske, the Marquess and Marchioness of Zetland's lovely home near Richmond. She was a very well-trained, sweet Yorkshire girl, and a real treasure, whom I was sad to part with when I finally left Yorkshire. Again I had a good soldier servant who could cook, so I was once more able to do quite a lot of voluntary war work in the camp. Our double spare room was quite popular for putting up the wives or mothers of our friends who were living in barracks. Peter usually played golf on Saturdays and Sundays, when his military duties permitted. When I could arrange something for Jim on Saturdays, I went racing with racing friends. I well remember racing at Stockton with a number of barrage balloons overhead!

THREE

War work and the *Tatler*
(1941–44)

Up until that point we had imagined that this war was going to be a short one. Instead it went on and on, and we lived with great uncertainty. Early in 1941 I realized, rather to my dismay, that I was going to have another child. I had had two miscarriages since Jim had been born, so I hoped there would be no complications this time.

Peter's drinking was the greatest worry in my life, and now when he had drinking bouts he became rather aggressive. One night in July 1941, when my maid was away on holiday, Peter came home late and very drunk and abusive. This terrified me, so I woke Jim and took him in to my room and locked us in. Then there was the most awful scene where Peter eventually battered the bedroom door down and came in with a revolver.

This incident so unnerved me that it finally finished my married life! Next day, when Peter went into barracks, I found and took charge of the revolver. Then I packed some clothes for Jim and me, and telephoned our Colonel's wife Gladys Weatherall – always such a true, loyal friend – and told her I was running away, taking Jim, and the car, and the revolver. At the same time I asked her to keep an eye on Peter.

I told no one else. I did not want to get friends in the district involved in my troubles, which I had always tried to hide as much as possible. I still received an allowance from my father which, in his generous, kind manner, he continued giving me until his death, and this was a great help.

I drove to Darlington and booked a couple of rooms in a hotel for the night, and from there I telephoned a great friend in the south of England and asked if Jim and I could come and stay for a few days. I was very frightened of the revolver – I do not know to this day if it was loaded or not. That evening I got hold of some corrugated brown paper and string and carefully made a parcel of the gun and addressed it to a local police station. I posted it in Yorkshire, on my way south next day, without enclosing any explanation!

On arrival in the south I telephoned my father, who was happily alone in the country, and my mother-in-law, and told them not to worry; but I did not disclose where we were, as then they could honestly say they did not know should Peter ring to ask.

I had been ill quite a lot while expecting this baby, and my London doctor had decided that I should have it by caesarian operation. My family were against my having the baby in a London nursing home because of the bombing, so I had to give in, and was booked into a nursing home at Beaconsfield which my docter chose, as it was near to London.

I left Jim with very dear friends in Warwickshire, Captain Gar and the Hon. Mrs Emmet, who had a son, Simon, of his age, where I knew he would be safe and happy. On 2nd September 1941 I went into the nursing home feeling desperately down. I had a feeling something was wrong and that I might die, and I worried about what would then happen to Jim. This premonition was wrong; but I never saw my baby, a little son who died within a few hours. There were various complications, and for a few days I was seriously ill. I got a typical child's letter from Jim, who had been told his baby brother had died. 'I am sad that my baby brother has gone back to God I had grouse for lunch today'! All in one sentence!

I was hardly out of the nursing home before I had to see Jim off to prep school for his first term. I had got all his school uniform and marked it before I went to the nursing home. He went off on the school train from Paddington to Newbury full of good cheer – St Andrews of Eastbourne had moved to Chaddleworth for the war.

I am afraid that as I made my way back to a taxi I started crying. I then realized how ill and lonely I felt. I longed to throw myself into some very hard work to forget everything, but my doctor would not allow me to work for at least four months, which proved sound advice, as I eventually returned to good health.

Early in 1942 I started divorce proceedings; the following spring I got my divorce and full custody of Jim. Peter married again twice. His second wife, Patricia, suffered as I did from his drinking until she died very young of cancer. His third wife, Bridget, persuaded him to join Alcoholics Anonymous, which worked miracles, and he was completely teetotal for some years before he died. Peter very kindly told Bridget how he deeply regretted making me so unhappy with his drinking.

It was during my months of convalescence that I realized the great value of good health and good friends. God had, up until now, blessed me with both, and thankfully he has done so all through my life. My friends were truly wonderful to me during this time. I spent my time between them, visits to my in-laws and very brief visits to my parents in Warwickshire – usually when my mother was away. My mother was more than difficult at this time, and always liaised with Peter, giving him inaccurate information about Jim and me! I only went home for the sake of my beloved father, who was now retired and getting old and spending more of his time in the country.

Towards the end of my convalescence, in January 1942, the Christmas holidays, I took Jim to a children's party. Someone present said that it was such a social party it should be written up in the *Tatler*. I was told that I wrote a good newsy letter, and they suggested that I do it, as at that point I had more time than any of them. Rather reluctantly I wrote a rough piece, then telephoned the hostess for her to check it, before sending it off to the editor.

In due course I got a charming letter enclosing a cheque for ten shillings and sixpence, and asking me to send him any more pieces I could write!

In November that year, I had written to my dear friend Alan Butler, who was still Chairman of de Havillands, saying I wanted a job that would help the war effort, and could he find me work in one of the D.H. factories. He replied that none of their factories were in very suitable places for a mother with a young son to bring up! He had written instead, he said, to a friend of his, a Mr Gordon, who, with his brother, ran a small factory for aircraft and naval work not far from Godalming, to ask him to take me on. So in January, the Monday after Jim went back to school, I started working at the Weyburn Engineering Works at Elstead. I worked on night shift from 7 p.m. to 7 a.m. five nights a week. I had found a bedroom and sitting room in which to live with a charming old couple about a mile from the factory; he drove a bus and had a garden full of flowers. His wife produced breakfast for me when I got home each morning, and a sort of high tea before I set off on my bicycle for the factory each night.

The factory was extremely hard work, which was just what I wanted. Each morning I fell asleep, exhausted, directly I put my head on the pillow! It was also most interesting, and I was paid a lot of money, which I badly needed.

I had absolutely no previous mechanical experience, but by looking and listening very carefully to the foreman and to the setter I learnt a surprising amount, quite quickly, including how to use precision tools, and how to set up my own job so that I did not waste valuable money-earning time having to wait for a setter. We were paid on piece work. Before many months I was doing rather specialized work, including milling aluminium 'boosters', which were small parts for the Rolls-Royce engines in Spitfires, for which complete precision was all-important.

There was a good variety of work, and a variety of machines. On some of these jobs I had to stand on a wooden box to reach my work, as a taller man was working the same machine by day! I worked here from January 1942 until the end of July 1943. During that time, in term time, I usually spent weekends at the United Hunts Club in London (it no longer exists), or I would sometimes go racing or do something that was fun. Once or twice I wrote this up and sent it to *Tatler*. Readers would have been amused if they had known that my little piece had been written in a factory canteen during the long break at midnight. The *Tatler*'s editor, Reggie Hooper, sent me an old copy of *Debrett*, which I sometimes took to the factory in a basket on the handlebars of the aged staff bicycle my sister-in-law had very kindly loaned me (which I later brought to London, but I was too frightened to ride it there, after a few near misses).

I had very dear friends in the district, Mr and Mrs Tom Berington, with an only son of Jim's age called Tim. They would always have Jim to stay in the holidays, and I could also stay there at weekends whenever I liked. They were very rich, and very sweetly would not take a penny for having us. Tom Berington had his roots in Worcestershire, and Olguita Berington was an American by birth. They had a very nice home near Farnham, where it was very handy for me to join Jim when I was working at the Weyburn Engineering Works.

As I arrived there one Saturday morning, off my night shift, I was greeted by Tom Berington, a kind, very gentle man, looking very worried. When he said 'I gave your son and my son a good thrashing last night!' I was amazed and wondered what was coming next. Then I discovered that the two boys, both still only around nine or ten years old, had stolen some cigarettes from the drawing room and taken them to have a smoke behind a haystack on the farm. Trying to light up in a wind they had set the haystack alight. The whole haystack was lost, which in those days, with the great shortage of food for animals, was a very serious matter. The police had of course come to enquire as everyone had seen the flames, and Tom had very sensibly taken the policemen up to the boys' room as he thought they would make them realize more forcibly than he could what wrong they had done. I don't know if this early incident had anything to do with my son never smoking, even as a teenager. I have always been truly grateful to Tom Berington for the way he dealt with Jim, and grateful that Jim never acquired the habit of smoking.

Two other friends who were so kind in having Jim and me to stay during the war were Mr and Mrs Geoffrey Grinling, who had a house on the Sussex-Hampshire border, where Jim and I were paying guests for part of several school holidays; from there I could also easily commute to the factory.

In these war days at weekends during the term I went to Newbury quite often and stayed at the Chequers Hotel, near where Jim was at school, and took him out. I was also given time off from the factory in the summer holidays to be with my son. Then I took Jim to stay with friends at Barmouth, and on to my sister-in-law's family in Scotland, where her parents, Mr and Mrs Kenneth Hunter, so kindly lent Jim and me a tiny, very sunny cottage. We went there for several summers and loved it. I was terrified at night, as it was very isolated, but it was a wonderful holiday cottage and so good for Jim to be with his cousins.

In the summer of 1943 when my divorce was finally made absolute I was awarded only one hundred and fifty pounds a year for myself and the same amount for Jim – because Peter had by now left the army, and claimed he had no income! (They did not have him back in the brewery.)

By this time I was getting rather tired of my factory job. I had paid up all my doctor's bills for my baby's birth and my illness, and I thought I might make a change. Doing continuous night work was affecting my eyes, which was worrying. But it was not easy to get released from a war job, especially if you were on specialized work. While I was in Barmouth that summer, I met a friend called Joan Kenyon, whom I had known at dancing classes as a child in Warwickshire. She was working as a dame in a house at Eton, where the staff, with the exception of the cook, were, like herself, amateurs, with children at school. She suggested that if I would like to come and work at Eton, I would be released from the factory, as education had a certain priority.

In September 1943, I arrived at Evans, then one of the oldest and most out-of-date houses at Eton College, for the start of the autumn term. I was to work for Mr Cyril and the Hon. Mrs Butterwick, who were absolutely charming, and became lifelong friends. I had a very varied job. I looked after the pantry and the boys' dining room, and at times looked after the Butterwicks' private dining room, often waiting at table when the Butterwicks had a dinner party. I never aspired to being a 'boy's maid', as has been frequently claimed in the penny press.

There were four boys' maids at Evans, all of them like myself, with children at private boarding schools. I had an unbelievably cold and uncomfortable bedroom in the attic, but it was all the greatest fun, as the others working here were all so nice. I also saw quite a few of my friends when they visited their sons, and stole away on my bicycle for several good afternoons' racing.

Désirée Butterwick was a darling, and also a tremendous snob. Sometimes she would come into my pantry and discuss endless people in *Debrett*. She was also a very strict disciplinarian. One Saturday morning I told her in a casual way that after I had finished my work that evening I was going out to have a late dinner with friends who were staying at the Bridge Hotel for Windsor races. She looked at me sternly and said I could not go, that I had already had my half day off that week and that if she allowed me out, it was a bad example to the others! I said no more.

That evening after work I saw the lady who did the night watch and said I was off out and that on my return I would knock twice on the staff sitting room window which overlooked the pavement. That evening luck was not altogether on my side. I had just finished a happy dinner with my friends when the air raid sirens went. My host would not let me go back to Evans and said I was to stay with them until the all clear, which I did. Luckily I stayed on a little longer talking.

When I arrived back I found a distraught night watch lady. She told me that everyone had been brought downstairs to the air raid shelter when the sirens went off, and that when someone had suddenly said 'Where is Mrs K?' she had replied 'Oh, she never wants to be disturbed if there is a raid'. When the all clear sounded, to her dismay Mrs Butterwick decided some of them should go into our staff sitting room and have a hot drink. The poor night watch thought that at any moment she would hear two knocks on the window and all would be lost! Happily, by the time I got back everyone had gone to bed, and dear Mrs B never knew that I had been out that night.

It had been understood when I started at Eton that I would only work there for one term. During my short period there, I found myself a job in London working for the Soldiers, Sailors and Air Force Families Association, in one of their workrooms run by friends of mine in Cadogan Square. These friends, Mrs Seary Mercer and Miss Brue Hollebone, could also rent me a very nice bedsitting room at the top of the house. I was rather frightened at the idea of bustling noisy London, and the bombs that were still falling.

I left at the end of the autumn term, and spent the Christmas school holidays with Jim, staying with various relations and friends.

Soon after I started working in London, thanks to my always untruthful and difficult mother exaggerating my salary hugely to Peter, he stopped paying my share of the settlement, leaving only the one hundred and fifty pounds towards Jim's keep and schooling, which was to continue until Jim left Winchester College in July 1951. My father, thank God, still gave me an allowance, and the odd extra cheque, but I always knew that would stop when Daddy died, as he had left everything to my mother for life.

My job for SSAFFA was to cut out clothes for the troops' families with an electric cutting-out machine. I had never seen such a machine, let alone used one! But in those war days one had to have a go at everything! I learnt how to use the machine, and how to lay the cardboard patterns on the material so as to get as many garments as possible out of the precious rationed material. I would draw round the patterns with chalk and then start cutting, often through thirty or more thicknesses. This terrified me each time I did it! – often several times a day – but miraculously I managed never to ruin any cloth, or to cut off any of my fingers!

At the end of my first week's work at Cadogan Square, I found I could feel very lonely in the evenings if I was not dining out, even though my friends were all being so very kind, inviting me out to dine, as was my beloved brother George when he could get a few hours' leave, as he was stationed in London at the time. Determined not to get depressed alone, I decided I had better get an evening job, as well as my nine-to-six day one. This could not be too far away, as getting about in London in those days with the ever constant threat of air raids was not easy. I heard of an American canteen near Cadogan Square, at which there was a very well-paid evening job, so I decided to apply to work there.

They were very nice and said I could have the job, but I must produce a reference. I rang Harry Yoxall, the much respected and beloved managing director of *Vogue* in England, whom I had known when I worked in their information bureau before the war, as I thought a reference from *Vogue* would carry more weight since the magazine was loved by all Americans. He at once said to come along and see him the next day, which was a Friday. When I arrived, he was kindness personified, and wrote me a wonderful reference. Then, in a chatty way, I told him, as I thought it would make him laugh, how before I had heard of the SSAFFA job Reggie Hooper, then editor of the *Tatler* (which was then owned by Illustrated Newspapers), had asked me if there was any chance of my working for them at the *Tatler* office to do their social pages, which were called 'On and Off Duty'. I had turned the offer down as I did not feel it was in any way war work; also my family, especially my beloved brothers, were horrified at the thought of my writing a social diary for any publication. (I had never been asked or allowed to write a word when I was with *Vogue*!)

Harry then, to my horror, quietly tore my form and reference in two! 'Betty,' he said, 'Reggie Hooper is in great difficulties, he is desperately short of staff and really needs your help. I know you, and I know you can do the social side for him better than anyone.' He suggested I could do my SSAFFA cutting-out job in the mornings and evenings, and go to the *Tatler* part-time by day. I was to wait until Monday morning, then ring Reggie Hooper and say I had changed my mind, and that I would go and work at the *Tatler* part-time. What I did not know then was that Harry Yoxall had spoken to Reggie Hooper – a great friend of his – that morning, and had heard from him that the *Tatler*'s fashion editor had just committed suicide, and that Reggie Hooper was now without anyone to do the fashion, as well as the social copy! The woman who was writing the social copy had been sacked for tactlessly describing a party in the country the night of the bombing of Bath, mentioning well-known guests who should have been on duty.

As Harry Yoxall predicted, the plan – his way of helping two friends – worked out for both of us! I duly rang Reggie Hooper, who was to my amazement delighted, and on Monday 24th January 1944 I started working at the *Tatler* five mornings a week, and in the evenings for social events when needed. I was paid four pounds a week, not nearly as much as the American canteen would have paid me!

My first year at the *Tatler* was a very worrying one. When I started, I found that no invitations at all were coming into the office. I had to find everything to fill the social pages, and we were weekly! Soon I found myself doing much of the fashion page of the magazine as well. This meant I often worked at my SSAFFA job, for which I was also paid a tiny salary (I think two pounds a week), until well after midnight, after I had been working at the *Tatler*.

One week I was so desperate for copy that I had the idea of standing at the bus stop outside the Ritz Hotel after luncheon, as so many people met at the Ritz bar or lunched in the Ritz Grill during the war. As I had hoped, it worked well. I met and chatted to a number of friends and filled a lot of space, not naming, of course, those who had jumped the bus queue, among whom I am afraid a prominent and very dear peer, who is now dead, was the worst offender! One had in those days to be extremely careful not to give away anything that anyone was doing in terms of war service, or where they were stationed.

One day I heard the assistant editor asking someone on the telephone if the social editor could go to a certain function at a services club. When I arrived at the All Services Canteen Club I was greeted, to my amazement, by Mrs Anthony Eden, whom I had met on several previous occasions. Her husband was then Foreign Minister in Churchill's government. Beatrice Eden was just as surprised to see me as I was to see her! She had no idea I was writing for the *Tatler*. She was helping Mrs Littlejohn Cook, who founded this canteen club, to run it, and after my first visit she invited me to anything she arranged and was always so kind and helpful. So many friends helped me when I started, including Lady Tedder, wife of the air marshal, who invited me to various meetings and fund-raising events for her Malcolm Clubs, which she opened for men of the RAF in many parts of the world.

Countess Mountbatten of Burma, then Lady Louis Mountbatten, whom I had met before I started working on the *Tatler*, was also very helpful. Once she knew I was doing this job, she always invited me to any St John Brigade or other charity fund-raising events she was interested in, and to some of her family events as well.

The first wedding I wrote about for the diary, the marriage of the 15th Lord Dormer to the present Earl of Gainsborough's sister, Lady Maureen Noel, was in February, a few weeks after I had started.

During the war SSAFFA held their annual bazaar at Rootes car salerooms in Piccadilly. I went along quietly on my own in my working clothes to help on one of the stalls and possibly to write a little piece about it. Suddenly, to my great surprise, I found myself having the great honour of being presented to The Queen by Mrs Seary Mercer, who was head of the SSAFFA workrooms. She kindly told Her Majesty that I was doing a quantity of cutting out for them at all hours of the night! Her Majesty was, as always, so kind, and interested in my cutting-out work.

During that period, when I was working at the *Tatler* and for SSAFFA in Cadogan Square, my only neighbour at the top of the house was a dear pre-war friend called Mrs Bay Garle, who had joined the MTC for the war. She was far better off than I was, so she had a sitting room as well as a bedroom, and we shared the bathroom. Later, in 1947, when I had left Cadogan Square, I had the very difficult task of breaking the news to Bay Garle that the then Sir Walter Monckton, for whom she had left her very nice husband John Garle, was going to marry Bridget Countess of Carlisle He had left for India without telling her. But Bay had the sweetest nature and after his remarriage they still went on meeting.

The only snag to my room in Cadogan Square was that each time an air raid warning was sounded, and there were many, especially during the mini blitz in February, we were supposed to go down to the basement. I got so tired of having my sleep constantly broken that I asked if I could put a campbed under the stairs on the ground floor, so that I could sleep there at night and stay there during raids. I slept there for weeks, with a thick coat, strong shoes, a torch, and my tin hat beside me! At least like this I got some badly needed sleep.

That year, 1944, really was one of the most frightening periods of my life, particularly during the summer, when we had the V-1 flying bombs, which I found terrifying.

It was also one of the saddest. On 18th June 1944 my beloved brother George Kemp-Welch, who was then thirty-six years old, and who had joined the Grenadier Guards when war broke out, was killed when a V-1 flying bomb landed on the Guards Chapel.

George was by ten minutes the younger of my twin brothers. He was tall and athletic and had, as I said earlier, worked hard going right through the firm of Schweppes, from the very bottom to being a director on the board when war started. In 1934 he had married Mrs Diana Munro, who was the eldest daughter of the then Prime Minister, Mr Stanley Baldwin, later Earl Baldwin of Bewdley. They had no children, but enjoyed ten years of very happy married life living in Wellington Square, Chelsea.

Di, who had a son by her first marriage to Gordon Munro, later Sir Gordon Munro, went to live in Worcestershire when war broke out.

George was always so kind and good to me, especially after my marriage ended. We had dined together, on our own, only three days before the dreadful bombing, as we were then the only two members of our family living in London.

The bombing happened on a Sunday morning. I was away that weekend staying with friends for the Derby which was run at Newmarket on the Saturday. When the news came through, I had a presentiment that George had been killed. I telephoned everyone I could think of but could get no news. I returned to London on Sunday night, and early Monday morning I managed to get hold of the duty officer at Wellington Barracks, who told me my brother was missing, and then George's soldier servant contacted me. When two people were dug out alive on the Wednesday, my hopes rose that my brother might still be alive, but in vain. We had five days of agonizing suspense until George's body was dug out of the debris the following Friday.

Then came another terrible moment when I had to go to the mortuary to identify my brother. His twin brother Peter, who was in the Coldstream Guards, was on the staff at Wilton House in Wiltshire, where they had spent a lot of time planning for D-Day and were now planning the advance that followed, and as he could not get leave I was the next of kin. Peter only just managed to get leave the following week for his twin brother's cremation and the family luncheon with just my parents, Peter and his wife Peggy, and my uncle Brigadier Martin Kemp-Welch in the Grill Room at the old Berkeley Hotel. In those days there was a high brick wall built on the pavement to protect the windows from bomb damage, so no daylight entered.

At the end of luncheon I said goodbye to my beloved brother Peter not knowing if I would ever see him again, as I knew it was only a matter of days before he went overseas to France and Belgium. I went straight to my office feeling desperately sad. I will never forget my arrival there to collect some clothes to take to a photographic session. The assistant editor, who knew where I had been but was such a hard person to work with, gave me a terrific ticking off as I was fifteen minutes late. I remember taking it quietly then, but I burst into tears when I got outside the office.

Flying bombs added to the fashion side of work problems when getting clothes photographed outdoors for the fashion pages. I can remember telling the models never to lie flat on their faces as some people liked to do when the flying bombs came over, as the clothes were all on loan from various shops. We sometimes found ourselves, when sirens sounded, in very funny places, rushing into shops and buildings and taking refuge until the danger had passed, then quickly back to work before another siren!

In 1944, I wrote about a race meeting at Ascot, where we were still dodging V-1 flying bombs! A racecourse was then the one place where one hardly heard a reference to Hitler's V-1s. That day, both Sir Malcolm McAlpine and the then Viscount Astor brought off doubles. Other famous racing personalities I recorded as present that day included the Hon. Dorothy Paget, as always wearing her famous blue tweed coat, which I think must have been air-conditioned or thermostatted, as she wore it summer and winter in all weathers! Dorothy Paget, owner of the grand chaser Golden Miller, was a great patron of the turf for many years. She never seemed to buy any new clothes, and had a very sweet tooth. I remember someone laughingly saying that they thought she must swop her clothes coupons for sweet coupons! Fulke Walwyn had received instructions that summer from a Mr Gordon Roll – a prisoner of war since 1940 – to buy him twenty yearlings to put into training. This showed what Gordon Roll, and possibly other prisoners, thought of Germany's chances!

On the social side, things were brightening up. Quite a few invitations were by now coming in and during Jim's term time I still went racing most Saturdays at either Ascot, Windsor, or sometimes Salisbury, which had remained open – unlike many courses – for the duration of the war. In the summer holidays I continued to take Jim to the sea at Barmouth and the tiny cottage in Perthshire. It was up here that Jim learnt to shoot and to fish. I was able to carry on my social pages with news from North Wales and Scotland. I made sure I had taken enough fashion pictures in advance to keep those pages going while I was away.

By the late summer of 1944 everyone began to sense that the war was drawing to an end. The Normandy invasion had been successfully completed and the troops were advancing and clearing up pockets of resistance. In London, the V-1s and V-2s were mercifully less frequent.

Dining out was still very popular because of the rationing of food and the shortage of servants in private houses, so all the restaurants were packed, as were the top nightclubs such as the 400, where dear Rossi kept everyone's bottles of drink labelled with their name, and always knew which of your friends were in London or on leave. Ciro's was also popular. I seemed to be taken to both clubs quite often in those days. I lunched or dined most frequently at either Claridge's, with my father, or the Berkeley, the Ritz, the Dorchester, the Mira-belle, Bucks Club, the Cavalry Club, the Guards Club or Wiltons.

In the war days, and for some time after, when lunching or dining at Claridge's you often saw members of European royal families who were making their home in England while their countries were over-run. These included King George of the Hellenes, Crown Prince Paul of the Hellenes, the King and Queen of Norway, Queen Marie of Yugoslavia, King Peter and Queen Alexandra of Yugoslavia, and others.

That year, 1944, Monsieur René Massigli came to London in the very difficult appointment as representative of the Provisional Govern-ment of France. The government of General de Gaulle had yet to be recognized. He was received by the King but, being neither ambassa-dor nor minister, he was not accredited to the Court of St James's. This choice was one of General de Gaulle's better moves, as René Massigli was a charmer and a great diplomat. When the de Gaulle regime was recognized, René Massigli at once became their Ambassa-dor, and he and his very attractive and tremendously chic wife Odette soon became leaders on the London diplomatic scene. The Massiglis rented Lowndes House as the French Embassy residence, as the pre-war French Embassy had been bombed; and it was during his term of office here as Ambassador that the French Government bought the fine pre-war London residence of the Duke of Marlborough, in Kensington Palace Gardens, which is still the French Embassy residence, and which Odette Massigli redecorated with her impeccable taste. Unlike England at that time, France seemed to have no shortage of beautiful silks and textiles, and the curtains and covers in this Embassy were the envy of all who saw them!! After the war, the Massiglis gave some wonderful parties here: I was lucky enough to be invited to most of them and later to their home in Paris, and kept in touch with them both long after they left London.

That year the Diplomatic Corps at the Court of St James's were all very cultured career diplomats, with charming wives who entertained graciously, so a lot of the limited social life took place in the various embassies.

By autumn 1944, after eight or nine difficult months, I had begun to get into my stride with the diary, though I still found it a problem to make the extra time to help with the magazine's fashion page. My work continued to increase, as more and more of the fashion work was landed on me, although my name never appeared. At least there was only one page a week to fill, but it took a great deal of time finding clothes to photograph, then persuading the shops to lend them, as they were all rationed, collecting them, arranging sittings with models and photographers, and being present at sittings when the clothes were photographed, sometimes with the bombs overhead. Jean Simmons, then a very pretty teenager, and later a most successful actress, modelled some young people's clothes for me at this time.

I went to the first big charity gala that autumn in aid of the Red Cross and the St John Ambulance Brigade Fund, who in those days worked far closer together. Today they work as two organizations with separate benefits. Among those present at this gala was Lady Louis Mountbatten, whom I then described as 'Head of the Red Cross and St John in Britain'. She was certainly Superintendent-in-Chief of the St John Ambulance Brigade. Lady Louis was still in uniform, and so were quite a few of the women at this gala, after a long day's work.

Lady Louis' party included the Hon. Kay Norton, who ran a very successful pre-war couture salon in Sheridan's old home, where Hardy Amies's showrooms are today. At this point in 1944 Lady Louis' elder daughter Patricia Mountbatten, now Countess Mountbatten of Burma, had joined the WRNS, and her other daughter Pamela, now Lady Pamela Hicks, was still at school.

My first really 'big' wedding for the *Tatler* was the marriage in the autumn of 1944 of Lt-Colonel Harold Phillips, Coldstream Guards, to Miss Georgina Wernher, daughter of Sir Harold and Lady Zia Wernher, at St Margaret's, Westminster. There were only two brides-maids, Princess Alexandra of Kent, now Princess Alexandra the Hon. Lady Ogilvy, who was fulfilling this role for the first time, and wore a white net frock; and the bride's sister Miss Myra Wernher, now Lady Butter, who wore a shell-pink satin dress – the latter had been made out of the bride's coming-out dress, to save coupons!

The guests included King George of the Hellenes, the Duchess of Kent, Prince Dmitri of Russia, and Prince Bertil of Sweden, all cousins of Lady Zia Wernher. This wedding, I wrote, 'was beautiful in its simplicity and quiet dignity'. Looking back, it is amazing how very well dressed the guests were after nearly five years of clothes rationing! Quite a few of the guests of course came in their uniform, especially the Red Cross, as Gina Wernher had worked as a VAD at Langton Hall, where Lady Zia Wernher was the Commandant.

I remember being very worried that I would not get all the details right, so Lady Zia Wernher very sweetly invited me the following day to the Dorchester, their temporary home since their London house had been bombed, to help me.

During the late autumn of 1944 I was going to so many functions for the *Tatler* that I often had to get up very early and go down to the workroom and do my cutting out for SSAFFA from 6 a.m. until perhaps 11 a.m., and then go into the office.

The King and Queen spent most of the war living at Buckingham Palace during the week. Princess Elizabeth, now our beloved Queen, and Princess Margaret were living at Windsor Castle, where their parents joined them at weekends. Queen Mary was living in the West Country. Young friends of the Royal Family who were at Eton were often invited up to join the young Princesses at Windsor Castle on Sundays after church. I well remember the younger of two brothers who had been invited to the Castle telling me what fun he and Princess Margaret had had with a hose, targeting among other things one of the sentries' feet, which they were stopped from doing, but not before the feet came in for quite a splash.

That Christmas of 1944, Princess Elizabeth and Princess Margaret both appeared in one of their amusing pantomimes at Windsor Castle. This time it was Old Mother Red Riding Boots. The King and Queen saw one of the performances, and so did many members of the royal household and their families. The Princesses had the help of Mr Hubert Tanmer, then headmaster of the Royal School, Windsor Great Park, in their production. Children from the school provided the chorus, and there was a ballet devised by the famous teacher of ballroom dancing Miss Vacani, whose dancing school is now successfully run by Lord Eden's sister Miss Elfrida Eden, in private life Mrs Richard Fallowfield, and Miss Mary Stassinopoulos. After the final performance, Princess Elizabeth gave a Christmas tea party for all the village children and for others who had taken part.

Just before Christmas there had been the first night of Terence Rattigan's new play, *Love in Idleness*, at the Lyric Theatre, with the famous pair Alfred Lunt and Lynn Fontanne in the leading roles. It was a very social occasion, as Rattigan first nights always were. In those days first nights and film premieres were very much part of the very limited social life.

On 10th December 1944, I rented a small furnished flat from a friend in Hill Street for the school holidays. Jim and I spent that Christmas with my sister-in-law Peggy Kemp-Welch and her two children John and Penelope at my Uncle Martin's house near Winchester.

My dear bachelor uncle was always away staying with one of his sisters for Christmas. Everything was in very short supply, and Peggy and I struggled to decorate the Christmas tree, as both our pre-war Christmas decorations were in store. On Christmas Eve, my sister-in-law received a letter from my brother Peter who was on active service in France; he sounded miserable, living in bad conditions in the middle of the Battle of the Bulge.

The Hill Street flat was such a success that I arranged to stay on, and within a year I moved into an unfurnished and slightly larger flat across the corridor. This had belonged to friends who kindly told me (before telling the landlord) that they were leaving, so that I could apply for their three-year lease before anyone else. Many years later, when it became available, I bought a long lease for the flat, and it is where I still live forty-eight years later!

FOUR

War ends
and the social world reawakes

(1945–46)

It caused quite a sensation in the spring of 1945 when it was announced that Princess Elizabeth, now eighteen years old, having already trained as a Sea Ranger, was training to join the Auxiliary Territorial Service as an honorary second lieutenant. Up to then, she had been specially tutored by Sir Harry Marten, the Provost of Eton, but this had to stop for the moment, as she was to take up full-time training with the ATS.

The 'Priscilla in Paris' article, a pre-war favourite with *Tatler* readers, had suddenly stopped in 1940, when Paris fell, with the brief statement 'No Priscilla'. In March 1945 'Priscilla in Paris' returned again under the heading 'Paris During the Occupation'. Priscilla was a charming English lady who had lived in Paris nearly all her life. She took the greatest care of me on my first post-war visits to Paris; I learnt a great deal from her and appreciated her very loyal friendship. She continued her very popular 'Priscilla in Paris' feature weekly in the *Tatler* until she died.

On Easter Monday, I went to the opening of the flat racing season, which was then at Ascot. It was a splendid day's racing with a large attendance. The Duchess of Kent, not a regular racegoer, was there looking very elegant in a long, well-cut camel hair coat and felt hat, a classic that would look right today! The war news by now was getting better and better, and we were all becoming more hopeful that peace was in sight.

In April that year we were all saddened by the news of the sudden death of President Franklin D. Roosevelt. The King immediately ordered court mourning for a week, and many private parties and other functions were cancelled or postponed. Mr Anthony Eden, the then Foreign Secretary, headed a delegation to Washington for the funeral. A most moving memorial service for the President was held at a packed

St Paul's Cathedral. The King, in the uniform of Admiral of the Fleet, and The Queen, in deep mourning, attended, as did Princess Elizabeth in her ATS·uniform with a black band on her arm, the Princess Royal, the Duchess of Kent, and Princess Juliana of the Netherlands and Crown Prince Olav of Norway, who were both living in exile in England then. The Prime Minister, Mr Winston Churchill, who was a great personal friend of the President, and all his Cabinet, were present.

By now, not only Paris but also Luxembourg had been liberated. I was delighted when Sir Thomas Cook, as Chairman of the Luxembourg Society, invited me that April to a farewell party for the Grand Duchess of Luxembourg. After her country was invaded by Germany in 1940, the Grand Duchess and her family spent the rest of the war years in England, at their house in Hampstead. I believe they still keep this house for family visits to England.

In spite of endless piano lessons all through my youth I knew nothing about music, or the world of music. I well remember the agony I went through in April that year at a committee meeting for a charity concert, when I was introduced to Doctor Malcolm Sargent, later Sir Malcolm Sargent. I had no idea whether he was a pianist, violinist, trumpeter, or conductor! I was terrified I would put my foot in it, so I followed the golden rule of keeping my eyes and ears open and my mouth shut, and let him do the talking, which he did very easily with the greatest charm. I soon discovered his line!

Over the years, I met Malcolm Sargent quite frequently and got to know him quite well, as he was perhaps the most social of all conductors. He was very good-looking and an absolute charmer. Sadly he died of cancer far too young in 1967.

Each day now the news was getting better. We heard that the American and Russian forces had linked up, and gradually prisoners were getting released. Then came the tremendous excitement of Peace in Europe. On VE Day and the following day, London went mad rejoicing! There were crowds everywhere in the streets laughing, cheering and waving flags or anything else they had to wave. Most public transport had stopped, and most offices were closed.

For some unknown reason the *Tatler* office kept open, and we all had to go in to work. I know I got a bus to work, but coming home in the evening I had to walk from the office, which was at the far end of New Oxford Street, to my flat. As I passed Claridge's there were crowds outside dancing and singing in Brook Street – a sight I thought

I would never see. As I walked on I suddenly felt rather sad, remembering those dear ones who had died in the war whom we would never see again, including my beloved brother George.

There had been tremendous crowds outside Buckingham Palace all day. In the morning the King and Queen and the two Princesses came out on the balcony and received tumultuous cheers. Later The King and Queen left the Palace and drove along the Mall, which was lined with thousands of well-wishers, to make a three-hour tour of the East End of London, which had suffered the worst bombing. When they returned, the crowds were still lining the Mall, and thousands were outside the Palace, so the Royal Family came out on the balcony numerous times until after midnight.

It was the same scene around the Palace the following day, when Their Majesties made a tour of the south side of London across the river. I had no engagements on either evening for the *Tatler*, so I stayed at home, as I am rather frightened in big crowds.

From the moment of Victory in Europe social life increased. The first victory film premiere was the film *Czarina* at the Odeon Theatre. On this occasion evening dresses and lovely jewels made their first appearance! Unlike film premieres today, which are usually attended mostly by the film and stage world, the audience in those days included many more members of the diplomatic and social world. The Royal Family had endless VE celebrations to attend all over the UK, and gradually more pre-war ceremonies returned. Historic treasures like the Old Masters of the National Gallery, safely hidden in Wales during the war, were returned to the National Gallery, and the Royal Family attended the first Private View. Princess Elizabeth was already undertaking quite a few engagements on her own.

The first two royal garden parties to be held at Buckingham Palace after Victory in Europe were held for mostly repatriated prisoners of war of all ranks from the three services, and men and women of the Red Cross and St John who had been working so long and so hard on behalf of the services.

Princess Elizabeth accompanied her parents on both occasions, greeting a number of guests at the parties. These included some very gallant men, including the legless pilot Group Captain Douglas Bader, who fought in the Battle of Britain; Lt-Colonel Charles Newman, who won a VC at St Nazaire; Lt Geoffrey Place RN and Lt Donald Cameron RN, heroes of the midget submarine attack on the *Tirpitz*, who were awarded the VC; and Lt-Commander Stephen Beattie, who also received a VC. There were to be no purely social garden parties until after the war in the Far East was over.

That month I went to the third Royal Windsor Horse Show, for which the Duke of Beaufort was President and Mr Geoffrey Cross, the joint founder with Count Robert Orssich, was Chairman. It was held in the Home Park, Windsor Castle. It was extremely well run by the most efficient chairman and secretary Mr Ian Hazlett, and the profits were given to war charities. It is amazing to think of the show making a profit. For all shows now, it is a constant worry to find sponsors to meet expenses, even to break even!

After luncheon The King and Queen arrived, taking their seats in a small enclosure on the lawn in front of the marquee with large umbrella canopies. In those days there were no stands; today there is a fine, spacious royal box, and stands nearly all the way round the arena.

During the afternoon, the King and Queen had the joy of seeing their daughters competing in the private driving class for the best single turnout, which had a very big entry. Princess Elizabeth, who had Princess Margaret as a passenger, drove her pony to a phaeton with coolness and good judgement, showing the pony off beautifully. She really won the class on merit. After receiving the cup from the Duke of Beaufort, Princess Elizabeth drove a lap of honour round the show ring, so that everyone could see the winner and the cup that was on Princess Margaret's knee. There were quite a few Eton boys present, wearing top hats and tails.

That year's Fourth of June at Eton was an exceptionally happy one as many families were reunited, and there was a tremendous mood of Peace in the air. The recent return of the basic petrol ration meant that many could come by car for the first time for five years. However, the Eton boys in the lower boats had not that year got back to wearing the traditional clothes for the Procession of Boats, and there was no firework display.

That year Princess Elizabeth, in her ATS uniform, accompanied The King and Queen to the Derby at Newmarket, and looked to be thoroughly enjoying herself. I noticed her talking to the Earl of Rosebery, who was a pillar of the turf, and always a fount of racing information. Perhaps that day at Newmarket first inspired our beloved Queen in her love of racing!

Both the Derby and the Oaks were still run at their wartime venue, Newmarket. The women looked smart though not dressy. White hats were a feature; many hundreds wore them at that meeting, with well-tailored long coats, or thin tailored suits. A familiar racing character present both days was Prince Aly Khan, who was wearing battle dress and greeting many friends with his great charm, which always made you feel you were the one person he most wanted to talk to! He was also expressing his joy at being back on an English racecourse after five years' absence in the Middle East, and was delighted at his father's horse doing so well in the Oaks. There was such a different feeling here from the previous year's Derby, which was run soon after our forces landed in Normandy, and as the flying bombs had started to land on London. This year many families were enjoying their first day's racing together for five years, and five favourites won!

The biggest wedding that summer was when the Hon. William Astor, then Member of Parliament for East Fulham, and son and heir of Viscount and Viscountess Astor, married the Hon. Sarah Norton, daughter of Lord Grantley, at St Martin-in-the Fields, with the reception at Admiralty House. The bride had no problems over coupons for her wedding dress, as it was made out of exquisite ivory brocade satin that was over fifty years old and had belonged to her grandmother. There were no bridesmaids. At the wedding I could not help thinking of a story I had been told the previous spring about young friends staying at Cliveden one weekend telling Bill Astor, then in his late thirties, that it was time he got married and suggesting quite a few young ladies that Bill had shown interest in, including Sarah Norton. Apparently this advice sank in, and he invited Sarah Norton out to dinner that week and proposed to her! Sadly the marriage only lasted until 1953.

In June The King and Queen gave a small private dance at Buckingham Palace for Princess Elizabeth and Princess Margaret, who were then nineteen and nearly fifteen years old. That was the first year that I remember Wing Commander Peter Townsend carrying out his duties as equerry to The King.

For all of us that year there was the General Election. I was too busy at work to get very involved, other than to cast my vote, but like many others I took it for granted that the Conservatives would win, though possibly with a smaller majority. It was a great shock when the Conservatives lost. It was a very poignant moment when Mr Winston Churchill, who had led the country so brilliantly for five years through the war days, went to Buckingham Palace to hand in his resignation to The King. He had had an audience with His Majesty the previous evening when he gave him a report on the Berlin talks, from which he had just returned. Here he was back again at the Palace within twenty-four hours!

The King, I was told at the time, was very moved by his resignation, as not only had Mr Winston Churchill been his Prime Minister for five years, but he had always been his staunchest supporter and had guided his country steadfastly through the most terrible and darkest days of his reign. A very sad moment to be saying goodbye to such a dedicated citizen. As our constitution decrees, The King had already sent for the leader of the Labour Party, Mr Clement Attlee, to ask him to form a government, and he came to the Palace shortly after Mr Winston Churchill left. Mr Attlee had an exceptionally busy first week as he had to go out to Berlin to carry on the talks as well as form a new government.

Shortly after the Election, the eagerly anticipated first state visit from a president of the United States of America, Mr Harry Truman, took place. He was on his way back from the talks in Berlin with Generalissimo Stalin that Mr Winston Churchill had been at. There had been plans for state functions, and American-born hostesses and other leading hostesses had been trying to arrange parties, though nothing had been finalized as no one knew the duration of the Berlin talks. In the end it was a very brief visit without any ceremony. Plans for parties were put aside. The King met President Truman – this was for the first time – on board the battle cruiser *Renown* off Plymouth Sound. The two heads of state of course discussed the war with Japan, which both their countries were still fighting. Later in the day The King went on board the US cruiser *Augustus* to pay the President a courtesy call of ten minutes, but so much did both men find to talk about that The King spent over half an hour on board, so that the US cruiser sailed on her homeward journey three-quarters of an hour later than scheduled!

That July, I went to the wedding of one of London's richest, kindest and most flamboyant pre-war and post-war hostesses, a widow called Mrs Reynolds Albertini, who married Lt-Colonel James Veitch at the Brompton Oratory. During the war Norah Reynolds Albertini devoted her time to the organization of entertainment for the troops. She also paid for the equipped ambulances and mobile canteens which were sent all over the world where men of the Allied nations were fighting.

Norah Reynolds Albertini was also for some years a governor of the Star & Garter Home at Putney, and on her wedding invitations a little note asked friends to make a small donation to the Star & Garter Home in lieu of a wedding present. She had a heart of gold, but a very flamboyant streak, which was in great contrast to her second husband (I never knew her first husband). Jim Reynolds Veitch was a very quiet man, a typical Guards officer, and was wonderful with Norah, managing to reduce the masses of wide and exquisite diamond bracelets she habitually wore almost from wrist to elbow to two or three at a time!

That summer quite a lot of private cocktail parties were given before everyone left for the summer holidays. One week, I went to a cocktail party in Chelsea given by Mr and Mrs David Rawnsley, whom I hardly knew but whose invitation I had accepted. The party was for Liam Redmond who was appearing in the film *I See a Dark Stranger*, for which David Rawnsley had done the settings. Most of the guests were from the film world, and I looked round and realized I did not know a soul in the room! It was amazing that my host and hostess, having invited me to their party, made no effort to introduce me to even one guest! I was just about to bolt when suddenly a good-looking young man came forward and said 'You look rather lost. Come and sit and talk to me.' I had no idea who he was. Then I discovered he was Michael Wilding, who was then working on location on the film of Compton Mackenzie's *Carnival*. He could not have been kinder.

During the party he introduced me to Ann Todd, who was looking very glamorous – she had just finished the film *The Seventh Veil* with James Mason; to Trevor Howard, and to an American couple called Mr and Mrs David Hand. He, David Hand, had been Walt Disney's righthand man, and Mr Arthur Rank had just brought him to England to make cartoons in this country.

In the first week in August that year I had another most enjoyable day's racing at Ascot. The highlight of the afternoon was the exciting victory by a head of The King's good-looking colt Rising Light, in a mile-and-a-half race. The King and Queen, accompanied by Princess Elizabeth, who one realized by now was becoming very keen on racing, like her father, were all present. It was a great joy to them, as The King had not seen any of his horses win since his good filly Sun Chariot had won the Oaks at Newmarket in 1942.

Having just had an election and a change of government, it was decided that there would be an Opening of Parliament before the summer recess. By a happy coincidence the day chosen happened also to be the day that final victory was at last proclaimed. The King had decreed that it would not be a full dress ceremonial affair and that peers would not wear their robes of state. This decision was good news to old and young peers as it relieved them of finding their robes, or of having to obtain any, as all clothes were still rationed. Many peers wore uniform, the others morning coats. The Household Cavalry escort wore their workday khaki, instead of their scarlet and blue tunics, shining cuirasses, and plumed helmets. The Guardsmen lining the route were also in khaki. For The King and Queen, it was the first state drive in peace time. They drove in a semi-state landau, which The King ordered to be kept open in spite of the rain! Inside the House of Lords, His Majesty, who wore his uniform of Admiral of the Fleet, did not wear his royal robes or the Imperial Crown; the latter was carried in front of him on a red velvet cushion. The Queen wore a long frock of turquoise blue and a little hat that was a frothy mass of blue to match. The peeresses wore day dresses and hats, and the ladies of the diplomatic corps excelled themselves with their millinery creations!

Shortly after the Opening of Parliament, having fulfilled a few more engagements and finished all his other work, The King left with The Queen and the two Princesses for their annual holiday at Balmoral. During those summer holidays at Balmoral Princess Elizabeth had a fall while out riding. Happily she broke no bones, but it left her very stiff and bruised, so Princess Margaret for the very first time took her sister's place at an official engagement of a youth parade in Scotland.

On 12th August that year, the Scottish and Yorkshire moors showed the effects of six years of war and little keepering. Bags were very disappointing. But for many the joy of being home and able to go out shooting on the Glorious Twelfth was a happiness on its own.

I could not get away until late August that year, so I cut out our usual visit to friends in Barmouth, and Jim and I went straight to the little cottage at Garrows in Perthshire, where we had a few very happy weeks. As before, I managed to keep my diary going from the north.

While I was in Perthshire I went over to the Earl and Countess of Mansfield's lovely home, Scone Palace, which had been used as a girls' school during the war. The object of my visit was a cricket match between Lord Mansfield's 'The Hills' eleven and 'The Carse' eleven captained by Major James Drummond-Hay, a very amusing character who had just returned from the Far East, where he had been on active service with the Coldstream Guards. His eleven, many of them still at their preparatory schools, were all very jokey, most of them wearing top hats with the Drummond-Hay emblem – sprigs of holly tucked into their hat bands. They included Douglas Mackintosh, Malcolm

Drummond-Hay, David Walter, Ewan Davidson, Robert de Pass, Richard Leach, Ian McKellar and Keir McKellar.

The Earl of Mansfield's eleven included Neil Ramsay, Lt-Colonel Charles Anderson, Viscount Stormont, John Douglas, Captain Ralph Stewart-Wilson, and his younger brother Blair Stewart-Wilson, now Lt-Colonel Blair Stewart-Wilson, who, since 1976, has been Deputy Master of Her Majesty The Queen's Household, and an equerry to the Queen, Peter Tower, and Jocelyn Stevens.

During the summer of 1945, while on holiday in Scotland, I received a telegram to tell me that my kind editor Reggie Hooper, who had helped me so much when I started at the *Tatler*, had died suddenly of heart failure. It was a sad shock. I was going to miss him dreadfully, and he would be a great loss to the *Tatler* – he had been with the magazine all his working life, having joined it directly he came down from Oxford.

The assistant editor, a woman, was made temporary editor. That was a very trying period! As I have said, she was a difficult woman to work for and regularly had the editorial staff in tears. A new editor was eventually appointed. He had been a crime reporter until the war, and during the war he had edited a soldiers' paper; he knew nothing about glossy magazines and the world that *Tatler* portrayed.

One very good thing he did was bring with him a wonderfully reliable sub-editor called John Mann, who was still with the *Tatler* when I left in 1959. It was an interesting change! The assistant editor who had been in charge did not get on with the new editor, and after a few years she eventually left for another magazine. Soon after his arrival, the editor relieved me of the business of helping on the fashion side so that I could give all my time to the social side.

It was he who gave me the name of 'Jennifer'. That October he came to me and said that now that the war was over he thought it was time to change the title of the social pages from 'On and Off Duty' back to something personal. He wanted to call it a 'A Social Diary' with my signature at the end. I flatly refused, as I did not like personal publicity; also I knew my family would be furious if they saw my name appearing! So that week the copy went off with the title 'A Social Diary', and unsigned; that was on 31st October 1945.

The following day my editor came to see me and said that to him I looked like a Jennifer, and would I agree to 'Jennifer writes her Social Journal' heading my pages. As I knew that no member of my family was called Jennifer, and as it seemed to me a simple old-fashioned name, I readily agreed. The title has varied from time to time over the years since then, but the name Jennifer has always been there.

Soon we were to learn that this new editor had rather lengthy luncheons, and frequently did not return to the office until between 4 and 6 p.m., sometimes very wobbly and in a merry mood, and sometimes in a very bad temper! It was exasperating for our poor art editor, a dear man called Bill Yearly, who often wanted decisions on pictures in other parts of the magazine, so eventually he used to ask me to come and choose them and make the decisions.

I heard later that the editor was a little frightened of me; happily I never incurred his wrath. He lasted a few years.

Our next editor was Philip Youngman Carter, who was a clever artist and had been assistant editor for some time. He was married to Margery Allingham, author of many successful crime novels. Pip Youngman Carter was a good editor who, all-important, had the feel of the magazine, knew his job, and was very nice to work for. I was sorry when he left.

In autumn 1945 Mr Ernest Bevin, who was then Foreign Minister, was host at a reception given by the Government at the House of Lords for delegates of the first meeting of the Council of Five – the all-important conference of the Foreign Ministers of the United Nations. He received the guests in the Royal Gallery with Mrs Bevin. It was an illustrious evening and one of friendly understanding.

I met Ernest Bevin on quite a few occasions, and once sat next to him at dinner. I always found him a most entertaining and charming man with far more of a conservative outlook than you might expect in a socialist. I also met his very dear wife 'Flossie', who was a great and loveable character. After a party they would sometimes sit down at a piano and sing popular old songs together.

I met both the Prime Minister and Mrs Attlee, later Earl and Countess Attlee, on numerous occasions, and I went to many of Mrs Attlee's charity meetings at 10 Downing Street, but I could not say that either of the Attlees was a very amusing character. I found both of them pretty heavy going! I remember that the first of Mrs Attlee's meetings was around teatime, and we were shown in by what looked like a daily (gone were the liveried footmen of the Baldwin, Chamberlain and Churchill eras). For tea there were thick schoolroom sandwiches and little cakes in paper cases. Mrs Attlee soon learnt; in six months this had all changed to a uniformed staff, thin sandwiches and home-made cakes!

A charming royal occasion I attended that autumn was the christening in Westminster Abbey of the infant son of King Peter and Queen Alexandra of Yugoslavia. The baby was christened Alexander and had The King and Princess Elizabeth among his godparents. His mother, who was most attractive, was, before her marriage, Princess Alexandra, the only daughter of King Alexander I of the Hellenes. It was a truly royal occasion. The King was wearing naval uniform and The Queen the then very fashionable long silver fox stole over her black velvet coat.

The ceremony was conducted by the Patriarch Gavilo, who was one of the most courageous men in Yugoslavia when the Nazis occupied the country. He came to London especially for the christening, and was assisted by Bishop Nikolai, the Metropolitan Germanus, and Father Nikolic, in the presence of the Archbishop of Canterbury, the Dean of Westminster, and Archpriest Theokritoff.

Unlike a christening in the Church of England, when the senior godmother holds the baby, on this occasion it was the senior godparent, who was our King. The King was also godfather to King Peter, and had been best man at King Peter's wedding. His Majesty had to carry the baby three times round the font, following the officiating priest, which he did with care and precision. At the end of this part of the service His Majesty gently handed the little Prince back to his nurse. It was then that Crown Prince Alexander started crying, as all babies should do at their christening. When I meet Prince Alexander, Crown Prince of Yugoslavia now, with his second wife and his three beautifully mannered young sons, I often think of his christening.

That year, those of us who loved racing heard with joy the good news that the Duke of Norfolk had been appointed The King's Representative at Ascot, which gave all of us hope of a return to a meeting there something like the royal meetings of pre-war days. This was the first time that The King, who owned Ascot racecourse, had appointed his own Representative.

In December, The King celebrated his fiftieth birthday with a family dinner party at Buckingham Palace, followed by a small dance for his and The Queen's friends, and many of the Princesses' young friends. Dancing took place in the Bow Room and the Grand Hall, as the state ballroom was still under dust sheets, having been shut up throughout the war.

The King and Queen spent Christmas at Sandringham, which

had been closed during the war. With them were Princess Elizabeth, Princess Margaret, Queen Mary, and the Duchess of Kent and her three children. Also with the Royal Family party for Christmas were Lady Constance Milnes Gaskell, who came with Queen Mary, the Hon. Mrs Geoffrey Bowlby, who was in waiting on The Queen, and Sir Eric Miéville, making his last visit to Sandringham as The King's Assistant Private Secretary, as he had resigned to start working in the City. Also one of the newer circle at court, Wing Commander Peter Townsend, who was originally appointed as the last of the war series of 'equerries of honour'. He had stayed on at Their Majesties' request as a permanent member of the royal entourage, and was already very popular in the royal circle.

In January 1946 I attended a big Anglo-Argentine wedding. It was the first marriage of Viscount Ednam, now the Earl of Dudley, to Señorita Stella Carcano, the elder daughter of Señor Miguel Carcano, who was then the Argentine Ambassador at the Court of St James's, and Señora Carcano, which took place at the Brompton Oratory, with the reception at the fine Argentine Embassy in Belgrave Square.

The bride wore a dress that I will always remember, as it was the first really lovely wedding dress any of us saw after the war. It was made of white satin with high neck, long sleeves, and a full skirt falling into a long train. The tight-fitting bodice and the long sleeves were quilted, with a single pearl in each corner of the diamond quilting. Her tulle veil was held in place by a little Juliet cap of the same quilting. It had been designed and made in Paris, where there was no restriction on material or embroidery, by Pierre Balmain, and was quite exquisite. Short white gloves, which I have seldom seen brides wear, gave an added chic to the whole effect.

The bridegroom was wearing the uniform of the 10th Hussars, with whom he served on active service in Italy during the war. The Earl of Dudley was present with his second wife; his first wife, the bride-groom's mother, who was a sister of the Duke of Sutherland, had been killed tragically in an air crash in 1930.

Early in 1946 the Egyptian Ambassador Mr Abdel Fattah Amr Pasha was At Home at the Egyptian Embassy to nearly a thousand guests, in celebration of the birthday of King Farouk of Egypt, who liked everything done in a large and flamboyant manner! It took hours getting up the wide marble staircase to be received at the very fine embassy in South Audley Street. It was also hard work trying to get around in the rooms upstairs or downstairs, for it seemed that all the diplomatic corps, Members of both Houses of Parliament, leaders in commerce and industry, several members of the royal household and many others had braved the crush! There was the most lavish display of food. I remember being rather shocked when I saw an elderly peeress filling her rather large handbag with goodies.

At the end of February came the re-opening of the Royal Opera House, Covent Garden, which had happily escaped bomb damage during the war, even if it had undergone some strange transformations, such as becoming a wartime *palais de danse*! For the re-opening, all the seats and covers were cleaned or renewed, and the famous stage curtains bearing the royal cypher put back in their place.

As the first really glamorous evening in the West End, it brought home the realization that the war truly was over. It was a sparkling scene: all the women were wearing beautiful dresses and sumptuous furs, with exquisite jewels. The Royal Family were present, including the two Princesses, who were making their first ever visit to the Royal Opera House. The King was in naval uniform and The Queen wore a dress of pale grey, with a diamond tiara and pearl necklace. Queen Mary also wore a diamond tiara and lovely jewels, and, over her evening dress, a sable-trimmed blue evening coat which she kept on all the evening.

The Royal Family sat in the Royal Box, and members of the Cabinet in the front row of the Grand Circle. There were many members of the diplomatic corps present. The ballet chosen for the re-opening was also star-studded! It was *Sleeping Beauty* with music by Tchaikovsky, decor and costumes by Oliver Messel, and dancing by the then Sadlers Wells Ballet Company.

The cast was sensational too. It was headed by Margot Fonteyn, later Dame Margot Fonteyn, as Princess Aurora – her dancing was absolutely superb – and included Beryl Grey, later Dame Beryl Grey, and Moira Shearer, later Mrs Ludovic Kennedy.

In the interval of this memorable occasion, I strolled round meeting friends and marvelling at the many beautiful clothes and jewels. For me the most outstanding looking were Mary Countess Howe in a long black velvet dress over which she wore a full-length white ermine coat, a magnificent diamond tiara, and fine diamond corsage ornaments, and the Countess of Rosse, justly proud of her brother Mr Oliver Messel, whom I met that evening. She looked very striking, wearing all the Rosse family emeralds and diamonds, including a tiara, necklace, bracelets, and so on! Another was Mrs Wellington Koo, the very chic wife of the Chinese Ambassador, who wore her famous jade jewels set in sparkling diamonds.

At about this time The King and Queen gave a small dance of around two hundred and fifty guests for Princess Elizabeth at Buckingham Palace. The guests were nearly all her contemporaries; some of the girls had already had coming-out dances at which Her Royal Highness had been a guest, and many of the young men were in the Brigade of Guards, and were friends of the two Princesses.

In March I went to the lovely dance at Claridge's that Wing Commander Gerald Constable-Maxwell and his very dear American-born wife Carrie gave with Mr and Mrs Anthony Buxton for Miss Anne Constable-Maxwell, now the Duchess of Norfolk, and Miss Elizabeth Buxton, later Mrs Michael Bonn. Gerald Constable-Maxwell, who was one of the most entertaining as well as kindest men I ever met, was one of our greatest pilots in the RFC in World War I, and had shot down thirty-one German aircraft.

This dance was arranged to perfection with beautiful spring flowers everywhere, a good band, delicious supper, and a very special guest list. Princess Elizabeth was present, looking radiant in a dress of the palest pink tulle. She danced every dance and stayed until nearly 3 a.m. Her partners that evening included the Hon. Charles Stourton, now Lord Mowbray Segrave and Stourton, Mr Boyce Richardson of the US Navy, and a childhood friend, Lord Ogilvy, now the Earl of Airlie, and Her Majesty's Lord Chamberlain since 1984.

Also in March I went to the first post-war three-day Cheltenham National Hunt Festival. I went up and down from London by train except for one day when I stayed down for the race week dance at Rossley Manor. On one of these train journeys I travelled with Sir Alfred Munnings, who was also going up and down each day. He was not going to watch the racing, but to watch the horses with his sketching outfit, in the paddock, at the start, and jumping different fences.

On the day I travelled with him, we both had window seats opposite each other. When we had been going for more than an hour and were passing through good hunting country, he suddenly said 'Betty, let's have a hunt.' I did not know what he was talking about. Then he explained that we each chose a line of country and where we would jump each fence, or in some cases a stone wall, and you got a very bad mark if you chose a bad landing! It was the greatest of fun, but very exhausting, especially for me as I was sitting with my back to the engine!

After racing that day I passed 'AJ', as he was known to friends, sketching the hills around Cheltenham racecourse and I flippantly said 'Don't miss the train'. His quick reply was 'Go on and keep us two seats together' – a very tall order on a race train, crowded as they were in those post-war days.

However, I was lucky, as I got two seats side by side. This was fortunate in more ways than one, as travelling in the same carriage just opposite us was a charming young American couple. AJ of course started chatting to them and asked if they had enjoyed the meeting, and so on. After a while they got a suitcase down from the overhead luggage rack. In it were masses of sandwiches, sausage rolls, and champagne, which they immediately very generously asked us to share with them.

We chatted most of the way back to London, during which time we discovered that this charming young couple were called Phipps. They were members of the famous American Ogden Phipps family, and AJ had painted his grandmother or aunt, or some near relation, in America just before the war. Young Phipps knew the painting and was obviously delighted to meet the great artist. I treasure the picture AJ Munnings gave me as a wedding present. It is a signed print of a painting he did of Frank Thatcher, the famous Pytchley huntsman. It hangs today, in my tiny dining room, in the same frame it arrived in.

The racing was interesting. The Hon. Dorothy Paget, who was present in her famous dark blue tweed coat, won three races on the opening day. In contrast to this very rich owner were the success stories of two farmers, a young one and a retired one. The young farmer, Mr Billy Hobbs, won the United Hunts Challenge Cup with Rearmament, who was given to him during the war for a couple of sacks of corn by a member of the Warwickshire Hunt. Rearmament was ridden by a young friend, and started at 100–8. So little was he fancied that Billy Hobbs nearly went to Stratford-upon-Avon market with some of his stock instead of going racing!

The older retired farmer, Mr E. Manners, had bought a horse called Prattler for twenty pounds when horses were selling cheaply during the war. To his owner's surprise and joy, Prattler, extremely well ridden by Major Dermot Daly, a great character in the Heythrop country, won the National Hunt Steeplechase! He started at 33–1, and paid a dividend of over 100–1 on the Tote.

This year, 1946, saw the nineteenth and twentieth Queen Charlotte's Birthday Balls for debutantes, in aid of Queen Charlotte's Hospital.

This ball, which began in the reign of Queen Anne, was revived in the twentieth century under the presidency of Lady Hamond-Graeme, the tall and austere wife of Sir Egerton Hamond-Graeme, who had the able help of Mr Seymour Leslie. They ran these balls with no committee, no posters or leaflets, and almost no expenses, as they worked through the hospital office. What a contrast to the public relations and high-cost overheads of so many of today's charity functions! The Queen Charlotte's Balls, which carried on with two or three balls a year throughout the Second World War, but in the ballroom rather than the Great Room at Grosvenor House, raised a great many thousands of pounds for charity.

This year there were fifteen hundred applications for tickets, so it was decided, as before, to hold at least two balls. At each ball nearly three hundred debutantes were selected as Maids of Honour to take part in the traditional march with the giant birthday cake, which six of them then pulled, with white satin ribbons, right up the dance floor to where the ball's President and guest of honour stood in long evening dresses and tiaras.

On arrival all three hundred debutantes curtseyed simultaneously to the Guest of Honour and to the President. The former was sometimes a member of our Royal Family, or a foreign royal lady, or the wife of a member of our peerage. The Maids of Honour always curtseyed to the two ladies, *never* to the cake, as I have seen written so often.

There were then many mothers queueing up to present their daughters at court! Many had been hoping that the pre-war evening courts, when young girls and young marrieds were presented to their Majesties by their mother or a sponsor, the men wearing court dress and the ladies evening dress with three white ostrich feathers on their head, would soon be resumed. However, after consultations with the Earl Marshal, the Duke of Norfolk, and the Lord Chamberlain, the Earl of Clarendon, The King decided early in the year not to hold any evening courts in the first year of peace. Although a lot of people were disappointed, this was a wise decision. The idea that evening parties at Buckingham Palace, instead of courts, with ordinary evening dress and no feathers or frills, would count as presentation was also abandoned. There was, however, an idea around at that point that The King and Queen might hold one or more Royal Presentation Garden Parties that would count as presentation, but no decision had been made.

Little did anyone realize then that there would never again in England be another 'court' as in pre-war days.

The Grand National at Aintree was, in those days, as much a social event as the National Hunt Festival at Cheltenham. Everyone in the district had house parties for the meeting, the largest of these being usually the Duke of Westminster's at Eaton Hall, the Earl and Countess of Derby at Knowsley, and the Earl and Countess of Sefton, who then owned Aintree racecourse, at Croxteth. Most hosts and hostesses had boxes and luncheon rooms at the racecourse where they held big parties. Besides private entertaining, many racegoers stayed at the Adelphi Hotel in Liverpool, where they always had special dinners the night of the Grand National, which in those days was always run on a Friday. Others stayed at the Grosvenor Hotel in Chester and many came by train for the day from London. That year the day returns were third class only, with no food, but that did not deter the real enthusiasts!

Before I was married, I always stayed with dear friends in Cheshire for the Grand National, but after the war, when I was working on my Jennifer's Diary, or Jennifer's Journal as it was then called, I decided I would see much more of what was going on if I stayed at the Adelphi Hotel. This arrangement also meant that I was able to get up early, and go out to Aintree to watch the horses have an early morning gallop. I had a badge and a very good reserved seat in the County Stand, and happily plenty of invitations to luncheon in one or other of the private luncheon rooms. Also, after a couple of years, Mrs Mirabelle Topham, who ran Aintree with a rod of iron, invited me each year to watch the racing from her very spacious box, where she also had a television. She was a great character, who had many rows with many people!

That year, when I came back to the Adelphi after watching the horses work, I joined Captain and Mrs Bobby Petre for breakfast in the hotel. Bobby Petre, who was always rather highly strung, was riding Mr and Mrs John Morant's Lovely Cottage in the big race, and he was very over-excited and worrying about the race. In the middle of breakfast he said to his wife and me 'In so many hours and so many minutes I shall just have jumped the fourteenth fence.' I thought he was being a bit optimistic and laughingly – and perhaps rather unkindly – I said 'By that time you will probably have fallen off!' Bobby Petre won the Grand National later that day! There was tremendous cheering as the Morants were very good owners, and Bobby Petre was a very popular amateur rider. No one joined in the cheering more heartily than I did, as I had known Bobby Petre since before he went to

Sandhurst, and his dear wife since she was a teenager, and I went to their wedding. Alas, I did not have a penny on the winner!

Point-to-points resumed that year, and that spring saw the re-opening of the Tate Gallery, which had been bombed and closed for seven years. Colourful confirmation that the war really was over was the wonderful display of tulips of every colour in the long border at Buckingham Palace. (Nowadays, these are herbaceous borders much admired by guests to Royal Garden Parties.) During the war, like all the borders at Buckingham Palace and Windsor Castle, the long border had been used to grow vegetables. Another plus was that once again newly marrieds were able to go abroad on honeymoon.

The spring meeting at Newmarket that year was memorable in that The King had three winners! Sadly he was not there to see them win, but Princess Elizabeth was. By now the racing world was waking up to the Princess's real love of racing, and there was great speculation as to whether she would soon have her own stable of race horses.

A few weeks later I went to Lingfield Park racecourse for their Derby Trial meeting. Although the stands still lacked a little paint, they were in splendid repair, and the lawns and flowerbeds and paddock all looked most attractive, with the flowering chestnut trees in full bloom. That day it really lived up to its pre-war name of Leafy Lingfield. It was hard to believe that it had been a prisoner-of-war camp for six years. I wonder how many racegoers there today know that part of Lingfield's history. It has, in recent years, become one of the first racecourses to have an 'all weather' course.

The first semi-royal wedding I ever went to was the marriage at St Margaret's, Westminster, of The Queen's nephew, the Hon. Andrew Elphinstone, the younger son of Lord and Lady Elphinstone, and the Hon. Mrs Vicary Gibbs, widow of Captain the Hon. Vicary Gibbs, who had been killed in the war on active service, and daughter of Captain and Mrs Angus Hambro. The bride was a lady-in-waiting to Princess Elizabeth, who, with the bridegroom's sister, the Hon. Margaret Elphinstone, now the Hon. Mrs Rhodes, was one of the two older bridesmaids. I remember being very shy and rather frightened at the very small reception in the River Room at the Savoy, as there were so many members of the Royal Family present, and I was trying to take in the whole scene quietly. The royal guests included The King in naval uniform, The Queen in blue, Queen Mary, Princess Margaret, King George of the Hellenes, and Prince Philip of Greece, later the Duke of Edinburgh.

After a gap of six years, the Derby returned to Epsom on the first Wednesday in June. In those days private horse-drawn coaches still drove on to the centre of the course with a coachman blowing his horn, and took their place beside the buses that had been chartered for the day for parties. Sadly today these horse-drawn coaches have all disappeared at Epsom, although quite a few private coaches still come to Royal Ascot. The King and other members of the Royal Family came to the 1946 Derby, and drove up the course to the Royal Box, as they did again on the Friday for the Oaks.

Unlike today, when all the royal party go down to the paddock before the big race, only The King and Princess Elizabeth and The King's sister the Princess Royal, the Earl of Athlone and the Hon. Gerald Lascelles went that year. Derby day was very wet and windy and very cold. Many of the ladies wore their fur coats! Most of the men were in uniform, the others in lounge suits, not morning coats.

The great Victory Parade took place in London that summer in June. The royal party watched the parade from a flower-bedecked saluting base at Marlborough Gate. With tireless courtesy and his tremendous sense of duty, The King took the salute of each individual contingent in the very long procession. With The King and Queen on the royal dais were Princess Elizabeth, Princess Margaret, Queen Mary, the Princess Royal in the uniform of the ATS, the Duchess of Kent in her WREN's uniform, her daughter Princess Alexandra, the Earl of Athlone, Princess Juliana and Prince Bernhard of the Netherlands, the young King Faisal of Iraq, and his Regent, and Lady Louis Mountbatten in her St John uniform. Mr Winston Churchill, Mr Attlee, Mr Mackenzie King and Field Marshal Smuts sat on the left of the royal party with the chiefs of staff, including Lord Louis Mountbatten.

After the parade The King and Queen entertained a luncheon party of around sixty guests at Buckingham Palace. In the evening there was a marvellous firework display over the Thames, which the Royal Family watched from the Lord Chancellor Lord Jowitt's flat overlooking the terrace of the House of Lords.

By far the most important wedding of that summer was the marriage of the Duke of Northumberland to Lady Elizabeth Montagu Douglas Scott, elder daughter of the Duke and Duchess of Buccleuch and Queensberry. This took place at Westminster Abbey in the presence of The King and Queen, Princess Elizabeth, Princess Margaret, Queen Mary, King George of the Hellenes, and the Duchess of Kent.

As the bride, who looked beautiful, had been a WREN during the war, the First Lord of the Admiralty lent nearby Admiralty House for the reception, which was attended by around 1500 guests, including WRENS who had worked with Elizabeth Montagu Douglas Scott during the war, both here and in Australia, where she did a magnificent job. Also indoor and outdoor staff from the two families' estates in England and Scotland, and nannies, governesses, hunt servants – in fact no one connected with either family was left out.

I remember the mothers of the bride and bridegroom, both beautiful women, looking wonderful that day. The royal party all came on to the reception, where they mingled in an informal manner with the guests. There were two wedding cakes at this wedding! One was a wonderful four-tiered cake which had been sent as a present from Australia, and only arrived the day before the wedding! The second one was only two-tiered but beautifully iced and decorated and made by the cook at Drumlanrig Castle.

The bride and bridegroom motored down to Albury Park in Surrey, which was one of the bridegroom's seats, for the first part of their honeymoon. Later they were going to make their homes at Alnwick Castle in Northumberland, and Syon House, Brentford, where the present Duke of Northumberland and his mother live today. I came away from this very happy wedding, which had united two of England and Scotland's oldest and most respected families, with the strong feeling that this marriage would last. Happily I was right. Hughie and Elizabeth Northumberland were blessed with a splendid family of three sons and three daughters. They, and their children, radiated kindness, contributed to the good of the country, and were happily married for forty-two years, until Hughie Northumberland died in 1988.

It was about that time that I first became interested in the work of the St John Ambulance Brigade. Lady Louis Mountbatten, who was then Superintendent-in-Chief of the Nursing Corps and Divisions of the St John Ambulance Brigade, invited me to go along to the St John headquarters, which is the historic Gate House of the Grand Priory, at Clerkenwell. Here, speaking magnificently without a note, Edwina Mountbatten told us about the work of this wonderful organization both in Britain and all over the Empire, and how it had quickly switched from war-time to peace-time work. She then gave a vivid account of all she had seen in the Far East, Australia, and New Zealand.

She told us of her visit to a leper colony, and how brilliantly St John workers had moved a colony of 500 sufferers a considerable distance under most difficult conditions with great lack of transport. Edwina

Mountbatten so inspired me that evening that I have been a firm supporter ever since. A few years ago in the 1980s I was very honoured when I was made an Officer Sister of the Order of St John, and I attended an investiture at Gate House when the Lord Prior Sir Maurice Dorman pinned on my award. I thought of that evening in 1946 which led to my great, and I hope helpful, interest over the years.

Not surprisingly, there was a very big application for entrance to the Royal Enclosure for the first post-war Royal Ascot. The Duke of Norfolk as The King's Representative had the very tricky task of sorting out the doubtful starters! The same rules about no divorcees were applied that year as in 1939. How empty the Royal Ascot Enclosure would be today if those rules still applied! The King had been firm that with clothes rationing still in existence no top hats and morning coats should be worn; instead it was to be service uniforms or lounge suits, with bowler hats. In fact, it was announced that if a man turned up in a morning coat with a top hat he would be asked to change, but I cannot remember that happening! For the women there was a change too, as short day dresses and hats were to replace the long, ornate dresses of the pre-war Royal Ascots.

His Majesty decided that the Royal Family would drive down the course in open landaus. In the first carriage, drawn by the famous Windsor Greys, were The King in naval uniform, and The Queen in a lovely shade of blue. In the carriage with them on the opening day were the Master of the Horse, the Duke of Beaufort, and The King's nephew Viscount Lascelles. Princess Elizabeth and the Princess Royal were in the second carriage, with the Earl of Euston, now the Duke of Grafton, and the Earl of Ellesmere, now the Duke of Sutherland. The Royal Family and their guests watched the racing from the Royal Box, and there were club marquees again.

The flowers round the Royal Box were beautiful, the lawn meticulously mown and green, and the course was in wonderful condition. I remember surveying the scene in the Royal Enclosure on the first day, with everyone so well dressed, and thinking what a contrast it was to meetings at Ascot during the war years, when anyone could buy a badge to get in, and then could watch from any stand that was derequisitioned! You would see men in tweeds and cloth caps, and stockingless women in cotton frocks and no hats. With a war on, this had been acceptable, but it was so very good to see Royal Ascot beginning to recover its pre-war glory.

At one Royal Ascot a few years later, I observed five ladies in the

Royal Enclosure wearing a navy blue and white dog's tooth check silk suit, from the great designer Edward Molyneux, on the same day! I don't think the ladies were too pleased!

The most awkward moment of duplication I ever remember was at one of Mrs Gilbert Miller's evening parties that she and Gilbert Miller gave each year in the River Room at the Savoy. American-born Kitty Miller, who dressed exceptionally well, had been to Paris and had given up her time for fittings at one of the top couture houses. She was standing receiving her guests, wearing the most beautiful stiff white wild silk dress, when in came the Duchess of Windsor wearing the same dress. It was no laughing matter for either of them! Happily Charlie Chaplin and his lovely wife Oonagh came right behind, so Kitty soon had someone amusing to take her mind off her dress.

During that Royal Ascot, the first post-war Ascot dance was held at the Guards Boat Club at Maidenhead on the Wednesday night, for 700 guests. It was most beautifully done. The club, which overlooked the river, was wonderfully lit, and so were the trees and the motor boats, which were at the disposal of the guests. The ballroom was banked with pink and blue hydrangeas, a wonderful dance band was playing, and at midnight two pipe-majors in full dress played an eightsome reel, and, if I remember rightly, several Scottish dances. Princess Elizabeth, who was the guest of honour, brought a large party of young friends, several of whom were staying at Windsor Castle. Everyone in the social world was there!

The first big country dance I went to after the war was a ball given at Sutton Place, the home of the Duke of Sutherland, by his second wife Clare, formerly Mrs Vincent Dunkerley, for her very attractive daughter by her first marriage, Miss Wendy Shakespear. As we drove up to the house, which was built by Sir Richard Weston in about 1523, it looked like fairyland floodlit. The Duke and Duchess of Sutherland, the latter in a white dress, stood in the Great Hall with Miss Wendy Shakespear, who was, I think, in a cloth-of-gold dress, receiving their guests. It was a beautifully arranged ball, with exquisite flowers everywhere, everyone in the social world that you could imagine present, and a good dance band and dancing that went on till dawn.

Two Royal Garden Parties took place at Buckingham Palace that July. At the first there were a number of our Royal Family, as well as royal families from other parts of the world, who had been taking refuge in England while their own countries were occupied or otherwise in turmoil. The King wore naval uniform, and The Queen a silk dress and jacket and little feather-trimmed hat. Princess Elizabeth and Princess Margaret, who walked just behind their parents when they came out on to the lawns, both wore silk dresses and straw hats, while Queen Mary was an upright figure in a printed chiffon dress, one of her very special swathed toques and an eight-row choker pearl necklace. She was accompanied by her daughter the Princess Royal.

The Glyndebourne Musical Festival re-opened that summer. Mr John Christie, whose wife Audrey had a beautiful, well-trained voice, built a theatre beside his historical Sussex home between the two wars. He and his wife, who was beautiful as well as musical, started a small opera season here, with operas by Mozart. These soon became very fashionable and Glyndebourne became part of the English summer season; seats there were and still are at a premium. Audrey Christie put a great deal of effort into making a visit to Glyndebourne a memorable experience. Inside the theatre everything was spic and span. In the interval there was an excellent cold dinner served in a dining hall, or you could picnic if you wished in the beautiful garden. Hours of work had been put into the garden: it was a picture, with rolling lawns, tidily clipped yew hedges and beautiful herbaceous borders.

That season I went to Glyndebourne for the opening night of Benjamin Britten's new opera *The Rape of Lucretia*, which, like everything at Glyndebourne, was beautifully produced and received tremendous applause. I dined and watched the opera with John and Audrey Christie. At the end of the performance John Christie went on to the stage and made a brief speech, and said they had started the theatre with Mozart, and then had two great Italian composers. Now they had a young English composer who he was sure would prove a tremendous success. All the men wore black tie and dinner jackets and the women wore evening dress, as, happily, they still do at Glyndebourne today.

The very briefest of foreign royal visits took place in July that year. Queen Wilhelmina of the Netherlands flew over from Holland for one night in London. The object of her visit was to decorate The King with the Order of Wilhelmina, and to present His Majesty with the black and the grey Dutch horses that were her gift to the Household Cavalry and to the Royal Mews. The King and Queen gave a very distinguished dinner party at Buckingham Palace on the night of Queen Wilhelmina's arrival, at which Queen Mary and other members of the Royal Family, ministers of state, and the Master of the Horse, the Duke of Beaufort, were present.

The next morning many members of the Royal Family, including the Earl of Athlone, who was then Colonel of the Life Guards, were assembled in the Inner Quadrangle at Buckingham Palace to watch Queen Wilhelmina present the fine horses to The King.

I always heard that Queen Wilhelmina was a most interesting raconteur, and The King must have enjoyed her company, as I was told that on that occasion he very courteously drove with her to Croydon airport, and saw her into her aeroplane for her return flight to the Netherlands. As far as I know, he never did this before or after for any royal visitor.

FIVE

The first of my travels

(1946–47)

At the beginning of August, in 1946, a big event occurred in my life. I flew for the first time! I had always said I would never fly unless my father, brothers, or my son were seriously ill and I urgently needed to get to them. I was absolutely terrified at the thought of flying, as Alan Butler, the Chairman of de Havillands, had found out years before, when I was staying with them at Bembridge.

By now, however, I had realized that my Jennifer's Social Journal, as it was then, would be very dull if I never wrote about anything overseas. So when I was invited by the Hon. Mrs Emmet to stay at Altidore Castle, Co Wicklow, for racing at Leopardstown and the Dublin Horse Show the following week, I said 'Yes'. As it came right after Goodwood, I decided I had so little time that I must fly.

I booked myself on an Aer Lingus flight. When the Friday afternoon arrived, and my Goodwood copy had been put safely to press, I felt sick with fear! I said nothing to anyone, and went to Airways House and at 4.30 p.m. caught their bus to Croydon airport. In those days there was no allocation of seats on any flight: you simply rushed to get on board and sat where you could. They were quite small aeroplanes with one very narrow aisle down the middle.

I had decided that if I sat by the aisle, I could not see out and that would be the best seat for me. When we had been flying for about half an hour, the husband of a couple on the other side of the aisle, who I knew by sight from race meetings, leant across to me and said 'I am just going to order drinks for my wife and myself. Would you have one with us? I would advise you to have a brandy and ginger ale.' I was rather surprised, but I accepted. When we landed, he asked me if I had ever flown before. I answered 'Actually, no!' He then told me they had noticed how frightened I looked, since I was nearly the proverbial 'green with fear'!

I found out that he was Mr Darby Rogers, who then trained in

Ireland. He and his dear wife Doll had come straight from Goodwood; they were the kindest couple you could meet, and became great friends of mine for many years. Sadly they are both dead now.

Once having taken the plunge, I started to travel frequently by air, and I have since flown many thousands of miles in every kind of aircraft!

This was the first Dublin Horse Show for six years. The showground and stands at Ballsbridge were then among the biggest in the world. A great character of the Dublin Horse Show, then and for many years, was Judge Wylie, whose son Mr John Wylie later helped his father, and eventually succeeded him as Chairman of the Executive Committee. After the show each day there were evening race meetings as well as hunt balls, so it really was non-stop. As I was over in Dublin for the whole of show week, I could not go to Cowes for the regatta, which also took place for the first time in six years, but without any of the really big pre-war yachts competing.

I went to the cottage in Perthshire as usual that summer, and while I was there drove over to the Princess Royal Park, Braemar, for the first post-war Braemar Gathering and Games, which were the wettest in living memory! This did not deter 25,000 spectators coming from all over the world to cheer The King and Queen and the two Princesses (who wore the kilt with neat jackets), and to watch these fabulous Scottish Games. The roads were jammed for miles, and although I started out from the cottage at around 7 a.m. I did not get to my seat until around noon. The royal party arrived at 3 p.m., bringing with them Prince Philip of Greece. Even if it was wet, it was a colourful scene, with the royal party sitting in the little Royal Pavilion decked with tartan and branches of rowan berries, and the Highland lairds and their ladies wearing the tartan of their clans. The Marchioness of Aberdeen also had a tartan umbrella!

As in the South that year, the North also resumed their annual entertainments. Besides Braemar, Aboyne, Pitlochry, and other gatherings, there was the Black Watch Memorial Fund Ball, the Angus County Ball (very well run that year by the Hon. Mrs Duthac Carnegie), and the Perth Hunt Balls. I went to two out of three of these balls.

Soon after I returned from Scotland, I dined one evening with the Chairman of the Association of British Aero Clubs, Mr Whitney Straight, who directly after the war dropped using his rank of Air Commodore. He told me of the goodwill tour he and Colonel Mossy

Preston, who was previously in the Grenadier Guards, and now very popular Secretary-General of the ABAC, had just made in a de Havilland Dove, to private clubs and aerodromes to monitor the amount of private flying in England since the war – the ban on private flying had been lifted in January.

After he had described the scheme to me, Whitney told me of a funny incident during the tour when the whole party were spending the night with Sir Lindsay and Lady Everard at their beautiful home, Ratcliffe Hall, where Sir Lindsay Everard, the Member for the Melton division of Leicestershire from 1924 to 1945, had for many years had his own aerodrome and had done a great deal for civil aviation.

During dinner it came up in conversation that Sir Lindsay had too many cygnets on the lake at the Hall. So Whitney Straight said he would like a pair for his lake at home, where he had a collection of rather special wildfowl. Immediately Sir Lindsay's son-in-law, Lord Newtown-Butler, now the Earl of Lanesborough, one of the funniest men I know, offered to lasso a couple of cygnets off the lake after dark! Much to everyone's surprise, he accomplished this unusual feat with the aid of a long pole, a rope, and an electric torch, returning with a cygnet under each arm ready for the journey next morning. They travelled well, and I heard later that they were living happily on Whitney's lake.

That autumn the Duke and Duchess of Windsor made their first visit of any length to this country since his abdication in 1936. The Earl of Dudley lent them Ednam Lodge at Sunningdale. They kept a very low profile, the Duke of Windsor refusing any public engagements. He spent some of his time sorting out his possessions from Fort Belvedere, which had been in store, and saw a few of his closest friends.

That month was the first time that I met Prince Philip of Greece, later the Duke of Edinburgh. It was in Romsey Abbey before the marriage of Lord Brabourne to the Hon. Patricia Mountbatten, elder daughter of Viscount and Viscountess Mountbatten, at which Prince Philip and the Marquess of Milford Haven, both cousins of the bride, were ushers.

On arrival in the Abbey I saw a very good-looking young naval officer with a piece of paper in his hand. As I passed he was saying 'Does anyone know what Mrs Kenward looks like as I have to find her?'! I stopped suddenly and said 'I am Mrs Kenward', then he put the piece of paper in my hand and said 'My uncle asked me to give you this list, and said I was to be sure you got it safely'. He was very kind and helpful then about my seat, and we greeted each other briefly at the reception.

This was a beautiful wedding in Romsey Abbey, at which the then Archbishop of Canterbury, assisted by the Bishop of Winchester, the Vicar of Romsey, Canon W.H.B. Corban and the Reverend A.B. Ronald, officiated. Arum lilies were the only flowers in the Abbey and graced the altar and the chancel steps. The bridegroom wore the uniform of his regiment, the Coldstream Guards, and the bride, who was given in marriage by her famous father Viscount Mountbatten, wearing naval uniform and six rows of medals, was a radiant figure wearing a classical wedding dress made of exquisite Indian silver and gold brocade. Her lace and tulle veil was held in place by a pearl and diamond tiara, a recent gift from her mother. The bride was attended by four bridesmaids – Princess Elizabeth, Princess Margaret, Princess Alexandra, and the bride's sister the Hon. Pamela Mountbatten, now Lady Pamela Hicks. The King, in naval uniform, and The Queen, in pale grey, were present at the marriage, also the Duchess of Kent, Prince Philip's mother Princess Andrew of Greece, and Admiral the Hon. Sir Alexander and Lady Patricia Ramsay. The Abbey was filled – not with all the usual socialites to be seen at weddings, but with close relations and friends of both families, tenants, estate workers and employees from the Mountbatten and Brabourne estates, five hundred townspeople of Romsey, representatives of all the local organizations, and men and women who had served alongside the bride's parents and with the bride and bridegroom during the war years, when, as I have already mentioned earlier, the bride was in the WRENS overseas. I remember thinking that day how lucky I was that the bride's parents had given me a wonderful seat in the Abbey, and invited me to both receptions.

After the ceremony there was only a comparatively small reception at the bride's home, Broadlands, near Romsey, as most of the house was still being used as a hospital. Here Viscount and Viscountess Mountbatten, the latter looking enchanting in a pale blue dress and little feathered hat, received the guests with the bridegroom's mother, Doreen Lady Brabourne, and the bride and bridegroom. Guests then passed members of the Royal Family who were talking to friends. I remember an American-born wife turning to me as she saw The King and Queen ahead and saying 'Do I baab?' I quickly and quietly replied 'Bob twice and walk on.'

After the bride and bridegroom cut their wedding cake with a sword, The King proposed their health, wishing long life, every happiness and the best of luck, and the bridegroom replied briefly. After this Their Majesties, with the bride and bridegroom and their attendants, the bride's parents, the bridegroom's mother, Sir Felix Cassel and one or two other close relations, went on to Crosfield Hall in Romsey, where several presentations were made from the estates of both families. The King again proposed the health of the bride and bridegroom. I think this must have been the only time in history that a reigning monarch went to two receptions for the same wedding and twice toasted the bride and bridegroom. After the bridegroom had replied to the toast, the new Lady Brabourne, now Countess Mountbatten of Burma, made a really warm little speech saying she had just fulfilled a lifelong ambition to be married in beautiful Romsey Abbey, and with so many friends present. At that exceptionally happy reception I found myself talking to a Mr Bracken, who was then in charge of Viscount Mount-batten's Irish estate, Classiebawn Castle, Co Sligo, and who had been with the family since 1901. I always remember he was bubbling over with joy when he told me it was his first visit to England and the proudest day of his life, as he had been presented to The King.

A couple of weeks later I found that in spite of taking the greatest care when writing about the Brabourne-Mountbatten wedding I had made one of the biggest mistakes of my diary days. Although general knowledge, it had also escaped the editor, sub-editor and the reader they then had at the printers. I had described Field Marshal Sir William Slim as Admiral Sir William Slim! I only discovered this when an unknown reader telephoned after seeing an early copy, and pointed out my mistake. I was mortified and wrote the dear Field Marshal a letter of apology and delivered it by hand to his club.

I got the kindest reply saying 'Not to worry, I have been called many things worse than that.' General Sir William Slim, later Field-Marshal Viscount Slim who, after he retired, was Governor and Constable of Windsor Castle, and his wife Aileen were a very dear and special couple, whom I was to have the privilege to know much better in later years.

I had no car and chauffeur in those days. I had to rely entirely on driving myself in borrowed or hired cars, or go by train, taxi and an occasional car hire in the evenings. I noticed in my 1946 pocket diary that I averaged £1.12.6 a week for taxis, that a car hire for the evening cost £1, my rail ticket to Liverpool for the Grand National (I expect it was a return) £3.0.6, and a return air fare Aer Lingus to Dublin for the Dublin Horse Show £11.15.0. My Derby Day Members badge cost £3, my Royal Ascot four-day badge £7, and luncheon bills for two at Claridge's or the Berkeley were mostly under £1.5.0.

I was usually invited to both private and charity dances with a partner, and at first I invited a number of friends to escort me; but in time I realized that at most dances I could probably see and take in everything I needed to by 12.30 or 1 a.m., and that if I took a partner he usually wanted to go on dancing far later. Very soon I used to say I would rather come alone, as that way I was free to leave when I wanted to. Of course one could not do this if staying in a house party; then one had to stay until others wanted to leave.

At the end of 1946, it was announced that The King had decided there would still be no Royal Courts in 1947, the reasons given being the continued austerity, the shortage of goods, and the growing need for exports.

The list of those wishing to make their curtsey had been increasing, so The King and Queen wisely chose as a solution a series of Royal Presentation Garden Parties at Buckingham Palace, the attendance at which was to be recorded as the equivalent of presentation at court. It was also decided to hold one of the Royal Presentation Garden Parties at Holyrood House, Edinburgh, when the court was in residence there in July. Applications came pouring in to the Lord Chamberlain from ladies wishing to make presentation at the Presentation Parties, which was what they were called.

On 1st February 1947, The King and Queen, accompanied by Princess Elizabeth and Princess Margaret, left England to make a tour of South Africa. It was the first time such a royal visit had been made to the Union, and in contrast to overseas royal visits today, which usually take three to four weeks at the most, on this occasion The King and Queen were not due back until May! They had planned a semi-state drive from Buckingham Palace to Waterloo, but the roads were so icy that The King decided they should travel by car instead of the horse-drawn landaus. Queen Mary, the Duke of Gloucester, the Princess Royal and the Duchess of Kent were at Waterloo station, and members of the Royal Family travelled down to Portsmouth with The King and Queen and the two Princesses. Mr Attlee and members of the Cabinet were also at Waterloo to see them off. Quite a contrast to the quiet departures today of The Queen and the Duke of Edinburgh when they leave on royal visits: now they drive to London airport, and a handful of officials and possibly the ambassador of the country they are visiting see them off there.

February is always a dull social month in England, so I decided that from now on I must try and go abroad during that time. On St Valentine's Day I took off by train and boat for St Moritz. It was the height of a coal crisis in England, and everyone was shivering. I had a very sad and rather guilty feeling in my heart as I left London, rather as one felt during the bombing when one went for a weekend in the country, and left one's friends to carry on.

The boat train from Victoria to Folkestone was barely heated, and although there was a restaurant car on the train, they could not produce enough lunch to go round! At Folkestone I boarded the Channel steamer, cold and hungry! Luckily a kind and efficient steward soon produced a sandwich for me. Except for my return journey from New York in 1929, when so many people had kindly been alerted to look after me, and my short trip to Dublin, this was my very first trip abroad alone, so I was a little apprehensive.

When we landed, there were no customs to cope with before boarding the warmth and comfort of the Engadine Express, on which I had a very comfortable sleeper. Breakfast next morning of coffee, croissants, and black cherry jam, with brilliant sun shining into the carriage, was very cheering.

On arrival at Zurich, where we had to change, I bought a Swiss newspaper, whose headline was *La Crise Charbonnière en Angleterre*; another was *La Bataille de Combustible en Angleterre*. Several practical-minded Swiss said to me that it was incredible to think that England could have so much of her industry brought to a standstill by this strike.

My train from Zurich wound its way up the Engadine in glorious sunshine, and we arrived in St Moritz in the late afternoon. Horse-drawn sleighs met the train as well as the hotel buses.

I went straight to the Palace Hotel where I was warmly greeted by Monsieur Hans Badrutt and his good-looking son Monsieur Andreae Badrutt, who together ran this hotel so superbly. In St Moritz you could not possibly guess there had ever been a war! There were very few English here, as the foreign currency allowance was so small, but there were masses of foreigners, who seemed to have plenty of money to spend. Before I left England, I had been kindly invited to join a party to dine that night at the Chesa Veglia, then very fashionable, especially on Saturday nights. It was such a cheerful sight inside the restaurant, which also functioned as a tea-room and a nightclub.

All the waitresses and some of the guests were in national costume, and there were brightly coloured tablecloths on all the tables. An enchanting Hungarian band, also in national costume, was playing all the latest Continental tunes. Idely, the head waitress, worked miracles fitting everyone in, and then produced delicious food. She was remembered by many of our soldiers and airmen who had managed to get to St Moritz while they were interned in Switzerland during the war, as Idely then always had a cup of hot chocolate and some of her good cakes for them.

On my first morning I came downstairs to find King Peter of Yugoslavia in the hall, just off to Celerina, where he hoped to fit in two runs that day. A little later the Gaekwar of Baroda, who was staying at the Palace with the Maharanee and their suite, came down with his camera and told me he was off to find a good spot from which to photograph the Schlitteda Engadiadinaisa, which I was also off to watch. This was a most picturesque parade of ornamental sleighs, some over 100 years old, drawn by horses wearing fabulous trappings, with their drivers and passengers in nineteenth-century costumes.

From here I went on up to the fashionable Corviglia Club, in those days so well run by Vicomte Charles Benoist d'Azy. I had lunch out of doors on the terrace in brilliant sunshine, overlooking the snow-covered mountains. Also lunching were the Duque d'Alba, and his only child the Duquesa de Montoro, who had just become engaged to Don Luis Martinez de Irujo. They stayed at the Palace Hotel for many years, and the Duque would sit at a special table in the corner of the huge lounge playing patience, or, if he could find an opponent, chess, a game at which he excelled. He was a very courteous and charming man, whom I enjoyed meeting.

On my second evening in St Moritz I went to the Sunday night candlelit dinner at the Palace, which was very chic, with everyone in evening dress. Among those dining that night was the famous skater and later film star Miss Sonja Henie, who, looking very pretty, arrived wearing what in those days was rather unusual, a platinum mink coat over a black dress with a magnificent diamond necklace and brooch, and huge ruby and diamond clip earrings.

On the Monday morning I went on to Davos, which I found a tremendous contrast to St Moritz, where life was all glitter! I had not skied since my visit to Wengen in the twenties, but before coming on this first winter sports trip for the magazine I had decided I had better not ever think again of skiing myself, as I could not afford to break a leg or hurt myself and lose my job. At St Moritz this hadn't mattered a scrap, as the majority of visitors to St Moritz are always there for the social life and seldom think of actually skiing! Davos was quite different: people really go there to ski. In those days, runs were discussed at breakfast, lunch, and dinner, when it was telemarks around the soup, slaloms through the main course and christianas with the sweet! It was early to bed and early to rise, and when I went up the funicular without any skis, I was looked at very strangely, as if I was something that had come out of the cheese! This made me feel very self-conscious and rather miserable at first, but I knew that my job required me to get used to it.

During my first visit to Davos I was shocked and saddened by the sight of so many hospitals or clinics for sufferers of tuberculosis. Switzerland specialized in the care of this disease; the patients used to be brought out on their balconies in their beds, in the pure clean air and sunshine. The sight of a hearse going down Davos High Street was a frequent one, and I remember contrasting all these sad people suffering and dying with others nearby more fortunate who were full of life and skiing. Happily, not long after, a cure was found for the dreaded tuberculosis, and the hospitals and clinics vanished or were turned into modern hotels whose happy visitors could enjoy the sunshine and winter sports.

That year I went on from Switzerland to the South of France. I arrived in Cannes after a twenty-seven-hour train journey via Landquart, Zurich, Lausanne, and Geneva; at the latter I had time to stretch my legs and take a walk to see some of the fine buildings. I then boarded my sleeper and woke up on the Riviera. In Cannes it was raining, and I learnt I had arrived on one of the two days of the week on which they had electricity cuts from 7.30 a.m. to 3.30 p.m., not because of shortage of fuel, but because the electricity plants were worn and needed resting!

I stayed at the Carlton Hotel. I remember being so cold that first day in the hotel that I didn't take my coat off until I had a hot bath before changing for dinner!

My first evening I went to a recital given by a famous Hungarian pianist, and on the Saturday night I dined at Les Ambassadeurs, at a gala in honour of the French artist Monsieur van Dongen, who was there with his lovely young wife. We had a five-course dinner, of a kind we had not dreamt of in England for years!

During that evening I met the great French hotelier and resort creator Monsieur François André, and his charming and able wife. He told me that wonderful repairs had been done to the war damage in Deauville, where he also ran the casino and three big hotels, and that he planned a really pre-war season there that summer. This led to my visiting Deauville, and for nearly ten years the Deauville Air Rally became an annual feature of my diary for the *Tatler*.

At first I used to fly over with Mr Angus Irwin, who was Deputy Chairman of Illustrated Newspapers, who owned the *Tatler*. Angus Irwin had been a pilot in both world wars, but had not flown much for several years when the prospect of our going to Deauville for the Air Rally first cropped up. Typically, off went Angus to Luton Flying Club, which was near his country home, to hire a machine for some practice. Then on the Saturday of the rally he picked me up at Croydon in a small two-seater Auster. We took off for Deauville – with the map on my lap! Other years we flew in a variety of hired light aeroplanes, including a de Havilland Moth.

The rally was sponsored by the Royal Aero Club in Piccadilly. This club was very fortunate in having Colonel R.L. Preston, late of the Grenadier Guards, as its general manager. Before the war 'Mossy' Preston took a leading part in running the Brigade of Guards' very popular flying club at Heston. One of the most efficient men, he was full of imagination. Shortly after the war when he was in Deauville playing golf, Mossy met Monsieur François André. Between them they decided to revive the Deauville Air Rally for members of the Royal Aero Club, and associate clubs, which had just started as war broke out – also to invite the Aero Club of France.

The rally was to take place over a weekend in the first two weeks in July. The first one was such a tremendous success that the Air Rally became an annual event thoroughly enjoyed by all who took part. The same programme was followed year after year. You were invited to arrive at Deauville airport on the Saturday morning, and it was a splendid sight as you came in to land to see scores of small aeroplanes parked in rows below. We were welcomed at the airport by Monsieur André, and taken in buses to our hotels in time for luncheon. The afternoon was free. In the evening there was always a wonderful gala at the casino, complete with cascades of fireworks outside the huge windows at midnight. You were given a card of entry to the casino, so that if you wanted to you could gamble.

On the Sunday, there was a golf match between the Royal Aero

Club and the Aero Club of France, played on the very fine Deauville golf course. Everyone was invited to Sunday luncheon up at the Golf Hotel, and to attend the prize-giving. In the evening there was a dinner, usually at the Hotel Royal, and you took off for home on Monday morning. At the dinner a leading personality of the Royal Aero Club made a speech and thanked dear Monsieur André on behalf of all the guests. And his guests we certainly were, from the moment we landed, to the moment we took off! All we were expected to do was to leave a voluntary tip at the hotel for the staff, who always treated us as if we were royalty or millionaires! It really was a fantastically generous gesture of François André, as at each rally there were always over a hundred light aeroplanes and well over a hundred guests.

The speech at the Saturday evening dinner was usually made by that outstanding personality the first Lord Brabazon of Tara, President of the Royal Aero Club, who frequently came on the rally with Lady Brabazon. One year when making his speech 'Brab' with great charm added 'To many British visitors Deauville has become Andréville', about which we all agreed; François André looked delighted.

When I was about to fly home with Angus Irwin on one occasion the fog was so bad at Deauville and across the Channel that we were all grounded at Deauville airport, which in those days was a couple of small huts, with no runways, just a small airstrip made of iron gratings. At 12.30 p.m., news came that we could fly as far as Le Touquet with the possibility of flying on to Lympne. So we took off and landed at Le Touquet, where we found the forecast very gloomy.

I was getting in a panic as I had promised to be down in Surrey by lunchtime next day to help Sir Adrian Jarvis, who was High Sheriff of Surrey that year, with his big official High Sheriff's luncheon. By around 3 p.m., Angus Irwin, Brab and Hilda Brabazon and many others had decided they would probably stay in Le Touquet for the night. Suddenly, to my joy and relief, Mr Jack May, who was a member of the Redhill Flying Club, came along and said he had permission to fly as far as Redhill, but his wife did not want to go across in this weather, so he had a spare seat. I jumped up and said: 'Please take me.' I had no idea what sort of pilot he was, or what type of aeroplane he flew. Angus was not pleased with me! Anyhow, in no time we took off. It was pretty bad over the Channel, where we flew low, and it was worse when we saw England, but we were lucky in finding the Folkestone-to-London railway line, which we followed. Happily we spotted the fork in the railway line to Redhill, and on we went. Then it was a case of Jack May knowing the various red lights on his local roads, which got us safely to the little airfield where by now everything was locked up. In time, someone appeared, keys were found, our little aircraft was put to bed, then Jack May drove me to the station to catch a train to London, and happily I got to the luncheon next day in plenty of time.

One year, when Angus Irwin was ill, the club arranged for me to fly with a colonial member I had never heard of, but who I discovered was very bad-tempered (not to me) and always ready for a fight! This was at times very unnerving, as I found when we landed from Luton at Croydon airport to clear customs. Here my pilot was asked, I think, to pay a landing fee, or some quite regular charge, and he refused. I offered to pay but I was not allowed to. There was a scene: coat off, sleeves up, and ready to fight such as I had never seen before! He was a very big man. Eventually the problem was resolved, we got back into the aeroplane and took off and finished the journey in silence – I flew home with another pilot!

Another year in the early sixties, I flew on this Deauville rally in a small Brantley helicopter, with no floats and no radio, but brilliantly piloted by Mr Tommy Sopwith. This was an idea of Mr Tony Everard's, who had just taken over the chairmanship of the Helicopter Club of Great Britain, which only had a very few members. Tony was desperately trying to build up the membership and asked if I would help by writing about the club in my diary. The club then had fewer than ten members; today there are nearly two hundred. I am very proud that in the sixties I was made an honorary member for life. Over the years I have always tried to attend their functions and keep in touch.

Tommy Sopwith, who is the best helicopter pilot I have ever flown with, uses his helicopter as anyone else uses their car. We had a slow but amusing flight over, with a lot of happy laughter, and arrived in time for luncheon. There were only two helicopters, including ours, but over a hundred fixed-wing light aeroplanes at that rally. We had an equally amusing flight home on the Monday, when Tommy dropped me off, just as he had collected me, at Battersea airport.

Another smaller air rally I went to before this was in England, when Major David Constable-Maxwell, a keen amateur pilot, and Mrs Constable-Maxwell invited a number of members of the Royal Aero Club to their home Bosworth Hall, where they had an airfield, for a rally and a party one Saturday evening. David Constable-Maxwell arranged for me to fly up with Mr John Houlder, whom I had never met before, in his Miles Gemini.

It was at luncheon in a marquee that day that I had my first flight in a helicopter. Mr Dick Fairey, son of aircraft designer Sir Richard Fairey, who had lost a leg in an accident, suddenly arrived after luncheon and asked if anyone would like to come up in his helicopter. To my surprise I heard myself saying that I would like to! The only other acceptance was the Constable-Maxwells' very dear old nanny! Dick Fairey took me for a most interesting flight closely looking at various beautiful gardens and estates of interest around Leicestershire, which I thoroughly enjoyed. I landed, having been completely won over to helicopters. Since then I have flown many miles in them and found them tremendously useful.

John Houlder, whom I knew nothing about, I found a very shy man, and on our way up we hardly spoke. In twenty-four hours this shyness had eased a little, and we talked quite naturally on the short flight home to Luton. To my surprise John Houlder suddenly suggested I might like to fly the machine; he would, he said, have a dual control. So, rather frightened, I took over, listening to all his instructions. We wobbled a bit! and as we were coming towards Luton I wanted to hand over to land, but John said to carry on and that he would help me. I learnt a lot in those few minutes! – how to keep my eye on the point where I wanted to land, to watch the falling speedometer and height recorder. He, I think, worked the wing flaps for speed. Eventually we made a safe but very bumpy landing. Rather unfortunately that landing was watched by Mr Kenneth Davies, the then Chairman of the Royal Aero Club, who jokingly remarked to John on his bumpy landing when we went into the clubhouse! We both kept very quiet!

A few months later John Houlder very kindly flew me over to Paris for the day for Christmas shopping, when he was going over on a business trip. Once again he said I must have a spell at flying the Gemini. This time it was a much longer flight, and one I found more unnerving as we had to keep to a given height, and at that height we flew through thick cloud the whole way. Visibility was only a yard or two; to me that was a great strain, as all the time I feared something would suddenly appear in front of us. After half an hour or more at the controls I asked to give up.

The only other time I have taken the controls of an aeroplane was several years later when I was staying with the Alan Butlers in

Rhodesia, now Zimbabwe. As I wrote earlier, Alan Butler had tried in the 1920s to get me to fly with him in his de Havilland Moth without any success; now, at last, he had got me airborne. Having heard from me that John Houlder had persuaded me to try flying his Gemini, once we had left the precincts of Salisbury he suggested I should have a go at flying his Cessna, which I did. It was a bit frightening at first, as there are small mountains around Salisbury and it often meant flying along a gully between two mountains; as the Cessna was a much faster machine, one's reactions had to be faster too. I remember enjoying myself, and being amazed at the contrast in the two aeroplanes. The Cessna was so light to handle, to me it felt like riding a polo pony after riding a hunter!

I have rather strayed from February 1947 with my little airborne stories.

On Sunday morning, I left Cannes and joined the Blue Train on which my brother Peter Kemp-Welch and his dear wife were travelling, and we arrived in Monte Carlo in comfy time to unpack for luncheon. We were all staying at the Hôtel de Paris. Monte Carlo then only had a population of between 17,000 and 18,000, of whom around 400 were British, and 60 American citizens. The colourful army, or Royal Guard as I think they called them, were only about twenty strong. It was a very pretty little principality – none of the high concrete buildings existed then – with a fairytale atmosphere, and flowers everywhere. A little world of its own, with no income tax, no taxes on real or personal property, and no electricity cuts! To all of us from England it was indeed another world, with apparently plenty of everything! The only thing that was missing that year was sunshine. Just as I had had bad weather in Cannes, it was cold and wet all the time I was in Monte Carlo, but happily for others it improved after I left.

Sadly I had to leave this joyful scene after a few days. I caught the overnight Blue Train to Paris, and happily found no heating or lighting cuts at the Ritz Hotel, so I was quickly able to enjoy a lovely hot bath, always for me the best thing after a long journey. Before lunch I found friends in the Ritz bar, where I met the Hon. David Herbert with a party of friends including Sir Michael Duff, also Miss Nina Leclerq, then one of *Vogue*'s fashion editors, and The Queen's couturier, Mr Norman Hartnell, later Sir Norman Hartnell.

During my brief stay, I was able to fit in two spring collections at Pierre Balmain, and at Christian Dior. Monsieur Pierre Balmain, I remember, had unfortunately had his leg broken in a car accident the previous day, so was not present, but I met Monsieur Christian Dior, whose friendship I later enjoyed until his death in 1957.

Both collections were superb. Christian Dior had hit the headlines with his sensational but wearable 'New Look' collection that spring. We were then still rationed for clothes in England as well as for many other commodities, so to see these lovely clothes was an added joy. We were also very strictly rationed with foreign currency, so few of these lovely models came to England, but the Americans were buying them in a big way. After the collections I joined friends for supper at Maxim's, which had just reopened after a complete renovation.

During the war Maxim's was taken over entirely by the Germans and was a favourite haunt of General Goering. From here we went on to the 'in' place of the moment, the Club des Champs Elysées, which was under the Champs Elysées Theatre, with two good bands and a slick, well-dressed floor show.

Next day I lunched at the Officers Club with Baronne de Wardener, who supervised it so well. The club was then open not only for serving officers, but also for ex-officers living in Paris, and Pammy de Wardener, who was quick and intelligent, was so helpful in advising members on where to buy, what to see, and where to go. Later that day I went with 'Priscilla' to a French engagement party given by Monsieur and Madame Jules Simon for their daughter in Avenue Bosquet. Their home had three huge reception rooms adjoining each other, with exquisite tapestries on the walls, and large bowls of white lilies and pink tulips everywhere. The buffet was out of this world. It was so interesting to me to see this very elegant French party. Our hostess, who looked very chic in black, had driven across the Sahara with only a woman friend as her companion in the thirties, and during the war had driven an ambulance.

From here, I went on to dine with that jovial and very dear personality, the Princesse de Croy-Roeulx, at her beautiful home in Avenue Foch, where she had priceless treasures which she had managed to save from damage during the German occupation. The house in those days was freezing cold with only a small stove in each room for heating!

My hostess, who spoke perfect English – she had not been to England since The King's Coronation – was a wonderful hostess, and it was a most amusing dinner party. The guests included Comte de la Forest Divonne, a renowned brilliant conversationalist; Monsieur Willy Durand, who was always the life and soul of any party; my hostess's brother and sister-in-law the Marquis and Marquise de

Pomereu, who had just flown back from Morocco, where they then owned big estates; the Duc d'Harcourt, whose lovely Château de Thury-Harcourt, in Normandy, was one of the showplaces of France until destroyed by the Germans; and Comte Philippe de Brissac.

Next day I travelled home on the luxurious Golden Arrow train, enjoying a super dinner and a comfy sleeper on the French section before crossing the Channel on the *Invicta*, then the last word in Channel steamers, and on up to Victoria by Golden Arrow, which arrived on time. Although it took a little longer, how comfortable and enjoyable travelling was in those days!

My impression during my first post-war visit to France was of poverty on one side of the street and plenty on the other. In those days, in most parts of France there was a black market where you could buy anything from butter to rice, blankets to mackintoshes – at a price. You frequently saw notices on the grocers' doors saying 'no fats, or sugars' and so on. In the poorer parts of Cannes, I felt sad when I saw some of the children looking thin and undernourished, but what made me even sadder was that their parents seemed quite lethargic and resigned to the situation.

In March 1947 the first Grand Military Meeting for eight years was held at Sandown Park, and for the first time the Grand National was run at Aintree on a Saturday, to comply with the government ban on mid-week sport. It was like a charge of the Light Brigade when fifty-seven starters lined up that year! The race week entertaining had resumed in a limited way in luncheon rooms and in private boxes.

On 21st April, Princess Elizabeth celebrated her twenty-first birthday while in South Africa with her parents, on their long official tour. On that day, many of us heard on the radio Princess Elizabeth make that wonderful speech, dedicating her life to her country, a promise she has truly fulfilled in every way.

In May, I had my first look at Perth races, run then as they are still over the Earl of Mansfield's land around Scone Palace. My memory of that day was that the ladies as well as the men were very well wrapped up, wearing their clan tartans as suits, coats and shawls, with Newmarket or Wellington boots, as in spite of it being May it was icy cold and very, very muddy underfoot. The racing was not of a very high standard! It was however a great social gathering. I have since been quite a few times to Perth races, in both April and September, staying always with two very dear friends, Earl and Countess Cadogan, at their Perthshire home Snaigow. It has always been a social gathering and a wonderful chance to see friends who live up north.

The King and Queen, on their return from South Africa, made their traditional official drive through the City, and attended a state luncheon at Guildhall. As we still had food rationing, the banquet was restricted to three courses, instead of the ten or twelve courses served to Their Majesties when they returned from Canada eight years previously. Happily for those attending banquets, menus have generally never returned to more than five courses, at the very most.

That May, the whole country wished Queen Mary a very happy eightieth birthday. We all thought then that it was wonderful how at that age Her Majesty still frequently went to the theatre and cinema, and fulfilled more tiring engagements such as visiting the British Industries Fair, and other official engagements. Recently we have seen an even greater royal miracle in our beloved Queen Elizabeth the Queen Mother, who since her ninetieth birthday in 1990, with her tremendous charm and interest in everything, has continued to fulfil a great number of official engagements, including a few abroad.

At about this time I had one of my most absent-minded moments! A few months before, a charming young lady called Lambton had come to ask my help arranging her London wedding as she was an orphan and an only child, and had no one really to help her. I gave her all the help I could and told her absolutely everything I could think of. She very sweetly invited me to her wedding, at which her cousins the late Earl and Countess of Durham were going to receive the guests. I arrived at the Knightsbridge church rather late. As I drew up I saw no wedding awning, and thought how stupid I had been not to mention an awning. I then went inside, where the congregation were singing a rather sad-sounding hymn, and I was handed a service sheet. I knelt down for a moment, and then stood up to join in. When I looked at my service sheet I saw it was a thanksgiving service for a poor woman that I had known by sight racing!

I crept out of the church and hailed a taxi, whose driver was very helpful and suggested other churches in the neighbourhood. At the first one we tried I happily found a wedding awning and Miss Lambton's wedding service in full swing. The flowers and service were beautiful, and when the bride and bridegroom and her attendants came down the aisle afterwards it was all as I had visualized. I went on to the reception at the Hyde Park Hotel where I found a happy bride and bridegroom, and everything that I had suggested. I felt very relieved.

The London season that summer, as in pre-war days, officially started with the Private View at the Royal Academy. The big excitement that year were two pictures painted by Mr Winston Churchill. The 'season' had actually got off to rather a slow start, as the Royal Family had not returned from their South African tour until the middle of May. The Chelsea Flower Show returned to the grounds of the Royal Hospital, Chelsea; the first post-war May balls were held in Oxford and Cambridge; the Royal Richmond Horse Show took place at Richmond, and the first post-war Royal Tournament; and the first afternoon Royal Presentation Garden Parties were held in the gardens at Buckingham Palace, one at the end of May, and the second in June.

The first Presentation Garden Party took place in glorious sunshine. Just a few of the girls being presented wore long dresses with hats, as did a few of the mothers, and these found themselves very incorrectly dressed. The Queen looked radiant in pale blue, with a very dressy hat of blue ostrich feathers and tulle, Princess Elizabeth looked very attractive in a pink and white silk dress and jacket, and Princess Margaret was in white – but these were all short dresses. Queen Mary wore her usual lower-calf length, and the majority of older and younger ladies present had skirts just below their knees. The King was in naval uniform.

The royal party came out on the terrace and stood at the top of the steps while 'God Save The King' was played. When they came down on to the lawns, Princess Elizabeth and the Lord Chamberlain the Earl of Clarendon, accompanied The King down his lane. Princess Margaret and the tall, elegant Helen Duchess of Northumberland, the Mistress of the Robes, accompanied The Queen; and Queen Mary took her own lane, accompanied by her lady-in-waiting, Mabell Countess of Airlie, grandmother of the present Lord Chamberlain, who was wearing one of her super jaunty hats perched at an angle! As I have already mentioned, attending these parties counted as having been presented at court.

There were many starry-eyed young people present, who were enjoying seeing the Royal Family at home, and the colour of the scene. Quite a few of these had served in the Forces during the war.

That evening Mr Alan and Lady Patricia Lennox-Boyd, later Viscount and Viscountess Boyd of Merton, gave a young people's dance at their home in Chapel Street, with candlelit tables in the garden. This was for his god-daughter, the much publicized Miss Raine

McCorquodale, later the much publicized Countess of Dartmouth, and even later the much publicized Countess Spencer, now Raine Countess Spencer.

Other social events held that summer included the Royal Caledonian Ball, the Fourth of June, the Derby and Oaks, Royal Ascot, the Lawn Tennis Championships, Royal Windsor Horse Show, the Glyndebourne Opera Festival, Henley Regatta, the Eton and Harrow match, and the International Horse Show. Then it was off to Goodwood for Race Week, Cowes Regatta, the Dublin Horse Show, and up to Scotland for the 'Twelfth'.

There were quite a few debutante dances that season and for the first time I started to make a list of the girls coming out. Life was nearly back to normal, except that we still had quite a lot of rationing!

One evening I went to the American Embassy to have a drink with the new American Ambassador and his wife, Mr and Mrs Lewis Douglas, a charming, friendly couple who were a tremendous success during his three-year appointment here from 1947 to 1950. Lew Douglas was not a career diplomat, but a very successful banker and businessman, and London was his first appointment. It was such a pleasure to have a chatelaine once again at the American Embassy, as no ambassador's wife had been in residence at the embassy since the Kennedys before the war. With the Douglases was their attractive blonde eighteen-year-old daughter Miss Sharman Douglas, who was to become a great friend of Princess Margaret, and for many years one of the most popular girls in the Princess Margaret set. I well remember Peggy and Sharman Douglas that evening asking me about several points of English social etiquette. Later that evening, Sharman was going to the Royal Opera House to join Sir John and Lady Anderson's party, to see Massine dance in a Royal Gala Performance of *The Three-Cornered Hat*, in the presence of the Duchess of Gloucester.

For the first time since 1939, The King's birthday was celebrated with the pomp and pageantry associated with birthdays of a head of state. Everyone in the Brigade of Guards was delighted with the revival of Trooping the Colour on Horseguards. Princess Elizabeth made her first appearance at a Trooping as Colonel of the Grenadier Guards. She rode side-saddle and wore a very smart dark blue uniform and peaked cap.

That year for the first time ever the French won both the Oaks and the Derby. Epsom racegoers really looked smarter than usual, as there were quite a few very chic and well-dressed French racing ladies there, including Madame Léon Volterra and her husband, who had come over to see the French horses run.

Others racing on both Derby and Oaks days were the Aga Khan and the tall and handsome Begum Aga Khan, and his good-looking son Prince Aly Khan, who had more charm than anyone I can remember. The Aga Khan had a lot of horses in training here before the war, and was at that time rebuilding his racing stable. During that Epsom race week, there were parties every night. The first dance was shared by ten hosts!

Although they are two, or some years three, weeks apart, Royal Ascot always seems to come right after the Derby. That year Royal Ascot had returned to normal with the men wearing top hats and morning coats. There was the usual state drive up the course.

I went to a very good dance given by Viscountess Knollys and Mrs Edward Compton for the Hon. Ardyne Knollys, now the Hon. Mrs Owen, and Miss Zoë d'Erlanger, now Mrs Paul White-Thomson, a niece of Mrs Compton. This took place at Hurlingham on a glorious summer's evening. Princess Elizabeth was the guest of honour, and Philip Mountbatten Lt RN, who had that year been nationalized as a British subject, and adopted the name of Mountbatten, and whom I had seen at several of the young people's dances, was also there.

That was the first post-war year that Henley Regatta, known then as the Ascot of Rowing, got into full swing. What a different scene it is today! The men wore suits and felt hats or panamas, or blazers and their old rowing caps or boaters, sometimes faded with age. The women all wore their prettiest dresses or smart linen suits, and all of them wore hats and gloves. It was nearly as difficult to get an invitation to the Stewards' Enclosure as it was to get into the Royal Enclosure at Royal Ascot!

Then, in July, there was much rejoicing when the engagement of Princess Elizabeth to Lt Philip Mountbatten RN was announced. The young couple made their first public appearance together the day of the announcement at a Royal Garden Party at Buckingham Palace. As she had done before, Princess Elizabeth accompanied The King along his lane on the lawn, but this time with her fiancé beside her, who, like The King, was in naval uniform. The young couple received congratulations all the way. Lt Mountbatten was at that time at the Petty Officers Training School at Corsham, and was hoping to get summer leave to spend time with his fiancée and other members of the Royal Family at Balmoral. Before the Balmoral holiday, he accompanied the

My father, Brian Kemp-Welch (1878-1950), in his twenties.

My mother, Verena Kemp-Welch (1884-1968), in her late forties.

My twin brothers George (left) and Peter Kemp-Welch in their teens at Charterhouse.

My step-grandfather, General Sir George Greaves, GCB, KCMG.

My grandmother Lady Greaves, when she was presented at Court after her second marriage.

Netherwood, where my grandmother and step-grandfather lived, and where I spent many happy times as a child.

The training account document reads:

TRAINING ACCOUNT

Mrs Kemp-Welch.

In Account with
P. Behan,
Moonsjoy Lodge,
Kildare.

September 11. 1916

Left: My mother's bill for racing in Ireland – training and expenses – in 1916.

Above: Riding my champion show hack, *Rising Star*, winner of many prizes in 1931 and 1932.

Below left: My elderly cousin, Mrs Richard Morten, in her WVS uniform during World War II. She took me in when I ran away from home.

Below: In Switzerland with Lois Butler (Mrs Alan Butler), one of my greatest friends from 1923 until she died in 1970.

With Peter, leaving St Margaret's, Westminster, on our wedding day in June 1932.

Above left: My beloved bachelor uncle, Brigadier-General Martin Kemp-Welch, DSO, MC (1885-1951).

Above: My son Jim after shooting his first grouse, aged nine years, in Scotland in 1942.

Left: Jim and me outside St Michael's Church, Chester Square, after a wedding in the fifties.

The first Royal Garden Party at Buckingham Palace after the war. The King and Queen and the Princesses are followed by Queen Mary and the Princess Royal.

Top left: With Angus Irwin, deputy Chairman of Illustrated Newspapers, off to a Deauville Air Rally in a little hired aeroplane (piloted by Angus) in the early fifties.

Above: A cocktail party in Ocho Rios, Jamaica, in the fifties. *L. to r.* Sir Alfred D'Costa, me, the Countess of Mansfield, Mr Hugh Tilley and Lady Mitchell.

Left: Mr Jocelyn Stevens, whom I worked for so happily at *Queen* magazine from 1959 to 1968. *(Lord Snowdon)*

Scottish reels being danced.
Queen Elizabeth can be seen in the centre. *(Bill Bates)*

Royal Family to Scotland when the court, as usual, moved into residence at Holyrood Palace, Edinburgh, for a week in July.

On that occasion Princess Elizabeth and Lt Philip Mountbatten – it was just after their engagement was announced – dined at the Caledonian Hotel with the Duke and Duchess of Buccleuch, before they all went on to a charity ball, and were able, for the first time, to dance together in public. Up to then they had only danced together at private dances, at several of which I had mentioned them both being present, but not dancing together!

The Eton and Harrow two-day match at Lords returned in all its pre-war glory, with all the men in top hats and morning coats and the women in their prettiest dresses, many of which had been worn at Royal Ascot. In those days there was a lot of entertaining in boxes, in arbours, and in coaches drawn up at the side of the ground; here their owners dispensed hospitality – the seats in the coaches offered a wonderful view of the cricket. As in pre-Second World War days, the object of going to Lords for the Eton and Harrow match, for which you had to get tickets from a member of the MCC, was to dress up and go to see your friends, many of them old school friends, and of course to be seen!

I remember when we were very young, around six and seven years old, my brothers and I – all of us were keen cricketers in those days, though I was only ever allowed to field – were taken to the Eton and Harrow match one year by our parents. We were all three very excited, as we thought we would see some real cricket. Alas, we never saw a ball bowled or a run scored! We just followed our parents round, frequently stopping for them to talk to their friends. All we ever saw of the cricket, through a small gap in the crowd, was a young Etonian fielding in the deep; we knew which side from his pale blue cap.

That year in my 'Jennifer's Diary' I mentioned over seventy socialites who were also present. What a change today! Had I gone to the match in 1991, I doubt if I would have been able to see seven! The Eton and Harrow match has, over the years, lost status socially, and is now only a very unsmart one-day affair, with a very poor attendance. I recently heard, in fact, that it may no longer even be played at Lords, but played alternate years at Eton or Harrow, as Eton does with the Eton and Winchester matches.

After Goodwood, I again flew over to Dublin for the Dublin Horse Show, which had bigger entries than ever. All the usual hunt balls were held each night, sometimes two a night. On the same night as the

Galway Blazers ball, a wonderful ball was given by Mrs Aileen Plunket at her beautiful home Luttrellstown Castle, just outside Dublin, now a country hotel. For once I did not go to both! I only went to Luttrellstown, which was truly magnificent. I went to one or two balls every night that week! Whereas we in England were in a state of economic crisis – The King, who was at Balmoral with his family, was ready to come south at any moment if needed – Ireland did not seem to be suffering at all, with the exception of fuel: peat, which they then used more than coal, was rationed. Food of every description was not rationed, and was plentiful, with all the small luxuries you could not yet buy in England.

The big excitement in Scotland that summer was the first Edinburgh International Festival of Music and Drama, which went on for three weeks. It has of course become a great annual event and a feature of the international calendar.

I stayed at the Caledonian Hotel, in Princes Street, and I well remember unpacking in my room with a feeling of great depression and apprehension. I knew so little about music, but I felt the Edinburgh Festival should be covered in my diary. Luckily, kind friends came to my rescue! The then Countess of Rosebery, who was very musical, was angelic and immediately took me under her wing. She told me what to write about, and took me to some of the Festival parties, always collecting me from the hotel and seeing that I got home safely. The Roseberys – he was not musical and never came to the Festival – had Sir John Anderson, later Viscount Waverley, then Chairman of the Royal Opera House, and Lady Anderson staying with them at nearby Dalmeny House, and they also gave me guidance on the musical events. Every hotel in Edinburgh and the district was packed, and there were house parties for miles around. In the evening the men wore dinner jackets and the women evening dresses, often with beautiful jewels.

From Edinburgh I went south to Yorkshire, for two days of the York summer meeting, known as the Ascot of the North. I went back to Scotland later in the season on a round of visits. I stayed with Viscount and Viscountess Tarbat (he became the Earl of Cromartie) at Castle Leod; and with Captain and Mrs Jack MacLeod at Culloden House – he was the Member for Ross and Cromarty. That year we all motored over to Skye, a drive through magnificent country, for the Portree Balls. Accommodation was at a premium and very primitive! I found I had been booked into a tiny white-washed cottage where on one side of the front door there was a window with a plant, and on the other side a cow! The owner took me up to a spotless room, where I had the light of only one candle by which to get dressed for the ball.

The balls, which were held on two nights as there were so many applications for tickets, took place in a village hall decorated with tartan rugs and branches of rowan berries. They were then very efficiently run by Mr Iain Hilleary. As at all dances in those days, especially those in Scotland, we had programmes. The Tarbats had organized several evenings to practise Scottish country dances and reels, so I was made to take part, and somehow managed to get by with a little guidance and pushing into place!

Soon after my return to London I went to see Captain Edward Molyneux's winter collection, which was beautiful in its simplicity; and to see Madame Angela Delanghe's collection. Both, with Norman Hartnell, Hardy Amies and John Cavanagh, were leaders in the world of couture. The very chic women looking at the clothes were all anxious, not about the prices, as we might be today, but about how best to invest their coupons, which seemed scarcer than ever.

The great highlight of the winter of 1947 was the marriage, in November, in Westminster Abbey, of our beloved Princess Elizabeth to Lt Philip Mountbatten, on whom The King bestowed the titles of His Royal Highness and Duke of Edinburgh just before the wedding. Unlike many royal marriages, some of which are arranged, one felt that this young couple met naturally and were really in love. The whole country was thrilled, and there were celebrations throughout the UK. I only saw some of what was going on in London. I heard before the wedding that Lt-Colonel the Hon. Sir Piers Legh, then Master of the Household, was having an anxious time with the interior decorators getting the Belgian suite and the other royal spare rooms and other parts of the Palace refurbished and ready in time for the wedding. Although the state rooms had been restored after being dismantled for the war, quite a lot of the Palace was still being redecorated. This was not easy with materials and skilled workers still scarce. But happily all was finished in time.

With all the royal and other guests to cater for, special applications had to be made from the Palace to the Westminster Food Office for extra ration permits, which had of course been unnecessary for the previous big royal influx, the Coronation, in 1937. The Lord Chamberlain the Earl of Clarendon, and his Comptroller Lt-Colonel Sir Terence

Nugent, were also busy at their office with wedding invitations and lists of guests for the various parties.

In the run-up to the wedding there was a succession of royal parties. The King and Queen gave three afternoon parties at St James's Palace to show the display of lovely wedding presents given to the young couple. These included an exquisite ruby and diamond necklace and earrings, two rows of pearls, and a pair of drop earrings in a modern design given by The King and Queen to their eldest daughter. More beautiful jewellery came from Queen Mary from her own collection, including a superb tiara, an enormous corsage ornament, a ruby and diamond bracelet, two diamond bracelets and lots more. A fine canteen of rattail-patterned silver, four silver statuettes of Grenadiers, a pair of silver candelabra, six silver menu holders, and two silver grenade light-ers were the gift from the Grenadier Guards to their Colonel-in-Chief Princess Elizabeth. There was also masses of superb china, glass, and furniture.

On the Monday night, The King and Queen gave a small dance at Buckingham Palace, preceded by a dinner party attended by many of the twenty-eight royal guests from overseas. The following evening, Their Majesties held an evening reception at Buckingham Palace for over a thousand guests. This, I heard, was a glittering scene. Although the men did not wear court dress, they did wear their orders and decorations, and the ladies their prettiest dresses, with truly magnifi-cent jewels. All the family heirlooms – of which England has more than any country – were being worn that evening.

The Queen looked wonderful, in one of her gorgeous crinolines embroidered in gold, with which she wore the blue ribbon of the Order of the Garter, the wide diamond band of the Order above her elbow, a diamond tiara, a diamond necklace, diamond earrings, and bracelets. Princess Elizabeth, who looked very pretty and radiantly happy, accompanied by Lieutenant Mountbatten, also wore the blue ribbon of her very recently received Order of the Garter on her cream tulle evening dress. Queen Mary also wore the blue ribbon of the Order of the Garter on her gold brocade dress; also a diamond tiara, and other magnificent jewels.

Lovely parties were given that week in a number of the embassies as well as at Buckingham Palace and St James's Palace. The whole of the country felt in a joyous mood, for the wedding of our future Queen. It was the first marriage of an heiress to the throne of England for over 800 years.

On the Monday before the wedding, I was lucky enough to be able to go to the rehearsal in Westminster Abbey. This was my first really big royal wedding, and I was so keen to get everything right, that I had worked myself into a great state of worry!

On the great day, I left the flat by car at 7.30 a.m. on a typically cold dark November morning with a slight drizzle. The route was lined all the way by crowds waiting to see the bride, most of whom had slept there overnight. I was well wrapped up in a new mink coat, which I had borrowed from a dear friend, which was a real godsend. I arrived at the Abbey before the doors were open! There were quite a few strange faces who had also arrived early. Then, to my joy, I saw that cheery familiar face of the then Lord Hazlerigg, who suggested we stroll around to keep warm. I remember we talked about cricket until the doors were open. That was so lucky for me, as he was such a dear jovial man that he made me feel completely relaxed before I entered the Abbey.

The setting was magnificent, with the gold plate of the Abbey all displayed, lots of candles, and two very tall flower arrangements. Colour was provided by the scarlet and gold uniforms of His Majesty's Body Guard of Honorable Corps of Gentlemen at Arms, the magnificent vestments of the clergy, and the lovely clothes of the guests. The service was memorable in its simplicity, with beautiful music, all of it chosen by the bride. When the guests were seated, Princess Elizabeth, looking radiant but rather nervous, walked up the aisle with The King, who was in naval uniform, while the choir and congregation sang that lovely hymn 'Praise My Soul, the King of Heaven'.

The bride wore an exquisite pearl- and crystal-embroidered wedding dress designed by Norman Hartnell, with a long silk net train with the same embroidery. Her tulle veil was held in place by a fine diamond tiara. Her Royal Highness was attended by two pages, Prince William of Gloucester and Prince Michael of Kent, who wore white silk shirts with lace jabots and kilts of the Royal Stewart tartan. There were eight bridesmaids headed by Princess Margaret: Princess Alexandra of Kent, Lady Mary Cambridge, Lady Caroline Montagu Douglas Scott, Lady Pamela Mountbatten, Lady Elizabeth Lambart, Miss Diana Bowes-Lyon and the Hon. Margaret Elphinstone. They wore Winterhalter-style dresses of ivory silk tulle over satin, with clusters of orange blossom in appliqué satin, a motif which was repeated on the bridal train; their headdresses were tiaras of flowers. The then Marquess of Milford Haven was best man to his cousin, Prince Philip. The service was conducted by the Archbishop of Canterbury, the Most Reverend Geoffrey Fisher, assisted by the Dean of Westminster and the Precentor of Westminster. During the signing of the register in the Chapel of St Edward, the beautiful anthem 'Blessed be the God and Father' was sung.

The service over, a fanfare of trumpets announced to everyone that the bride and bridegroom were coming. Then we heard the first notes of Mendelssohn's *Wedding March*, and we saw the radiantly happy young couple, who stopped to bow and curtsey to The King and Queen, and to Queen Mary, as they walked to the West Door of the Abbey. They drove away from Westminster Abbey in the Glass Coach with an escort of Household Cavalry through Parliament Square, up Whitehall, along the south side of Trafalgar Square, past the Victoria Memorial, and on to the gates of Buckingham Palace. There were tumultuous cheering crowds along the whole route.

The King and Queen followed the same route in the Irish Coach, with another escort of Household Cavalry. When the royal party got back to the Palace everyone went straight up to the first floor to the white and gold Throne Room where, I was told, The King himself marshalled everyone together for the photographers. I published a lovely photograph above my story of the wedding, which I captioned 'The Royalty of Europe'. This was of our own Royal Family, including the bride's elderly cousins Princess Marie Louise and Princess Helena Victoria, and her grandmother Queen Mary, who was standing beside the beautiful and very gracious Queen Victoria-Eugenie of Spain, the bridegroom's mother Princess Andrew of Greece, King Haakon of Norway, the King and Queen of Denmark, the Queen of the Hellenes, King Michael of Roumania, King Peter and Queen Alexandra of Yugoslavia, Prince Bernhard and Princess Juliana of the Netherlands, the Count of Barcelona, Prince Georg of Denmark, Prince and Princess George of Greece, Prince and Princess René of Bourbon-Parma, Prince and Princess Michel of Bourbon-Parma, Prince Jean and Princess Elisabeth of Luxembourg, and others. Only royals were in that picture, so only two of the bridesmaids, Princess Margaret and Princess Alexandra, were included.

After the photographs had been taken, the bride and bridegroom and her attendants and other members of the Royal Family appeared on the balcony of Buckingham Palace, much to the joy of the many thousands waiting outside to see and cheer them. Later, many readers will remember, Princess Elizabeth and the Duke of Edinburgh drove in an open carriage to Waterloo station to catch the train to spend the first part of their honeymoon at Earl and Countess Mountbatten's Hampshire home Broadlands, near Romsey. The royal couple spent the second part of their honeymoon in Scotland at Birkhall, where The King and Queen had spent such happy summers before he came to the throne. It is where Queen Elizabeth the Queen Mother now spends her summer holidays.

It had been arranged that Clarence House would be rewired and redecorated as a home for Princess Elizabeth and the Duke of Edinburgh, but as it would not be ready for some months, Princess Alice Countess of Athlone, and the Earl of Athlone, who were returning after the wedding to South Africa where he had been Governor General from 1923–31, kindly suggested that the young couple went to live temporarily in their home the Clock House, in Kensington Palace. Princess Elizabeth accepted, and they stayed there until they moved to Clarence House.

On the evening after the royal wedding, a car came to collect me at the flat at 11.20 p.m. to take me to Broadcasting House, Langham Place, as I had been asked to broadcast my account of the wedding for the BBC World Service. I eventually got to bed sometime in the early hours of the next morning. It had been for me a long, memorable, at times worrying, but on the whole very happy day.

SIX

My first state visit

(1948–50)

Some people may wonder how I was able to fit my job in while bringing up my son Jim, who always came first in my life.

When I started at the *Tatler*, Jim was nearly eleven years old and already away at his preparatory school, St Andrews, so it was only at half-terms and in the school holidays that I had to make arrangements for him. It was the same when he went on to Winchester College, as in those days both public and preparatory schools did not give the boys all the weekends, long half-terms and extra holidays that they have today.

Jim had his own little bedsitting room in my flat in Mayfair. I made him a member of Queens Club when he was still only ten years old, so that he could go off there to play squash and watch squash and rackets among other young people. He used to have lunch at a little restaurant near the club, run by two dear old ladies; I used to go to see them from time to time with a small present, as they always gave Jim a wonderful luncheon at an extremely reasonable charge (for which he used to leave a tip of a penny halfpenny!). Jim was always very careful over keeping account of every penny I gave him. I was desperately hard up in those days, for although I still had my dress allowance from my father, my salary at the *Tatler* was very small (it was four pounds a week when I started in 1944) and my only other income was £150 a year allowance for Jim from Peter. The board of the *Tatler* were very good in allowing me to write articles on the social scene for French and overseas publications, which helped my finances quite a bit.

On one or two occasions I had to resort to pawning a diamond brooch which my Kemp-Welch grandmother had left me to pay school fees, but I always redeemed it in time, usually by writing an extra article or doing a radio interview. A few years ago I gave that brooch to my eldest Kemp-Welch great-niece, as I thought it had been such a friend to me that it should stay in the family. My flat was so reasonable when I first came here as the rent was controlled. It cost me then less than £300 a year inclusive of all rates and service charge. Now I own the lease, but I have also to pay ground rates, water rates, rates or poll tax, and service charge. The latter alone has risen to nearly £3000 a year!

When Jim was fifteen years old, I made him a junior member of the Lansdowne Club, which is very near to the flat, so that he could have exercise by playing squash and swimming. As he grew older, the Lansdowne Club was somewhere Jim could take his friends for a meal, instead of having to bring them to the flat, which I must say was constantly full of his contemporaries in the holidays! I was very fortunate in having two daily treasures. Mrs Mott looked after my flat from the day I went into it for thirty-five years until she retired. Mrs Perry was a wonderful daily cook, who cooked for Jim and his friends, whether I was at home or not. Mrs Perry had been with my brother George before the war. As I did not think it was very good for a young boy to spend too much time in London, I always broke up the holidays for him with visits to my father and mother-in-law, until they died. He also stayed with my brother and sister-in-law Peter and Peggy Kemp-Welch, and his two young cousins John and Epony Kemp-Welch, at their home at Great Hallingbury, where he had stayed since he was a baby.

Jim sometimes went to stay with my parents in Warwickshire, but not very often, as my mother was always so difficult. When Jim was on these country visits, I usually managed to join him for part of each weekend. When his father married the Hon. Patricia Eyres-Monsell in 1947, I then let Jim go to stay with them as well, as I knew Patricia, who was an exceptionally sweet and kind young woman and had nothing to do with our divorce, would take care of Jim, who by then was fourteen.

Jim was lucky in spending the first two years of his life at Winchester College in Furleys House, under the guidance of a great sportsman and fine personality, Mr Harry Altham, who was an outstanding housemaster. His dear wife fed the boys better than in any other house; in spite of rationing, she always seemed to be able to get plenty of the nutritious food the boys needed.

I shall always be grateful to Harry Altham for the splendid example he set my son, and the very good influence he had on him over two very impressionable years of his school life, and as a friend for many years later. Sadly Harry retired, and Furleys was then run by Mr Eric Emmett and his wife, who were very nice but quite different. I well remember Jim saying to me before my first visit to see him under the new regime 'Please don't get on to politics with Mr Emmett as he is very left'. I heeded his request and I got along quietly with the Emmetts, but I sadly missed the dear Althams, who happily still lived quite near, so that Harry Altham was always available to his former pupils for help and advice.

When my son was leaving Winchester at eighteen and a half years, I was anxious that he would not sit about doing nothing until he was called up for National Service, an experience which several of my friends had found very trying with their sons. In the circumstances I decided to take a completely unorthodox line. I found out that Jim would be called up from the Winchester area, not London. I wrote to the officer in charge at the calling-up office and said that my son was leaving Winchester at the end of July, that I considered one month's holiday was adequate, and could he please arrange for him to be called up as soon after 1st September as possible as I was a working mother.

I never had a reply, but Jim got his call-up papers to report for military service the first week in September! He was sent straight up to Catterick for training, which was where he had been with us as a small boy at the beginning of the war. Jim had a very good two-year National Service, with no setbacks. He passed out as an officer at Mons Barracks in the minimum time.

As a subaltern he joined the 14th/20th Hussars, who were then back in England and stationed at Lulworth. For his second year he went overseas by ship with the regiment to Libya, and towards the end of his two years' National Service he was chosen as one of two officers and a small number of men to go by battleship down the Mediterranean with Admiral Earl Mountbatten's farewell trip before 'Supremo' retired as Commander-in-Chief, Mediterranean in 1954.

It was during Jim's last year at Winchester that a careers specialist went to the college and gave a talk to the boys on their future. Among other things, he advised any boy who did not have capital behind him to emigrate to the Commonwealth, as he would never get anywhere with the high taxation in this country. This made a strong impression on Jim, and he came home and told me that when he had finished his National Service he was going to emigrate to Rhodesia or Canada. Thinking that that time was some way off, and that he would surely change his mind, I did not worry. Alas, he didn't change his mind, and more and more Canada became uppermost in his thoughts.

When he was going overseas with his regiment he went to say goodbye to my brother Peter Kemp-Welch, who had been like a father to him and whom Jim respected more than anyone. My brother advised Jim not to emigrate anywhere unless he had some qualification to offer. Jim decided to qualify in accountancy, and my dear brother then said he would have the *Financial Times* sent out to him in Libya once a week so that he could learn a little from reading it while on his National Service, and that he would also help him to get into a good firm of accountants. Peter as always kept his word, and arranged for Jim, on leaving the army, to start work at what was then Peat, Marwick and Mitchell, now KPMG Peat Marwick. Jim's wish to emigrate to Canada, sadly for me, never wavered. Soon after he had sat his final exams, I saw him off by ship from Southampton, on 1st June 1959. As that ship got smaller and smaller on the horizon, my heart nearly broke, and I knew that was the saddest day of my life. The one person I had loved and devoted twenty-six years of my life to, and worked so hard to educate properly, had now gone for ever. I returned to my flat where Jim had been living for the past five years (having decided he would get better looked after here than in a flat of his own while he took his exams) knowing it would never again be full of the happy laughter of Jim and his friends, who had somehow seemed to be able to pack into the tiny space, and to enjoy themselves.

After a few months I turned Jim's bedsitting room into a tiny dining room and kitchen, as having a spare room in London when you are working is rather a trial! After Jim left I threw myself into my work harder than ever, so as to try not to think of my personal sorrow.

As I write, it is nearly thirty-three years since Jim sailed for Canada, and I still miss him desperately. I have always tried to look on the good side of life, and now I feel that I am lucky to know that Jim has an interesting job which he enjoys, with splendid employers; he is healthy and happy with a wonderful English-born wife whom he met in Canada, and who loves Canada as much as he does. They have been blessed with two very healthy, attractive and intelligent daughters, aged nineteen and twenty-one as I write, who are both doing very well at a Canadian university. These dear granddaughters, Lucy and Sophie Kenward, are completely Canadian and, I regret, have no interest in England.

*

In 1948 the foreign currency allowance for travelling abroad was still a pittance, so I decided in February 1948 not to go abroad, but to go to what was known as the English Riviera, i.e. Torquay. I took the Torbay Express, a journey of four hours from Paddington, and stayed at the then very well-run and comfortable Imperial Hotel, which was the equal of any grand Continental hotel. It was happily very mild and sunny, and although one missed the mimosa, the orange blossom and the flowers of the Côte d'Azur, in Devon there was japonica, forsythia and masses of prunus blossom, and flowerbeds full of wallflowers and daffodils in bloom. Many guests were playing golf and tennis in summer sportswear.

On my first evening, I bravely went down to the restaurant for dinner alone, in order to catch the mood of the place. Usually in a hotel I have dinner in my hotel room, if I am not dining with friends. To my horror that evening, as I was finishing dinner, a very pushy lady, who I learnt was the 'hostess' of the hotel, came over to my table accompanied by a male guest, and said she would like to introduce him to me, as she was sure I would like to dance after dinner! I was absolutely amazed and horrified, as I had never dreamt of such a situation. I at once declined, I am afraid very abruptly, and said I had been travelling and that I was off to bed early. Then I bolted to my room. The next evening, happily, I had planned to dine with friends.

I found that Torquay and the English Riviera was indeed flourishing. Quite a few well-known people had also decided to change overseas plans, and were staying there.

At the end of May I flew to Paris to write about the the official visit of Princess Elizabeth and the Duke of Edinburgh, Their Royal Highnesses' first official visit overseas since their marriage. Paris was bathed in sunshine and decorated with flags everywhere, and there were pictures of the royal couple in every shop window. The warmth of the welcome given to them by the people of France was very moving. They flocked to cheer them from the moment they arrived at the flower-bedecked Gare du Nord, until they left Le Bourget five days later. The President of France, Monsieur Vincent Auriol, gave a banquet for them at the Elysée Palace on their first evening, and earlier in the day invested Princess Elizabeth with the Grand Cordon of the Legion of Honour, which she wore with its riband across her white satin evening dress at the banquet.

On the first afternoon of the visit Princess Elizabeth stood at the top of the high steps of the Galliéra Museum to open the exhibition called 'Eight Centuries of British Life in Paris'. As Her Royal Highness started to make her speech, the bells of an adjacent church and the bells of all the churches nearby started to peal loudly. The Princess gave one worried look, then bravely and wisely raised her voice and, speaking in fluent French, carried on.

Although those of us who were present did not, because of the bells, hear every word, the speech came over brilliantly on the wireless. I learnt later that the bells were being rung for confirmation services, many of which traditionally take place in France that weekend.

The British Ambassador and Lady Harvey gave a dinner party followed by a reception at the fine British Embassy in honour of the royal couple. On the final night of the royal visit, there was a brilliant gala at the Opera House. For this and all the evening events Princess Elizabeth wore diamond tiaras and magnificent jewels with her sumptuous Norman Hartnell embroidered satin evening dresses. The royal visit also included trips to Versailles, Fontainebleau, racing at Longchamp in the President's box, and a journey down the Seine in a motor launch.

This was my first royal visit overseas as well as the Princess's, and it taught me a lot. All-important, I found, is your accreditation, and seeing that you get the necessary tickets and car stickers for the events you want to attend. I found this can be hard work. On this occasion it was easy, as I had friends in the Embassy, and I had good influential friends in Paris who were all sweet and kind and ready to help me in every way. I learnt that you must stay centrally, in an efficient hotel, with an able concierge, as there is a lot of quick changing and telephoning to do on a royal tour. I stayed at the Ritz, so I had no problems. Also you must have reliable transport, and a really good driver who knows his way around, and who can talk his way through often awkward officialdom!

Another week that summer, I went to watch the polo at Roehampton Club, which had just got going again for the first time since the war. I watched Viscount Cowdray's team, which was very much a family team, comprising himself, his two sisters the Hon. Mrs Gibb and the Hon. Mrs Lakin, and his brother-in-law Mr John Lakin, beat the Cotswold team by three goals to one. John Cowdray did more than anyone in this country to revive the sport after the war. He got his pre-war polo grounds at Cowdray Park back into good condition as soon as possible, and he invited some of the best polo players in the world to play there. That year during Goodwood Race Week John Cowdray put on a really pre-war polo week at Cowdray, with matches starting after racing each day and the finals on the Sunday afternoon. The same polo week at Cowdray Park still takes place each July. I always feel rather sad that when the Guards Polo Club started at Windsor, it took some of the sparkle out of Cowdray Park polo, as it was so much nearer London for spectators. Windsor has also had the attraction of the Duke of Edinburgh, and later the Prince of Wales, playing there. There is no longer polo at the Roehampton Club. It ceased in 1950.

That year during Goodwood Race Week, the Duchess of Norfolk, who had a big house party with the Duke of Norfolk at Arundel Castle, organized a wonderful ball at the castle on a glorious hot summer's night in aid of the Sussex Association of Mixed Clubs and Girl Clubs. Driving over the drawbridge into the vast turfed courtyard of the castle with its encircling drive, you saw hundreds of chairs in the centre of the grass for sitting out. Near the front door were three long buffet tables, all lit by candles in silver candelabra, which burnt gaily until daybreak. Not often do you see candles burning outdoors like this in England.

This was the first big ball to be given at Arundel for many years, and guests were eager to see all the beautiful pictures and other priceless treasures. The Duchess of Norfolk, looking very attractive in a dress of scarlet lace and chiffon, with a superb diamond necklace, was a marvellous hostess; and the Duke of Norfolk, with his wonderful wit and dry humour, I noticed dancing happily much of the evening. Everyone in the district had brought their house parties, and many of the guests begged Lavinia Norfolk to make this an annual affair. She did run a successful charity dance there in Goodwood week for several years.

That year was one of the first really splendid post-war Goodwoods. The Duke and Duchess of Richmond and Gordon had a house party of young people at Goodwood House, friends of their two sons the Earl of March, now Duke of Richmond and Gordon, and Lord Nicholas Gordon Lennox, and their luncheon room and box at the racecourse was packed each day. Although there were no Bucks Club or Cavalry Club tents there was a members' marquee, and numerous private luncheon tents as well as the very attractive chalets where one was invited to a seated luncheon for ten or twelve.

For several years I stayed with friends at Angmering, which is comfortably near, so that we could bathe in the sea each morning and arrive at the racecourse in time for luncheon. Other years I stayed with Mr and Mrs Ralph Hubbard at their house in the grounds of

Goodwood. Ralph Hubbard was at Eton with the Duke of Richmond and Gordon, and was later his agent at Goodwood and one of his closest friends for many years. There is a race named after Ralph Hubbard at the summer meeting.

In August I flew over to Deauville, to join friends who had gone ahead for a long weekend there. I travelled on the regular air service from Croydon to Deauville, which left a lot to be desired. We started late, in an old-fashioned seven-seater with six ordinary single seats. The seventh seat, which was occupied by a six-footer, was what the Americans so aptly called a 'jump seat', i.e. it was a flap that lets down from the side, with no upholstery. The passenger on this seat was paying a full fare! There was no rack for hand luggage, so we sat with that on our laps, and to add to the discomfort the ventilators above the seats did not function! I was grateful to know I was travelling home in a chartered plane.

After reaching Deauville, it was like being in another world. It seemed an oasis in what was still a troubled Europe, especially after the austerity still apparent at home. Deauville seemed to have healed very quickly the scars of war and occupation. The fine hotels, the Royal, the Normandy, and the Golf, were spic and span with every luxury for visitors.

We stayed at the Golf Hotel, which is high on the fine eighteen-hole golf course. Lord Iliffe's wonderful yacht *Radiant* was among several big yachts anchored a little way out from the town. Before racing each day, we went down to bathe on a quiet part of the beach, and on our way back looked in at the fashionable Plage Fleurie, with its little coloured tents. It was packed with visitors, many of them French, tanning themselves in the latest Paris swimsuits – the local shops were full of glamorous holiday clothes so tempting to buy, but my special travel allowance was for travel expenses, not for buying clothes!

The racing was of a very high standard; we watched it comfortably from seats in the stands and private boxes. There were also plenty of seats under the trees in the paddock. After racing, we walked across to the centre of the course to watch the polo, and saw a British team, captained by that fine player Colonel Humphrey Guinness, play a South American team captained by another high handicap player, Mr J.C. Alberdi. This team had the well-known playboy 'Ruby' Rubirosa playing at No. 1. I was amused to see that one of the grooms looking after one of the polo-playing Balding family's ponies was wearing the kilt, which seemed strange in Deauville!

On the Saturday night we went to the Grand Gala at Les Ambassadeurs called Le Bal de l'Ombrelle. It was organized by the Comtesse de la Falaise, who had lost her husband when he died in a concentration camp during the war. There were 600 guests. No one sat down to the five-course dinner until 10 p.m., and many were still dining three hours later. Unlike Paris, food was plentiful in Deauville, as it was in the heart of the Normandy farming district; there was also wonderful local fish. The entertainment that evening included a ballet and very large floor show. The women guests were very glamorous and beautifully dressed – many of them in white. The Shahanshah of Persia was among the many men wearing white dinner jackets. The casino was later a great meeting place, although not everyone was there to gamble, especially the English, who still had very limited foreign currency allowances. There was quite high play among foreigners.

The Prix Morny was won on the Sunday by Monsieur Léon Volterra's Amour Drake. We flew home on Monday afternoon in a chartered Dover aeroplane from Morton Airways, landing first at Eastleigh to drop off some of the party, and then on to Croydon.

That autumn I was very kindly invited by Sir Eustace Pulbrook, then the Chairman of Lloyds, to a very impressive reception given at Lloyds in honour of the visiting Commonwealth Prime Ministers. All the women had dressed up and the men wore their decorations with their white ties and tail coats; these, sadly, are so seldom seen these days. On arrival the 2,500 guests walked down the marble corridors, through the bronze gates into the immense underwriting room fondly known as 'The Room'. Here they were received in front of the Lutine Bell by Sir Eustace and Lady Pulbrook, the latter looking most attractive in a black velvet dress with a superb diamond necklace and earrings.

After receiving guests for over an hour, the Chairman and Lady Pulbrook and the Deputy Chairman Sir Stanley Aubrey went to the entrance to meet the Duke and Duchess of Gloucester, and the Duke of Edinburgh. The arrival of the royal party in The Room was heralded by two strokes on the Lutine Bell. The flowers at that party had been supervised by Lady Pulbrook and were sensational, so none of us were surprised when, following Sir Eustace's death in 1953, Susan Pulbrook started a flower shop, Pulbrook & Gould – now very well known — which was an instant success.

That November, flags flew over London, guns were fired, and church bells rang to herald the birth of a son to Princess Elizabeth and the Duke of Edinburgh, at Buckingham Palace. This baby is now our beloved Prince of Wales. Looking after Princess Elizabeth and the baby at Buckingham Palace was Sister Rowe, one of the most experienced and charming maternity nurses in the country. Sister Rowe was also one of the most fashionable monthly nurses, and to get her to look after you and your baby in the forties and fifties, you had to book her months ahead.

In contrast to the happy news at the birth of Princess Elizabeth's son and heir, there was deep worry at The King's sudden illness. Although he was forbidden by his doctors to undertake any activities involving exercise, The King was carrying on with state business in his suite, and continuing to give private audiences. His illness had caused his doctors to veto the long tour of Australia and New Zealand which he and The Queen and Princess Margaret were due to start at the end of January, and which they had all been so looking forward to.

That year had been one in which entertaining had been on a much smaller scale, except at some of the embassies. This was not surprising with the current high taxation, rationing of food and shortage of staff, and the very high cost of entertaining in restaurants.

Among the weddings that took place that year was the marriage of Mr Gerald Legge and Miss Raine McCorquodale at St Margaret's, Westminster, and Londonderry House. Before that engagement was announced, the bride's mother Mrs Hugh McCorquodale very kindly rang me to tell me that the engagement would be announced that week. She made me laugh when she added that it was better than it sounded, as his mother was a Horlick (wealth) and that he would become the Earl of Dartmouth in due course!

In the Christmas holidays, both before and after World War II, the Bertram Mills Circus at Olympia was a hardy annual to which everyone took their children. Each year it started with a reception and luncheon before the afternoon opening performance. This luncheon was a very social occasion, always attended by the Lord Mayor and Lady Mayoress of London, members of both Houses of Parliament, the diplomatic world, the sporting world, and leaders of commerce and industry. Mr Bertram Mills, who also exhibited Hackney horses in the driving classes of the big summer horse shows, was a great character, who I believe had made a fortune during the First World War. He started this wonderful circus in 1920, which was run to the very highest standards, so that it became a much-loved feature of childhood for several generations. It had a six-week season at Olympia each winter, when he hired the greatest international circus stars to augment his regular team.

After Olympia, the circus went to its country home where it stayed, when not touring the country, in a fleet of the most luxurious motor caravans and horse boxes, all marked Bertram Mills Circus. Bertram Mills had two very efficient sons, Bernard and Cyril Mills, who grew up to help him. They also showed his driving horses at the shows, and they carried on the circus after their father's death. Sadly, around the sixties, times changed and circuses rather went out of fashion as there were not the big audiences to keep them going, so in 1967 the Bertram Mills circus packed up.

In 1949 Margot Fonteyn was prima ballerina of the Sadlers Wells Ballet, which also had Moira Shearer dancing with them following her starring role in the film *The Red Shoes* in 1947. They were having a tremendous success both at Sadlers Wells and at Covent Garden. The theatre was thriving too. In 1949 we saw Laurence Olivier and Vivien Leigh, to whom he was then married, appear in a play together for the first time when they opened at the New Theatre in Sheridan's *The School for Scandal*, with costumes by Cecil Beaton. This was shortly after their Old Vic tour together in Australia. Sir Alexander Korda, Sir Michael Balcon, Mr Terence Rattigan, Sir Ralph and Lady Richardson and Mr Oliver Messel were in the audience that evening; I was lucky to be there too. Cecil Beaton missed the opening as he was in New York working on another stage production.

A couple of weeks later, I went to one of the best and most amusing parties that London had seen for a long time. This was a costume ball given by the Swedish Ambassador Monsieur Gunner Hägglöf and his dynamic and very attractive Italian-born wife Anna at the fine Swedish Embassy in Portland Place, where the Hägglöfs, who had only arrived in London from Washington the previous October, entertained very well and very frequently. I usually hate any sort of fancy dress event, but this one was fun, and a most amusing evening.

Our good-looking host wore the costume of an eighteenth-century courtier, complete with white wig, and Anna Hägglöf was in daffodil yellow, with a feathered mask. Everyone arrived masked, and on arrival was handed cards by means of which you found your partner for the evening. There were some beautiful costumes: many of them crinolines in fabulous silks and satins, some hundreds of years old. One of the most beautiful was a bottle green crinoline worn by Donna Josephine Gallarati Scotti, the second daughter of the very popular Italian Ambassador of that time. It was two hundred years old, and had belonged to her great-great-grandmother. It won first prize that evening. The Queen's niece, Anne Viscountess Anson, who came as the young Queen Victoria, won the third prize of a super green suede beauty case. That evening I introduced Anne Anson to Prince Georg of Denmark, who was wearing a Regency costume. Later in the evening he was her partner in one of the Scottish reels which Anna Hägglöf had, to everyone's surprise, organized. A couple of weeks after the dance I saw them dining happily à deux at the Four Hundred. Later that year they announced their engagement, and were married in 1950.

Early in 1949 I flew out to Zermatt for two or three days among the really keen skiers. The weather was wonderful, the sun shone, the snow was perfect, but so many would-be skiers were laid low by an influenza epidemic that the ski slopes appeared rather empty.

When I left Zermatt, I spent a night in Geneva, then went on to Wengen, which I had not visited since the twenties. I stayed, as before, at the Palace Hotel, which still reigned supreme with the Borter family in charge. Skiing conditions were quite good and everyone seemed in happy holiday mood. Wengen was a ski resort that families used to return to year after year. On that visit I remember dining in a party of ten who, with the exception of myself, had all come to Wengen each year for over twenty years, with a break for the war years. The Downhill Only Club, which was founded in Wengen in 1925, was going stronger than ever and is going strong today.

At all three of these skiing resorts there were a number of British visitors, but they all still had the same problems, however rich they were, of having to eke out the then still very small travel allowance.

From Wengen, I went on to St Moritz, a twelve-hour journey with six changes that I was dreading. In those days there were no helicopter services at Swiss resorts. In St Moritz I stayed once again at the Palace Hotel which was so full that weekend that Hans Badrutt and his son Andrea, who for so many years ran the Palace Hotel so well, had to turn sitting rooms into bedrooms. St Moritz was totally different from other resorts. The few English there were mostly with some service scheme. I had not been here for two years, and I found it a luxurious and rather fabulous oasis such as I had forgotten existed anywhere. The shops were full of glittering goods which would even have caught one's eye in the Rue de la Paix, and huge Cadillacs, Buicks and other big cars filled the streets. The new ski lifts were always packed both ways; and the clothes, both day and après ski, were much more exotic than at the other ski resorts.

I remember feeling that the German and Italian visitors who had lost the war nevertheless all had so much more money to spend than the English!

That spring The King's health was worsening, and in March he underwent an operation, so official engagements were rather in the air. The Queen gallantly fulfilled quite a lot on her own, and Princess Elizabeth suddenly seemed to undertake many more engagements and provincial tours, often accompanied by the Duke of Edinburgh.

In May, The King made his first social appearance after his operation and convalescence. This was at the marriage at St George's Chapel, Windsor, of Mr Antony Lyttelton, son of Mr Oliver and Lady Moira Lyttelton, to Miss Caroline Lascelles, daughter of The King's very popular secretary Sir Alan Lascelles and the Hon. Lady Lascelles. He and The Queen also went on to the reception held in the Waterloo Chamber at Windsor Castle. His next appearances were at the two presentation garden parties at Buckingham Palace, which were rather large affairs and must have been tiring for His Majesty, as I recorded in my diary 2,300 guests on the first day, and a hundred more than that on the second!

The ladies of the diplomatic circle had the pleasure of making their curtseys individually to The King and Queen as they passed by the Throne, with the Lord Chamberlain, the Earl of Clarendon, announcing the names of the various ambassadors, ministers and high commissioners. After this brief return to ceremony, The King and Queen on both days made a slow progress through the room, stopping here and there to talk to guests singled out by the Lord Chamberlain and his aids. So great was the crush in the state rooms on both days that although the debutantes and young marrieds enjoyed the stately scene inside the palace, and the thrill of Their Majesties being present, and being at a party which counted as 'being presented', many of them left without seeing The King or The Queen.

In August I made my first post-war summer visit to the South of France. I flew to Nice and stayed at the wonderful Hôtel du Cap at Antibes, where I was greeted by Monsieur André Sella, who was born there and who ran the Hôtel du Cap so superbly for many years. The hotel, I was told, was originally built to entertain the Grand Dukes of Russia in France! From friends who have stayed at the Hôtel du Cap in 1990 and 1991 I hear it is still outstanding in its comfort and the leisure life it provides for guests. On that visit I found very few English visitors, because of the continued currency restrictions. Most of the

English were staying in villas with friends. Instead, film stars abounded around the 'Cap'. One of the first I met was Merle Oberon, who had great charm, and whom I liked better each time I met her. Later, when I joined friends at their cabana, Norma Shearer was there, looking lovely in white shorts and a red and white striped blouse. Constance Bennett was at the Cap on a three-day visit, and film producer Mr Darryl Zanuck said he hoped to stay for a month.

I visited Americans Mr and Mrs Charles Murphy at the Clos de la Garoupe, which they had rented from Lady Norman while Charles Murphy was helping the Duke of Windsor with his memoirs. He took me to luncheon with the Windsors at the Château de la Croë, which they had rented. We were just four, and our hostess had everything arranged to perfection. Her repartee, I remember noticing, was quick and often cruel, like pebbles on a corrugated tin roof.

At the end of my usual visit to Scotland, and in the 5th October Jennifer's Diary, I put a note saying I was going on holiday for a fortnight and that my diary would be resumed on my return. I did not lose any readers!

After my blissfully restful holiday in the depths of the country, I flew over to Paris for my first Prix de L'Arc de Triomphe, which was won by Monsieur Marcel Boussac's filly Coronation V, ridden by Roger Poincelet. At that time Monsieur Boussac, who had a big racing stable in France, was still winning most of the big races both sides of the Channel. That year the first prize for the winner of the Prix de l'Arc de Triomphe was £30,000. In 1991 it was £500,000.

I was amazed to see how many of the French women were wearing black suits or black coats that year, and always with a very tight-fitting small black hat, sometimes trimmed with a feather or with sequins. I stayed at the Ritz which was packed, and Monsieur Auzello, who then ran the Ritz so well with his invaluable assistant Monsieur Zambroski, was being asked to work miracles to fit guests in. I stayed over for the Monday and Tuesday, and went to see as many winter collections as I could.

Towards the end of July I went to a beautifully arranged dinner dance given by the Cygnets at Claridge's. Cygnets House was a very exclusive finishing school in Queens Gate, started after the war by Mrs Rennie O'Mahony, who ran it so well with great charm and also with a rod of iron! At the end of each world war, the group of girls who had missed out on 'finishing' in France or Switzerland were very notice-able. Mrs Rennie O'Mahoney, who was widowed without children when quite young, and was a tremendous snob, rather reversed matters. Her pupils included quite a few young foreign ladies, whose parents wanted them to learn perfect English, and finish here. At this party at Claridge's, she had pupils from Geneva, Paris, Amsterdam, Brussels, Athens, and Rome, which I thought must be so good for her English students.

A private dance that I will always remember most vividly was a lovely ball which took place at the fifteenth-century Oxburgh Hall in Norfolk, which has a moat all round it. This was given by Sir Edmund and Lady Paston-Bedingfeld to entertain officers of the 1st Battalion Welsh Guards, who were on exercise in the district. Everything was most beautifully arranged in this magnificent setting, with masses of wonderful flowers in all the rooms, a delicious dinner for those of us staying in the house, a hot breakfast in the early hours, and an especially good band for dancing. For me it was all the greatest fun, except for the cold!

I arrived by train with several other guests from London, and we were met at the station and driven to Oxburgh. Here I was shown up to a very large high-ceilinged room with a four-poster bed, Persian rugs on a polished floor, and a one-rung electric fire, but no central heating. I managed to keep warm by having a very hot bath when I dressed for dinner, but when I came to bed around 1 or 2 a.m., my hot water bottle was tepid, and the room icy, so I got into bed in my dressing gown. After a while I realized I was still very cold. I felt rather desperate, as I badly needed a few hours' sleep, and nothing makes me more miserable than being cold. I suddenly had a brain wave. I got out of bed and put one of the Persian rugs from the floor on top of the bed, and set my alarm clock for ten minutes before I was due to be called so that I could remove it before the maid came in.

It worked like a miracle. I had several hours' good sound sleep and came down to breakfast full of cheerfulness, able to say I had slept very well! The Paston-Bedingfelds were a dear kind family, who I don't think felt the cold.

For my 1950 winter sports trip, I decided to start off in Kitzbuhel. To do that I had to fly from Northolt to Zurich and then go on by train. I decided to stay the night at the Baur au Lac in Zurich and to dine with Mr and Mrs George Sulzer at their charming home at Winterthur, where they entertained many English friends.

Next day I took the train that crossed the Austrian frontier at Buchs, then climbed to the top of the Arlberg Pass through the seven-mile-long tunnel which brings one right into St Anton, where I saw many skiers coming down the Galzig. From there we went on down through the Inn Valley and on to Innsbruck, where we stopped for half an hour. Here I took a quick walk through the town and saw the tremendous damage done by bombing during the war. Then on I went, eventually arriving at Kitzbuhel.

I found Kitzbuhel enchanting. It was full of happy skiers but light-hearted skiers who, while they went skiing daily, didn't take it seriously as they did at St Moritz. The wide village street was packed with horse-drawn sleighs with their bells jingling, huge sports cars bearing the registrations of many countries, and skiers in the latest and brightest ski clothes off to the Hahnenkamm, where a cable railway then took everyone up the mountain. The men who were not going skiing were all in their picturesque Tyrolean costume. At Kitzbuhel I could go up the mountain on the cable railway without skis without everyone noticing I was a non-skier. I would meet friends at the top for luncheon, and come down on the railway. At night, when everywhere was lit up, Kitzbuhel looked just like fairyland.

The après ski and the evenings in Kitzbuhel were such fun. There was usually some form of music in the very colourful cafés where one enjoyed hot chocolate and far too delicious Austrian patisserie. The restaurants were also attractive and fun and the food delicious. Everyone wore chic and pretty clothes in the evening, but nothing was sophisticated. The Goldene Gams was a great rendezvous for aperitifs, and Tony Praxman's for après ski hot chocolate, and later for dinner and dancing. The Austrians, in spite of all they had suffered in the war, and were still suffering, were in contrast to the Swiss such light-hearted people. The evenings were always full of soft Tyrolean music and happy laughter.

From Kitzbuhel I went on to Wengen for a few days. Here among the guests I found Air Chief Marshal Lord Tedder and Lady Tedder, for whom the Swiss Railway Executive had arranged a special trip up to Jungfraujoch, and on to see the very advanced and well-equipped International Institute of Scientific Research which was being used by scientists of many countries. This was to take place the the day after I arrived, and they very sweetly invited me to join them.

In April, going up here is a haven for spring skiers, but February is not really the time. The morning we started the weather was bad. We went by the normal train to Scheidegg and there we entered the special train. A snow plough had been sent up ahead of us to clear the line as trains had been unable to reach the top for three days. Our first stop was Eigergletscher where, when we looked out of the window, we could see the huskies sitting in the snow outside their kennels. These polar dogs are used to draw small sleighs around this isolated spot. Then the train entered the tunnel, which is through many miles of rock.

We climbed slowly until we reached the Eigerwand Station, then a tiny siding cut in the rock. Now at 9,400 feet we turned to the south through the hundreds of passes from the Eiger to Eismeer. Then on again for the last lap to Jungfraujoch where at 11,333 feet there was a good modern hotel, at that time the highest in Europe. We got out of our train, and at first we had to make our way slowly along a corridor cut in the rock; to start with the walls were rough granite, then by degrees they became ice, as did the floor and ceiling, from which hung icicles.

At last we entered the Ice Palace. Here in a vast room supported by ice pillars were flowers in ice vases, and in one of the alcoves the life-size model of a modern car in ice. From here we returned to the hotel for a well-earned early hot lunch. Then we walked further through the mountain in what I thought were quite scary conditions to the beautifully equipped International Institute of Scientific Research, in which laboratories scientists from all over the world were at work on experiments.

A lift then took us up to the sphinx, the meteorological observatory 11,723 feet up in the mountains where we found two young enthusiasts experimenting in a small room on a high-powered, short-wave telephone service. Though a very cold and at times rather hair-raising trip, it was well worth having been able to see the many brilliant feats of engineering on the way, and the progress of high-altitude research on the roof of Europe! We eventually got back to the Palace Hotel at Wengen in time for a rather late dinner.

When I got back to England in March that year, we had the state visit of the President of France and Madame Vincent Auriol, which I always think was the grandest and most colourful of all state visits within living memory. There were flags flying everywhere and spring flowers and blossom in the parks.

The visit took the usual pattern. On the first night The King and Queen gave a brilliant banquet at Buckingham Palace, where around

170 guests sat down to dine off gold plates. On each side of the room, beautifully displayed on red plush cushions, was an exquisite royal collection of George III gold plate.

The following evening, the French President and Madame Auriol gave a wonderful banquet at the new and only just decorated French Embassy in Kensington Palace Gardens. Here only around 70 guests sat down to dinner and around 150 came in after dinner. Here again everything was arranged to perfection by Madame René Massigli, who was such an elegant and gracious Ambassadress, with perfect taste, and a brilliant organizer.

I was very kindly invited to this memorable party after dinner. Both evenings The Queen looked wonderful, wearing a magnificent tiara and beautiful jewels with her crinoline evening dresses; Princess Elizabeth was a picture, and all the other royal ladies had excelled themselves, knowing that all the French ladies would be looking very chic. Both Madame Auriol and Madame Massigli were beautifully dressed and looked very elegant on every occasion. On the third and last evening of this state visit there was a brilliant gala at the Royal Opera House in honour of the President and Madame Auriol. The Royal Box had for the first time been built in the centre of the Royal Circle and covered quite a wide space. It was decorated with the Royal and Republican cyphers and swags of flowers. The Royal Box and the whole auditorium was decorated by Mr Oliver Messel, so you can imagine how marvellous it was.

I have never seen a gala at the Royal Opera House to rival that one, and I have been to many! Not only was this fine opera house looking its best, but so were the audience. Every man in the audience wore a white tie and tails with orders and decorations which seemed to cover their chests! The King wore the scarlet riband and the Order of the Legion of Honour, and Monsieur Auriol wore the riband of the Order of the Bath. I noticed Mr Winston Churchill, who arrived late from a division in the House of Commons, wearing the Cross of his Order of Merit round his neck. He also wore the medallion of the French Croix de Guerre.

Both The Queen and Princess Elizabeth wore pastel-coloured satin crinolines embroidered with crystals and pearls, designed by Norman Hartnell, with diamond tiaras and diamond necklaces, and the scarlet riband of the Legion of Honour across their dresses, and long white evening gloves. Madame Auriol and the ladies of the diplomatic corps all looked wonderful, and every woman in the Opera House seemed to be wearing her best dress and long white gloves and the most fabulous jewellery.

England, then, had probably more beautiful family jewels than any other country. They were all at Covent Garden that evening! They made such an impression on me that a few nights later I had a nightmare and dreamt I was somewhere where even bald-headed men were wearing tiaras!

When the royal party arrived, trumpeters of the Household Cavalry standing on the stage played a fanfare and floodlights played on the Royal Box until the royal party were seated. Then the curtain went up on the stage and we saw an hour and a half of superb ballet danced by the Sadlers Wells Ballet, with Margot Fonteyn, Moira Shearer and Robert Helpmann in the leading roles. It was, I think, the most glamorous gala in living memory.

Shortly before that state visit, Mr Robert Menzies, the Prime Minister of Australia, had announced from Canberra that The King and Queen might visit Australia in 1952. On the last night of the French visit I remember thinking how tired our beloved King looked, and I wondered if he would ever be able to take on another long royal tour.

It was also announced early that year that there would be three afternoon Presentation Parties instead of two. It was announced quite early that the strict rule of morning coats and top hats for Royal Ascot would still be left in abeyance, as The King, thoughtfully, was reluctant to force young men into buying Ascot outfits at the present formidable price; but it was hoped the number of lounge suits would be kept to the minimum.

In 1950 Lady Hamond-Graeme, the President of the Queen Charlotte's Birthday Ball for Debutantes, was able to hold it once again in the Great Room at Grosvenor House. This had been closed during the war and the ball had taken place in the much smaller Grosvenor House ballroom, where there were so many applications for tickets that it was decided to hold two if not three Queen Charlotte's Birthday Balls each year!

This ball had for many years been held to raise funds for the Association of Friends of Queen Charlotte's Maternity Hospital and the Chelsea Hospital for Women, and they needed funds to carry on their good work, war or no war.

The Queen Charlotte's Birthday Ball at Grosvenor House gets its name from the ball that was held to celebrate Queen Charlotte's birthday each year at St James's Palace at the beginning of the last century. At the Grosvenor House balls after the war, the huge birthday cake was drawn in by four debutantes each side, with another hundred or more debutantes walking slowly behind in rows of eight, all wearing long white ballgowns and long white gloves, who had walked down the two wide staircases four abreast and joined up when they reached the dance floor. Then they all walked slowly forward to the tune of the March from Handel's *Judas Maccabaeus*, which was always played at Queen Charlotte's Birthday Ball at St James's Palace, until they came up to the guest of honour, to whom all the girls curtseyed simultaneously.

It was a picturesque sight never to be forgotten, especially when you watched from the balcony. Only a certain number of the debutantes attending the ball took part in the historic birthday cake ceremony, but every debutante present had to wear a long white dress and long white gloves, and all their names were in the programme. On the morning of the dance, there was always a rehearsal at 11 a.m., when the leading girls were chosen mostly on their height – a tall girl was seldom up front – and they were made to do the march over and over again until it was perfect. I went to several of the rehearsals, which I found amusing to watch. It was amazing to see the differences in the smoothness of this ceremony after they had been rehearsing for an hour and a half or more. Both Lady Hamond Graeme and Margherita Lady Howard de Walden, who succeeded her as President in 1952, were very strict about the birthday cake ceremony being carried out with almost martial discipline. If you had been chosen to be a maid of honour, and you did not turn up for the rehearsal, you did not take part at the ball.

During the fifties, and up to 1965, there were around 350 debutantes each year at the Queen Charlotte's Birthday Ball, with a record 432 in 1964. After 1966 numbers dropped to around 250 in 1969, which was Margherita Lady Howard de Walden's last year as President. Then in 1970 Miss Sylvia Darley took on the role of President until 1975.

The last year I went to the Queen Charlotte's Birthday Ball for Debutantes was, I think, in 1972 when the number of debutantes present had fallen to 145. In 1975 it was decided to stop the Queen Charlotte's Birthday Ball altogether as there was not enough support. In the late 1980s, a new committee got together, arranged modern sponsorship, and organized what was called a Queen Charlotte's Ball

for Debutantes in the Great Room at Grosvenor House, again in aid
of Queen Charlotte's Hospital.

I went to the ball, and having been to many real Queen Charlotte's
Birthday Balls, with all their glamour and pageantry, I felt this was a
sad and pathetic evening. There were around twenty-five rather reluctant girls, so-called debutantes in white, none of them nearly as well
turned out as in the old days. There was also a large cake, as before,
but the meticulously regimented pageantry had gone, and the whole
evening seemed rather shoddy to me. As the debutante of the fifties
and sixties no longer exists, it seemed to me a strange idea to try and
resuscitate the ball as a debutante ball. I am all for raising money for
wonderful Queen Charlotte's Hospital, but organize a really good
charity ball and forget so-called debutantes!

In the fifties and sixties, as in the twenties and thirties, the London
season was a hectic time for eighteen-year-old girls and for young men.
There were often two or three private dances on one evening. During
May, June and July they did little else but dance most nights until the
not so early hours of the morning, sleep very late, and go to girls'
luncheon parties, or to Ascot, Wimbledon, Henley, or one of the other
fashionable hardy annuals. Then they would go away to country house
parties, probably with a Saturday night dance, each weekend, ending
with Goodwood. From 1948 I made a list of the girls who were
coming out each year, which was a godsend to their mothers wanting
to arrange mothers' lunches, cocktail parties, house parties, and then
eventually their daughter's coming-out dance. (I stopped the lists
altogether in the early eighties, as the whole scene had changed.)

Then came a summer break – unless they went to Cowes or Dublin
– at either Frinton or Bembridge or some foreign resort with their
family in August, until it was time to go to Scotland for another round
of dances and house parties. In the autumn they might begin to think
about taking a cooking or secretarial course.

Those days are finished. Since the seventies, young people have
grown up much earlier. By eighteen they have had a spate of teenage
dances, so these are no longer the excitement to them that they were
to their seniors. The majority of teenagers today are much more
serious-minded than they were in those days. Most eighteen-year-olds
are working towards getting accepted for one of the universities, so
most of them want to spend a gap year, before going up to university,
travelling the world or going abroad to one country to learn a language
fluently.

During the eighties and nineties there has been a much greater number of teenage dances in the Christmas holidays, and a few in the Easter holidays, so that most of the eighteen-year-old boys and girls already have quite a large circle of young friends. Nowadays, eighteen-year-olds' parents are more likely to give a cocktail party for them, usually during the summer or Christmas holidays; then if they are going to have a dance this comes later, when they are nineteen to twenty-one, and that is often shared with a brother's coming of age, or the parents' silver wedding, or all three together.

At the end of June, I flew over to Paris for twenty-four hours to go with friends to the first big ball held at the Travellers Club in the Champs Elysées. Club members at that time came from fourteen nations. I also went to watch the Grand Prix run at Longchamp next day.

Paris was full of visitors and every moment I was there was fun. The ball was a most elegant occasion. I had never seen more chic women, or more beautiful dresses, and the jewellery was exquisite. The Travellers Club salon had been transformed for the evening into a ballroom with Deuxième Empire decor, and the card room into a supper room. There was plenty of sitting-out room in the house and in the flower-filled paved courtyard, where we sat and sipped champagne under a cloudless sky.

The former British Ambassador Sir Alfred Duff Cooper, the then President of the Travellers Club, and his beautiful wife Lady Diana Duff Cooper, who was wearing a dress of white faille with a strapless top, with a circlet of stephanotis entwined with diamond stars on her head, received the guests. Among the guests I met were the Duke and Duchess of Windsor. He, like Duff Cooper, was wearing his orders and decorations, and she was looking very chic and was surrounded by French friends. It was the only occasion on which I ever saw the Duchess of Windsor wear a tiara: it was quite a small diamond and emerald one, and with it she wore a rather original boat-shaped single strand diamond and emerald necklace which lay horizontally across her neck. Her dress was white corded silk, rather tightly draped, and buttoning up the back. The only other tiara I saw that evening was a fine aquamarine tiara, worn by Maureen Marchioness of Dufferin and Ava with an ice blue satin dress.

In spite of His Royal Highness looking at me rather sternly when, after curtseying to him, I only shook hands and did not curtsey to his wife, he asked me later in the evening to come and sit and tell him all the news from home. I was amazed at the number of people he enquired about, even going back to the hunting field many years before. At times his eyes had a sad look, as if he was wistful about the English life of which he was no longer a part. We also discussed his memoirs, *A King's Story*, which the brilliant American writer Charles Murphy was helping him write. Charles Murphy, with the full agreement of the Duke of Windsor, later that year asked me to read the manuscript of that book, as I would probably catch mistakes which he, as an American, could so easily make. I did this, and I also proposed cutting sections that I knew were inaccurate and rather unkind. When they very sweetly sent me a copy of the book, which was published in 1951, I saw, to my surprise, that all my suggested cuts had been made!

To return to the Travellers Club Ball, before the Duke of Windsor left me, he asked whether I had ever seen the club's famous and beautiful La Paiva's silver bath. I hadn't, so he took me to see it, and there we met Mr Cecil Beaton, who was also admiring this famous bath. I have been told that the Travellers Club has never had quite such a brilliant party since! How lucky I was to be there.

Next day Longchamp was bathed in sunshine. The men were in morning coats and top hats, although some Frenchmen wore grey bowler hats with their morning coats. The women were in beautiful dresses, and large velvet or tulle – not straw – hats; blue mink stoles were much in vogue. The Grand Prix produced a very popular result as Baron Guy de Rothschild's two colts Vieux Manoir and Alizier filled first and second places, and Comte Edouard Decazes' Lacadur was third. Guy de Rothschild and Eddie Decazes and Eddie's dear American-born wife Caroline were then, and still are, much loved and respected in the French world of racing.

That year was the first time I could remember Queen Mary missing any of the Royal Garden Parties. It was considered that those long and rather tiring afternoons might be too much for her.

At the end of July, I flew over to Bordeaux on a BEA flight, and from there went by a special bus to Biarritz for the opening of the season. I stayed at the Hôtel du Palais, once the summer palace of the Empress Eugénie. This had been cleverly converted into a luxurious hotel retaining all the old-world charm of lofty rooms and ornate mouldings, and the cypher 'N & E' appeared frequently on the ceilings and fitments.

Biarritz at the beginning of this century was a very fashionable summer holiday resort for many of the crowned heads of Europe, including our own King Edward VII. In the Hôtel du Palais I was shown a large plaque with the inscription 'This was where King Edward VII of England formed his Cabinet with Asquith in 1908'. This could have been a slight overstatement as I don't think the ruling monarch of the United Kingdom has formed a cabinet since Queen Anne.

I found Biarritz in very festive mood. All the hotels were full, as were the private villas, some of which were used by their owners all the year round. A splendid programme of attractions had been arranged, including an international lawn tennis tournament, in which Jean Borotra and Jean Bernard were to play, an international horse show, and numerous golf competitions, ending with the Biarritz championship, followed by the International Grand Prix of the South West. The fashionable Chuberta golf course was, I heard, nearly back to its pre-war perfection.

On the night I arrived, there was a great gala to celebrate the Opening of the Season. The cabaret was the first performance of Roland Petit's new ballet *Musical Chairs*, in which he danced with Violette Verdy, who, then only sixteen, had just finished making the film *Ballerina*.

I had meant to stay longer than the forty-eight hours I was there, but after I got back to the hotel from an evening in St Jean de Luz, I received a message that my beloved father, who had had a stroke two weeks previously but had seemed to be making a good recovery when I left, had had a relapse. His doctor thought, quite rightly, that I would like to know this – my mother would never have bothered to get in touch with me, and my brother was up in Scotland. The concierge was wonderful and somehow got me on to the first flight on Monday morning, and I was at my father's bedside by early afternoon. Happily he was conscious, and showed how pleased he was to see me, but sadly he died very peacefully two days later. I miss him to this day. After his funeral I once again threw myself into my work, which is always a great salvation when you are suffering sorrow.

There was much rejoicing when on 15th August it was announced that Princess Elizabeth had given birth to a baby girl. Congratulations showered in to Clarence House for Princess Elizabeth and the Duke of Edinburgh, who was due to take over his first sea-going command, HMS *Magpie*, at the beginning of September. The Queen went up to join The King at Balmoral a few days after the arrival of the baby.

Princess Elizabeth waited until the Duke of Edinburgh had gone off to join his ship, then went up to join the Royal Family at Balmoral, with Prince Charles and the baby Princess Anne.

After Edinburgh I flew over to join racing friends at the Golf Hotel, Deauville. This elegant resort was once again packed. There were flowers galore in all the window boxes and gardens, and the biggest cars you could imagine appeared, gleaming in the sunshine, and cruising along the front bordering the Plage Fleurie. At night, as in the previous year, the dresses and the jewels were sensational in their beauty.

This year the centre of attraction in the evenings was King Farouk of Egypt, who was playing *chemin de fer* for extremely high stakes. A real exhibitionist, he was always laughing loudly, showing off, and generally enjoying the limelight! Several members of his entourage were playing at the same table, including one woman, the attractive French-born Mrs Charles Clore, looking as always extremely chic, with a different diamond necklace and other jewels each evening! Françine Clore was having to concentrate on playing at this big table while her husband sat beside her, probably giving advice! She told me years later how frightened she was playing so high, and what a terrible strain it was.

After Deauville I went back to Scotland, this time to the Highlands, for some of the Scottish balls, and an odd day or two out with the guns on the moors.

One morning in November, I went to the State Opening of Parliament by The King accompanied by The Queen. I watched the procession go through the Royal Gallery, which is always deeply impressive. Before the procession starts, or the peers and peeresses take their seats in the chamber, they usually come through in all their robes and splendour to talk to friends.

That was a busy day for me. I went straight from the Houses of Parliament to the flat and I wrote my copy on the Opening of Parliament and got it typed and off to my office! Around 4.30 p.m. I left for London airport. I boarded a British Overseas Airways stratocruiser for New York. Like other passengers I went down to the little bar lounge for an aperitif before dinner, which was served to our seats. After dinner you moved out of your seat while an upper and lower bed was let down by the cabin staff. If you had booked one of these beds, which I think in those days cost only £12 10s extra, you climbed in and enjoyed a comfortable night's sleep. We took off around 7 p.m.

in the evening, landed at Reykjavik in Iceland to refuel, and arrived in New York around 7 a.m. next morning.

On this visit New York was enjoying an Indian summer, and I was going about in a thin black silk suit. After luncheon on my first day, I went along to Madison Square Gardens where the National Horse Show was in full swing. For the first time since the war, an English team was competing in the show jumping.

I went each day, and watched the show part of the time with the British team from their box, and partly with the Irish team in their nearby box. I had got to know most of the latter at the Dublin Horse Shows.

One evening after the show I went to the Horse Show Ball, held in the Starlight Room at the top of the Waldorf Astoria. This large room was decorated with the flags of all the nations. Seven hundred guests sat at candlelit tables, and the ball finally got started at 1.30 a.m. I left around 3 a.m., but the ball, I heard, went on until 7 a.m!

A spectacular evening I enjoyed was the opening night of the Metropolitan Opera. Mr Rudolf Bing, who had been such a success at Glyndebourne and the Edinburgh Festival, had taken over the administration of the Metropolitan Opera as general manager, and there was great excitement over changes he had made. Verdi's *Don Carlos* had been chosen for the opening and it was a production worthy of that great theatre. But on the opening night in those days, as probably also these days, people went more to be seen than to see or listen! Unlike the Royal Opera House, latecomers that night were allowed to clatter in and take their seats long after the curtain had gone up, and flashlight cameras clicked inside the theatre during the performance as well as the interval. All the boxes in the first tier of the circle known as the 'Diamond Horseshoe' were, as were all the other seats in the theatre, full. Thanks to the kindness of Rudolf Bing, whom I had known at Glyndebourne and Edinburgh, I had a wonderful seat where I could see everyone and everything!

The furs that evening – chinchilla, silver blue mink, and snowy white ermine – were superb, and there was some exquisite jewellery, though not as much as I expected, and no tiaras. Mrs Cornelius Vanderbilt Whitney's magnificent diamond necklace, diamond earrings, and diamond bracelets were, I think, the most beautiful jewels I saw. Escorted by her husband, she looked very elegant wearing a sumptuous platinum fox stole over her faille dress.

While I was in New York for these busy few days, I dined at the 21

Club which was fun to revisit after twenty years – the last time had been during Prohibition when it was Jack and Charlie's. I had a warm welcome from the Kreindler brothers who ran the 21 so well, and produced really excellent food; they had, I was told, the best cellar in the city!

After this very happy brief visit to New York, I went on for an even briefer visit to Washington. During my stay I visited a wonderful old lady called Mrs Truxton Beale in her lovely house in Jackson Place. She was one of the most respected and beloved ladies in Washington, with all the charm of the great Edwardian hostesses. I felt very honoured that she had invited me to tea; this was served as it was in my grandmother's day, with silver tray and silver kettle. I also went to a very frightening ladies' luncheon at the Sulgrave Club.

I flew back to New York to fly home in one of BOAC's superbly comfortable stratocruisers to the usual spate of pre-Christmas cocktail parties and charity dances and bazaars.

SEVEN

Exploring new territory

(1951–52)

The New Year came in with the Festival of Britain, to be held in London in May and June, very much at the forefront of everyone's minds.

Early that January, I enjoyed a happy reunion with old friends when I went up to Yorkshire for one night for a ball given by Lt-Colonel R.J. Stephen and officers of the 14th/20th Hussars at the Officers Club at Catterick. I had mixed feelings about returning to Catterick, where, during the war, I had had some very happy, but also some very unhappy, times.

This was a happy twenty-four hours and I was glad I had gone. The ball was beautifully arranged and colourful. The blue and gold, and crimson and gold drum banners of the 14th Hussars and the 20th Hussars hung on the walls. The magnificent regimental silver, which includes some massive pieces, was all on view, and all the serving officers of the 14th/20th Hussars wore their regimental evening dress. Added to this, there were perhaps more pink coats worn by local guests than seen even at a hunt ball.

Lt-Colonel and Mrs Stephen received the guests, and Lt-Colonel Basil Woodd, who commanded the regiment after Lt-Colonel Stephen, and his attractive wife Diana, were busy looking after everyone. Bobbie Stephen was best man at my wedding, and Basil Woodd was one of the ushers, so I really was among old and true friends! I stayed the night with Bobbie and Alison Stephen, who had a dinner party at Haig House before the ball.

When I got home from St Moritz, I had to begin thinking about the London season for that year. This was another busy year for debutantes; there were 220 on my list, and there were so many debutante dances arranged for May, June and July that quite frequently there were three in an evening.

For this year's Presentation Parties there was a much better arrangement for the debutantes. Instead of the few who previously were individually presented to The King and Queen, all the debutantes, without their sponsors, were lined up to walk past Their Majesties, who were seated, each girl curtseying twice. Thus each debutante saw their King and Queen quite close. The two first Presentation Parties were to take place in March, and only one in May, so as to lighten the load for Their Majesties in May when they had so many Festival of Britain engagements.

The Festival of Britain was officially opened in May by The King, who spoke from the steps of St Paul's.

In 1951 I went for the first time to the International Trophy meeting at Silverstone Motor Racing Track. The day before racing, I motored up with Mr Dick Wilkins, a very old friend of mine and my brother's, who used to race an Alfa-Romeo at Brooklands in pre-war days. We stayed most comfortably with Lord Wardington and his very dear mother in their attractive home in the picturesque village of Wardington.

Next morning we were able to motor over to the course early, in less than an hour. The first person I met on arrival at the circuit was the Duke of Richmond and Gordon, a steward of the British Racing Drivers' Association – a racing driver himself in pre-war days, who had done so much for post-war motor racing with his motor race circuit at Goodwood. I also met Mr John Cobb, who then held the world speed record of 394.2 mph, which he achieved in his Napier-Railton.

It was John Cobb who had persuaded me to come to Silverstone. When I had met him the previous weekend through Dick Wilkins, who lived next door to my brother, he had said that if I did everything else I simply must do Silverstone too, and gallantly promised to drive me from point to point inside the circuit once the racing started. Dick Wilkins and I first had a walk round about. We saw the Italian mechanics guarding the scarlet Alfa-Romeo, and a little further on another mechanic who was busy with a small saw cutting across the back tyres of a Maserati. I gathered this was to prevent skidding, as one scratches the soles of a new pair of shoes.

Then we went up to the pits to see the little 500 cc cars known as the 'mighty midgets' having their final tune-up before the first race. Sadly, the weather was bad – it started to rain and rain. With John Cobb, whose very pretty wife was also there, I watched the first five laps of the first race from Club Corner, where there was a hazardous damp patch which caused some exciting skids; happily without mishap. From here we drove across to Stowe Corner, where you can watch the cars come with great speed down Hanger Straight, then back to the Stewards' Enclosure to watch the finish. The winner was Eric Brandon, driving a Cooper, with a Norton engine. I noticed a young American driver, Henry Schell, who was driving with great dash.

After our rushing about from point to point watching some exciting heats of the International Trophy race, a storm with lightning, hail and torrential rain broke as they started the final. Reg Parnell, wearing an exceptionally deep visor, drove magnificently in these nightmare conditions and was soon well in the lead. The race was eventually cancelled, and after a long conference the Stewards decided to award Reg Parnell the trophy and the £500 prize-money. I had thoroughly enjoyed every moment of the day in spite of the storm. It was a really well-organized meeting; exciting and interesting racing, superb driving to watch, and an excellent luncheon.

That year Mr Jimmy Jarvis, later Sir Adrian Jarvis, invited me to join his party of friends going to Le Touquet for Whitsun and I gladly accepted. Le Touquet was so popular with the British, especially golfers, in pre-war days, partly because it was easy to reach, and secondly because, though it was an elegant little place with everything of a high standard, life was much more informal than at Deauville. Many people owned villas there, including Gertrude Countess of Dudley, and Mr and Mrs P.G. Wodehouse.

Le Touquet had taken a terrible pounding in World War II, in which it had played a gallant part. However, the reconstruction had been done well and promptly. For instance, although we saw two wings of the giant Picardy Hotel only as empty shells, over a hundred rooms in the centre had been refurbished and were fully occupied. I left London at 11.15 p.m. and drove to Croydon where Jimmy Jarvis had chartered a Dove from Norton Airways, which took the party of six over to Le Touquet aerodrome very comfortably and swiftly. We were sitting down to luncheon at 1.30 p.m.

From 1st June that year, BEA were running a regular service to Le Touquet where a four-day return ticket would cost under £6. We stayed at the Westminster Hotel, which had been completely rebuilt on modern lines and was very comfortable. Some visitors were staying at the Hôtel Bristol, others at the much smaller, very comfortable Le Manoir, which was on the edge of the forest overlooking the golf course. The original eighteen-hole golf course, laid out in 1906 by an assistant master at Eton, Mr R. H. de Montmorency, who was also an amateur golf champion, and by the great golf professional Harry Vardon, was back to its pre-war condition. Quite a few competitions had been arranged for that summer, including an inter-club tournament which the Guards, the Cavalry and the Junior Carlton Clubs had entered. A magnificent new casino had been built on the site of the old one.

Each morning I walked round the golf course with Jimmy Jarvis and others of the party playing golf. On Saturday night we went to the gala at the Casanova nightclub at the casino, which was very well done with a good dinner, Paris mannequins showing Jean Desse's collection, and a cabaret given by the Karwi dancers.

One day we motored out to a fascinating inn in the heart of the country near Montreuil called La Grenouillère, where the speciality was frogs' legs. Another day we drove to Montreuil where we saw the fine statue of Field Marshal Earl Haig on his charger in the main square. We went on to luncheon at the magnificent Château de Montreuil, which was originally built with the 'best of everything' as a luxury home by a member of the Rothschild family who lived there before the war. It had a glorious garden, where we sat and enjoyed our coffee after luncheon.

We flew back to Croydon just as comfortably as we had come out, on Tuesday afternoon. This was the first of a great many Whitsuns I spent in Le Touquet with Jimmy Jarvis and his friends and sometimes his family, right up until he sadly died very suddenly of a heart attack in 1965.

That summer, The King's health again caused consternation. His Majesty, following his doctors' advice, went up to Balmoral for ten days quietly after the opening of the Festival of Britain engagements and the state visit to avoid over-strain. He seemed rested on his return, but to everyone's dismay he quickly developed influenza which was difficult to throw off, so his doctors ordered rest again, this time for at least four weeks. This meant cancelling his projected visit to Northern Ireland, among other official engagements. The Queen quickly stepped into the breach and went to Northern Ireland, taking Princess Margaret with her. A short while later, The Queen attended the Festival Derby. Her Majesty was then accompanied by Queen Mary, which delighted everyone present; also by Princess Elizabeth, Princess Margaret, and the Duchess of Kent. No men of the Royal Family were present! Princess Elizabeth, although with a very full list of official engagements herself, also immediately stepped into the breach for her father with calm assurance, and her tremendous charm. To me, it was fascinating to watch how well she grew up from girlhood into womanhood, to shoulder the great responsibilities ahead of her.

All royal plans that summer remained uncertain, as the doctors said after a couple of weeks that The King must have a long convalescence, probably with a complete change of scene. In the end this idea was abandoned and The King and Royal Family went to Balmoral.

That season I went to masses of debutante dances, to Glyndebourne, and to most of the hardy annuals. One of the charity dances that stands out in my mind took place on a Saturday evening at Sir Anthony and Lady Doughty-Tichborne's historic home, Tichborne Park, in aid of the Hampshire branch of the Red Cross. The Tichbornes are one of the oldest Hampshire families, owning great estates in the county since before the Norman Conquest.

It was a fine summer's evening with a full moon. The house's floodlit silhouette was reflected in the moat and on to the waterfall near the lake, which made a truly beautiful picture. This charity dance was run entirely by the Chairman of the Committee, blonde Lady Smiley, one of Cecil Beaton's two sisters, with the help of brunette Lady Doughty-Tichborne, both very attractive young marrieds, who had their husbands to help them on the evening. They not only supervised all the arrangements, but also provided the excellent supper without any caterers. It was all cooked at home and varied from cold salmon to hot curried game! There were beautiful flowers all over the house, and all the women wore their prettiest dresses and masses of beautiful jewels.

Everyone in the neighbourhood had dinner parties and many had house parties for this dance. I stayed nearby with very dear friends, Mr and Mrs Robin McAlpine. Next day the house-party went to one of the several buffet luncheon parties being given by friends in the district.

The second dance I remember that year was the most brilliant ball of the season, given by the Earl and Countess of Haddington for their only daughter, Lady Mary Baillie-Hamilton. This took place at the Duke and Duchess of Northumberland's historic home Syon House, on the outskirts of London. This was given to an ancestor of the Duke of Northumberland by James I in 1604, and rebuilt by Robert Adam for the first Duke of Northumberland about 1760. Syon, with its Roman Great Hall, Greek statues, wonderful pictures and so many beautiful treasures, is a superb setting for any party, and on this particular evening there were the most exquisite flowers everywhere. Lady

Haddington was a tremendous perfectionist and everything was perfectly arranged. The house and grounds and even the fine old trees in the park were floodlit, and the Roman Great Hall with its classical statues was transformed into a conservatory.

In the grassed courtyard in the centre of the house a mass of mixed flowers were arranged on the tall stone urn in the centre, and the four large flowerbeds were filled with polyantha roses and masses of flowering pink lilies which scented the whole area. A wonderful dance band played for dancing, and there was a delicious supper at candlelit tables in two rooms.

Outside on the lawn were seats and plenty of colourful deck chairs to sit on, and gypsy musicians strolled around with violins and accordions softly playing lilting romantic tunes on this really warm summer's evening. Mary Baillie-Hamilton, who is dark and very pretty, stood between her parents to receive the guests, and wore a white tulle dress embroidered in mother-of-pearl sequins; she wore white flowers at the back of her head.

The Queen, who wore a white tulle crinoline, with a magnificent diamond tiara and necklace, was present; also Princess Elizabeth, looking radiant in an orchid mauve dress, and diamond tiara and other lovely jewels; Princess Margaret, looking pretty in a strapless white satin dress, and the Duchess of Kent, looking beautiful in an exquisite white lace dress, a high diamond tiara, a diamond necklace and her long diamond earrings. The royal ladies had dined with their host and hostess and the Duke and Duchess of Northumberland at Syon in a big dinner party before the ball.

The jewels at this ball were unbelievable in their beauty. The Duchess of Northumberland wore a superb family tiara with her red dress, and her beautiful mother the Duchess of Buccleuch, now Mary Duchess of Buccleuch, wore the exquisite Buccleuch emeralds and diamonds. The Duchess of Roxburghe, later Mary Duchess of Roxburghe, wore huge diamond bows on her dress and diamond cupid bows in her hair. The Countess of Ronaldshay, later Penelope Marchioness of Zetland, wore a pearl and diamond tiara, necklace and earrings, and the very large and beautiful family diamond corsage ornament.

During the Royal Family's stay at Balmoral Princess Margaret came of age; but there were no great celebrations. While he was at Balmoral, The King, with the help of his invaluable Land Rover, did manage to get out on the moors to shoot, which he so enjoyed, even if at first it was only for a few hours.

This improvement in The King's health was not to last. At the end of September he had a relapse, and had to have a serious operation at Buckingham Palace. The Queen was among the Counsellors of State appointed then to deal with documents which needed The King's attention, but His Majesty insisted on being kept fully informed of all that was going on. At the last minute Princess Elizabeth and the Duke of Edinburgh had to postpone their official visit to Canada; they did however go after The King was safely over his operation.

During the summer I travelled down to spend a few days at Bembridge. I had not visited this small English seaside resort since the late twenties, but I found it quite unspoilt and very little changed except that the very exclusive Garland Club had been rebuilt. There were still members of those three great Bembridge families – the Moretons, the Thorneycrofts, and the Woodruffes – playing a leading part in the place.

Other families too spent many summers here with their children, as their children in turn still do.

The teenagers were still busy sailing dinghies, and the more modern smaller scows. The older generations were sailing Red Wings, which made a lovely picture when they were racing. There were still plenty of nannies sitting on the sandy beach with the smaller children. All the houses and furnished rooms were full, and so was the pre-war-built Spithead Hotel.

After Bembridge, I flew over to Ireland for the coming-of-age ball given by Oonagh Lady Oranmore and Browne for her son Mr Gay Kindersley. This took place at their home, Luggala House, right in the Wicklow Mountains where they go down to Loch Tay. A huge marquee on the lawn held a dance floor and long buffet, all beautifully decorated with flowers. Oonagh Oranmore and Browne wore, as she usually did, a very 'youthful' white broderie anglaise dress, and received the guests with Gay Kindersley, who was an exceptionally busy young host looking after his friends. It was a most enjoyable ball which went with a swing until the early hours of the morning, when a wild young guest thought it would be amusing to drive his car full tilt into the marquee. Miraculously, few people were hurt, though one girl was hit by the car and had her leg broken. I did not mention this incident in my diary.

I decided towards the end of September, when Jim had gone back to Winchester, that I must have a breather, but it must be in the sun. I chose the Formentor Hotel at Formentor, looking over Pollensa Bay, on what I then described as 'the little island of Majorca'. In those days the island had not been discovered by the masses of tourists. At Formentor there was this one very comfortable, not too large, luxury hotel, with an uncrowded private sandy beach; and seven houses. For me it was a wonderful choice, a haven of rest with a week of unbroken sunshine. Here time meant nothing, no one ever hurried, few ever carried a watch or knew the hour – such a contrast to one's busy life always rushing around back home.

The election that autumn resulted in a change of government, Mr Winston Churchill replacing Mr Clement Attlee as Prime Minister, which was a great relief to everyone as Britain was not prospering and many people had gone to live abroad.

I was very kindly invited to the 1st Viscount Camrose's wonderful election night party at the Savoy, at which there were around two thousand guests. His election parties were always a model of good organization and were attended by everyone who was anyone, so you were bound to meet interesting people with tremendously varied occupations.

On arrival guests were given a book with all the statistics of the election clearly tabulated so that one could follow the results easily. In the main reception room constituencies were arranged on the wall; by the end of the party the results of quite a few had come in and been noted down. Another room was set aside for dancing, with a results board at one end, and there was a delicious buffet supper.

One of the two most important weddings of 1951 was the July marriage of Mr Ian Gilmour, later Sir Ian Gilmour (and in 1992 created a Life Peer), to the Duke and Duchess of Buccleuch's younger daughter Lady Caroline Montagu Douglas Scott at Westminster Abbey, with the reception at Syon House, the home of the bride's brother-in-law and sister, the Duke and Duchess of Northumberland. Prince Richard of Gloucester, later the Duke of Gloucester, was one of her pages. I remember being seated in the Abbey with guests from the Commonwealth each side of me, and the Duchess of Buccleuch telling me that she had done this specially so that I could make the wedding more interesting for friends who had come so far, by telling them who everyone was. Such a typically kind thought of Molly Buccleuch, to whom I have always been devoted.

The Queen, Princess Elizabeth and Queen Mary came to the wedding; sadly, Princess Margaret was ill and could not be present. Also the Duke and Duchess of Gloucester, and I am sure nearly every old family in England, as well as many personalities and over 500 from the various estates in Scotland, for whom transport and accommodation had all been arranged. Transport was also arranged both ways between the Abbey and Syon House for those who did not have cars. I remember appreciating this kindness. It was a glorious day, so the 1500 guests were able to stroll on the lawns at Syon, as well as enjoy the house and all its treasures. Very sensibly, the bride and bridegroom cut their cake outdoors; it had been placed in the centre of the long colonnade running down the lawn side of the house. I remember distinctly that there were no speeches!

The other big wedding I went to was the October marriage of the Marquess of Blandford and Miss Susan Hornby, which took place at St Margaret's, Westminster, where they had a long guard of honour from the bridegroom's regiment, the Life Guards; the reception was at the Goldsmiths' Hall. Princess Elizabeth missed this wedding, as she and the Duke of Edinburgh were away on her official visit to Canada and North America. The Queen was present with Queen Mary, Princess Margaret, the Duke and Duchess of Gloucester, Princess Alice and the Earl of Athlone, and their daughter Lady May Abel-Smith. The Prime Minister Mr Winston Churchill, who was a distant cousin of Sunny Blandford, and Mrs Churchill were present.

At the end of January 1952, Princess Elizabeth and the Duke of Edinburgh set off on their five-month journey to the far south, for their official tour of Australia and New Zealand, deputizing for The King. On their way they were calling in at Kenya, Mombasa and Ceylon. Princess Elizabeth's lady-in-waiting on that trip was Lady Palmer, widow of Major Sir Anthony Palmer, who had been killed on active service. Henriette Palmer was appointed in 1949. In 1953 she married widower, Mr Alexander Abel Smith, later Sir Alexander Abel Smith, who died in 1980; as I write Henriette Abel Smith is the Queen's longest-serving lady-in-waiting.

Soon after Christmas, I left in a BOAC Stratocruiser on the Monarch Service for New York, with Mr and Mrs Robin McAlpine, their seven-year-old daughter Carolyn, now Mrs Nigel Elwes, and her French governess. It was a very disrupted flight! We were to have boarded and taken off as usual between 6 and 7 p.m., but after some delay at the airport we were told the flight was delayed until 9 a.m. next morning, so we went back home. Next morning we took off a little late.

Then, after we had refuelled at Prestwick and were well out over the Atlantic, we had to turn back and again land at Prestwick owing to the terrific gales.

On our second attempt, before I tucked up for the night, I gave firm instructions to the stewardess that I did not want to get out at Reykjavik, Iceland, where we were due to refuel, and that she was not to disturb me until we were one hour out of New York, as I wanted to sleep. I was fast asleep after our landing at Reykjavik when the stewardess started shaking my shoulder. I am afraid I gave her a very grumpy reply, as it was then about 1 or 2 a.m. However, it seemed there was a blizzard raging outside and there was no hope of our refuelling and taking off for some hours, so everyone was to go into the airport hotel.

Getting off the aeroplane was quite a feat, as it was hardly possible to stand, so strong was the blizzard. None of us had overboots as when we had discussed what to bring we had not imagined we would need them. Stewards carried Mademoiselle and Carolyn, then Norah Mc-Alpine and I had a steward each to hang on to us and get us down the steps and across the snow into the hotel. Robin McAlpine had done a bit of quick thinking, and said he was going ahead to try to book three bedrooms, which he luckily got with three bathrooms.

I personally had a long sleep, and as I had a good book I did not surface until lunchtime, having heard there was no chance of us getting airborne until the evening. On take off from Reykjavik the following evening we had a splendid view of the aurora borealis, a wonderful sight. We eventually arrived in New York on New Year's Eve, nearly forty-eight hours late.

I was staying with dear American friends, Mr and Mrs Henry Seigbert, who had a very spacious apartment on East 54th Street. New York was covered in snow and looking wonderful with all its fabulous Christmas decorations still up.

I had been invited to four New Year's Eve parties, but I only accepted two.

I dined with my host and hostess, who had their daughters Pat and Claire Seigbert and a group of friends with them; some came to dinner and some came later.

I left the Seigberts around 11.30 p.m. and went on to Mr and Mrs Gilbert Miller's annual New Year's Eve party. This was held at their fine Park Avenue apartment, which was full of works of art; it was one of the most beautiful homes in New York. This apartment previously belonged to Kitty Miller's famous financier father Mr Jules Bache, who also for many years gave a New Year's Eve party here. This year Kitty Miller had chosen pink, white and silver for her decor – quite a relief from red and green and holly! My hostess looked very chic in a beautiful Balenciaga dress of black lace over white satin, and this time no one wore a duplicate! The guests were all rather special, and included publisher Mr Henry Luce, who had such a successful diplomatic career and his wife Clare Booth Luce; she was wearing a magnificent sapphire and diamond necklace. Also present were designer Mr Edward Molyneux, and Mr Ronald Tree, who had a brilliant political career, and his wife Marietta.

From the theatrical world there were Sir Laurence and Lady Olivier, who were then playing in *Caesar and Cleopatra* and *Antony and Cleopatra* in New York, which Gilbert Miller had presented; Alfred Lunt and his wife Lynn Fontanne; Miss Audrey Hepburn, who was then appearing on Broadway in *Gigi*, another of Gilbert Miller's presentations; Mr Rex Harrison and his current wife Miss Lilli Palmer; Miss Anita Loos, whose amusing book *Gentlemen Prefer Blondes* was a bestseller; Mr Cole Porter, whose tunes have kept many toes tapping; and Mr Robert Helpmann. I remember it was a stimulating and very friendly evening.

Miss Gertrude Lawrence had given me a seat for the matinee of *The King and I* (a sell-out in New York) the next day on condition I came round to her dressing room after the show to tell her all the London news! She gave a wonderful performance in this super musical. I found dear Gertie Lawrence, who usually lunched with me or I with her when she came to London, as beautiful as ever in a red flannel housecoat, but far too thin. I sat with her while she ate her evening meal between shows. She asked about a mass of friends, seemed rather homesick, and said I was to do all I could to see that *The King and I* got a big theatre when it came to London later in the year. She kissed me goodbye and said what fun our hour together had been. Alas, that was the last time I was to see her as she died, far too young, in New York, in September that year.

The following day, I flew on with the McAlpines to Nassau. This was my first visit to the Bahamas. We arrived after luncheon in glorious sunshine, with bougainvilleas flowering everywhere, the temperature in the high seventies, and no currency problems as this was a sterling area. Robin McAlpine's parents, Sir Malcolm and Lady McAlpine, who had always been angelic to me, and who always spent several months each winter in Nassau, were already installed in their Nassau home, Graham House, which had another family house next door. We were not staying there, however, as this year Mr Harold Christie, later Sir Harold Christie, a great and dynamic personality, then a bachelor, had lent Robin and Nora McAlpine his very comfortable fully staffed house Breezy Ridge, which was right on the sea. Harold Christie was living at his town house, Cascadilla.

During this trip I dined at Government House with the Governor Major-General Robert Neville; and I met Eunice Lady Oakes, widow of Sir Harry Oakes who did so much to develop Nassau. I also visited Sir Francis and Lady Peek, who I knew from before, at their enchanting town house Tamarind; and I met Major and Mrs Herbert Holt (his family I was told founded the Royal Bank of Canada); and I met his sister-in-law, Mrs Robert Holt, who lost both her husband and her son in World War II. Babbie Holt was left extremely comfortably off, and enjoyed having friends around her; she was a wonderfully kind and thoughtful hostess. She had a super, well-trained staff organized by her housekeeper Ina both at her Lyford Cay home and at her house in Canada, where I also stayed with her. Babbie Holt had another much smaller Bahamian home in the Exhumas where she would go for a rest. For many years until she died, Babbie lent this calm retreat to Princess Alexandra and the Hon. Angus Ogilvy for a quiet holiday in February.

On a later visit to Nassau, I spent an afternoon, during which I got desperately bitten by sandflies, out at Lyford Cay with Robin McAlpine and Harold Christie. The latter was showing Robin where he proposed that a golf course should be built, with a club house beside a sandy beach, a swimming pool, tennis courts, a yacht marina and a shopping centre, and he pointed out various sights for building attractive luxury houses. Harold wanted Robin's advice on the construction side, and the possibility of dredging the swamp. I thought it sounded crazy, as part of it was a swamp, but Robin said it was all possible. Within a year or two Harold had got the great Canadian tycoon Mr E.P. Taylor interested. Eddie Taylor, who had made a fortune in beer and business ventures in Canada, always did things in a big way to the highest standard. He developed Lyford Cay on those lines, and for a number of years he saw that it was run most efficiently.

Soon after the Lyford Cay Club was opened Eddie Taylor asked me to go and stay there for a week as his guest, and let him know what was wrong. I found very little wrong! Typically, when Eddie needed a manager he rang Monsieur François Duprée, who then owned some of the best hotels in Paris, also the Westminster Hotel at Le Touquet, and the Ritz Carlton in Montreal, and said he wanted him to send him a really top manager. There was no limit on salary. François Duprée certainly did Eddie a good turn in sending him Maurice Neyrolles, who was a wonderful manager and stayed there after he opened it for many years.

Lyford Cay quickly became one of the most fashionable winter resorts for Americans and the English. Houses sold like hot cakes, and the Lyford Cay Club, for which the entry fee was high and the entrance exclusive, became difficult to join. Happily this has, in a more limited way, continued, and although Lyford Cay, like everywhere else in the world, is rather different forty years on, it still has a very high standard, and is a luxury resort I love visiting.

Eddie Taylor and his wife Winnie became great friends of mine, and I stayed with them at their comfy Toronto home on several occasions. I also visited Eddie's wonderful and very large stud at Willowdale, where the greatest of all stallions, Northern Dancer, was foaled. I saw his victorious son Nijinsky at the stud when he was a foal.

During that first visit to Nassau, I flew over one weekend to stay with Mr and Mrs Robert Rea at the Everglades Club in Palm Beach. I was met at West Palm Beach airport by Bob Rea in the most enormous Cadillac, bigger even than King Farouk's at Deauville. I remarked as I got into it, 'Oh, what a lovely car', and was told proudly that it was the biggest car in Palm Beach! Dear Bob was a terrible show-off; his wife Hélenè was the contrary, quiet and gracious.

I had two amazing days, during which I was absolutely wide-eyed at the wealth everywhere! The dresses at the Everglades on Saturday night were all Paris couture, with lovely jewels, including Mrs Randolph Hearst's pearl necklace, which she wore with a black lace dress. On Sunday, we lunched with a charming couple called Newman from Philadelphia who had a super house here. We lunched out on the patio starting with a huge glass salad bowl full of caviar! My host then had two yachts in the marina, one for him and his wife, and one for his teenage sons and their tutor and friends. I returned to Robin and Norah McAlpine, saying I had had a lot of fun and luxury; now all I wanted was something simple, a glass of water and a boiled egg.

After that visit to the Bahamas, I stopped off in Bermuda on my way home to stay with Mr and Mrs Stanhope Joel, who had recently emigrated to live there because of taxation. They had a most attractive large and comfy house full of fabulous treasures on Perrots Island, which was around eighty yards from the shore – you had to get across by motor or rowboat. Stan Joel also always had *Gryla* standing by. This was a fast speedboat on which they would go out to greet friends arriving on one of the big liners.

Lt-General Sir Alexander Hood was then Governor of Bermuda; he came to dinner one evening. I also met Mr Alec and the Hon. Mrs Mitchell who had just bought Mr Vincent Astor's house. His brother Sir Harold Mitchell already had a lovely house here. Stan and Gladys Joel were both in good form, and in those days giving a lot of parties. One night while I was there, when a restaurant we were at was closing around midnight, Stan said that the band and all his party were now to come to Perrots Island, which it did – and we danced until 3 or 4 a.m. He still had a stud and a string of race horses in England, and they would come over to England each year for the Derby and Royal Ascot, before taking off to Paris and Deauville for French racing, returning to England for York and Doncaster, before finally going back to Bermuda until the following June. They were very loyal friends, who loved having their friends around them. I had been at their wedding, and I enjoyed lots of good parties with them over the years.

I arrived back from this lovely trip in the sunshine towards the end of January. After ten days or so in the office, I was off again for my annual visit to Switzerland. The morning before I was due to leave, we heard the very sad news that The King had died suddenly at Sandringham. As many will remember, Princess Elizabeth heard the news while at Tree Tops game reserve in Kenya.

I decided to carry on with my Swiss trip, but to reduce it to just three days in St Moritz. In those days the *Tatler* appeared weekly, so I had to keep going to fill my pages, which by this time were usually four or five each issue.

While in St Moritz, I went up to the Cresta Run each morning, where the race for the Curzon Cup was being run. The Cresta is never a frivolous or noisy gathering while the racing is on, no doubt as everyone is aware of the risks the riders are taking, but this year it seemed quieter than usual with the Union Jack flying at half mast beside the timekeeper's box.

On my way home from Switzerland that spring I spent twenty-four hours in Paris where the showing of the couture collections was in full swing and everyone was talking clothes! I only had time to visit one collection, so I chose Christian Dior in the Avenue Matignon, which everyone told me was the best. Also, it was always a joy to be with

Christian Dior himself. The collection was superb. Before the show, I enjoyed a privilege shared, I know, by very few English visitors. I had lunch with the Maestro in the wonderful, very chic canteen that Christian Dior ran for his entire staff, from the highest executive to the youngest working girl. At that time they numbered nearly 1000.

The canteen took up the greatest part of the basement of this fine house in Avenue Matignon. The atmosphere was crisp and very alive with cream walls, cherry red top and tables, modern chromium-plated chairs with cherry red seats and excellent modern daylight lighting. There was always a hot or cold menu to choose from; I can say both were delicious as I lunched here with Christian more than once. Fresh fruit and coffee ended a luncheon beautifully served at your own table. I learnt that the food was the same for everyone, that you paid according to your wage or salary. This meant that the youngest apprentice could afford as good a lunch as the highest executive. Christian Dior told me this was his special wish. I remember being very impressed meeting Madame Longuet, a quiet and intelligent trained nurse who was always on duty to look after the staff. She was lunching with Monsieur Gueniot, then a brilliant young doctor, who attended there for a couple of hours each day – he was then busy, he told me, on diabetic research. I hope for the sake of the staff working at the House of Christian Dior that the very high standard that dear Christian Dior personally insisted on, for both the canteen and health care, has been maintained today.

I did not attend The King's funeral in February, but I watched the cortege and procession pass from a window in Fountain House, Park Lane. There was court mourning until 31st May, which cut out many social events. The Queen graciously said functions arranged in aid of charities could still be held, so Queen Charlotte's Ball and other charity balls in May did not have to be postponed; a lot of debutante dances had to be fitted into June and July, though, and some were held in the autumn.

In April I went to Goodwood for the first international car race meeting that season. Here, in the first race, I noticed a clever very blond young driver who was driving a new British engine Formula 2 Cooper with which he won. I was amused to see him wearing a black bow tie with his white shirt and white overalls! He was 23-year-old Michael Hawthorne, until then practically unknown in the motor racing world. He soon became the personality of the afternoon in spite of the world champion Juan Fangio from the Argentine, and his compatriot driver Froilan

Gonzalez. The latter, driving a Ferrari, won the twelve-lap Scratch race for the Richmond Trophy, with Mike Hawthorne second. Another winning driver that afternoon was Stirling Moss, who won the Earl of March Trophy driving a Kieft. After that afternoon, Mike Hawthorne went from strength to strength with many victories until he was tragically killed in a road accident near Guildford.

That year was the first of many during which The Queen and the Duke of Edinburgh stayed privately with the Duke and Duchess of Beaufort at Badminton House for the Badminton Three Day Event. The trials started in a small way in 1949, and became an international event in 1951, mainly thanks to the generosity of 'Master', as the Duke of Beaufort was fondly known, for so gallantly lending his land.

In 1952 they were called the BHS Olympic Horse Trials, as it was an Olympic year (Whitbread had not then come into the picture as sponsors). In fact sporting sponsorship was hardly known in those days.

I was always at the Horse Trials at Badminton for the last two days each year during the fifties, sixties, seventies, and eighties, when I started cutting out cross country day as the crowds were so big; by that time I knew most of the jumps so well that I watched it on television instead. I then went to Badminton only on the Sunday, for the show jumping and prize-giving. For many years when I did two days, I stayed with friends in the district, including Captain and Mrs Charles Tremayne at their lovely home Easton Grey, and Major 'Cuddy' Stirling-Stuart near Malmesbury; each of my hosts was for many years a steward, in charge of one of the jumps on cross country day. There was often a charity dance at Westonbirt on the Saturday night, and always numerous house parties and dinner parties given for the event, which was great fun.

By the beginning of June, court mourning had ended and The Queen once again had very full weeks ahead of her, including The Trooping, the Royal Tournament, the two Presentation Parties at Buckingham Palace, the Chelsea Flower Show, Royal Ascot, and a week at Holyroodhouse, Edinburgh, which includes a Royal Garden Party and other official engagements. Also a visit to the West Country, a tour of the Duchy of Cornwall, a visit to the Royal Show, investitures, three Royal Garden Parties at Buckingham Palace, and other official engagements, as well as all the affairs of state to attend to daily.

During a quick trip to Ireland for part of Horse Show week, I also went evening racing at Phoenix Park. This was fascinating. The racecourse was laid out so that it came right at the stands. It was in those days all owned by the Arnott family. When I went racing there, I was kindly invited to Sir Lauriston Arnott's box, which, if I remember rightly, seemed up on stilts, and you had to climb up a very steep wooden staircase. Here he generously dispensed hospitality to a large group of friends at every meeting until sadly his box was burnt down. Here I used to meet his nephew Mr Eric Arnott, who had left Harrow and was studying at Trinity College, Dublin. Little did I think then that that charming young man would one day become one of the world's leading eye surgeons. Today I am one of his patients. I am so grateful to him for taking such care of my eyes for many years now and for the wonderful eye operations he has performed so successfully on some of my friends.

After Dublin, and a couple of days in my office, I flew down by night, to save time, in a BEA Elizabethan to the South of France to stay for a few days with Mr and Mrs Antony Norman at their enchanting villa Clocher de la Garoupe, on the Normans' Garoupe property. Antony Norman's mother, Lady Norman, a great character and a true Victorian, was then living in the big Château de la Garoupe, where the Princess Royal and Viscount Lascelles spent their honeymoon. Lady Norman lived there during the winter and spring, and in the summer she moved out to a small villa on the estate and then cleverly let the château each summer for a big rent to a millionaire. They were queuing up to rent it!

Giovanni Agnelli of Fiat fame had rented the château for several summers, but had just bought the beautiful villa La Leopolda, near Beaulieu, where one year I went to luncheon with him and his beautiful wife. This year Mr Stavros Niarchos and his very sweet wife Eugenie and their little son Philippe were in residence, along with a party of friends. On his mother's death Antony and Anne Norman moved into it, and have never let it since. They live there part of the year, and at their home in Lausanne for the other part of the year. Anne and Antony Norman are a marvellously hospitable couple, and so generous in having friends to stay in both their homes. I have visited them many times, and always think Château de la Garoupe is my very favourite home to stay in.

Villa life had returned to the pre-war heights. There was a tremendous amount of very chic entertaining by a number of internationally well-known hostesses. I could have filled page after page with social news from there!

After three nights with Anne and Antony Norman, I went on to stay with the Swedish Ambassador and Madame Hägglöf at the charming Villa La Punta, at St Jean Cap Ferrat, rented by them for a second summer.

Anna Hägglöf was a great card player, and would sometimes start before luncheon – though more often afterwards – and go on until late at night with a break for dinner. Alternatively the card-playing at home would end by dinner time, and then we would all go either to the local casino at Beaulieu, or to the Monte Carlo Sporting Club. The other guests staying also played cards and gambled at the casino.

As neither my host nor I either played cards or gambled at the casino, each evening around 4.30 or 5 p.m., when it was getting cooler, we would go for a walk. Gunnar Hägglöf was such an interesting man; he knew far more about people and what was going on in England, as well as other parts of the world, than any Englishman I ever met!

Anna Hägglöf, who was Italian by birth, and extremely attractive, was also the greatest fun and quite unpredictable, when not glued to the card table. A lot of their guests were attractive and fun-loving Italians, so I always enjoyed being with Gunnar and Anna. I was sad when they moved on from London to Paris, as so many friends in the diplomatic corps do. I have never since known any of the Swedish Ambassadors or their wives, other than perhaps to be introduced to them at a party.

From Cap Ferrat I went on to Monte Carlo, which was much as usual, and then I spent a few days in Deauville on my way home. Here I enjoyed all the usual attractions of the Plage Fleurie, of golf in the morning, racing and polo in the afternoon, and a gala ending with a shower of fireworks.

On my return I flew up for the opening day of York races and went on up to Scotland to spend a few days at Gleneagles. Here one of the first people I met was Mr Harold Macmillan, then Minister of Housing and Local Government, who was looking very tired. He told me he had just visited the devastation at Lynmouth caused by the storm and floods, and afterwards reported it to a Cabinet meeting in London. Lady Dorothy Macmillan had already arrived a few days earlier, so they were able to relax together.

In those days Gleneagles was run by British Railways. They had never heard of conventions, symposiums, or package tours; in the summer it was always full of very social guests, many of whom enjoyed the two superb golf courses, shooting, fishing, painting or driving round the countryside. Some stayed for a couple of weeks' holiday, others perhaps only for a couple of nights on their way up north and on their way back south. People who lived in the district came to Sunday lunch here, sometimes bringing house parties, and to dine and dance here on Saturday nights during the summer.

The great piece of news buzzing round Gleneagles when I arrived was that Queen Elizabeth the Queen Mother had bought the ancient Barrogill Castle, Caithness, later called the Castle of Mey, which Her Majesty had first seen when she was staying with her great friends Lt-Commander Clare and Lady Doris Vyner.

On Monday morning I had breakfast with racing driver Mr John Cobb and his wife, and a Mr Railton, who were on their way north to Inverness, where John Cobb was to try out his new jet-propelled boat on Loch Ness in an attempt to gain for Britain the world water speed record; he already held the world record for speed on land. He was a big, quiet, solid gentleman, thoroughly dedicated to his endeavours for Britain. Sadly this was the last time I was to see him; he was killed about a week later during one of these attempts.

Lord Derwent, President that year of Scarborough Cricket Festival, very kindly invited me to stay with him and his very chic wife, French-born Marie-Louise, at their beautiful home Hackness Hall in Yorkshire, for the opening of the ten-day festival. Unlike a lot of women, I love watching good cricket. My brother George had played on two occasions at the Scarborough Festival in the past, though I had not been present. The Scarborough Festival produces the top players and usually wonderful cricket.

A couple of weeks later I went to Hampshire for part of a farewell regimental weekend given by Lt-Colonel Basil Woodd and officers of the 14th/20th Hussars. My son, Jim Kenward, who passed out at Mons Barracks, Aldershot, that summer, was now serving with the 14th/20th, who were off to Tripoli the following month. Basil Woodd and his attractive wife Diana were a wonderful host and hostess, and had organized all the young officers to look after the guests. The programme began with an 'all ranks' dance on Friday night, then a cricket match next day, followed by a cocktail party on the floodlit lawn outside the Officers' Mess, and a cold buffet supper before another dance. On Sunday there was a church service, and General Sir Richard McCreery, Colonel of the Regiment, took the salute at the Regimental March Past.

That year I stayed for Doncaster races and sales with Sir Malcolm and Lady McAlpine, who always rented a house there for race week. This year The Queen had her colt Gay Time running in the St Leger and came down by train overnight to see him run. On arrival in the paddock she met her trainer Mr Noel Murless, later Sir Noel Murless, and her jockey Gordon Richards, later Sir Gordon Richards, whom she watched mount Gay Time before she returned to the Royal Box. The presence of Her Majesty had attracted the biggest crowd I have ever seen at Doncaster. If I started to tell you who I saw I would fill several pages!

That year I also went to the Ayr Western meeting and stayed at the very comfortable Turnberry Hotel with a party of friends, including Mrs Lowis and her brother Mr John Baillie, a great character of the racing world, who had several runners and one winner at Ayr; and Sir Adrian Jarvis, always known as Jimmy. The latter had two runners at the meeting, who finished first and second in their respective races, so our party was a very happy one. The hotel has a fine championship golf course, where the men played golf each morning. I was only allowed to join them when I had collected the *Sporting Life*. I then had to take it out and answer to John Baillie and Jimmy Jarvis and others whatever racing queries I was asked. Not always too easy when a high wind was blowing off the sea!

Ayr is a charming small racecourse, which in those days attracted the Newmarket trainers to run some of their best horses there. The Ayr Western meeting was a very social occasion, with hotels full and everyone in the district having house parties and parties. Although smart, it was not as dressy as Royal Ascot or the York Summer meeting.

That Christmas I spent in Malta. Until then my son Jim and I had never spent Christmas apart. This year he was, as I have written, with the 14th/20th Hussars in Libya. I gave this matter a little thought, and decided that if I went out to Malta – where there were no currency problems! – for Christmas, Jim might get leave to fly across to join me. I cabled his commanding officer, Colonel Basil Woodd, saying I was planning to spend Christmas in Malta, and asked if Jim could join me there. I got a splendid cable back from Basil Woodd saying 'Jim can join you for Christmas and New Year, Basil'. So I cabled Jim to apply for leave, which of course he was granted. He did not know about my cable to his Colonel! I flew out on Christmas Eve to Rome in one of BOAC's Argonaut Speedbirds, travelling at 18,000 feet. After a few hours in Rome, I flew on in a smaller plane, landed at

Luqa airport, and motored in to the Phoenicia Hotel in Valetta, where we were going to stay.

Jim joined me here an hour later, and we decided to go to the midnight Christmas Eve service at the Valetta church, instead of early church on Christmas morning. We had adjoining bedrooms with a door between. His room somehow seemed to fill quickly next morning with young men – friends of Jim's or sons of my friends – all of whom were doing National Service out there, and some of whom had come to collect family Christmas presents that I had brought out for them.

I found several letters of welcome, but the first one I opened was from Countess Mountbatten of Burma saying she had heard I was arriving with Jim and asking what we were doing for Christmas luncheon and dinner, and would I ring her on my arrival. This was so typical of Edwina Mountbatten's kindess – I had purposely not let her know we were coming, as I knew how busy her life was there as Lord Louis was then Commander-in-Chief Mediterranean Fleet.

I rang her right away and told her what we were doing on Christmas Day, and we then found we were going to the same friends for drinks after church and before luncheon, so we would meet there. She told me they were giving a dance during the week for their younger daughter and that Jim and I must come to that too. On Christmas Day we went to the Christmas Day morning service and on to drinks with friends, then on to Christmas luncheon with Commander Henry Wilkin and his attractive and very sweet wife Anne, who were old friends.

In the evening, Colonel Sir Peter Grant Lawson, who was in the Blues, and his very attractive American-born wife Ginny had asked us to dine. Peter Grant Lawson was out in Malta as Colonel-in-Chief Administrator of the Malta Garrison. They were living in the House of Four Winds, high up on St Michael's Bastion, with a wonderful view over the Harbours. After dinner we went out on to the balcony in the moonlight, with a clear starry sky, to look at the ships lit up. They included several submarines and their parent ship the *Forth*, and destroyers including HMS *Darwin*, which was new, and their parent ship the *Tyne*; and the giant aircraft carrier *Ocean*, just back from Korea, which was decorated with a huge Christmas tree in red lights with a star on top.

During our stay I was quite overwhelmed with everyone's hospitality and kindness; invitations flowed in! I had booked a drive-yourself car in advance, so we were mobile. The Governor and Commander-in-

Chief Sir Gerald Creasy and Lady Creasy kindly invited us to a wonderful dance they gave for their daughter Miss Juliet Creasy at their winter residence the Palace, at San Anton, which was most attractively decorated for the occasion. The Creasys were a charming couple and a lot of fun. Although the dance started off a little formally, everyone was soon dancing a hokey cokey, then reels, and the Governor led a conga into supper!

The dance that Admiral Earl Mountbatten and Countess Mountbatten gave for Lady Pamela Mountbatten at Admiralty House was also the greatest fun and very memorable. Edwina Mountbatten, who had exquisite taste, had redecorated and refurnished the house specially for the occasion, and had brought quite a few pictures out from Broadlands as well as superb pieces of silver which we saw in the dining room at supper. It was a colourful scene, as most of the men were in uniform and the ladies in their best dresses. Our hostess looked very chic in orchid satin, and Pammy Mountbatten was in pale blue tulle. Here again they had pipers playing for reels and Scottish country dances; it was altogether a very joyful scene. Lord Louis insisted that the party end soon after 1 a.m. when, as at all good parties, everyone wanted more.

One afternoon I went alone and had tea and spent a couple of hours with Edwina Mountbatten, quietly catching up on news from home, including her charities as well as her friends. On two afternoons we went to the Marsa Club to watch the polo. Lord Mountbatten, a good player with a handicap of seven, played most afternoons.

Another day I made a tour of the big airy wards at the Royal Naval Hospital at Bighi, and went up to the top floor where I found naval wives and their children. The sailors in the wards were unanimous in their praise for the nursing and care they were receiving. This was not my first visit to the hospital, as one morning I had gone there to watch an operation to which I'd been invited by a naval surgeon at the Mountbatten dance. Two days later, when I was being put into a white gown and cap and shoes, I asked myself why I had accepted the invitation. But I had no time to think as we were soon in the operating theatre. The surgeon who invited me (he was not operating but was present) said they had hoped for an appendix operation, but instead the operation I was to watch was to put a new bone in the nose of a sailor, who had broken it badly in an accident. I was told that if I felt like fainting I was not to clutch at anything, as everything around me was sterilized, and they would have to resterilize! Luckily I was so very interested in all I saw, including the anaesthetic, that I never felt queasy for a moment. I was impressed with the precision and care with which the operation was carried out by the surgeon, and by the constant monitoring by the anaesthetist. I was grateful, too, that I had been given the opportunity to watch their work, as it took away any fear I might have had of having an operation, as I had now seen exactly what happens.

At the end of these very full and happy eight days in Malta, I said goodbye to my beloved son, who returned to his regiment in Tripoli. I then flew to Rome for two very busy days, during which I managed to see quite a few friends.

Then I had the great thrill of my first flight in a BOAC Comet 4 jet liner. As I wrote then, 'It came beyond my highest hopes'. I had by then flown in a variety of machines, from a tiny de Havilland Moth to the huge and comfy Stratrocruiser, but I never dreamt that any aeroplane could be as quiet and comfortable as the Comet 4. We took off in thirty-three seconds and were soon flying at nearly five hundred miles an hour at 38,000 feet, with absolute smoothness. After a breakfast in Rome, I spent an hour in my office in London before luncheon!

The Comet 4, I think, was my very favourite aeroplane. I flew in this first commercial jet everywhere I could until, alas, it was grounded following a bad crash, with tragic loss of life, after taking off from Rome airport to fly to London in 1954. I had been on the same flight from Rome in a Comet 4 the previous day.

EIGHT

The Coronation

(1953–55)

I went up to Edinburgh in January 1953 for a very special wedding. This was the marriage of the Duke and Duchess of Buccleuch's only son, the Earl of Dalkeith, to Miss Jane McNeill, whose parents, Mr and Mrs John McNeill, lived in Argyllshire.

The bride looked so beautiful, so radiantly happy, and so elegant as she arrived punctually at St Giles Cathedral with her father. Her wedding dress, which had been designed by Mr Hardy Amies, now Sir Hardy Amies, was a dream. It was made of white lace woven in a mayflower design, the Buccleuch emblem, picked out with a silver thread. Her tulle veil was held in place by a superb Buccleuch tiara, also in a mayflower design.

The Queen and the Duke of Edinburgh and Princess Margaret had travelled to Edinburgh by the royal train from Sandringham. In spite of thick fog and cold, thousands had lined the streets to see the royal party – it was the first time a reigning queen had been to a wedding in Edinburgh.

As at all big functions in the Buccleuch family, everything was organized to perfection. The ushers were well briefed and coped with the 1600 guests in St Giles Cathedral most efficiently. I well remember nearly getting squashed leaving St Giles, until Mr Paul Channon, then an Eton schoolboy, very gallantly took my arm and made a way for me.

The Duke and Duchess of Buccleuch, and his mother the Dowager Duchess of Buccleuch, had, I am sure, every member of the Buccleuch family around them as well as tenants and people who helped on all the Buccleuch estates. It was a wedding I shall always remember as a particularly happy occasion.

That year I went to Manchester Square, where Mrs Gordon Leith had lent her charming house for a special showing by Bellville et Cie of their debutante and spring collection. The clothes had all been designed by Belinda Bellville, by then the newly married Mrs David Whately, whom I had known since she was a child. It was her very first dress show! She had then just opened a shop in Knightsbridge, with a Mrs Synda Scott, where they specialized in clothes for young girls.

I wrote at the time 'It was a fresh and youthful collection, and the prices would suit all parents', as they ranged from a day dress at eight guineas to the most expensive evening dress at forty-five guineas. This really was reasonable as they were all made to measure with the necessary fittings. That day Belinda Bellville had a couple of models showing the clothes and only her very attractive and dear mother, the Hon. Mrs Peter Pleydell-Bouverie, and her aunt, Mrs Rupert Bellville, to help her. To me it was so wonderful to watch Belinda Bellville blossom out, thanks to her hard work and artistic talents, and develop the wonderful retail and wholesale business she built up as Bellville et Cie. It is also good to see the business still flourishing today as Bellville-Sassoon, still one of England's top designers. Also what was so truly splendid was that Belinda Whately, who is now retired and living in the country with her husband, managed to have a happy marriage and to bring up a fine, healthy family.

At the end of March the whole country was saddened by the news of the death of Queen Mary at the age of eighty-six. Her Majesty was a regal personality of the old school, but underneath that upright severity she had a heart of gold. I wrote at the time, 'Queen Mary knew what it was to be poor, she knew what it was to lose one's dearest, she went through great anxiety when her eldest son abdicated, and she knew the worries of war, but she knew no fear.' Her Majesty was going to be sadly missed. I knew I would miss seeing her at the theatre, which she loved. On those occasions she was often accompanied by Brigadier Sir Norman Gwatkin, a very cheery personality with a fund of very fresh stories which I am sure amused Queen Mary, as she would often chuckle at his remarks. As a mark of respect for her grandmother, The Queen ordered one month's court mourning.

Being Coronation Year, hotels were heavily booked, and charities were getting on the band wagon with Coronation balls for every good cause in the land. Sir Simon Campbell-Orde was once again running the Caledonian Ball, which dates back to 1849, and the tickets, he told me, had been sold out early. A record number of 144 dancers were to take part in the famous Set Reels, which always open the Caledonian Ball. It was the same for Queen Charlotte's Birthday Ball, which sold out a record number of tickets early. Parties and celebrations were being arranged in every city and village all over the country.

In 1953, for the second year running, I published a list of private dances and social functions taking place throughout the year. My first list of social functions was such a tremendous success, and so many readers asked me to do it every year, that I have now published this list without a break for forty years! The only difference is that in 1975 I was forced to omit the private parties, because gatecrashers were using the list for information.

There were a record number of Coronation debutantes. Besides the eighteen-year-olds, there were also seventeen-year-olds and nineteen-year-olds, who had come forward or held back! For Coronation Year, Margherita Lady Howard de Walden, President of the Queen Charlotte's Birthday Ball, had persuaded the Duchess of Gloucester to be that year's guest of honour, so the debutantes had a royal lady to make their curtsey to.

Regiments also had Coronation balls. I was kindly invited out to Germany by the Colonel, Lt-Colonel Anthony Llewellen Palmer, and officers of the 9th Lancers, who were then stationed with the BAOR at Detmold, to their Coronation Ball. This was my first visit to Germany, and I found it intensely interesting. I noticed every yard of the land was cultivated – by horse- or oxen-drawn cultivators, not mechanical tractors!– and the women of the families were all working in the fields. The Germans were working happily with our troops, some on the telephone exchanges.

The refugee problem at that time was colossal, but was being dealt with wisely, every area having to take its quota of refugees from the Eastern zone. What impressed me was how everyone was working! Our army, anyhow in that area, was kept extremely busy, and the wives were all working in one way or another. My hostess for that weekend, whom I had never met previously, Mrs David Belchem, whose husband, Brigadier David Belchem, was in charge of a brigade out there, had a very busy life. She had taken over a farm where she raised pigs and fresh farm produce for the benefit of the British families, and she also ran a well-stocked shop.

I had been personally invited out to the ball by Major the Hon. Christopher Beckett, later Lord Grimthorpe, who was then second-in-command of the 9th Lancers, and had a lot to do with organizing the ball, which was on a Saturday night. It took place in the Officers' Mess. It was most beautifully organized, and to help him with the arrangements Christie Beckett had Major John Reid, and the Reids' house guest Miss Gillian de Burgh, who did the flowers so beautifully; also the Hon. Mrs Llewellen Palmer, who was a talented artist and did some clever decor. Among them were exquisite flower arrangements, including 'ERII' in mixed flowers in the place of honour over the very wide staircase. The troopers on duty were all wearing full dress uniform and the regimental regalia, and the magnificent regimental silver was all on show. Dancing took place non-stop on three floors. The regimental band and the Rhine Army Alamein Band played on the ground floor and basement – in which there was a mural of the Royal Coach and Household Cavalry escort nearing Buckingham Palace on Coronation Day – and on the first floor Mr David Yorke, a guest from England, played the piano indefatigably so that the dance floor was always full.

I went to all the hardy annuals in May, starting with Chester race week, then the Caledonian and the Queen Charlotte's Balls, and many other charity balls as well as a great number of private dances. That season I think I was out every single night, often fulfilling three or four engagements.

Once again I joined Jimmy Jarvis's party for a happy Whitsun weekend at Le Touquet. While I was there, I was terribly teased about my flamboyant bearded friend. This was that very colourful personality Nubar Gulbenkian, the son of the famous art collector Calouste Gulbenkian, whose Gulbenkian Museum in Lisbon is such a joy to visit. Nubar, who had a thick black beard and was a tremendous extrovert, married a very dear French-born friend of mine, born Mademoiselle Marie Ayala, then Miss Samuelson.

At Le Touquet, Nubar would wear a French beret on the golf course, and had one of his rather 'show-off' cars out there. Some readers may remember the London taxi he drove about in, which was painted in a basket design on black and had two carriage lamps. His Rolls-Royce in Paris had a clear roof so that as a passenger you could be seen inside it; for good measure, Nubar would insist on the inside light being on, in the evenings!

This year for the first time Hutchinson House in Stratford Place, for many years the home of the Earls of Derby, was used for private dances.

The second of two dances I went to there was a very grand evening. In fact it was the biggest and most resplendent private ball of Coronation Year. It was given by the Hon. Lady Ward and Mrs John Ward for Colonel and Mrs John Ward's daughter Miss Elizabeth Ward, who was always called 'Diddy' Ward, and was arranged to pefection. Mr Felix Harbord had done extremely clever decor to transform the house and garden. As well as the main ballroom in the house, which was lined with priceless tapestries, there was a dance floor in the garden with a canopy overhead. The Queen, looking radiant in a cream satin dress with gold embroidery, with a pearl and diamond tiara, and a two-row pearl necklace, arrived at the ball with Queen Elizabeth the Queen Mother, who looked wonderful in a pale blue tulle crinoline, with a satin bodice, and a diamond tiara and a ruby and diamond necklace. This was one of the last private functions the royal ladies attended before the Coronation.

The Hon. Lady Ward, a regal figure wearing a diamond tiara with her gold dress, was accustomed to entertaining in a big way, as before she married she acted as hostess for her father, American millionaire Mr Whitelaw Reid, when he was American Ambassador for several years here.

It was quite an original idea for mother and daughter to wear nearly identical dresses. Diddy Ward looked enchanting in a white satin and tulle dress with trailing green leaves across the skirt. Her beautiful mother Susan Ward wore the same dress in bottle green satin and tulle, but instead of the trailing leaves hers had huge white roses on it.

It really was a glamorous scene, as all the married ladies wore tiaras and exquisite jewels, with gorgeous dresses, most of them crinolines, which sometimes caused congestion in a doorway! The men, including our host Colonel Jackie Ward, all wore their orders and decorations with, of course, white tie and tails. Most of the young girls were in white.

It was a warm evening and Queen Elizabeth the Queen Mother was among those waltzing on the outdoor dance floor. Both The Queen and Queen Elizabeth danced quite frequently that evening, which is one I shall never forget for its beauty, and for the warmth and friendliness of all the guests, who were obviously enjoying themselves as much as I was.

When I am asked what event was the most important in my forty-five years of Jennifer's Diary, without any hesitation I always reply 'The Queen's Coronation'. I felt so tremendously grateful and privileged to be present.

I started my description in the *Tatler* by writing 'A thousand years of history woven into one gigantic blazing tapestry, now animated, now still, now wrapped about with splendid music, now hushed, now silent, and in its very centre the serenely lovely young Queen Elizabeth the Second'. We who were privileged to be at Westminster Abbey for her Coronation can never forget the sight of The Queen, first in her beautiful robes, then divested of all but a severe long white pleated linen dress – this, perhaps, above all other moments in the hour-long ceremony, was that which most intimately touched my heart and mind. All about her at one moment glittered and glowed. Then suddenly she sat there, alone, without ornament save for her true beauty, the inheritor of a nation's honour, fame, and future. To me that was the most moving scene I have ever experienced in my life. It seemed incredible that that young girl (sitting in that simple linen garment, The Queen looked about sixteen years old) was, alone, officially taking on the tremendous burden she had inherited. My goodness, we as a nation are fortunate in having had such a wonderful Queen, who has kept her word and dedicated her life to her country, and has shouldered that burden that she inherited so magnificently, for already forty years.

That day the sun shone through the windows of Westminster Abbey, and a fanfare signalled her arrival with the Duke of Edinburgh, who was in the full dress uniform of an Admiral of the Fleet. Her Majesty was wearing a royal robe of crimson velvet, trimmed with ermine and bordered with gold lace, over her heavily embroidered long white satin dress designed by Norman Hartnell. Round her neck was a beautiful diamond necklace and on her head a diadem of diamonds. The Queen's six train bearers, who wore long cream satin dresses embroidered in gold, with gold leaves in their hair, were all attractive girls – Lady Jane Vane-Tempest-Stewart, Lady Mary Baillie-Hamilton, Lady Rosemary Spencer-Churchill, Lady Anne Coke, Lady Moyra Hamilton, and Lady Jane Heathcote-Drummond-Willoughby. The Archbishop of Canterbury, Doctor Fisher, was wearing a magnificent cope of gold and cream, and stood with the Archbishop of York, Doctor Garbett, both carrying mitres. This was the first time, I was told, that mitres had been worn at a coronation for many years, if ever. All the many other clergy present wore magnificent vestments. One of the most outstanding was the then Dean of Westminster, Doctor Alan Don, who wore a superb cope of red velvet which had been worn at the Coronation of King Charles II.

The Lord Great Chamberlain, the 5th Marquess of Cholmondeley, grandfather of the present peer, looked magnificent in his gold-braided scarlet full dress uniform and robes of state; and the Earl Marshal the

Duke of Norfolk, who was in charge of all the proceedings, wore a special uniform comprising a scarlet coat richly embroidered in gold, with white knee breeches and stockings under his robes of state. The peers sitting in the South Transept were wearing their ermine-trimmed crimson Coronation robes, or the very dignified dark blue Garter mantles, over morning dress or uniforms. Opposite, in the North Transept, the peeresses were wearing their crimson velvet ermine-trimmed robes over shimmering evening dresses and truly magnificent jewels. It is really staggering, the exquisite and magnificent heirloom jewellery that English ladies wear on state occasions. Sadly nowadays, these jewels spend the rest of the time in the safe custody of banks.

The Prime Ministers of the countries of the Commonwealth had taken up their places with our Prime Minister Sir Winston Churchill, who was wearing the uniform of Lord Warden of the Cinque Ports under his Garter Mantle, and Lady Churchill. Their grandson Winston Churchill was present as page to Marshal of the Royal Air Force Viscount Portal, who carried the sceptre with the cross. Queen Elizabeth the Queen Mother, Princess Margaret, wearing an exceptionally long crimson velvet ermine-trimmed train that was carried on her way to the Royal Gallery by her lady-in-waiting Miss Iris Peake, later the Hon. Mrs Dawnay, and the Princess Royal and other members of the Royal Family arrived in procession and took their seats in the Royal Gallery. The Duke of Gloucester and the Duke of Kent sat beside the Duke of Edinburgh nearest the altar. It would take too long to describe the whole scene and the ceremony, but the next most memorable moment for me was when the Archbishop of Canterbury, having blessed the crown, came with other clergy from the High Altar to King Edward's Chair, where The Queen sat holding the sceptre with the cross in her right hand, and the rod with the dove in her left hand, and with great solemnity crowned her with St Edward's Crown. At the same moment the Prince and Princesses and the peers and peeresses put on their coronets and caps. Prince Charles joined the royal party for a short while and stood between Queen Elizabeth the Queen Mother and Princess Margaret to see his mother crowned. The benediction followed, then the enthroning, when The Queen was lifted up into her throne by the archbishops and bishops and peers of the Kingdom.

The Duke of Edinburgh was the first to pay homage, followed by the Duke of Gloucester and the Duke of Kent, followed by the Premier Duke, Marquess, Earl, Viscount and Baron. The long and impressive service over, The Queen, crowned and still wearing her exquisite gold raiment, and carrying the sceptre and rod in her hands, went through into St Edward's Chapel. When she returned to proceed in state procession to the West Door, she had changed to the Imperial Crown with a magnificent robe of purple velvet. It was dressed like this that, after her return to Buckingham Palace in the State Coach with the Duke of Edinburgh, Her Majesty appeared on the balcony of the Palace with the Duke of Edinburgh, Prince Charles, and Princess Anne.

I received such wonderful help and kindness over the Coronation. Firstly the Earl Marshal the Duke of Norfolk offered to let me attend the final rehearsal, so that I could see exactly what was to happen. (The Duchess of Norfolk, later Lavinia Duchess of Norfolk, took Her Majesty's place at all the rehearsals.) Then a very dear peer and his wife sweetly invited me to breakfast with them in the House of Lords before the Coronation, before everyone took up their places in Westminster Abbey, which I think we all had to do soon after 9 a.m. I know I ordered a car for 6 a.m. as I think I was to be in the dining room of the House of Lords by 6.45 a.m., and I was anxious in case I would be delayed by the crowds.

Breakfast was served, I remember, very early. It was a most amusing scene. Most of the men had taken off their coats and were in shirt sleeves (it was mid-summer). The ladies at this time of the morning were of course already in evening dress, their tiaras and jewels glittering in the broad daylight; some were carrying their tiaras as these can be fairly heavy, and they were going to put them on at the last moment. There was a lot of helping each other after breakfast to put the final touches to all the finery. It was a unique and extraordinary scene of informality, but all done with great dignity. Then, with all their Coronation robes on, our peers and peeresses looked magnificent. I was so happy to have been invited to this amusing interlude behind the scenes of this historic event.

For The Queen, this was an exceptionally busy week as besides her Coronation there were three afternoon drives through different districts of London, two state banquets at Buckingham Palace and a reception for 2,000 guests at the Palace. The latter followed the big dinner given by the Foreign Office at Lancaster House, at which the Prime Minister Sir Winston Churchill acted as host in place of Mr Anthony Eden, who was ill. The banquets and the reception at Buckingham Palace are still remembered by those who were present for the gold plate, the full court dress worn by the men, the lovely dresses, the beautiful saris, and the fabulous jewels, especially those worn by some of the Eastern potentates and their wives, all in the regal setting of the brilliantly lit Palace, full of glorious flowers sent up from the gardens at Windsor Castle.

In that brilliant Coronation season I well remember the opening night of *Gloriana*, a new opera written especially by Benjamin Britten, at the Royal Opera House, which was beautifully decorated for the occasion by Oliver Messel.

It was another of those glittering evenings attended by The Queen and nearly every member of the Royal Family, with all the men wearing their orders and decorations and the women wearing tiaras and fabulous jewellery with brilliantly coloured evening dresses. I noticed that The Queen, who was received on arrival by the Chairman, Viscount Waverley, and Mr David Webster, for so many years the general manager of the Royal Opera House, wore the bright blue riband of the Order of the Garter, as did the Duke of Edinburgh and Queen Elizabeth the Queen Mother. As the royal party proceeded up the wide staircase to the Royal Box, it was lined with guardsmen of the Grenadier Guards in their scarlet tunics, and on the arrival of the royal party in the box, when the orchestra played 'God Save The Queen', the whole of the audience rose and faced the Royal Box. The audience too was a little different, with the presence of the Crown Prince and Princess of Norway and Princess Astrid of Norway, and others from overseas, including Mr Robert Menzies, then the Prime Minister of Australia, and Mrs Menzies, later Sir Robert and Dame Pattie Menzies, and other Commonwealth Prime Ministers, members of the Cabinet and of both Houses of Parliament, and nearly all the foreign ambassadors to the Court of St James and their wives, most of whom gave Coronation parties before or after the event. I thoroughly enjoyed the whole evening except for *Gloriana*, which I thought was laboured and not the right choice for this occasion.

That week the British social world were highly amused by a rather ambitious and flamboyant American lady called Mrs Perle Mesta, whose parties in America had been much publicized. She had until recently been American Minister in Luxembourg, where again she gave much-publicized lavish parties, often entertaining European royals. Perle Mesta was, I felt, a very warm-hearted woman and I am sure she entertained to give others fun, as well as for her own satisfaction.

Mrs Mesta decided that The Queen's Coronation would be the right time to throw one of her spectacular parties in London, and chose the night after the Coronation. She rented lovely Londonderry House, scene of some wonderful parties when the Marquesses of Londonderry lived there, and then must have gone through *Debrett* and the Diplomatic List before sending out her invitations: I had friends who had never heard of her, let alone met her, who received invitations. Some of these had other engagements in London that night, so accepted to just pop in and have a look; it was not a dinner dance so there was no seating and no one was expected before 10.30 p.m. Perle Mesta shared the party with a Mr and Mrs George Tyson, whom I never heard of before or after the party, at which, sadly, I never met or saw them!

I had been invited to a debutante dance at the Dorchester that evening, and to dine with the host and hostess at the Dorchester before the dance, so I accepted Mrs Mesta's kind invitation, and I went on around midnight to nearby Londonderry House and found the party at its height. The lights were blazing everywhere, a really good band was playing, the ballroom was full, and the house was buzzing with people, with a lot of coming and going up and down the fine staircase.

Many guests had just come on from the state banquet at Buckingham Palace, so some of the men were in full court dress, and many wore orders and decorations. A great number of the women guests wore tiaras and there were many beautiful dresses. The one I remember most vividly was a buttercup yellow slipper satin crinoline worn by the beautiful young Countess of Dalkeith, who also had on the exquisite diamond tiara she wore at her wedding. After a short search I found my hostess, Mrs Mesta, who had just been dancing with the recently married Prince Jean of Luxembourg, who was there with his bride.

Perle Mesta gave me a very warm welcome and immediately introduced me to charming American friends. She was wearing the riband of the Grand Order of Luxembourg across her beautiful evening dress, but – oh dear! – on her head she wore the worst imitation tiara I have ever seen. It looked as if it had been made by a dressmaker! It made me very sad that anyone could spend all this money on a big party, which was very glamorous, but not take a little trouble to borrow a beautiful tiara from a friend, or from one of the top jewellers, whom I have always found so kind about loaning a tiara.

The other royal guests at the party included the Crown Prince and Princess of Norway, and Prince Bernhard of the Netherlands. The diplomatic corps were headed by the doyen, the French Ambassador Monsieur René Massigli, and his wife, looking very chic. Strangely I did not see one member from either of our Houses of Parliament there.

The only other dress that really caught my eye was also in yellow slipper satin, very chic, and worn by Mrs Cornelius Vanderbilt Whitney, with a diamond necklace of large graduated pear-shaped diamonds, which was easily the most beautiful necklace at a very memorable party.

The following week I was up at dawn on Monday to catch a train at Waterloo to Portsmouth. Here, later in the day, Her Majesty, accompanied by the Duke of Edinburgh, was going to review her Fleet at Spithead. I had very kindly been invited to watch the Review in the cruiser *Swiftsure*.

I left London feeling very frightened, hoping I was correctly dressed, that I would find the ship, and that when on board I would feel a little more confident. This was an entirely new experience for me. I found the ship, and my two hosts were both charming and gave me a big welcome and delegated younger officers to take care of me. I did not know a soul among the other guests!

The first great moment came when, shortly after the frigate *Surprise*, with The Queen on board, left the jetty at Portsmouth Harbour, preceded by the Trinity House boat *Patricia* with the Prime Minister Sir Winston Churchill aboard, a Royal Salute of twenty-one guns was fired from every ship of the assembled fleet, a most impressive sound and sight.

The Queen wore a white coat and close-fitting hat, and, with the Duke of Edinburgh, who was in Admiral's uniform, reviewed her Fleet from a specially constructed glass-panelled saluting platform on board the frigate *Surprise*. Her Majesty stood here for an hour and a half as the *Surprise* cruised slowly along the sixteen-mile line of ships. When the *Surprise* entered the Review lines, she passed between the vanguard flagship of the Home Fleet and the US cruiser *Baltimore*, which, like all other ships, was dressed overall. All the way the ships' bands played the National Anthem, and the officers and men were manning the side of the ships cheering Her Majesty. It was another very memorable occasion; I was glad I had had the courage to attend it.

At the end of November The Queen and the Duke of Edinburgh set off on a long tour of the Commonwealth in the South Seas, including New Zealand and Australia. This was the first time a reigning monarch had paid a visit to the Dominions. This meant that The Queen had to make her Christmas Day Broadcast to her people from New Zealand and that she had to spend Christmas thousands of miles away from her two children, Prince Charles and Princess Anne, and her family at Sandringham.

That year I went out to Switzerland and the winter sports rather early as I wanted to get it over before going off to the sunshine. Watching ski-racing is the coldest pastime in the world, but it is much easier to write about if you have stood watching all the action, even if you do get absolutely frozen in the process!

I started in St Moritz where there were masses of Americans. I went on for the racing at Grindelwald, which, as the crow flies, is no distance, but is very indirect by train; it took ten hours and four changes! From here I went on to Mürren, which was enjoying good snow and having the best season since pre-war days. My first evening I dined with the 'grand old man of skiing' Sir Arnold Lunn, and Lady Mabel Lunn, who always went to Mürren. All the regulars were here, and many family parties.

Next day I watched the Lowlanders championships and the event for the Duke of Kent Cup, which was run under very trying conditions as it was snowing hard and visibility was bad.

Next morning it was still snowing hard, and Schlunegger, the famous concierge, told me my chances of getting to Wengen that day were slender as nearly a metre of snow had fallen in the night, it was still snowing hard, and trains were not running because of small avalanches which were blocking the line.

I had just started my luncheon when Schlunegger came to tell me that a train had managed to get to the top, and would be leaving for Lauterbrunnen, the junction at the bottom, in ten minutes. So I abandoned my lunch, asked the concierge to get my luggage down from my bedroom and to the station, put on my anorak and top coat and ran for the train which was, I heard later, the last for two days! My luggage was happily also on board.

I had little idea of the eventful journey ahead. There were only five other passengers, all Swiss. As far as Gutsch we went well. Then on the second lap we were suddenly halted at an alarming angle while men cleared the line of another slide of snow. It was nearly 3 p.m. when we arrived at Lauterbrunnen, where a train for Wengen had been waiting for a couple of hours. Thanks to my Swiss fellow travellers, I got my luggage across to the Wengen train. I was told that this train was expected to leave about 4 p.m., the delay being due to a small avalanche earlier which had derailed a truck full of skis further up. No passengers seemed to be on the platform or in the train except myself, when I suddenly saw Alan Crompton and some of the British skiers, who had left Mürren early in the morning before they stopped all

trains. Then dear Sir Wavell Wakefield and his daughter Mrs Richard
Hensman arrived on skis from Wengen, expecting to catch the train
back as usual. When we confirmed that the train was unlikely to start
for another hour, we all went across to the Stenboch Hotel beside the
station for hot chocolate. I was jolly cold and famished by then. We
found the hotel packed with stranded skiers, some of them British,
including a Mr Seligman who had skied down from Wengen with his
wife. He was playing the piano, and some of the men and girls were
dancing.

Suddenly Madron Seligman struck up the music for an Eightsome
Reel, and in a flash there was the most amazing sight – a Scottish reel
being danced extremely well by cheery young people in ski clothes
in the middle of a snowstorm in Switzerland! As it finished, we heard
the train was about to start, so we all bundled on board. Someone then produced a banjo and others started to sing. All went
well until we were brought to a sudden halt about five hundred
yards short of Wengen. Another avalanche had come down ahead
of us on the line. The driver came along and threw open the doors
and told us we had to walk the rest of the journey, which he said
cheerily was no distance at all! He made us leave our luggage in the
train.

Five hundred yards up the side of a mountain, part of it through a
foot-wide track of soft snow into which one sank at each step, with
snow nearly shoulder high each side, seemed like five miles to me! In
addition there was the rather frightening feeling that there might be
another slide at any moment. I was so relieved when I arrived at the
Palace Hotel, where I received a warm welcome from Mr Fritz Borter
and his wife, who ran the hotel so well. With usual Swiss efficiency
my suitcases arrived in around an hour. In my bath before dinner, I
thought of my dear father, who always taught me that if you had an
appointment to keep and your transport broke down you must always
try to get there somehow. I have gone through life with two short
sayings: 'There is no such word as cannot', and secondly, 'Any fool
can be uncomfortable'.

Next day the weather was grim, but racing for the British Ski Championships took place. As at St Moritz, Grindelwald and Mürren I only
stayed two days in Wengen. During the whole trip I hardly saw the
sun. I have learnt that visits to Switzerland in January and during
much of February are often sunless. Happily this time I had the joy of
knowing I had plenty of lovely sunshine ahead of me, as Sir Malcolm

and Lady McAlpine had so kindly invited me to stay with them at their house in Nassau.

My next adventure was my first visit to Jamaica.

I had been invited by Mr and Mrs Stanhope Joel, whom I had stayed with two years previously in Bermuda, and known since we were teenagers, to stay with them at Content Hill, their house near Ocho Rios in Jamaica. That year Stan and Gladys Joel had decided as an experiment to come from Bermuda to Jamaica on a banana boat. They never thought that it might be delayed in various ports, which it was! So when I arrived at Montego Bay I was met by a friend and neighbour of theirs, Mr Douglas Vaughan, who was very fed up at having to meet me!

He told me that Stan and Gladys had been delayed and did not know when they would arrive, so they had arranged for me to stay, as their guest, at the Shaw Park Hotel, Ocho Rios, and had alerted friends around that I was coming. The drive from Montego to Ocho Rios is about seventy miles and it was quite late and dark when we arrived. Douglas Vaughan left me at the reception desk. I was then taken to a nice large bedroom in a brand new annexe, away from the main hotel.

I felt a bit isolated and lonely, as I had not expected to be staying alone in a hotel. I then had one of the worst nights I can remember. Soon after I got into bed there was suddenly an awful noise of banging. I sat up and listened (there was no telephone in my room), then got out of bed and armed myself with a large wooden coat hanger, waiting for an intruder. The banging continued on and off. I was getting so tired that eventually I got back into bed, and clutching my coat hanger I fell asleep from sheer exhaustion.

Next morning I complained to the manager about the noise, and asked for a room in the main hotel. The manager was mystified until a few days later a couple who were given my original room also complained of the banging. It was finally found that there were a number of rats in the roof which had come there to enjoy the food left by the workmen building the annexe.

I found Jamaica the most beautiful of all the West Indian islands. After that bad first night, I had a super visit. Everyone was so hospitable and kind. Even Douglas Vaughan thawed! I met his beautiful Belgian-born wife Golly. On the second day he took me at 5 a.m. to watch banana cutting at Iron Piece and Trouble Ground, two of the banana walks on his Brimmer Hall estate. It was 'banana day' – which meant there was a banana boat in the wharf and everyone in the district was cutting, working early in the morning before it got too hot.

During the morning I saw how the trees were grown from suckers, how the fruit forms, how it is cut and carried, and I learnt that when a stem of bananas (a good one has nine large hands or bunches and they are all green) is gathered, the whole tree is cut down and only the stump remains at about five feet. This protects the new sucker which will grow up beside it from the wind, and in only a few weeks bear fruit.

In those days you would frequently see a Jamaican girl or youth carrying two stems, each weighing about fifty pounds, on their head, and running with them from the tree to the spot where the Busher stands. Here they were checked and graded for loading on the lorry. I expect that today the cutting and transporting is all done by machinery.

Four and half thousand stems of bananas were cut on the Brimmer Hall estate and loaded on the banana boat the one day I was there. I was out in those banana walks until 9 a.m., when, very hot, I was taken to the house to have a lovely tepid bath and change before I joined Douglas and Golly Vaughan for breakfast. After breakfast Douglas took me down to the wharf to watch the loading of the banana boats.

What has been for me a long and very happy friendship started here when, the morning after my arrival, Sir Harold and Lady Mitchell, who had been alerted by the Joels, arrived to see me at Shaw Park. They were so kind and thoughtful, inviting me to their beautiful home Prospect, near Ocho Rios, and to meet their little daughter Mary Jean. Mary Mitchell drove me round to several homes, and to see places of interest on the island. Over the years I have visited the Mitchells quite often, staying in the main house at Prospect, and once staying in their nearby guesthouse when there was a slight earthquake the first dawn of my visit. I have also stayed several times at their super guesthouse, Frankfurt, which is right on a sandy beach. This is where Sir Winston Churchill used to go and paint every day when he was staying at Prospect one year recuperating from an illness. Harold Mitchell died in 1983, and dear Mary Jean, who had grown into an outstanding young woman, died tragically in 1990 from cancer while in her late thirties. She left behind a devoted and splendid husband, Peter Green, and two fine young sons. Happily I still saw Mary Mitchell when she came on her flying visits to London, until her death in America in April 1992. I went to her funeral at Kincardine in Scotland, where she was buried beside Harold and Mary Jean.

After my brief stay at Ocho Rios I drove down to Montego Bay to stay with Mr and Mrs Antony Norman in their new house at Roundhill. This is another luxury development, which had only opened that January, comprising a small luxury hotel right on the beach with about twenty well-designed small houses. The development was originally started by nine British, six American and three Canadian families, who wanted their own cottages with security.

Roundhill is a few miles south of the town of Montego Bay, which in those days was very unspoilt. Roundhill is still a much sought-after luxury place to stay, and although a great number more houses have been built since that first year, it retains a very gracious atmosphere, the only drawback being that the beach is very small. While I was here we usually went out to lunch and dinner and one night my host and hostess gave a buffet dinner party at their house for twenty-four guests. All the catering for the houses is done by the hotel. In the evening we sometimes went to beach parties.

One of these was given by Mrs George Girard'et on the banks of Great River. After dining under a full moon, guests embarked in small native canoes and were paddled up the river where flaming torches were placed at intervals among the trees, their light reflecting in the river. On arrival we were met by a native band, given planters' punch to drink out of coconuts, and hot sausages on sticks. While an enormous fire blazed by the water's edge, we were entertained by calypsos and native dancers. Later, at around 1 a.m., we paddled home after a most novel and enjoyable evening.

From Montego Bay I flew home in one of BOAC's stratocruisers and we landed at London airport ahead of schedule after a wonderful flight and a good night's sleep.

I was invited up to the flight deck as I usually was when flying BOAC, and I asked the Captain, whose name, I think, was Jones, and who I was told had recently flown two members of the Royal Family, if he felt more nervous when he was flying such VIPs. His immediate answer was 'On every flight I remember Mrs Jones at home', a response I found very endearing and one I have never forgotten.

Soon after my return from the West Indies there was the National Hunt Festival at Cheltenham. That year Mr Dick Wilkins, a very kind, generous and jovial bachelor and a successful jobber in the City, whom I have already mentioned, invited me to join a party of friends at the very comfortable Bear Hotel at Woodstock.

Dick Wilkins had somehow achieved the impossible that year by renting a box for the week's racing. These were like gold dust and there was a waiting list. It was in a wonderful position, near the Royal Box, and it still had the original owner's name on it during the many years to follow that Dick, and all of us in the party, and numerous others who came up for drinks, enjoyed it.

Sir Nigel and Lady Mordaunt also had a very large box and a luncheon room at the far and rather unfashionable end of the stand where we lunched each day. When Nigel and Anne died, both, sadly, far too young, their family kept the box on, and very sweetly have for many years invited me to luncheon there during race week.

Another first for me that year was a wedding in two countries on one day! This was the marriage of Miss Anne Boylan, daughter of Brigadier and Mrs Edward Boylan, to Captain Michael Dewey of the 3rd Hussars. This was jokingly called 'Operation Orange Blossom' because of the complicated manoeuvres it involved. First of all, the 12 noon wedding ceremony was conducted by Father Sir Lewis Clifford, assisted by Father Lanfranchi, at the little St Anne Church, in Abbey Orchard Street, Westminster; as the bridegroom was not a Catholic, the service was fairly short. After the ceremony, the bridal party and about one hundred guests, including the Guard of Honour from the bridegroom's regiment, went down to Northolt airport, where they had a buffet luncheon and cut a wedding cake.

Then the bride and bridegroom, their pages, bridesmaids, the best man Captain D. Watts, and forty guests including myself, took off in one of Aer Lingus's new Viscounts for Collinstown airport, Dublin. We then went on by road to the bride's lovely home Hilltown, near Drogheda, where nearly 700 friends from all over Ireland had come to wish the young couple happiness. Brigadier and Mrs Boylan and the bridegroom's mother, Lady Bell, stood with the bride and bridegroom in the baronial hall receiving the guests, who afterwards went on to look at the wedding presents, which filled two large rooms.

After the reception the bride and bridegroom flew back to London, and then in the morning on to Majorca for their honeymoon. I too flew back to London that evening, but not on the same flight!

Another Anglo-Irish wedding I found a little different was the marriage in Dublin of Mr William Hanson to Miss Patricia Edge. The bridesmaids were all grown up, and wore very pretty dresses with very full crinoline skirts that would have got badly crushed in a car. So Patricia Edge decided to have one of their horseboxes thoroughly spring cleaned, and her bridesmaids were taken to church and on to the reception in a horse box, I believe standing up! It was a very picturesque sight as these pretty girls stepped out at their destination.

Everyone rejoiced in May at the safe return of our beloved Queen and the Duke of Edinburgh from their six months' tour of the Commonwealth. Her Majesty was home just in time to attend the wedding of Viscount Althorp and the Hon. Frances Roche, later the 8th Earl Spencer and the Hon. Mrs Shand Kydd, parents of the Princess of Wales, which took place at Westminster Abbey. Other members of the Royal Family at that wedding included the Duke of Edinburgh, Queen Elizabeth the Queen Mother, Princess Margaret, the Princess Royal, the Duke of Gloucester, the Duchess of Kent, with the Duke of Kent and Princess Alexandra, and the Earl of Athlone, who, like The Queen, all went on to the reception at St James's Palace. Johnnie Althorp was then one of The Queen's equerries, and was acting Master of the Royal Household.

I once again managed to fit in both the Dublin Horse Show and Cowes; I also went down to Monte Carlo to stay at the Hôtel de Paris, where among others I met Miss Gloria Swanson, and fitted in a very glamorous gala at the Summer Sporting Club, where I met Mr Aristotle Onassis and his beautiful wife Tina, who kindly invited me for a drink on board their yacht *Christina* the following evening.

On the day after her return from America and Canada, Queen Elizabeth the Queen Mother attended the marriage of the Hon. Anthony Berry, youngest son of Viscount Kemsley, to the Hon. Mary Roche, younger daughter of Lord and Lady Fermoy, which took place at St Margaret's, Westminster, with a reception for over 580 guests at Hutchinson House. This was the second wedding in a year for Lord and Lady Fermoy; their elder daughter had married Viscount Althorp earlier in the year. The bride looked lovely in a dress of slipper satin with a very full skirt falling into a train, designed for her by Mr John Cavanagh, and a diamond tiara holding a tulle veil in place. She was attended by three pages and nine child bridesmaids. Several of the guests did as I had done, which was to mistake the Hon. Francis Roche for his brother, as he and Maurice Fermoy were identical twins. Francis lived in Paris, and one year I saw him in a restaurant in Paris and greeted him as an old friend, thinking he was Maurice Fermoy – much to his surprise, and to my surprise too, when I discovered my mistake!

By far the best ball of that autumn season was the Balaclava Ball, given at the Hyde Park Hotel. The evening was to commemorate the Charge of the Light Brigade at Balaclava during the Crimean War one hundred years before. The ball was given by officers of the five regiments who took part in the charge, the 4th, 8th, 11th and 13th/18th Hussars and the 17th/21st Lancers.

It was a wonderful scene. In the flower-decked ballroom the regimental crests were all recreated in flowers on each pillar. In the alcove at the top of the stairs magnificent pieces of regimental silver were cleverly lit, and in a small showcase was the dog collar worn by Jimmy, the little terrier who went through the whole campaign and even took part in the historic charge.

Most of the men present wore the full dress uniform of their regiments, which added to the colourful scene. Some of these uniforms had belonged to those who had taken part in the famous charge. Perhaps the most striking of these was the heavily braided sling jacket originally in the possession of the 7th Earl of Cardigan, who commanded the Light Brigade during the charge, which Major-General John Combe, Colonel of the 11th Hussars, wore at the ball. This ball was attended by The Queen, who arrived looking absolutely fabulous in a full-skirted grey lace dress, with a diamond tiara, necklace and earrings and the blue riband of the Order of the Garter. With Her Majesty was the Duke of Edinburgh wearing the full dress of the 8th Hussars, of which he is Colonel-in-Chief, with the Garter riband across his tunic. Queen Elizabeth the Queen Mother also attended the ball wearing a pink crinoline, with a diamond tiara and earrings and ruby and diamond necklace, and the riband of the Garter.

The royal party danced happily for well over an hour in the flower-bedecked ballroom, then went through with some of their hosts to the candlelit dining room. I thoroughly enjoyed this Balaclava Ball, where I was surrounded by friends and danced a lot. I stayed until nearly the end!

Another day in November I went to the Opening of Parliament by the Queen. The moment when our beloved Queen, wearing her Crown of State, sits on the throne and reads her speech to her two Houses of Parliament is always very moving. This year it was as poignant as ever, and the precision and pageantry was perfection.

Many of those present from both Houses of Parliament went on to the historic presentation ceremony to the Prime Minister in Westminster Hall, to commemorate his eightieth birthday. This was one of the most embarrassing presentation events I have ever attended. The gift for the Prime Minister was a portrait of himself by Mr Graham Sutherland, and when it appeared there was an immediate gasp from everyone present. There are many stories going around as to what happened to that portrait, but I know it never hung in the Churchills' sitting room!

Just before Christmas I went to a delightful party given by Lady Illingworth and Mrs Percy Illingworth to celebrate their birthdays on the same day. This took place in Lady Illingworth's lovely Grosvenor Square home, then the last private house left in the Square. Now that has gone too. The two first-floor reception rooms were crowded with friends, many from the diplomatic corps, and others from all over the country. Margaret Illingworth was a charming hostess and a dear kind woman, and over the years I lunched with her quietly and went to many parties there until she eventually left the house. Then, like many others, I rather lost touch with her, and thought she was living most of the time in Switzerland. So I was sad and very shocked when, through a much-publicized court case in 1991, I learnt she had spent the last few years of her life without being able to see any friends and in such terrible unnecessary penury. Such a sad and terrible end for a good dear kind woman.

At a London wedding I went to early in 1955 I remember the bridegroom's mother passing the message back to the congregation to 'All sing up as there is no choir'. We never knew if it had been forgotten or if it was economy on the part of the bride's father, who was renowned for being very careful with his wealth. At the same wedding, one of the relatives pointed out to me that the bride's father was receiving the guests with a little calculator clicking each guest past, so that the caterers didn't charge too much! Another amusing incident occurred at a wedding between a French nobleman who had been married before and had rather a past, and an English bride much younger than himself. When it came to the parson asking the marriage vows, ending with 'forsaking all others, keep thee only unto her?', the bridegroom replied 'Perhaps.' The service went on without a pause. I think I must hold the record in wedding attendances. Twice I attended three weddings in one day, all in London, starting with a morning wedding followed by a luncheon.

Early in the year I caught a 10.30 a.m. Swissair flight to Zurich and caught the train on to St Anton, which I was visiting for the first time. St Anton was definitely for dedicated skiers, being one of the best skiing resorts in Europe. The skiers were up in the mountains from dawn to dusk, thus there was little hectic night life, although there was an enjoyable après-ski life. The snow was perfect while I was there.

I was very impressed with the wonderful ski runs and facilities for skiing, and the courtesy and the efficiency of everyone in St Anton, then a small village with one village street, a few hotels, a handful of shops and numerous chalets dotted around. An example of Swiss efficiency was demonstrated at this time by Ebster, the famous St Anton tailor. A client who was leaving on the Monday morning decided on Saturday that she wanted another pair of ski trousers, so, undaunted, walked into Ebster's shop to see if there was any chance of having them made in time. The answer was 'Yes, certainly', he would fit them at her hotel early next morning and deliver them at 8 a.m. on Monday – which he did.

Sadly I could only spend three nights here, where even after dinner the conversation would revert to skiing and whether you were using Gomme, Head, or Kneissl skis. I caught the Arlberg Express to Kitzbuhel, where they were suffering a shortage of snow. Two hours before I left it started to snow. Excited faces were everywhere!

The evening after I returned from Austria I went to a very special party. The 20th Lord and Lady Willoughby de Broke had very kindly invited me to a small dance they gave in honour of Queen Elizabeth the Queen Mother. This took place at their charming London home in Gilbert Street. This was not a very spacious house, but although there were more than a hundred guests the rooms never became overcrowded. I had never seen Queen Elizabeth looking more radiant or enjoying herself more. She was wearing a soft pink crinoline, and dancing all the evening. Our hostess, who looked beautiful in a white satin sheath dress embroidered with crystals, had arranged the evening to perfection.

In later years John and Rachel Willoughby de Broke, who were to me always very loyal friends, angelically invited me twice to dine at their Phillimore Gardens home when Queen Elizabeth the Queen Mother was their guest of honour, at a dinner party of ten or twelve. I greatly appreciated this honour, and both evenings were for me truly gracious and wonderful ones.

I enjoyed this lovely party in the middle of three busy days in the office getting my Austrian winter sports story off to press. Then on the Sunday I was off again to Rome, via the South of France, for a wedding. It was snowing hard as I arrived at London airport, where there was absolute chaos. There were no porters, and the police would not let the chauffeur leave the car to carry my bags inside. Fortunately for me Sir Noel Charles, our former Ambassador in Brazil, Italy and

Turkey, and the 9th Earl of Lanesborough, helped me by finding an empty barrow and moving my cases out of the snow and upto the check-in desk. I flew in a BEA Elizabethan to Nice.

Next day I flew on to Rome, for the marriage of Viscount Hambleden to Donna Maria Carmela Attolico di Adelfia, which took place in the beautiful church of Santa Maria in Dominica, Rome. The pews were all covered with crimson brocade braided with gold, and hundreds of white carnations studded in greenery decorated the magnificent gilded altar. Unfortunately, much of this beauty was spoilt during the short ceremony by the intrusion of European cameramen and women who clambered over this specially sacred part of the church, letting off their flash bulbs only two or three feet from the young couple. The church was so crowded, guests were standing everywhere. In Italy, I gathered, it is not customary to have a team of ushers as we do. The only people carrying out these duties were the bride's brothers, Count Bartolemo and Count Giacomo Attolico di Adelfia. It seemed such a pity that those three very experienced ushers the Earl of Wilton, the Hon. Peter Ward and Mr Billy Wallace, who arrived at the church together, were not asked to help place the guests, who numbered over a thousand. As the bride's father, Count Bernardo Attolico, formerly Italian Ambassador in Moscow and Berlin, was dead, she was given in marriage by her grandfather, Count Pietro-marchi.

The bride looked very serene and lovely in a beautifully made wedding dress of old family lace, her lace veil held in place by a coronet of orange blossom. There were no bridal attendants. The bridegroom's witnesses were his uncle, the Hon. James Smith, and Lord Herbert. I somehow was seated very close behind the bridegroom's tall and gracious mother, now the Dowager Viscountess Hambleden, who has been a lady-in-waiting to Queen Elizabeth the Queen Mother since 1937. I remember her irritation at the photographers and the swift, elegant way she removed a press photographer who came to stand in front of her as the bride and bridegroom were coming down the aisle.

After the ceremony, which did not start until 5.30 p.m., the bride's mother, Contessa Eleonora Attolico di Adelfia, gave a reception at their charming home in Via Porta Latina – happily it was warm enough to stroll on the floodlit terrace and in the gardens, as there were around 2,000 guests at the reception.

Harry Hambleden had always been a rather wild young man, but he was also a very endearing personality with a great number of friends, most of whom came to the wedding, as did all his family.

Maria Carmela quickly settled into English life; she was a wonderful, understanding wife and they had five splendid sons. Sadly, the marriage was dissolved in 1988 and Harry Hambleden has remarried. Maria Carmela Hambleden is, happily for all of us, still living here, where she has made a multitude of friends.

That year there were more debutante parties than ever. On the list I published on 2nd March there were already 78 dances arranged between 1st May and 30th July, and a few more earlier and in the autumn. It looked like being a very busy season as masses of parties besides debutante ones had also been planned.

One of the most outstanding private parties that spring was when Sir Winston and Lady Churchill entertained The Queen and the Duke of Edinburgh to dinner at 10 Downing Street on his retirement as Prime Minister. The Queen wore the blue riband of the Order of the Garter across her evening dress and a diamond tiara. Sir Winston wore his decorations and Lady Churchill also wore a tiara and an order across her evening dress, as the charming hostess at 10 Downing Street for the last time. I wrote at the time 'Perhaps the most stirring moment of this memorable and rather poignant evening was after the Royal toast when The Queen proposed the health of her Prime Minister, the first time, I believe, that this has ever been done by a reigning monarch.'

That month I went down one morning to Ascot racecourse. On the flight to Nice earlier that year, Lord Tryon told me that he had been at a meeting at St James's Palace the previous day discussing the new Queen's Lawn at Ascot racecourse, which had had such distorted and varied reporting in the press. Someone at that same meeting had suggested that I be asked to go down to Ascot to see the new layout, and write about it. They thought I would give a true picture to the public. I felt very honoured at being considered in such a light and told Charlie Tryon that of course I would. On my return from Rome I found a letter of invitation, and now I was met by the very popular Clerk of the Course Major John 'Crocker' Bulteel, who took me round and showed me the many alterations and improvements that had been made. The greatest of these alterations was probably the new course over a straight mile, which is now easily visible from all enclosures; it also gave far more room in all the existing enclosures. I had a most informative morning which enabled me to write fully about the changes, and happily all those concerned were kind enough to say I had got it right!

This summer saw the inauguration of polo at Smiths Lawn, Windsor Great Park. The Queen, accompanied by Prince Charles and Princess Anne, Queen Elizabeth the Queen Mother, Princess Margaret and The Queen's house party, came to watch the polo; and the Duke of Edinburgh was playing in his Mariners Team. I watched the Mariners Team play their match in the quarter finals of the Smiths Lawn Cup, where sadly they were beaten 3–1 by Polo Cottage, the Duke of Edinburgh scoring the only goal for his side.

The polo here should have opened during Royal Ascot, but this year Royal Ascot was postponed until the middle of July owing to the course being waterlogged.

Shortly after the Lawn Tennis Championships at Wimbledon and Henley Regatta I left for Oslo for The Queen and the Duke of Edinburgh's state visit to Norway. It was Her Majesty's first state visit outside the Commonwealth since her succession and the first of a British sovereign to Europe for many years. The Queen had got to know King Haakon quite well during the four war years he was in England; he was always 'Uncle Charles' to her. On the night of The Queen's arrival with the Duke of Edinburgh in the royal yacht *Britannia*, King Haakon gave a banquet in their honour at the Palace. The following evening there was a glittering gala performance of *Peer Gynt* at the National Theatre, where orders and decorations were worn, and a great number of tiaras and lovely jewels.

On the final evening, The Queen and the Duke of Edinburgh entertained King Haakon with other members of the Royal Family to dinner on board *Britannia* before sailing for home. Those busy three days were filled with many other engagements for the royal visitors, including a garden party for 1,600 guests given by the British Ambassador Mr Peter Scarlett (whom The Queen knighted during her visit) and Mrs Scarlett at the British Embassy. Many of the guests were members of the British colony in Norway. The day after the royal departure I lunched at the embassy with the Scarletts, who had their three pretty daughters Miss Jane, Miss Petronella and Miss Belinda Scarlett staying with them. They were a dear couple, and helped me so much over this royal visit.

That year I flew to Italy to make my first visit to Venice. I travelled from Nice to Milan in an Italian Airlines Convair, and I went on from there to Venice by train, as the flight from Nice did not connect with the little plane that went on to the airport at the Lido. I travelled by gondola from the station to the Danieli Hotel, my gondolier singing lilting tunes all the way.

I did a lot of sightseeing, which is not really my forte! I took the Danieli boat out to the Lido and rented a luxury cabana for sunbathing, and I took a motor boat to see the Palazzo Rezzonico, which Mr Oliver Messel, who was spending several weeks in Venice, said I must visit. Oliver was working on the set for *Arms and the Man*, which Sir Alexander Korda was shortly to make with Alec Guinness in the leading role. I lunched with friends at Harry's Bar, and dined at several of the then fashionable restaurants.

On the night of my arrival I got an invitation from Don Carlo Bestegui to come and see his Palazzo Labio on a certain evening when he had asked a few friends in. As I had heard so much about his palazzo and the famous parties he gave, I rang in the morning and told him I would love to come. He sounded pleased. On the night, I set off alone in a gondola, never thinking it would be anything bigger than a handful of friends. When I arrived there were torches burning outside this really superb palazzo, and flunkeys wearing very smart colourful livery with knee breeches and powdered wigs were helping an endless number of guests, all dressed in super couture clothes and lovely jewels, to alight from their gondolas. When I got inside there was a vast entrance hall with, I remember, a sedan chair at the end looking the size of a postage stamp. The wide staircase up to the first-floor reception rooms was lined with more flunkeys.

One left one's evening coat halfway up and I saw every well-known Paris couture label going in, while mine had some very humble London boutique label. By now, fear was in my heart. I was longing to run home. I felt extremely apprehensive and longed to turn round and leave, but I knew that was impossible, as my gondolier was not returning for a couple of hours, so I carried on up the stairs with tears flooding into my eyes. I was greeted by my host, Carlo Bestegui, who had great charm and the most super manners; he immediately put me at my ease, and handed me over to the care of a charming Italian gentleman who never left me. There must have been at least 200 guests.

I asked to make a tour of the high-ceilinged, very large reception rooms which were built round a candlelit courtyard. The rooms contained endless exquisite treasures. I always remember the painted ceilings, the fresco paintings by Tiepolo, and the exquisite Venetian glass chandeliers throughout the palazzo, also the tapestries, including some priceless Gobelins, the Canalettos, Reynolds, and other fine pictures, the lovely furniture, and the magnificent carpets and rugs which at times it seemed a sacrilege to walk on. Happily, I met a few friends, including Mr Stavros Niarchos and his very sweet and beautiful wife Eugénie, who had come off their fine three-masted schooner *The Creole*, which was anchored just in front of S. Marco.

Towards the end of the evening, my host came to find me and took me up to another floor where he said he wanted to show me something that would amuse me. There in the centre of another lovely peaceful room, obviously used as a library, was a circular table on which were arranged in a fan-like pattern about fifty *Tatlers*, right up to the latest issue! I left this party having enjoyed my evening meeting my host, and seeing his beautiful home and treasures, and feeling much happier than when I arrived!

From Venice, I did a similar round to previous years, up to Scotland for house parties and balls, and then to Doncaster for St Leger week, where I stayed with Sir Malcolm and Lady McAlpine, who had rented a house for the week, which meant we could go to the bloodstock sales as well as racing.

In the early winter I went on a specially chartered train to the launching of the world's biggest oil tanker, the SS *Spyros Niarchos*, which Vickers Armstrong had just built at Barrow-in-Furness for Mr Stavros Niarchos, who then had the biggest independent oil tanker fleet in the world. Mr Turrel, the very efficient station master at Euston, was there to see us off. Some of the passengers played bridge or canasta on the journey, others sat quietly reading, or walked about talking to friends, as the coaches were open vestibule ones.

We all stayed the night at the Old England Hotel at Barrow-on-Windermere and then motored over to Barrow-in-Furness for the launching by Lady Weeks at noon. There was a short religious service, then Cynthia Weeks made a charming speech asking for 'God's blessing on the *Spyros Niarchos* and all who sail in her'. The tanker had been named after Stavros's father. After saying those words, Cynthia Weeks then broke a bottle of Pol Roger over the bows and the giant tanker slowly glided down the stocks into the sea, where tugs were ready to take her to her moorings. I found it a very moving performance, and I am afraid I shed a tear. She was a wonderful ship and was built to carry 14 million imperial gallons of crude oil. One felt very proud of what our shipbuilders had done.

Lt-General Sir Ronald Weeks presided at the luncheon, which took place after the launching. We were joined by the Hon. Sir Frank Hopwood, then Chairman of Shell, and Lady Hopwood, who had flown up from London for the day. Ronnie Weeks proposed the royal toast, and speeches were then made by 'Edgie' Knollys, Cynthia Weeks, Charles Dunphie, and Stavros Niarchos, who made an excellent speech in which he said he had already had nine ships built in England by this firm, and they were the best in his fleet; but he said rather sadly that they took longer to build them than any other country! After luncheon, we returned to London in our chartered train. It was my first launching of a big ship, and I was most impressed.

The last big wedding of that year was in December, when the Hon. Patrick Lindsay married the 9th Earl and Countess of Hardwicke's very beautiful daughter Lady Amabel Yorke at St James's, Spanish Place. The bride wore the most exquisite Pierre Balmain wedding dress made entirely of embroidered white lace with a wide band of white velvet all round underneath the skirt. With this she wore a short tulle veil and a small coronet of white gardenias, and short white kid gloves. I can't think why more brides don't wear short white gloves, as they give such a chic finish to any wedding dress.

The Duque de Primo de Rivera kindly lent the Spanish Embassy for the reception. Here the Earl and Countess of Hardwicke, the latter as always looking chic and immaculate, received the guests with the bridegroom's parents, the 28th Earl and Countess of Crawford and Balcarres. The fine suite of reception rooms were soon full of relations and friends, all in a happy mood with Christmas very near. Having known the bride's parents and her paternal grandmother for some years, I particularly enjoyed this happy wedding, as I met so many friends here. The bride and bridegroom flew out to India forty-eight hours later, where they were the guests of the Maharajah and Maharani of Jaipur.

After my son left the army and started taking his chartered accountancy exams, and was being looked after at my flat by Mrs Perry, who cooked, and my faithful Mottie, he used to have young friends to dine with him most weeks. This year we decided he should also have a drinks party for around forty of his friends and this took place the next week. As it was a success, it was the first of several such parties until he went to live in Canada.

Since I had started working on the *Tatler*, with my son also to think about I had not had much time for any private life of my own. I tried, when possible, to get away to stay with kind friends in the country at weekends, but as I so often had to work weekends with weddings, dances, racing and polo, this was not very frequent. I have happily always had friends to stay with for my work all over the world; also two or three very dear friends where I can invite myself at the last moment! They have been a godsend to me, and have helped me to keep going.

NINE

My days at the *Tatler* end
(1956–58)

In 1956 I flew to Monte Carlo for the pre-wedding celebrations and the wedding of Prince Rainier of Monaco and the beautiful film actress Miss Grace Kelly. This was one of those occasions when I had left home without any official invitation. I had received letters and cables from the Palace at Monaco about attending the wedding, but no official invitation card. This, I was told, would be waiting for me at the reception desk at the Hôtel de Paris. I had been asked not to open the envelope until I got to my room as there would probably be a lot of the international press around the reception area. When I reached my room, I was delighted to find that my invitations included one to the pre-wedding gala at the old International Sporting Club that evening, in honour of Prince Rainier and Miss Grace Kelly. Before I unpacked I looked out of my window and saw the harbour was a wonderful sight with a great number of private yachts. The biggest was Mr Aristotle Onassis's *Christina*, which could carry a small amphibian plane on board. There were also naval ships from quite a few countries anchored further out.

It was a truly memorable gala in an exceptionally beautiful and festive setting. The vast ballroom had been transformed for the evening by Monsieur André Levasseur, who has done the decor for Monte Carlo galas for many years. The theme was the Palace of Versailles, cleverly carried out in a colour scheme of red and white. The string band of many violins, which played Mozart and other period music during dinner, wore powdered wigs and white eighteenth-century costumes and the dance band which played later wore the same costumes in red! On the low balcony at one end of the room opposite the stage, a long royal table had been arranged, with a background of cleverly lit red velvet draperies, and all along the front of the balcony was a solid bank of scented white lilies with red roses at intervals. The flowers at the dinner table were kept very low so that everyone could see the royal party easily.

I was seated at a table with charming French guests, friends of Prince Rainier's father, whom I had never met before. Everyone was at their table when Prince Rainier arrived escorting Miss Kelly, who looked dazzlingly beautiful in a white satin full-skirted dress, with a wide turquoise blue chiffon scarf fixed across the bodice and knotted at the back. With this she wore short white kid gloves, and carried an evening bag of petit point, which was fashionable in the fifties. Her hair was arranged in a single Alice band of tortoiseshell. Miss Kelly sat on Prince Rainier's left and on the right of his father Prince Pierre. Also at the royal table were Prince Rainier's mother Princesse Charlotte, his sister Princesse Antoinette, the bride's parents Mr and Mrs John B. Kelly, and her brother-in-law and sister Mr and Mrs George Davis and several others.

All guests present that evening had been personally invited by Prince Rainier and included members of his government and of the diplomatic corps and friends of both families. The superb dinner had been produced by Monsieur Broc, who for many years ran the Hôtel de Paris quite brilliantly. He always had the very best chefs.

There was only one embarrassing moment during this truly brilliant and happy evening. That came after the dance band had just started to play and everyone waited at their table for Prince Rainier and Miss Kelly to get up and lead the dancing. Suddenly a couple appeared on the dance floor. Everyone looked amazed. I remember someone in my party asking me '*Qui est cet homme?*' For a moment I was going to say I did not know, then I had to be honest and say 'It is Randolph Churchill, son of Sir Winston Churchill, dancing with Princess Bismarck.' He was always a law unto himself. Prince Rainier and Miss Kelly didn't go on the dance floor that evening, and left reasonably early with all their party. I personally slipped away soon after Prince Rainier and his party left, as I knew I had a busy couple of days ahead.

There were various other celebrations that week, including a gala at the Monte Carlo Opera House which I also went to. I did not go to the civil ceremony the day before the marriage, but I had kindly been given a wonderful seat for the wedding service itself in the cathedral. White lilac, lilies and lilies of the valley massed in profusion decorated the interior, and a guard of the Prince's company of *carabinieri* in red, white and blue uniforms, light blue helmets and red and white plumes lined each side of the aisle, and at one moment sounded a fanfare of trumpets. The music, with a choir of a hundred voices and soloists, was some of the most beautiful I have ever heard at any wedding.

I was interested to see that the bride and her retinue arrived first, as I was told is the custom if the bridegroom is a ruling prince. Grace Kelly, as you can imagine, made a fabulously beautiful bride as she walked up the aisle on the arm of her father, and looked serious and dignified throughout. Prince Rainier then arrived in a picturesque uniform of light blue trousers and a black jacket with touches of red and yellow and gold braid, on which he wore various orders and decorations. Prince Rainier walked up the aisle accompanied by his Lord Chamberlain, his aide-de-camp and two priests, Father Francis Tucker, his private chaplain, and Monsieur Gilles Barthe, Bishop of Monaco. It was a beautiful service. After the ceremony there was a buffet wedding luncheon, also produced under the eagle eye of dear Monsieur Broc, at small tables arranged in the picturesque courtyard of the royal palace. The bride and bridegroom came out and walked among their friends greeting everyone. Then they had their luncheon, and cut their cake, all quite swiftly – a good example to brides and bridegrooms, who often hang about far too long before cutting their wedding cake.

After they had changed, Prince Rainier and Princess Grace left with the sun shining brilliantly, to board his yacht *Des Juvanta II*, to spend their honeymoon cruising in the Mediterranean. I felt so lucky to have been present at this fairytale wedding which touched the hearts of millions who saw it later in photographs, news reels and cinemas throughout the world.

In June, I had quite a problem, as I wanted to fit in a dance being given at their home in Hampshire by the 5th Lord and Lady Chesham for their daughter the Hon. Joanna Cavendish, as well as The Queen's state visit to Stockholm, and the Equestrian Olympics, also in Stockholm. I decided the only way I could do this was to miss the first day of the royal visit, which was a Friday. I went to Charlie and Mary Chesham's dance near Petersfield, which I thoroughly enjoyed: I knew masses of friends there and it was beautifully arranged.

Soon after midnight I left the dance, and drove straight to London airport to catch the 2.30 a.m. flight to Stockholm. I checked in, still in my evening dress, having allowed plenty of time to change afterwards in the ladies' loo into day clothes which I had in a zip bag, into which my evening clothes then went so that by the time I boarded I looked normal. As far as I remember I arrived at Stockholm around 5 a.m. not having had much sleep on the flight, which, I was thankful, was not delayed, as I had to be at a state luncheon by 12.30. As I had left my booking too late to get into the Grand Hotel, which was at that time the city's best, I had booked my room through the BHS agent who was making all the Olympic bookings. When I arrived at my so-called hotel, I thought it looked a bit different from my usual sort. I signed in and was taken up to a small but light and clean bedroom and bathroom with two single beds along one wall, head to head, something I had never seen before. (I was told this was quite usual in Sweden.) When I unpacked, the drawer space and cupboard room was very limited. I then realized I had no dressing-table. and not one mirror, so I rang down to the reception – whose answer was that I would find a mirror on the wall inside the lift! I asked them if they expected me to do my face and hair in the lift, and the reply was, yes, if it suited me. By now I was fuming as I knew I had no time to go to buy a large mirror either then or later in the day, and I otherwise had only my travelling hand mirror. Somehow I managed over the weekend. I never knew if my skirt was even or what the back of my hair looked like! I discovered later that the so-called hotel was a youth hostel that had been put on the list for the Equestrian Olympic visitors, and probably the summer tourist season.

I enjoyed the civic luncheon in honour of The Queen and the Duke of Edinburgh. This was hosted by Mr Carl Albert Anderson, the Chairman of Stockholm's City Council, and took place in the truly magnificent and very lofty Golden Hall of the City Hall. Here three walls were all of gold mosaic, the fourth being a row of French windows opening on to a wide terrace. Candles in pedestal candelabra stood all round the room; and at the top of the royal luncheon table lay a long mirror on which were strewn the heads of yellow roses and blue violas, the Swedish national colours.

The Queen and the Duke of Edinburgh arrived in the picturesque royal barge with the King and Queen of Sweden. There were no speeches, but before we sat down to luncheon we drank a toast to The Queen, and to King Gustaf. During luncheon a soloist, Jussi Björling, and a choir sang at intervals. In the afternoon The Queen and the Duke of Edinburgh attended a reception at the Tennisstation given by the British Ambassador the Hon. Sir Robert Hankey and Lady Hankey. Returning to my very strange room to change for the state gala at the Royal Opera House, I discovered that there was no room service.

That evening red, white and blue flowers decorated the very ornate Opera House with its mirrors and gilded walls. Many of the women wore tiaras and lovely jewels, and the men wore their orders and decorations. The Queen, wearing a gold dress, a sapphire and diamond necklace and a diamond tiara, sat between King Gustaf and Prince Philip, who had his aunt the Queen of Sweden on his left. In the intervals I met the Swedish Ambassador in London, Mr Gunnar Häglöff, who had helped so much in planning this state visit, and had also helped me over my visit.

I was glad to get to bed that night, as I was dead tired having missed one night's sleep.

Next day, the opening ceremony of the XVI 1956 Olympic Equestrian Games at the stadium was a most impressive and colourful occassion. It was my first Olympic Games, so I was very excited. King Gustaf arrived to declare the games open in an open state carriage with our Queen sitting beside him. In front of the royal stand, King Gustaf greeted members of the international committees including Lord Burghley, who was to become the 6th Marquess of Exeter later that year, and the 2nd Lord Luke. Then we saw the Olympic teams, followed by the horses and riders of twenty-nine countries. When they were in place a rider entered the arena carrying the Olympic torch, kindled originally at Olympus in Greece. He galloped right round the arena with the flame burning brightly, then he lit the Olympic bowl which burns traditionally throughout all Olympic Games.

This opening ceremony was the last of The Queen and the Duke of Edinburgh's 'official' engagements. They then went from here to stay aboard the royal yacht *Britannia*, where they were joined by Princess Margaret and the Duke and Duchess of Gloucester. The Queen and her party were frequently present at the games and other festivities, but quite informally. The Swedish Royal Family and the number of foreign 'royals' staying with them, also visited the games quite informally, in fact I quite often found I was watching an event surrounded by royals. During the week, The Queen and the Duke of Edinburgh gave a cocktail party on board *Britannia* for British and Commonwealth competitors and officials.

The Sunday evening of the opening I went to have a drink and dinner with David and Diana Burghley, who were staying at the Grand. Here, so great had been the demand for accommodation that they too were pretty uncomfortable. They told me that they had such a very small bedroom that one had to dress before the other, as there was not room for both to dress at the same time. We had a good laugh over our accommodation. Happily they had a sitting room, which they shared with Lord and Lady Luke.

I had to leave Stockholm on Thursday before the end of the Olympic Games, at which our team did well and Lt-Colonel Frank Weldon won a gold medal. I wanted to get back in time for the marriage of Mr Jocelyn Stevens, whom I had known since he was a boy, to Miss Jane Sheffield that afternoon. I very nearly missed the wedding altogether, as I could only get on a morning flight, which meant changing at Copenhagen, where I had an hour to spare. I sat down to write and forgot to look at the time, and looking out of the window for a moment saw the steps being taken away from my flight to London! Happily airports were much smaller in those days, and I managed to get the steps pushed back and to board that flight, landing soon after 1 p.m.

Janey Sheffield, who had been one of the prettiest debutantes of the previous year, made a beautiful bride wearing a dress of white silk organza, with a coronet of pink and white flowers holding her short veil in place. She had twelve bridesmaids, including some of the prettiest girls then around London.

The marriage ceremony took place at Holy Trinity, Brompton, and the reception was held at Cleeve House, the Hyde Park Gate house of Jocelyn Stevens's uncle Mr Edward Hulton, later Sir Edward Hulton, where guests were able to go out into the garden, and where Jocelyn and Janey Stevens cut their wedding cake. The young couple left for a honeymoon in Jamaica, where the Earl and Countess of Mansfield lent them their lovely home.

It is very rare to have a dance at St James's Palace. In fact, with all the number of dances I have been to, I can only remember two. The first was the beautiful ball given by the Duke and Duchess of Norfolk for their eldest daughter Lady Anne Fitzalan-Howard, later Lady Herries. As Earl Marshal and Hereditary Marshal of England, Bernard Norfolk, having organized The Queen's Coronation, had gained the reputation of being an outstandingly brilliant organizer and the ball, which was magnificent, without any pomposity or ostentation, was arranged to perfection.

The stately rooms were filled with lovely flowers grown at Arundel Castle, and have never looked better. A dance floor had been laid in the Queen Anne state drawing room, and another larger dance floor was laid in a yellow and white marquee on the lawn, which you reached by a staircase beyond the Throne Room.

The host and hostess gave a dinner party in St James's Palace before the dance when their guests included The Queen, who looked wonderful in a crystal-embroidered pale blue satin evening dress, a diamond tiara and lovely jewels, the Duke of Edinburgh, Queen Elizabeth the Queen Mother, in a white tulle crinoline and a diamond tiara, Princess Margaret, the Duchess of Kent, her son and daughter the Duke of Kent and Princess Alexandra, also the Duke and Duchess of Gloucester and the Earl and Countess of Rosebery. There were a great number of guests present at the dance, including the Duke of Norfolk's three sisters, and many other relations, many members of the royal household, of both Houses of Parliament, members of the Jockey Club and other racing friends. It was another wonderful evening that I felt privileged to be invited to and will never forget.

There was a great oil shortage that autumn. The Queen gave instructions that except for official occasions she wished to use only a small car, and when possible to take as many of her entourage as possible with her. This set a good example for the whole country. Buckingham Palace, Windsor and Sandringham all had the same cuts in their oil as any other household, and The Queen asked that the use of petrol and oil throughout her estates be kept to the minimum. I remember lots of us thinking that the oil shortage would let us in for a chilly winter! But it was not too bad.

My last evening of 1956 was an exceptionally busy one as I had five engagements, including a cocktail party, as well as a visit to two friends in King Edward's Hospital for Officers – Sister Agnes's Home, which was looking very festive with Christmas decorations. From there I went on to the City where the Honorary Artillery Company were holding 'The Batterness Ball' at Armoury House, near Moorgate.

The HAC is the oldest regiment in the Territorial Army, and dates from 1537. This was one of those agonizing balls where I arrived and found I knew no one. But I was given a warm welcome and soon got over my fit of nerves. I spent a couple of hours here before I went on to the Savoy, where the Limelight Ball, in aid of the Royal Society for Blind Children, was being held for the fourth year running, and was in full swing. I found masses of friends here. Lady Pulbrook was Chairman, and Countess Mountbatten, who took a keen interest in the Society, was President of the ball.

After actually seeing the New Year in here, surrounded by friends, I went on to a party at Canning House given by Mrs Marie-Louise Arnold, at which most of the Latin-American Ambassadors at the

Court of St James's and their wives were present. I arrived to find the dancing had stopped for everyone to listen to the cabaret, which was given by the talented television star Carmen del Rio, who was singing and accompanying herself on the piano.

When I eventually got home, I hoped the New Year would not have many evenings with quite as many functions to fit in! As 1st January was not yet a Bank Holiday in England (only Scotland), and that year it fell on a Tuesday, I was up again fairly early and in my office for a busy day, as I was soon going on my first visit to South Africa and Rhodesia.

I set off in the middle of January 1957 from London airport at 9 a.m. in one of BOAC's Super Constellations for Johannesburg, where I was due to arrive at 5.45 p.m. the following day. I said at the time that this flight was the best rest cure I had had for very many months. I boarded the flight feeling desperately tired, and rather wondering how I was going to manage on my arrival, with a round of social activities and unfamiliar faces, in a temperature well up in the eighties. But I was determined to relax, so after breakfast, which was served directly after take-off, I had my leg-rest extended to make a sort of slumberette, closed my eyes and slept until I was asked to fasten my seatbelt to land in Rome, where we lunched in the airport restaurant. We then took off on the longest stage to Khartoum, landing around midnight. Again, I slept most of that flight, as I did the next one to Nairobi, where we arrived next morning. (I had decided to cut out dinner.) Our next stop was Salisbury, Rhodesia; and then on to Johannesburg, where we landed around 4 p.m. local time.

I stayed overnight with friends in Johannesburg in transit to Cape Town. After I had enjoyed a refreshing bath, my host and hostess took me on a round of visits. Our first stop was Mrs James Fraser at Court House, where she had Sir Ian and Lady Fraser, later Lord and Lady Fraser of Lonsdale, staying. He was a wonderful man, whom I had known since childhood. Ian Fraser was blinded in the First World War, and founded and was Chairman of St Dunstan's for the Blind. In spite of this handicap, he lived a normal life with the help of his wonderful wife 'Chips'. He was a qualified barrister, a Member of Parliament 1924–29, 1931–37 and 1940–58, and was on the board of several companies, including Illustrated Newspapers, who owned the *Tatler*. He was also one of the best ballroom dancers I have ever known, and somehow never bumped you into anyone or anything.

Ian Fraser in particular was a tremendous help to me when I started my diary, not only criticizing it in a constructive manner, but also making many helpful suggestions, including that when I wrote about an occasion, I should describe it thoroughly so that someone like him, although they could not see the scene, could imagine it. He always got his wife to read my diary out to him – in those days it appeared weekly.

Next morning I took off early for Cape Town, arriving at the Mount Nelson Hotel, where I was to stay, in time for luncheon. Captain and Mrs Gordon Kirkpatrick, very old friends from my Warwickshire days, lived here for six months every winter, and they very sweetly took me under their wing.

I was very fortunate in meeting, before I left England, the Deputy Leader of the United Party, Mr Harry Lawrence, and he very kindly gave me a ticket for the Opening of Parliament next day, which I found most interesting. The Governor General then was Mr Ernest Jansen, and he and his wife drove in an open carriage from Government House to the Houses of Parliament. Before he made his speech – in both Afrikaans and English – there was a salute of 21 guns outside, and after the opening, the band, also outside, played 'God Save The Queen'. The Lord Chief Justice, who ranks next to the Governor, was then Mr C. R. Swart, the Prime Minister Mr Johannes Strijtom, and the new Leader of the Opposition Sir de Villiers Graaff. There had recently been a change of government.

After the opening, we went into the Assembly and watched the work of the new session; then we lunched in the members' dining room. Hanging on the walls here were paintings of former Prime Ministers, including the late Mr Cecil Rhodes.

The next day I went racing at the South African Turf Club Course, Kenilworth, with Gordon and Muriel Kirkpatrick, and lunched very comfortably in the stewards' luncheon room. I was overwhelmed with kindness and hospitality during my brief stay. From here I flew up to Johannesburg, where again I was so grateful for the great welcome and tremendous kindness I received. While I never saw any ostentatious parties, the standard of living in South Africa was very high. All the men and some of the women seemed to be working, and working hard, whether it was mining, finance, industry or farming. The women were all very keen on their houses and gardens, spending a lot of time keeping both in immaculate order.

The highlight of this visit to Johannesburg was a visit to the Premier diamond mine near Pretoria. Mr Tony Wilson, one of the directors of De Beers and Anglo-American Corporation, kindly drove me the sixty-mile trip. Mr Sewell took us around the whole plant and down the mine, which was one of the best mechanized in the country. We went down the mine in one of the high-powered, very fast lifts. Once below there were long, high, whitewashed, well-ventilated tunnels with train lines through them to take the little twelve-truck train laden with blue soil along to the giant lifter (which I noted was made by Vickers). The soil was blasted out of the ground in huge lumps. Then it was brought to the surface, crushed and broken up, washed and run over the greasetable, where a diamond would usually stick and be identified for the first time. Then there was the sorting, to divide the industrials from the gems, and the weighing and so on. I realized after all this why it is that a diamond is of such great value. There must be more modern equipment today for mining diamonds, but I was very impressed with the method I saw and also the fact that the human hand never came in contact with the soil or stones. This limits pilfering and IDB (as illicit diamond buying is known), which has always been a problem in the diamond business, in spite of strict security.

Seeing that diamond mine was one of the most interesting days of my life. It was here that the famous Cullinan diamond was found in 1905 – the biggest diamond ever to be found, weighing 3,025¾ carats. The late Sir Ernest Oppenheimer was the brains behind this mine, and during this visit to Johannesburg I met his son Mr Harry Oppenheimer, who was educated in England, and was a Member of the South African Parliament from 1948 to 1958 as well as a very hard-working businessman. That year he became Chairman of the Anglo-American Corporation, and a member of other companies mostly connected with mining. Harry Oppenheimer, his wonderful wife Bridget, and their son and daughter Nicholas and Mary Oppenheimer later became, and still are, very dear friends of mine.

One morning, I attended a meet at 8.15 a.m. of the Rand Hunt, of which Mr Peter Wilson had then been the Master for twenty-five years. He had built up a brilliant pack by importing hounds from England. The Rand Hunt was a drag; the line of fifteen to twenty-five miles was changed each time they met. I followed in a car and was amazed at the great gallop at which the followers went over what looked to me a hazardous course, in which earth banks predominated. At the conclusion around 10.30 a.m. everyone gathered back at the meet for 'tea', though I noticed many more followers were drinking a long cool drink.

From Johannesburg I flew on to Salisbury, Rhodesia, to spend a few days with Mr and Mrs Alan Butler at their home, Nufaro, in Highlands, a fashionable part in the outskirts of Salisbury. Alan Butler and his son David, who was a page at my wedding, by now had quite a few interests in Rhodesia, including cattle farming on a 50,000-acre ranch in Matabeleland, tobacco farming in Bulawayo and other areas, and a light aeroplane charter company in Salisbury. They were all run very efficiently by David Butler, who lived out here with his attractive wife Joanna and two young sons.

During my visit I flew up to see the construction work on the hydro-electric project of the Kariba dam. I had been the day before to the Salisbury office of Sir Alexander Gibb & Partners, consulting engineers of London, who were working on the project in conjunction with two French firms, where a dynamic personality called Doctor Olivier explained the whole project to me with maps and drawings, so that on arrival I understood a little about what I was going to see – which was a fabulous feat of engineering. The rise and fall of this great river alone was a headache. The latter varied on average between 16,000 cubic feet per second in the dry season, to 200,000 cubic feet per second in the wet season. The peak recorded flow was 380,000 cubic feet per second over a short period! We saw the diversion tunnel constructed to take the flow when needed during construction.

I went down the circular concrete dam, and was one of the first to cross the very newly constructed bridge high up above the river. I enquired about the lifebelts dangling from this bridge and was told they were to throw to any workman unfortunate enough to fall in this fast-flowing river, in which normally there was little hope of survival.

I had a frantically social four days, including an afternoon's racing with Mr Keith Acott of Anglo-America at the Belvedere racecourse, luncheon at the RVWA Country Club, a drink with Sir Ulick and Lady Mary Alexander, whom I had known for many years, at their delightful house on the outskirts of Salisbury, and a super drinks party which Alan and Lois Butler and David and Joanna Butler gave for me at Nufaro. Sadly this was to be one of the last times I saw David Butler. He was killed in Germany when his Mercedes ran into the back of an unlit stationary lorry while he was on his way to the Munich Olympic Games in 1972, where he was to have represented Rhodesia in the yachting events at Keil.

On that four-day visit I was very impressed with the climate, and the progress being made everywhere, and the tremendous growth in the city of Salisbury at that time. I wonder if that progress has been maintained during all the changes that lovely country has been through.

From Rhodesia I flew home in one of BOAC's new Britannia turbo-prop airliners then called the 'Whispering Giants' of the air. They were the last word in luxury and gave one a standard of comfort and speed (400 miles an hour) never dreamt of before. As always with BOAC, and now with British Airways, the cabin crew provided the highest standard of courtesy and efficiency.

In 1957 there were more debutante dances than ever, and masses of cocktail parties, with the first of them starting in April. In addition, more debutantes than ever were applying to go to the two Royal Presentation Parties at Buckingham Palace. These were fixed for the first week in April. The idea of the autumn dance – which I had suggested in 1954, as the summer months were so congested – had caught on.

I had been horrified back in the autumn of 1956 to learn that mothers' lunches for 1957 debutantes had already started. This really was ridiculous. In my humble opinion the season was becoming rather a racket! More and more people were trying to buy their way in. Ten years after the war now, prosperity had returned to England. Ladies who had an entrée at court – in that they themselves had been presented as debutantes – were taking a fee for presenting girls who had no mother, or whose mother did not qualify, possibly by not having been presented herself, to present her daughter. I knew of two peeresses and a commoner who did this very successfully for several years, and there were probably masses of others. Some of these ladies would, in return for a fee, bring a girl out for a whole season. This meant arranging for her presentation at court, introducing her to lots of other debutantes and generally launching her socially. This might mean the girl's parents renting a London house or flat for the purpose if they had no London home. One father whose wife had died, who had charming sisters who could have perfectly well presented his daughter, nonetheless employed one of these ladies to bring his daughter out. He told me afterwards that the season had cost a fortune – especially when clothes for the girl and her sponsor were included. I remember one poor father spending a fortune on a spectacular dance for his daughter, who had very few invitations in return.

During that summer a friend of The Queen's whom I had known for many years came to have a drink quietly, and we discussed the debutante situation. I told her very frankly all I knew. I wondered later if this had partly led to the announcement that autumn, from the Lord Chamberlain's office: 'HM The Queen will hold no more presentation parties at Buckingham Palace after next year.'

What a furore that simple statement created! There was great consternation among future debutante mothers and 'presenters'. Many papers carried it as front-page news, and even radio and television took it up. I was telephoned constantly for my reaction and comment, which I always refused to give.

The next year's two Presentation Parties were put forward to March, and after that year The Queen held additional garden parties instead; in this way she was able to meet many more of her subjects from all walks of life.

In the first week in April, when The Queen made her first state visit to France since her succession, I flew over to Paris a day ahead of the royal party so that I had plenty of time to pick up my various passes, invitations and opera ticket and so on. At that point I was suddenly asked if in addition I would like a place for the royal arrival beside the wide marble steps of the Elysée Palace. This overlooked the gardens where the royal party would alight after their drive from Orly airport, so I accepted, as I had never been in the Elysée Palace gardens.

It was a glorious spring morning without a cloud in the sky. The Elysée Palace garden looked lovely, with the blossom out, chestnut trees in flower and the lawns very green with flowers banked up the wide marble steps. I was amused, while I was waiting, to see how frequently French men shake hands. This was true even of the police. Each time a French policeman left for, I presumed, the loo, he went over to tell his colleague and always shook hands before leaving, and on his return!

The Queen and Prince Philip arrived in open cars accompanied by the President of France and Madame Coty. The British Ambassador at that time was Sir Gladwyn Jebb, later Lord Gladwyn, and he and Lady Jebb entertained beautifully at the fine British Embassy.

The programme for this state visit was a very full one, taking the usual form of state banquet, visit to the opera and so on. There was also a luncheon at the Palace of Versailles followed by a performance of ballet in the recently restored small and very pretty Royal Opera House at Versailles.

Another rather unique engagement was when The Queen, wearing a silver and white evening dress with exquisite jewellery, accompanied by the Duke of Edinburgh, took an evening sail down the River Seine in a well-lit launch with the French President and Madame Coty. Thousands of cheering crowds lined the banks of the river, and all the major buildings were floodlit. This trip, which I did not go on, ended with a magnificent fireworks display. After The Queen had landed, she and the Duke of Edinburgh went straight to the British Embassy in time to welcome the President and Madame Coty, who were Her Majesty's guests at a reception for around 1,000 in the fine first-floor reception rooms, and later at a small supper party in the embassy. The arrangements at the embassy, all taken care of by the British Ambassador and Lady Jebb, were quite perfect.

I was glad I had not tried to fit in the river trip as well. I, like other Englishwomen present during this state visit, was so proud of our beloved Queen's appearance. Her Majesty had obviously taken a great deal of care in choosing her clothes and on each occasion they were perfection. They were the work of the royal couturiers Mr Norman Hartnell and of Mr Hardy Amies. Both, some years later, were knighted. At the Royal Gala at the Opera, our Queen outshone everyone.

Sadly I had to leave Paris early the morning after the British Embassy reception, so I missed the very glamorous reception at the Louvre on the final evening of this very successful royal visit.

I did not go over to Copenhagen for The Queen's state visit to Denmark the following month, as it came in the middle of the season when I had so many other commitments.

Possibly the most elegant debutante dance that season was given by Mrs Neil McLean for her twin daughters Miss Marina and Miss Tessa Kennedy. This took place at the Dorchester, where the ballroom and gold room had been cleverly transformed into a Yugoslavian classical garden. Superbly lit, this created the most becoming setting for all the lovely women and young girls present. The decor was the work of two clever young interior decorators, who at that time had a shop in Lowndes Street. They were Mr Tom Parr, who, later on, was to be head of Colefax & Fowler, and Mr David Hicks, who went on to build up his own international business. Lady Rose McLaren had done the fabulous arrangements of exquisite flowers, which included twelve-foot-high pyramids of pink flowers, and sweet-scented white gardenias which studded the blue gauze on the walls of the nightclub. The twins, who are not identical, though both are blonde, did not dress alike – Marina was in palest pink and Tessa in white. Tessa Kennedy is now one of the top and most successful interior decorators and has a lovely family of four sons and a very pretty daughter.

A rather unusual dinner party I went to that autumn was when the Iraqi Ambassador and Princess Zeid al-Hussein, whom I had got to know quite well, invited me to dine to celebrate the engagement of King Faisal of Iraq and Princess Fazila at the fine Iraqi Embassy in Kensington Palace Gardens. There were many Iraqi guests present, including King Faisal's Lord Chamberlain Mr Tashin Kadry, who was in London on a short visit. Our charming ambassador in Baghdad, Sir Michael Wright, and Lady Wright were also at this dinner, where we had a number of rather hot Middle Eastern and Far Eastern dishes.

I saw the New Year of 1958 in at Monte Carlo. I flew down in one of BEA's Viscount 802s for one night for the '*Réveillon du Nouvel An*' at the International Sporting Club, staying, as always, at the Hôtel de Paris. The demand for tickets had been so great that they had decided to arrange tables for another 500 guests in the restaurant of the Hôtel de Paris. In spite of the numbers, Monsieur Broc's wonderful staff produced a well-chosen delicious dinner which was served quickly and piping hot, unlike dinner at most galas. The beautiful decor and a fabulous cabaret had been arranged as usual by Monsieur André Levasseur. I sat next to Mr René Mayer, a former prime minister of France, who was interesting.

In the afternoon I spent an hour watching the rehearsal of a new ballet danced by the French Theatre Ballet Company. I also had a look at the recently cleaned and repainted Salle Privée of the casino, which had previously looked so dreary. Now, with new crystal chandeliers and a lot of gold leaf and cream paint, it provided a most glamorous setting. The casino officials were not so sure this brighter setting was such a good idea, as a few nights before my arrival, one player, who said he was enjoying the new decor, had actually 'broken the bank'!

Next morning I was up early as I had two things of interest to see. The first was a tour Monsieur Broc took me on of a whole new floor being built on top of the Ronde of the Hôtel de Paris. This included eighty new bedrooms, all with their own balconies, six new flats and a grill room with a wonderful view over the Mediterranean. (When these bedrooms were finished Monsieur Broc asked me if I would try out different rooms on six consecutive nights, which I did, with my remarks on their comfort or discomfort.) I then left for the airport at Nice where Monsieur Gaston Naniche of BEA was waiting to take me on a tour of the new airport buildings. These had been most cleverly designed and most attractively decorated. I never mind having to wait at nice Airport.

The following day I went up to stay with two very dear friends, Lord and Lady Stafford, at Swynnerton Park, Stone, for the North Staffordshire Hunt Ball, which, like many hunt balls, was held in an empty college during the Christmas holidays. Happily, in this case, the setting was a magnificent mansion designed by Samuel Wyatt, with one of the most perfect examples of a circular room, completed in 1798. Morag Stafford, who married when she was seventeen and was the youngest peeress at the Coronation, looked lovely and so youthful at the ball in a dress of lavender blue faille: she looked far too young to be the mother of four lovely children, then all under five years old! Her parents, Colonel and Mrs Alastair Campbell, were also staying at Swynnerton for the hunt ball, which was a joy for me as I had known Muffy Campbell since we were children in Warwickshire and I stayed with her and Ally at Ardhuncart Lodge, their home in Aberdeenshire, on several occasions. It was a very colourful and successful evening.

I had quite a busy start to this year, as twenty-four hours after leaving Staffordshire and finishing off my copy at the *Tatler* office, I was in the air on my way to Zurich and Gstaad to watch some of the winter sports events. As the *Tatler* was a weekly publication and I always had four to six pages to fill, as well as frequent extra pieces to write and photographs other than those in Jennifer to choose, I had to keep going. This left little time for any private life!

1958 was not an eventful year. I went to all the 'hardy annuals', which were as before. I remember one hunt ball, the opening of *My Fair Lady*, and a couple of attractive autumn weddings.

The Heythrop Hunt Ball was held that year at Blenheim Palace. I remember it in particular for the cold! We were going through a bitter spell with snow on the ground, and although the 900 guests were told that the heating had been on for four days, that part of the palace had not warmed up at all (the private side of the palace where the Duke and Duchess of Marlborough had a separate heating system was very warm and comfy).

It was quite funny to see in the beautiful long library women dancing with fur stoles or short fur jackets over their evening dresses. I wrote at the time 'I did not see the Duke of Marlborough at the ball, but I caught sight of the Duchess of Marlborough at one moment walking through the big hall wearing a fur-lined duffle coat over her brown faille evening dress!' The real crunch came for all of us shivering guests when we went down to supper hoping for hot soup to warm us up, to find it was a cold supper!

My Fair Lady opened in London on Guineas day at Newmarket, so Sir Adrian Jarvis, who was coming to the first night with me, decided that we would fly up and down to save time. He seemed to use one of Captain Sammy Morton's charter planes very frequently in those days, and on this occasion it was certainly a joy. The costumes, all designed by Mr Cecil Beaton, who was there with Lady Diana Cooper, were sensational and exquisite and he was receiving many congratulations. The show had a brilliant cast, and there was an illustrious audience headed by the Lord Chancellor and Viscountess Kilmuir, whose brother Rex Harrison was playing the lead. We went on to the Four Hundred, where Rossi was coping brilliantly, fitting everyone in.

The first of two autumn weddings took place in the beautiful little Queen's Chapel at Marlborough Gate, designed by Christopher Wren, which is very seldom used for weddings. This was the marriage of Queen Elizabeth the Queen Mother's nephew Earl Granville to Miss Doon Plunket, the younger daughter of the late Hon. Brinsley Plunket and Mrs Valerian Stux-Rybar. Exquisite flowers, mostly lilies, were arranged each side of the altar, otherwise there were no elaborate floral arrangements. The bride, who was an exceptionally beautiful girl, wore a classical ivory duchesse satin wedding dress designed by Pierre Balmain with a band of the same satin holding her veil in place. The wedding was beautiful for its simplicity. When Doon came out, she always looked quite lovely, she had perfect manners and was charming to everyone, but never wanted to be in the limelight. I can remember her at dances going off quietly to take her golden labrador, who she had left in her car or upstairs, for a run; and she always seemed to be happier doing that than dancing with all the other young people.

The other wedding I remember partly for the wonderful variety of guests, and also for the display of wedding presents, now sadly so seldom seen. This was the marriage of the Hon. Nathaniel Fiennes, later the 21st Lord Saye and Sele, to Miss Mariette Salisbury-Jones, daughter of the then Marshal of the Diplomatic Corps Major-General Sir Guy Salisbury-Jones and Lady Salisbury-Jones. This took place at St Margaret's, Westminster, with the reception at St James's Palace, which The Queen had kindly lent for the occasion. Here in the Throne Room guests could see the really wonderful array of wedding presents from all over the world. They included some beautiful jewellery, fine silver and everything you could imagine for a home.

The guests included a large number of friends, including tenants and employees from the neighbourhood of the bridegroom's historic home Broughton Castle, near Banbury, a large number of villagers from around the bride's country home at Hambledon in Hampshire, and a very large contingent of ambassadors and their wives and other members of the diplomatic corps from all over the world, some in their colourful national costumes. Princess Alice Countess of Athlone came to the reception, and a large number of relations on both sides and most of London's social world were there too.

In December, to round off rather a difficult year, I flew to Rome for a wonderful party given by Princesse Pallavicini at her lovely Palazzo Pallavicini, which is full of priceless treasures. It was a glamorous evening with the Italian ladies vying with each other in their gorgeous silks and satins, and the Italian men all so smooth and elegant.

This trip cheered me up, as at the time at the *Tatler* we seemed to be having a relay of editors, which was most unsettling. None of these seemed to understand how a social diary functioned, and just as I had explained to a new editor, there was yet another change! The latest arrival, who came from a daily newspaper and had no magazine experience, was very difficult to get on with, so I started 1959 feeling rather miserable. I also knew this was the year that my beloved son Jim would leave for Canada if he passed his accountancy exams, which he was due to take early in May.

One Sunday, Jim, who knew I was not happy at the *Tatler*, made me sit down and talk; he wanted me to leave. After fifteen years of working there, this was going to mean a tremendous break for me. Mr Hector Caird had tried for about ten years to get me to go to *Queen* magazine, which he had sold to Mr Jocelyn Stevens in 1958, but I had always refused as up until quite recently I had been quite happy at the *Tatler*. Since Jocelyn had bought *Queen* magazine, I had heard through others that he, too, wanted to get me to work on that magazine. Also, just before Christmas, when I was travelling back from Southampton having seen one of the Union Castle Line ships off to South Africa, I was in the same carriage as a Mr Frederick Pemberton, who was the managing director of *Queen* magazine, and during the journey (not knowing I was feeling unsettled) he too tried hard to persuade me to leave the *Tatler* and go to *Queen*.

So at the end of my talk with Jim that Sunday, on the spur of the moment I said I would go and ring Jocelyn and ask him if it was really true that he wanted me to work on *Queen*. His immediate answer was 'Yes, of course, how soon can we meet?'

He came to my flat the next afternoon, and after a short discussion it was decided I would make the move, but that I must first work out my contractual six months with the *Tatler*. I said he must keep this absolutely confidential for two or three weeks as I was due to leave on my usual winter sports round in Switzerland in two days, and if I resigned before I went, it rather looked as if I was running away from what I was afraid might be a bit of a storm.

Jocelyn as always was splendid and never said a word. Neither of course did Jim, who was delighted I was making a move. I flew home from St Moritz around the third week in January and on the following Monday morning went to see the Chairman of Illustrated Newspapers, who then owned the *Tatler* and quite a few other magazines. He was a dear fatherly man with whom I had always got on splendidly.

When I told him of my decision he refused to accept my resignation, which took me by surprise. He said he was sure I would settle down with the new editor in time. He also reminded me that the board had twice asked me to become editor of the *Tatler*, but that both times I had refused. The suggestion was that if I would not do the job myself, I must not criticize whoever was appointed. (I had refused the editorship twice because I knew my limitations. Whereas I had made a success of my 'Jennifer', I did not feel I had the all-round experience to be a good editor, although it would have been a good step up. My motto has always been 'If you cannot do something well, don't do it at all'.)

My Chairman went on to say that I must be crazy to leave a good job to go and work for Jocelyn, who had already got a reputation for firing his staff at a moment's notice. He again said he refused my resignation and that I was to go away and think it all over quietly and come back on Friday to see him.

A few hours after this meeting I had a telephone call from Angus Irwin, who was still Vice Chairman of ILN. He asked me to go out to dinner to talk the situation over, which I had to refuse as I was booked up each evening that week. In the end I agreed to have break-fast with him in the Dorchester grill room on the Wednesday morning.

On Tuesday evening I was dining with a dear Norwegian, Mr Norman Bohn, who had lived in Cadogan Square for years, and whom I had known since the war days. I told him of my decision to change magazines. He then asked me about my using the name Jennifer, and whether the *Tatler* had registered it. This was something I did not know. Norman Bohn had patented several things in his life, and he said that if they had not registered the name he thought it must be mine by some law, as I had used it for more than so many years, but he offered to consult his lawyer. I also rang a friend, Commander Kenneth Kemble, who was a lawyer, and he said he would verify it for me. They both came back saying yes, it was mine, unless it had been officially registered.

On the Wednesday morning I duly had breakfast with Angus Irwin at the Dorchester. He, like the Chairman, tried to make me change my mind about my move and went on to say something I shall never forget, which was that in six weeks after I had started with Jocelyn, I would be walking the streets looking for a job, and that by then they would have someone else installed in my place so I could not return. I must say, dear Angus did frighten me a little!

Towards the end of that week, I received the nicest letter imaginable, written in longhand by Jocelyn Stevens, who was then only just rising twenty-six years old, one year older than my son. In it he said that since I had rung him on Monday to tell him that I had resigned, he knew I must be worrying, and that I must be thinking 'What have I been and gone and done!' He ended up saying he was looking forward to my starting when I was free, and he hoped that I would be very happy working at *Queen* magazine.

That letter showed me immediately the caring side of Jocelyn. When Friday arrived, I felt pretty frightened, but determined. When I went to see the Chairman, I found I had to face the whole board! But I had made up my mind: I had given Jocelyn my word that I would move to *Queen* magazine, and I could not now break that.

The Chairman then asked me if I was going to use the name of 'Jennifer', to which I replied yes. (I registered the name myself soon after.) It was agreed that I would work out my six months' notice, but that if they found anyone to take my place earlier I could be released. So I carried on exactly as before, and kept right away from the editor!

In March I had a telephone call from a Miss Muriel Bowen, whom I had met on several occasions at the Dublin Horse Show, in which she rode, and which she also wrote about. Muriel was mad keen on hunting; she also wrote for one of the Irish daily papers on a lot of horse events. She was a very cheery girl, and had rung to ask me if I would mind if she applied for my job, as she wanted to come and live in England and she thought she could do it. I at once said I would be delighted, as it meant I could move to *Queen* earlier. She said she could start in April, and eventually, after her seeing the board and the editor, Muriel Bowen was engaged.

My last three months at the *Tatler* were happier than some of the previous months in the knowledge that my time there was nearly up. I went to numerous weddings and other functions before the third week in April, when I handed over my diary in the *Tatler* after over fifteen years to Muriel Bowen, to whom I wished the best of luck. Sadly her diary was not to last long, as two years later the whole of the *Tatler* magazine folded. There was no magazine of that name until a few years later, when a man, who then ran several county magazines, successfully bought the name of the *Tatler* for, I was told at the time, £5,000, to start up a new magazine in the form of the present *Tatler*. Since he started up the *Tatler* magazine it has changed hands several times. Now it has a permanent home among Condé Nast's publications.

I had rung Jocelyn to tell him I would be finishing on Monday night, which fitted in with my final page passing, and that I thought it would be a good idea if I took the rest of that week and the following week as a holiday and started with him on the first Monday in May (which was not in those days a Bank Holiday). Jocelyn, however, said he wanted me as soon as possible, so I eventually left the *Tatler* on Monday night, 20th April, and started at *Queen* magazine at 10 a.m. the next day.

TEN

My first years at *Queen*
(1959–64)

Moving to *Queen* magazine was a dramatic change. Not only was I years older than anyone else on the magazine (I was nearly fifty-three by then), but I was used to working on a magazine that was one of a big group, and in a building where all the other magazines worked, with the benefits of my own reference books, the firm's reference library, messengers to call on to collect pictures or any details, immediate secretarial staff to step in if my secretary was ill or getting married, as so many did, and a very comfortable office.

When I joined *Queen* their office was in a small high corner house on Burleigh Street overlooking the old Covent Garden flower market. As I did not want to work in the main office, Faith Mason, my secretary – who had asked to come with me from the *Tatler* – and I shared literally a slit with Jocelyn's very pretty secretary Mary Ann Murray outside his office. It was so small that while we were there Faith and I had to share a desk! Happily this was only for a matter of months, before we moved to new offices (with no central heating – Jocelyn, being twenty-six years old, had never thought of heating!) in Old Fetter Lane. Here at first I had a better office, but in between two other offices with clear glass all round so that you saw all that was going on all day, which I found very disrupting. After about a year Jocelyn moved me to a large and lovely office, furnished to my design.

When I joined Jocelyn, to my dismay I found that, except for a very old *Debrett* being used as a doorstop, there were no social reference books in the building! By degrees I collected enough, and then when the original *Tatler* folded, my former dear Chairman said I could come to their office and have any of my old reference books that I wanted. They are still with me today, and invaluable.

Jocelyn Stevens was an inspiration to work for. He persuaded me to go to the functions I did not want to attend and he was always right. He got me to work even harder than I had ever worked before

– and enjoy it. He was full of bright and sometimes outrageous ideas for the magazines, which he expounded at editorial meetings. He was always editor-in-chief, and often sparred with his editors; in my eyes he was nearly always in the right. When I went up to the editorial floor and saw the situation was stormy, I always retired until later.

But with all these exciting fireworks – so different from the solid *Tatler* days – Jocelyn was always someone I could discuss my work problems with and ask advice from, and in spite of his youth it never failed to be sound, and the right answer. Jocelyn and his very sweet wife Jane Stevens, both of whom I had known since they were children, lived a very social life. So when I went to Jocelyn with a problem he knew what I was talking about, whereas most editors never had a clue. Although Jocelyn had a succession of editors while he owned *Queen*, which he bought as a twenty-fifth birthday present to himself, he was editor-in-chief on the masthead, and really always edited the magazine.

Having worked for his uncle Sir Edward Hulton on his magazines, Jocelyn knew the working of a magazine better than anyone. When we had quite a serious printing trade dispute, Jocelyn got together a band of apprentices who were not affected by the strike, instructed them himself, and got the magazine out when all the others were stopped. He even went off abroad getting work done, and drove the lorries delivering magazines, as the drivers were also affected. He was forced off the road and ditched on more than one occasion!

The editor when I first joined *Queen* was Miss Beatrix Miller, later for many years the successful editor of *Vogue*. We never saw eye to eye! I always felt from the start that Beatrix resented me, as she had had nothing to do with my joining *Queen*. I came entirely through Jocelyn, and she had never even set eyes on me until I sat at my desk. It quite obviously irritated her that I worked independently, and that in spite of my not being a professional in any way, I had somehow managed to build up quite a big readership.

I soon discovered that in those days Beatrix did not have a clue about the real social world. My first Jennifer appeared in the 12th May 1959 issue under the heading 'People and Parties, a diary of social events by Jennifer', and was only given two pages, to include photographs. After one or two issues, I was cut to one or one and a half pages each time, and very often it was entirely in half-pages placed horizontally beside advertising. The all-time low was the 1959 Christmas number. Then I started halfway down a half-page under another article, with a very faint heading and a microscopic Jennifer. On the next page was a whole-page article on something else, then I had another half-page column and continued two pages on with another nine and a half lines, totalling in all under one page! I suppose all this was to irritate me and make me resign. Irritate it did, but I never had any intention of resigning. I was there to help Jocelyn build up *Queen* into a super magazine, which he did with a splendid team, so I went on quietly, with one or two exceptions when I blew up.

Jocelyn was always loyal, and I knew I had his backing, but I did not draw him into my problems. When I joined, Mark Boxer, who had been up at Cambridge with Jocelyn, was the art editor, and together they thought up so many hilarious best-selling features. Antony Armstrong-Jones, who by then had become a very clever photographer, was taking a lot of photographs for the magazine, so there was youth all round. There was never a dull moment, and a lot of happy laughter, as well as some anxious times.

It was the greatest fun working with Jocelyn, as you never knew what he would think up next to go in the magazine. In the summer of 1959 he published a four-page article headed 'The Establishment Chronicle', which was a wonderful, really funny skit laid out as the *Eton Chronicle*. In the centre was a two-page spread of a blown-up photograph of a house at Eton, complete with the tutor, the dame, and all the boys with all their trophies. The original faces had all been changed to the faces of personalities, which included the Prime Minister Mr Harold Macmillan, captioned as H. Macmillan, and next to him 'Mr Canterbury'. No one was given a rank or title, just their initial. By the end of the week you could not buy a copy of that issue of the magazine anywhere. It was an absolute sell-out.

In June during my first year with Jocelyn, my beloved son Jim emigrated to Canada. I have written about this sad moment earlier. Dear Jocelyn and his team, and lots of work, helped me forget about his going.

I continued at *Queen* writing about all the hardy annuals and other events as before, but everything had to be curtailed at first, because of Beatrix's tiny space allowance, which was a bit frustrating, but probably good for my self-control.

The sixties were most certainly for me the 'swinging sixties'. Now that my son, Jim, had left for Canada, I had no reason to refuse invitations or to take a weekend or an evening off. The sixties were a period of much entertaining; invitations flooded in, and Jocelyn encouraged me to accept far more, travel far more and attend more unusual functions than I would have done on the *Tatler*, so I soon found I was working harder than ever. I was also given more space.

The sixties weddings began with the 1960 marriage of Mr David Hicks to Lady Pamela Mountbatten, which, like her sister's wedding, took place in Romsey Abbey with the reception at Broadlands. It was in the middle of an exceptional spell of snow and ice, when trains and planes and most other forms of transport had been cancelled! Guests walked in a blizzard on an icy, snow-covered road and path to the church and then faced the same perilous walk afterwards to find their transport.

Wearing a mink-trimmed white slipper satin dress and an exquisite pearl and diamond tiara, the bride looked radiant as she walked slowly up the nave with her father. She was followed by five bridesmaids, one of whom was Princess Anne, a bridesmaid for the first time.

When we arrived at Broadlands for the reception, all the lights had failed! But with Mountbatten efficiency, everywhere was quickly candlelit, and two footmen appeared each holding silver candelabra, to place one beside the bride and bridegroom and one beside their parents.

When I reached the receiving line Edwina Mountbatten asked me what was happening outside, and whether there were enough candles about. I was able to assure her that all was perfectly in order.

The sixties started in St Moritz with a big bang! It was a packed season: I went out to Switzerland very early and found many of the best-known international socialites there; also the top skiers, as some of the most important ski races were to take place in the resort.

A week after my winter trip to Switzerland, I flew by BOAC Comet – one of the first aircraft to have really efficient leg-rests – to New York on my way south to Jamaica, where I stayed with Sir Harold and Lady Mitchell at Prospect. On one evening while I was there, the Mitchells gave a cocktail party and buffet supper at their beautiful beach house Frankfort. On that starry night, a wood fire burned on the sand and a calypso band played all the evening. I remember sitting talking to writer Ian Fleming; we were enjoying a most interesting conversation until his wife Ann Fleming came along to see what he was up to! We continued our conversation on a flight to Nassau the following week. The Flemings had a house nearby where he wrote his famous James Bond books.

On the second day of that visit, while being carefully driven by Mary Mitchell's very experienced chauffeur and sitting in the back, we suddenly came face to face with two cars coming towards us abreast round a bend. As we had a high rock on our near side, there was nowhere for us to pull into and we were hit head on! Luckily our chauffeur was unhurt. I cut and bruised one of my hands very badly trying to save myself, and my dear hostess's car was completely written off!

I went on to stay with the Antony Normans at Roundhill, and from there I flew on to stay at the then 'new' Lyford Cay Club, and found it one of the most comfortable places I had ever visited. One felt wrapped in luxury from the moment one entered the grounds. The decor, designed by Ann Lady Orr-Lewis, was exceptionally attractive and the French manager, Monsieur Maurice Neyrolles, had imported a top French chef so the cuisine was super.

Eddie Taylor had invited me to stay there to tell him what could be improved upon. I could find very little, if anything, that could be bettered! It was so interesting to me, having been in on the development from day one and knowing how much care and thought had gone into the project, to see it all start to function. Sir Raynor Arthur was then the Governor. He and Lady Arthur were both charming and were a great success. I still meet Lady Arthur from time to time.

By an extraordinary coincidence, many years later, in very cold weather, I came home to my flat and found, as I got out of the lift, a lady sobbing her soul out. I stopped to enquire if I could help. She then told me that she and her husband had come from overseas for a wedding and that they had just been burgled while they were out and had lost most of their clothes, including her wedding clothes.

As she was about my size I quickly said, 'Perhaps I can help, you are welcome to borrow anything I have.' Happily she did wear my coat. It was not until long after the wedding that I discovered they were close relations of Lady Arthur, and had come for a family wedding.

While I was staying in Lyford Cay that year I heard on the 6 p.m. BBC News that Antony Armstrong-Jones and Princess Margaret had announced their engagement. Jocelyn and Janey Stevens were also staying out at Lyford Cay in their enchanting little house La Carina. As they were having a cocktail party that evening, I thought they might not have switched on the news, so I rang Jocelyn, who had not heard. His immediate reaction was 'Splendid, I like my staff to marry well.'

When I got to their party, there were many happy toasts to the newly engaged pair.

It was just as I was taking off at Nassau airport for Hileagh one morning in February 1960 that I heard of dear Edwina Mountbatten's quite unexpected death. She had died in Jesselton, Borneo, while on a very demanding overseas tour on behalf of St John Ambulance Brigade Overseas. At first I simply could not believe it, as she had looked radiant and seemed in such good form at Pammy Mountbatten's wedding, less than six weeks earlier.

I was very sad that I did not attend Princess Margaret's and Tony Armstrong-Jones's wedding that May. I had applied to the Buckingham Palace Press Office in the usual way, and was to get my tickets, car park pass and so on in due course. But when I returned early from Chester race week, twenty-four hours before the wedding, to my dismay I found no wedding tickets. I learnt from Buckingham Palace Press Office that they had been sent, but they were nowhere to be found. There was nothing I could do: the Palace could not duplicate them as special numbered seats had been allotted. As it turned out, it was just as well they didn't. I discovered afterwards that my tickets had been given to someone else on the magazine! When I later spoke to the editor about this, she coolly told me she had thought I was going to be away! It was one of the few royal weddings I have not attended.

That summer I went to a ball at Sutton Place given jointly by Mr Paul Getty, the oil multi-millionaire, who had recently bought Sutton Place from the Duke of Sutherland, and by Captain Ian Constable-Maxwell for his daughter Miss Jeannette Constable-Maxwell.

I had been to many gracious parties in this house; this was a complete contrast. Firstly, it was far too crowded. Secondly, around the swimming pool that evening were stalls with milk shakes, soft drinks and a variety of other items, all advertising their wares – it looked like a market. Thirdly, the ladies' cloakroom was in an empty bedroom, and next door in another empty room was a row of creosoted loos in creosoted huts such as you had at point-to-points in the old days, which the ladies in their often very pale silks and satins were asked to use, as Mr Getty had had all the luxurious bathrooms locked! If you wanted to move about that evening you had to fight your way. I felt sorry for Jeannette Constable-Maxwell, who was a sweet girl, as she and her friends, who were in the minority, must have felt rather lost in all that crowd.

Jocelyn and Janey were also at that ball, and when Jocelyn and I discussed it next day, he and I agreed it should be featured as 'The Battle of Gettysburg', and that we would do a joint piece, with photographs we had. I am sure in the end Jocelyn wrote most of it as it really was hilarious, but we had a lot of fun over it, and readers were amused! Paul Getty's son Mr Paul Getty II is one of our most generaous philanthropists today.

In January 1961 I flew out to India as a guest of the Maharaja and Maharanee of Jaipur. They invited me to stay at Rambagh Palace, which had, before they moved into a much smaller house nearby, been their home, and which they had just converted into a hotel. I left London airport at 11.30 p.m., two hours late. I was due to arrive in Delhi at 7.30 a.m., but as we were nearly two hours late landing I had missed the then one and only daily flight from Delhi to Jaipur.

I knew that my host wanted me there by 4.30 p.m. for a rehearsal for The Queen's visit, so I could not stay the night and catch the flight next morning. I had no one meeting me at Delhi except an airline official, as I should only have been in transit. So without anyone to turn to for advice and without giving it very much thought, I asked the airline official to arrange for a car to drive me there right away. I left Delhi around 10 a.m., having no idea what was ahead of me, and luckily not thinking too much about it! All I worried about was how soon the driver could get me there.

In those days the roads were pretty awful, in some places being just a single track. When we saw anything coming, my driver drove straight at it, hoping they would give way and go on to the sandy dusty verge. Sometimes it was a near miss! (I expect by now the road to Jaipur is a wide double carriageway or even a motorway.)

My driver would stop quite often at a village – he said for a cup of tea – which I found very delaying. Also I would be surrounded each time by villagers begging either with a crippled man or woman, or with a poor little malformed child. I began to wonder if I would ever get there.

I made it by 2.45 p.m. Of course there was no one to meet me as they had met the flight I missed, and now expected me to come on the flight next day. When I had paid off my driver, I went to my room at Rambagh Palace and telephoned Jai, who was amazed I had got there; he arranged to send a car at 4 p.m. to pick me up and take me to their house and the rehearsal.

When I arrived at their house I found Mr Evelyn de Rothschild, who had been staying a few days. He very sweetly told me quickly that in Jaipur I should always refer to and address Jai as His or Your Highness – I was so grateful to be put right at the start of my visit as no one else had warned me. After the rehearsal, which went on for quite a long time, I went back to their house with the Jaipurs and later they took me to a cocktail party. Another evening I went with Ayesha Jaipur, Evelyn de Rothschild and the Jaipurs' schoolboy son, Jagat Singh, to see a colourful display of folkdancing and singing.

When I had originally fixed the dates for my visit, The Queen was not due to visit Jaipur until two weeks later. When Her Majesty's plans changed, I cabled Jai and Ayesha and asked if they would like me to postpone my visit, but received a reply telling me to keep to my original dates. The Queen and the Duke of Edinburgh's visit was less than twenty-four hours actually in Jaipur. They went to church on Sunday in Delhi, then flew to Jaipur, and made the eight-mile drive from the airport in an open car to a civic luncheon with the Governor and ministers, and a visit to a community centre in the late afternoon. Then they attended the Jaipurs' reception. After the reception they dined quietly with Their Highnesses at Rajmahal and later left, with their host and hostess and the four sons, by special train for two peaceful days at their shooting palace, Sawai Madhopur.

I felt so fortunate to be staying in Jaipur during The Queen's brief visit and very privileged to be invited to the reception given in her honour by the Maharajah and Maharanee of Jaipur. It was something I shall never forget.

This was a fabulous spectacle of unrivalled pageantry – in spite of the Labour Government in power in India then saying that evening dress must not be worn at the reception. Although most of the ladies wore exquisite saris and jewellery, the men outshone them. They wore their orders and decorations on the most beautiful *sherwanis* (brocade tunics), often gold embroidered, and they wore turbans of every hue, usually with a spectacular jewelled ornament pinned on the turban.

The Queen, who had followed the request that evening dress should not be worn, looked superb wearing an ivory silk coat over a short dress to match and a sequin- and crystal-studded pillbox hat that sparkled in the strong lights. This had been designed for her very specially by Norman Hartnell and it could not have looked more regal. The Maharajah was a magnificent figure wearing a blue and gold *sherwani*, an imposing row of medals, and a scarlet turban with a four-inch-wide long strip of diamonds right across the front and a bunch of ospreys up the side. They rode together from Their Highnesses' residence, Raj

Mahal, through the streets lined with cheering crowds, in an ornate silver and gold *howdah* on an elephant which was dressed all over in gold, silver and scarlet, with gold rings in its tusks, and wide fringed silver bracelets on its forefeet.

The Duke of Edinburgh, wearing a day suit, followed on another elephant with the Maharajah's eldest son, Maharaj Jumar Bhawani Singh, who, like his father, wore full regalia.

I remember feeling once again so very proud of our beloved Queen as, standing up in the *howdah*, she arrived on the elephant at the Sabata of the City Palace, which was lined on one side by three more elephants, and camels of the Camel Corps, all with brilliant trappings, and five or six bullock carts with bright canopies.

The Queen was greeted here by the Maharanee of Jaipur wearing an exquisite green and gold sari and a fabulous two-row necklace of pearls, uncut rubies and emeralds. Monkeys were skipping around the top floors of the adjoining Chandra Mahal, chattering with excitement at the glittering scene below. I had very sweetly been given a wonderful position from which to watch all this.

Around 6.30 p.m. the royal party entered the fairytale pink and white courtyard of the adjacent Moon Palace, bright with carpets all over the lawns, hundreds of cinerarias around the verandahs and beautiful roses in profusion on the long buffet tables. The whole palace was floodlit, and during the evening a new moon rose above, and Jaipur musicians played Indian music. Two gold chairs were placed in front of a mass of scarlet bougainvilleas. The Queen walked across to the chairs, stopping here and there to talk to a guest. When Her Majesty was seated, she had a good look round at the beauty of it all.

That was another evening I shall never forget. It was probably the last of the really glamorous occasions of the Maharajahs of India.

For the two days that they were going to be away, Ayesha Jaipur gave me a list of things she wanted me to see, and also allotted a bearer to accompany me, but I did not realize this, and instead went off alone in strange cars the concierge got me. Some of my trips were quite scary alone! I visited the museum in the City Palace, I went round inside the Moon Palace, I motored up to the Amber Palace perched high on the Rajputana Hills and saw the gem of a temple with embossed silver doors and marble interior that was restored by the Maharajah of Jaipur. I visited Galta and Sisodiya Ram's palace by night when lit up and floodlit. I spent an interesting time seeing some of the industries of Jaipur, I visited the bazaars and the Gem Palace, from where they export jewellery to all over the world, and I did a lot besides this.

When Jai and Ayesha returned I had a couple of very amusing days with them, including attending – sitting on the very edge, as women are not usually present – the engagement ceremony in the City Palace for the official engagement of the Maharajah of Jaipur's third son, Maharaj Kumar Prithviraj Singh, to Devita. The bride is not present on these occasions, but was represented in this case by her uncle. A pandit performed the rituals, and the bridegroom sat on a cushion in the centre of a carpeted Sarbata in ceremonial clothes with a magnificent osprey in his turban. His father, wearing a pink and silver *sherwani*, sat on a gold chair nearby and his three brothers were present, also all the male nobles of Jaipur in their ceremonial clothes. Laid out in front of the bridegroom were about forty large flat dishes of fruit, nuts, cereals, spices, and so on, all with a special significance. Musicians played softly throughout the ceremony. Women members of the family do not attend; they had their own party with Ayesha Jaipur in another part of the City Palace, and Jai and Ayesha gave a cocktail party that evening at Rambagh Palace for relations and close friends. The wedding was to take place two months later.

On my last evening, Ayesha said she had a headache and could not go out, but Jai called for me all the same and drove me himself to a wedding eve party that they had planned to attend. It was being given by one of his noblemen and his wife, for their daughter, who was being married that week. We arrived and were greeted by our host in full regalia. The hostess and bride-to-be wore the most beautiful Rajasthan dresses and jewels, as did all the other ladies. I was given a drink by my host and then he and Jai went off to another part of the house and left me with all the ladies in the drawing room, where musicians sitting on the floor played all the evening.

I was asked if I would like to dance. Luckily I said no, as soon six ladies got up, strapped little bells around their ankles and danced very prettily; little groups of ladies did this at intervals all evening. I soon realized that we ladies were all segregated from the men, and we even had to wait for dinner until the men had finished theirs in the large dining room. It was an interesting evening.

I flew home on a BOAC Comet and was accompanied by Jagat Singh, then about eight or nine years old, on his way back to his preparatory school, Ludgrove. When we got into our seats he started sobbing about leaving home. I tried to comfort him. Then he decided he would cover his head with a blanket and lean on my shoulder; he slept like that for nearly two hours, which I felt was the kindest thing to let him do.

One of the two royal weddings that I did attend in the sixties was the marriage of the Duke of Kent to Miss Kate Worsley, which took place in York Minster in June that year.

I went up by train, and it had been arranged that I should lunch with a most charming couple, the 6th Earl and Countess of Clanwilliam, and a party of friends, at the Station Hotel at York, which has always been an exceptionally well-run hotel. I remember Lady Clanwilliam, who already had five daughters, telling me that she hoped her next child would be a boy. When the baby arrived, I read it was another girl!

York Minster has never looked more beautiful than it did that day. Lady Pulbrook and her team of flower arrangers had taken as their theme the White Rose of York. This country wedding had a slightly different feeling from the London royal weddings. Formal pomp and ceremony intermingled with the simplicity and happiness of a family celebration. As we arrived the bells of the Minster were ringing, the lights were on and the ushers were already busy seating the 2,000 guests. I was very kindly placed in a lovely seat where I could see everything and everyone.

When everyone was seated, we had the official processions. First the choir, clergy and canons of the cathedral; then the two processions of foreign royal guests and some members of the Royal Family; then Queen Elizabeth the Queen Mother accompanied by Queen Victoria Eugénie of Spain; then the bridegroom's mother Princess Marina Duchess of Kent, looking very chic, with Princess Alexandra looking enchanting in coral pink. A fanfare announced the arrival of The Queen and the Duke of Edinburgh, accompanied by the Prince of Wales. Another fanfare heralded the bride and her father, Sir William Worsley. The bride was wearing a superb wedding dress designed, as were Princess Marina's and Princess Alexandra's, by Mr John Cavanagh. The bride had a retinue of three pages and eight bridesmaids headed by Princess Anne.

After the ceremony, there was a reception at the bride's home, Hovingham Hall, where the bride's brother, Mr Marcus Worsley, now Sir Marcus Worsley, proposed the health of the young couple, but there were no speeches.

The following evening Mr and Mrs Harry Oppenheimer gave a lovely dance for their only daughter Miss Mary Oppenheimer, for which the Hon. Hugh and Lady Helen Smith lent the Durdans at

Epsom, which had been in the Rosebery family for many years and was a perfect setting for a dance. A triple marquee had been built on to the house so that with 600 guests it was never crowded.

I was among the 120 friends dining there before the dance, and we sat at candlelit tables of eight or ten, then had a chance to stroll through the octagonal sitting room and other rooms to enjoy the beautiful Rosebery treasures.

I remember late in the evening strolling out with a friend towards the stables where there was a notice saying 'The Dopers' Den' – this was, for the evening, a nightclub in the stables, which had over the years housed many classic winners. Satin jackets and jockey caps adorned the walls, and the racing colours of many famous owners were cleverly lit. The lighting throughout was very special, as Helen Smith's half-brother Lord Primrose, now the Earl of Rosebery, who had studied all forms of lighting, was chief electrician!

Harry and Bridget Oppenheimer received the guests with Mary, who wore a beautiful white organza dress appliquéd with pink and blue butterflies. Hugh and Helen Smith were nearby also greeting many mutual friends. They and the Oppenheimers and Mary were the most super hosts, as they all looked after the guests – including a number from South Africa – throughout the dance, but still managed to dance themselves to a very good band which went on until 4 a.m. I clearly remember that either Bridget Oppenheimer or Helen Smith arranged for Mr Tom Blackwell, a very old friend who was also dining, to drive me there and back. Not many hostesses do that!

Nearly every debutante of that year was there, each very well dressed, and there were masses of good-looking young men, none of whom dreamt of taking their tail coat or dinner jacket off during the evening, as some of the young men have started to do at dances in the last ten years.

The following February, in 1962, after a visit to Barbados, I flew to Antigua in a BWIA Viscount. This was my first visit to this island. I managed to fit quite a lot into the twenty-four hours I spent there, and decided it was somewhere I wanted to revisit!

I stayed at the Mill Reef Club, which was founded after the war by a group of Americans led by the famous American architect Mr Happy Robertson Ward. The Mill Reef Club is a luxury club and owns 1,400 acres, including six miles of Antigua waterfront, with about a dozen beaches. In those days there were around forty-five enchanting small houses on the Mill Reef Estate, all owned by members and excluded from speculation, most of them designed by Happy Ward. Mr Paul Mellon was in the process of building quite a big one. In my twenty-four hours, I managed to see the three leading hotels, the Mill Reef golf course, Nelson's dockyard at English Harbour (a haven for boats during hurricanes), to have a bathe and drinks before luncheon with the President of Mill Reef, Mr John H.P. Gould from Massachusetts, and his wife, to lunch on the estate with Mrs Walter B. Allen from Hartford, Connecticut, to dine with Happy Ward and his wife Dolly, and to go on to a barbecue on the shore at the Mill Reef where a calypso band played. I met twenty or thirty interesting Americans, among them Mr and Mrs Walter Kohler – he was in the steel business and was the former Governor of Wisconsin – and Mr and Mrs Archibald MacLeish – he was the US poet laureate. Quite a contrast!

This year the Spanish Ambassador and the Marquesa de Santa Cruz, who gave a lot of really lovely parties, gave a flamenco party at the Spanish Embassy. Casilda Santa Cruz, who was a really attractive and elegant hostess, wore a beautiful Balenciaga dress with a white top and a yellow faille skirt. She and Pepe had handpicked their guests, who were all very chic, intelligent and most amusing, and not too many of them, so the numbers were just right.

The Manuela Vargas Company of dancers and guitarists from Seville came to entertain the guests. They danced superbly for nearly an hour on a two-foot-high stage, so that everyone could see. Then there was a delicious buffet supper followed by more flamenco.

During the second period of flamenco the dancers invited some of the guests to join them. The first to do this was Viscount Hambleden, who, one soon realized, was a flamenco expert! After one or two others had joined in, the 5th Marquess of Salisbury – such a dear and amusing man, then in his seventieth year – went on to the stage and danced a flamenco amazingly well.

Although this was a busy week for me, I was enjoying myself so much that I stayed until nearly the end and I did not get to bed until 3 a.m.

Three weeks later Earl Beatty gave a wonderful twenty-first birthday party for Countess Beatty at their attractive home, Chicheley Hall in Buckinghamshire. Diane Beatty, who was David Beatty's fourth wife, looked beautiful in a full-skirted very pale blue silk organza dress; she radiated enjoyment as she received the guests with her husband.

The decor, I remember, had been done by Mr Cecil Beaton and was fabulous. A huge marquee had been built out over the terrace and part of the lawn on three levels: first, the wide receiving room with pale yellow drapes overhead, then the supper room in palest blue with bobble-fringe blue swags around the dado, and blue velvet button-upholstered Victorian loving seats placed at intervals around the walls. Bowls of white flowers decorated all the white dinner tables and a thick bank of pink, blue and white hydrangeas, lit from beneath, separated the supper room from the very original black and white checked dance floor. This was the first and only time I have seen a black and white check dance floor. It was most effective.

Cecil Beaton was present at the ball and received a tremendous amount of congratulation for his decor. Outside on the far side of the house, the lake was lit and there was a second very good band and outdoor dance floor. Everything was quite perfect. The guests included masses of attractive young marrieds and a few older friends of the family.

That day, in spite of having been to my office, then to three weddings, starting at 12 noon, then in the evening to a cocktail party and on to dine with Mr and Mrs Vane Ivanović in London before we all motored out to this dance in Buckinghamshire, I thoroughly enjoyed every moment I was at that ball.

Six months later I was invited out to luncheon by a man I had known for years but not well. I thought this very strange and I refused the first date he suggested, then to my dismay he asked me to select another date. We eventually lunched at the Carlton Club and after I had chosen my luncheon, I asked him why he had invited me. His reply was: 'Why didn't you mention us at the Beatty Ball?' I quickly told him what I had done that day and that the simple answer was I had forgotten I had seen them, as I had probably done with twenty other couples I knew even better! I had, in spite of being pretty tired, mentioned over eighty guests from memory without ever ringing my host or hostess, but unfortunately I had missed this couple!

In the winter Hardy Amies gave a party with a difference, on ice! This took place at Queens Ice Skating Club and was most beautifully arranged. There was very soft blue lighting and red candles, and skating instructors in pale blue sweaters glided around on the ice with trays of vodka or hot red wine for the 900 guests as they arrived for the party. There were scarlet sleighs to sit in for those who wanted to take a rest.

Hardy stood receiving his guests, some of whom came in full evening dress, others in short evening dress, others in a variety of skating outfits. The most outstanding among them was Mrs Norman Parkinson in gold lamé from top to toe. I remember Lord Willoughby de Eresby arriving looking dressed for the Côte d'Azur, wearing a loose pale blue shirt and pale blue linen trousers on which were pink and white squares. The ice rink was soon packed with happy guests skating, falling and dancing to the music – it was a most attractive scene.

There were intervals when exhibition skaters performed and made skating look so easy. Bacon and eggs were served upstairs and downstairs, where there was a very good band and dancing on a dance floor.

Early in 1963, Mr and Mrs Hugh Barton persuaded me to go out to Hong Kong. Hugh was then head of Jardine Matheson out there, and they said they would take care of me, which they certainly did. I flew out in a BOAC Boeing 707 – with Rolls-Royce engines, I was glad to see. It was a very comfortable journey. In those days it took twenty-four or -five hours, stopping at Frankfurt, Rome, Tehran, Bangkok and Delhi. Today you can fly non-stop in thirteen hours fifteen minutes. I stayed at the Gloucester Hotel and during my visit I went over the famous Mandarin Hotel, where I have stayed on every further visit, which was then under construction. Several friends and others had been alerted of my arrival. When I got up to my room, I found it filled with vases of flowers, baskets of fruit and six invitations to lunch and dine. I got to bed at 3.30 a.m.

At 8.45 a.m. my telephone started ringing non-stop. I lunched with friends on the Peak and after lunch I made a recording for 'Today', one of the local radio programmes. I had tea with a very dear friend, Mrs Lo Hing Kwong, and joined other friends for dinner.

Next day Hugh and Rosie Barton invited me to lunch in their box at Happy Valley, the Royal Hong Kong Jockey Club racecourse, where Hugh Barton was a steward. Racing in Hong Kong takes place in the greatest comfort. There are no bookmakers, and the turnover of the totalizator is so great that when the Government has taken its taxes, and a large and ample sum has been given back to the racecourse and racing, there is a very big sum over to donate to further education and charities in Hong Kong. If only that could happen in England!

I later dined with Mr and Mrs Harold Lee – he was a great business figure in Hong Kong then – in a beautiful Chinese house. I arrived at the house at the same moment as Admiral Sir David Luce, the C-in-C Far East, and Lady Luce. I did not know them or who they were, but before we went into the house, Admiral Luce asked me if I had previously been to a Chinese dinner, as if I had not, I must be careful not to take too much of the first course as there would be as many courses as guests at the table. We were ten guests and my host and hostess. We had a Chinese dinner of twelve courses, including chopped quail eaten in a crisp lettuce leaf. I was so grateful for the Admiral's tip!

I was very impressed with how hard everyone works out in Hong Kong. You never saw anyone sitting about doing nothing, and there was a wonderful spirit of helping others. At that time Hong Kong was flooded with refugees from China – they were sleeping in the streets and in every kind of shelter.

I met Mrs A.K. Rudge at the St John headquarters and I saw the wonderful work they were doing. I spent a morning over at Kowloon with Mrs Harry Stanley, who was working for the Lutheran Department of World Service, which was sponsored by the US, Germany, Sweden and the UK, and was doing magnificent work rehabilitating refugees, getting students into colleges and planning trade centres. At the headquarters I saw health rooms, the tuberculosis rehabilitation section, and the registration department where they already had over 30,000 on their files.

Another day, Mr Horace Kadoorie took me all over the fabulous experimental farms of the Kadoorie Agricultural Aid Association, successfully run on terraces cut out of the mountains. More than 7,000 pigs had recently been given in a short space of time to refugees to help them make a start in farming. More than 30,000 had already been helped successfully, including 10,000 widows. I was taken to see the refugees farming and I came away very impressed with the fantastic way in which they were making full use of every inch of land allotted to them.

Wearing a navy blue coat and hat and trying to look like one of the Red Cross, I was taken on a tour of the much-discussed Walled City in the Kai Tak area near Kowloon. I was taken round by one of the Red Cross workers who was connected with the little school inside run by nuns and the British Red Cross. At times we got a hostile reception, at others we were offered boiled sweets or cups of China tea. I was told I must accept everything! There was open drainage and the whole place seemed to me at the time very sad.

We went on to look round the very well-run Haven of Hope Sanatorium where the British Red Cross were also running a school, and from there to the Red Cross-run Princess Alexandra Children's Residential Home for schooling handicapped children. Another day I visited the St James's settlement, another splendid organization in a very poor and overcrowded district made more congested by refugees.

I climbed up a narrow wooden staircase to a room where three families with children and grannies were living, with the loo in one corner and in another a cooking stove on which was the biggest frying pan I have ever seen, and shelves up one of the walls where the children slept.

One night I went to see the arrangements the Street Sleepers Shelter Association had made for street sleepers. I visited two shelters and was most impressed with what I saw. Thanks to wise building and development, and the reclamation of land from the sea to create the large acreage of the New Territories, Hong Kong is a different place today. I have been back many times, including quite recently, and each time I am amazed at the new buildings and the engineering – including the tunnel under the sea from the airport to the centre of Hong Kong. As I said before, everyone in Hong Kong works!

Some time in 1962 the editor received a letter from a reader in Yorkshire which said: 'Having read Jennifer's Diary for some years, I cannot wait to learn how many Jennifers there are. No one woman could keep up this pace and deal with the office work as well.' I replied 'Alas, I have no exciting news for you of a team of Jennifers. I am alone. I have been so for many years with the help of only one secretary, who never goes to functions for me. I often work a twenty-four-hour day several days a week; then there are some quieter periods.' Little did I think then that I would still be writing Jennifer's Diary nearly thirty years on!

The debutante seasons made a lot of extra work for me. At certain times of the year people telephoned all day asking for guidance on a date for a dance, where to hold it, what band to have and how to contact them, what caterers to use, where to get invitations printed – and then they would change the date! Also where to get Caledonian Ball and Queen Charlotte's Ball tickets, how to get to the selection party for the Berkeley Dress Show, how many dresses a girl needed for her season, how to get a debutante's photograph published, how to have a photographer at their dance. Each year many mothers and sometimes fathers came to see me about the season.

This took up so much time and was so disrupting that for one or two years I made Tuesdays the only day I could see debutante mothers; that day was always fully booked at the office, and I saw masses of them at the flat. These queries for a number of years were absolutely non-stop and the answers were provided completely free! Jocelyn Stevens and I discussed several times how to make some sort of charge, but we never worked anything out. After Liz Anson and Jessie Scott-Ellis set up Party Planners, I was able to switch a lot of the party queries over to them. They, of course, charged a fee in the normal way.

One night after dining late at the Guards Club, and having been escorted the short distance home, I switched on the television and while rather absentmindedly watching suddenly realized I was looking at a spoof Jennifer on the screen in *That Was The Week That Was*. I was being portrayed by Fenella Fielding with a dark wig, dangling earrings, and a long cigarette holder! After a certain amount of apprehension (a feeling shared at that time by Cabinet ministers and others portrayed in this programme) I was able to enjoy a good laugh at my many shortcomings, as then picked out and shown off by Messrs Frost and Company.

The next royal wedding I went to was the marriage of the Hon. Angus Ogilvy, now the Hon. Sir Angus Ogilvy, to Princess Alexandra of Kent in Westminster Abbey in 1963. As she walked up the aisle with her brother, the Duke of Kent, Princess Alexandra made the most beautiful bride, wearing a dress of crisp cream lace with a sunray diamond tiara holding her long lace veil in place.

My most enduring memories of this wedding were the solemn moment when the bride and bridegroom made their marriage vows in front of the Archbishop of Canterbury and the Dean of Westminster, imposing in their full regalia; the chief bridesmaid Princess Anne wearing her hair swept up for the first time; The Queen looking most attractive in a dress of the palest green organza with a lilies-of-the-valley print and a hat to match; the bride's mother Princess Marina Duchess of Kent, serene and beautiful, and as always superbly dressed in a tunic dress of gold tissue, with an off-the-face gold embroidered hat; Queen Elizabeth the Queen Mother smiling to all around; and the Prince of Wales wearing a very large carnation in his lapel and looking rather serious.

I remember the fanfares of trumpets and the very happy faces of the bride and bridegroom, and the cheering of the crowds outside as the bride and bridegroom drove off to the reception at St James's Palace in The Queen's Glass Coach. The bride and bridegroom have always been such a friendly couple, full of fun and caring, who have carried out their duties over the years with both charm and a real sense of duty.

In September, I got a call from the Spanish Embassy from the

Ambassador, the Marqués de Santa Cruz. The Marqués had been asked by the President of the big debutante ball, then held in Barcelona each autumn, to select three English debutantes to attend it, as that year it was to be an international ball. Pepe Santa Cruz had immediately responded that if English girls were to go to Barcelona for the ball they must have a chaperone. The President of the Barcelona ball had agreed to this.

Pepe Santa Cruz was ringing me to ask if I would take charge and chaperone these young ladies and would I help him to choose them! I was a bit shaken by the idea, as never having had a daughter of my own, or any experience of looking after young girls, I was not sure how I would cope. Also, it was a very busy week for me. I would have liked to refuse, but dear Pepe Santa Cruz was such an old friend that I eventually said yes.

A few weeks later, in my new role as chaperone and feeling very apprehensive, I took off for Barcelona with three very attractive young ladies whom Pepe Santa Cruz and I thought would be good representatives for the UK. My contribution to their choice was that not only were they attractive, but I had always seen them behaving well and looking exceptionally well groomed and well turned out during the season. Also, all three had especially good manners.

They were Miss Stephanie de Laszlo, now Mrs Roger Williams, Lady Melissa Bligh, now Lady Melissa Levey, and Lady Mariota Murray, now Lady Mariota Napier. The latter's mother, the Countess of Mansfield, had asked me to take special care of Mariota, and not to let her out of my sight.

We were invited from Wednesday to Sunday, and to stay at the Ritz in Barcelona, where I stipulated we must have a large suite with a sitting room, not single rooms, so that I had all three girls under my eye. This had been agreed to. We flew out in an Iberia Airlines Caravelle. I found Prince Frederick of Prussia on the flight on his way to Majorca and Germany, and he seemed highly amused at me with my trio!

On arrival at Barcelona airport we were met by a party, headed by Señorita Carmen Lagarde, other members of the ball committee, and three escorts for the young British debutantes, among them the very good-looking Don Luis Mata y Satrustegui, known as 'Chippy'. When we had collected our luggage I suddenly saw the three girls being whisked off by their escorts in separate cars! I felt exactly as I am sure a hen does who has been sitting on duck's eggs when the ducklings first hatch and take to the water. I immediately thought of dear Dorothea

Mansfield's words! (How Jocelyn Stevens, my employer, laughed when I returned and told him the story.)

I got into the car with Señorita Lagarde as quickly as I could, and set off for the Ritz, where I was relieved to find my protégées had all arrived safely. We went up to our palatial suite, unpacked, bathed and changed. At 8 p.m., I took the girls and their escorts to Sandos, where we had a light meal outside before the rehearsal for the ball at the Palacio National de Mountjuich, which began at 10 p.m. and went on until after midnight. Then we were taken to Tres Rolinos to see a cabaret of flamenco dancers, after which the three girls danced to a very good dance band until after 2 a.m. I of course had to stay on as chaperone. We got to bed around 3 a.m. I had an 8 a.m. call to get some writing done.

My trio were all fast asleep when I left at 11.15 a.m. to make a tour of the very modern exhibition hall of the silk and textile industry with Señorita Mercedes Tintore as my guide. I got back to the hotel about 1.45 p.m. and found my dear protégées just ready and the four of us went down to luncheon in the Ritz restaurant. In the afternoon we drove to see the Spanish village and the cathedral. Then it was back to change and on to an official reception at 6 p.m. at the Colegio del Aste Mayor de la Seda. From there we went to a much larger reception at the Town Hall given by the Mayor of Barcelona at which King Simeon of Bulgaria and the stately Begum Aga Khan were the guests of honour.

Afterwards we went on to a lovely apartment belonging to Señor and Señora Roca, whose young son Señor Rogelio Roca had arranged a buffet dinner for some of the debutantes and a number of charming young men, which was a very jolly party. At 10.30 p.m. there was another rehearsal, this one ending long after midnight.

Then I became a very strict chaperone! I firmly refused all pleas to allow the girls to go on to a nightclub to dance. I felt tomorrow's ball was the all-important event and the British debutantes must look fresh and rested for it. The girls again had a long lie-in, then we went to do a little shopping before lunching at 2 p.m. at the Ritz, where among others lunching were Salvador Dali and his wife, and film star John Wayne. I insisted on the girls having a siesta before going to the hairdresser, Carita, which was an absolute nightmare as they had to wait one and a half hours before they were started. Each debutante had to wear the same headdress: a band of white satin with two iridescent bobbles. This made it an awful rush to be on time, but we made it.

I felt very proud of the three UK debutantes, who all looked lovely and beautifully turned out in their long well-cut white dresses and long white gloves (Mariota wore her Murray tartan sash across her white dress). They all carried themselves so well as they walked down the wide crimson-covered staircase of the Palacio National de Montjuich, which is oblong and twice the size of our Albert Hall; 1,800 were seated for supper, and with a large dance floor there was no squash. The ball itself was a magnificent spectacle and exceedingly well run in every way. The debutantes walked slowly down the long stairs, made their curtsey to the guest of honour, who, if I remember rightly, was the Infanta Doña Pilar de Borbón, then took up their position each side of the stage with a given signal when, one by one, their escorts arrived; then together they walked down a long raised platform to the end of the hall to a raised dance floor. When they had all assembled, the band played an old-fashioned waltz, they danced, and when that ended they descended to their tables. I was very impressed by the beautiful dresses, especially those worn by the Spanish debutantes, mostly in the stiffest white slipper satin or wild silk. They all looked far better turned out than debutantes at Queen Charlotte's Ball.

After the first course, we had about forty pipers, drummers and dancers of the Argyll and Sutherland Highlanders Pipe Band, who had been flown out for the ball, then a dress show from the Spanish couture houses, followed by a young French crooner, Françoise Hardy. There were three different bands and dancing went on until 4 a.m! The debutantes were given a lovely gift pack of scent, toiletries, a pair of nylons and a super silk scarf. It was an extremely elegant and gracious evening. The Spanish papers all gave the British debutantes wonderful praise.

I was interested when, during the ball, a sweet debutante from Belgium came up to me and said how lucky the English girls were to have someone to protect them, as she had not wanted to go night-clubbing the previous evening, but no one would listen when she said 'no'. Also that my girls had had things arranged for them that the others were left out of. After this, I felt perhaps my trip had been worthwhile!

I think the three debutantes enjoyed themselves. I found it an interesting and enjoyable three days, but I was very relieved to leave Stephanie and Mariota, who had both been angelic and behaved impeccably, safely back with their parents. Melissa went on to stay with Spanish friends.

In 1964 I suffered great grief when my second beloved brother, Peter Kemp-Welch, died in the London Clinic of heart failure. He had had a bad coronary two years previously, brought on by years of overwork, and although he took six months off to convalesce before returning to the City, he never really got over it, dying at the early age of fifty-six years.

I still miss him dreadfully – his unfailing kindness, sound advice, and irresistible sense of humour. As children, George, he and I had never had a cross word. Fortunately, Peter's son John, my beloved nephew, has inherited much of his father and uncle's personalities and kindness and sense of humour, and he is very dear to me.

This was one of those times in my life when I was grateful to have a demanding job that simply had to go on, forcing one to hide one's innermost feelings. I had planned a trip abroad that January which had been postponed because of my brother's illness. Two days after his funeral, however, I took off as previously planned.

After four or five very social days in Barbados, I flew to Jamaica to make my usual round of visits. Next I caught a Mexicana Airways Comet from Montego Bay to Mexico City. We landed at Merida, where I found I should have had a tourist card with a Mexican visa to enter Mexico. I had nothing but my passport, valid for all countries, and my health certificates. Happily, after I explained, they issued the necessary entry and exit form.

I found this visit especially interesting. Firstly I learnt that in Mexico City you could not rush about, as with the great height you were soon breathless. I was staying with Mr and Mrs Patrick Tritton, whose house was fascinating: it had a swimming pool in its centre with a very wide surround where we could enjoy an informal lunch or dinner. Nancy Tritton very sweetly met me at the airport and we went straight off to a *despedida* (farewell) party being given by Mr and Mrs Toby Hildyard, now Sir David and Lady Hildyard; he was then the Counsellor at the British Embassy. I remember Toby and Millicent Hildyard had a fascinating Japanese-style house where, instead of a staircase from floor to floor, there was a wide carpeted ramp.

Patrick and Nancy Tritton very kindly also flew me down for the weekend, with two other couples, to Acapulco, and I had a guest cottage next to theirs at the Las Brisas Hilton, where each cottage has its own private swimming pool, sunbathing mattresses, a little lawn with a table and chairs for breakfast and any other meals you wanted sent up from the hotel. The room and telephone service were exceptionally good. Transport was then inclusive throughout the grounds and to and from La Concha Beach. The Las Brisas jeeps were very picturesque, painted pale mauve with a striped canopy and a fringe all round.

The rest of the party, besides swimming in their pools, swam in the sea from a boat, but as I can't swim, film star Dolores del Rio, whom I met the first evening, said I was to use her sandy beach in front of her house to bathe from, which I did, as well as using my own pool.

During our stay we visited several fantastic homes in the area; one had a waterfall and stream running down the centre. Another had the bedrooms all opening right on to a large swimming pool in the centre, the other side of the bedrooms looking out on to a garden. One night we dined around 10 p.m. at La Perlo, where the tables are arranged on terraces overlooking a narrow stretch of sea coming in between two high cliffs. The big attraction here is to watch a diver climb down one side, swim across to the other cliff, climb 160 feet to the top, then do a swallow dive from the top into the narrow stretch of water below. A hair-raising performance!

I met an amazing number of people that weekend, some with houses, some in hotels, but nearly all on holiday, from all over America and the rest of the world.

That July I visited Beirut for the first time, for the Bal des Petits Lits Blancs, to which I had been invited by the French organizers, who flew two aeroplanes of 200 specially chosen guests from Paris, plus hairdressers Alexandre himself, Carita, and André Flessati from Elizabeth Arden to do the wonderful coiffures. I flew alone from London.

I stayed at the Phoenicia Hotel where, when I arrived in my room, I was a bit shaken to see an Arab's white robes, headband and so on on the floor. Soon all that was sorted out and I had a comfortable stay in an airy room with a balcony overlooking the sea.

On the first evening, we were all invited to a reception at his lovely home given by Mr Henry Bey Pharaon. He bought this house originally in Damascus, and moved it to Beirut! From here around 10 p.m. we went on to a gala dinner at the casino at Maalmein, high up eighteen kilometres from the city. There were around 400 guests, all seated outdoors, and the longest buffet possible serving Lebanese specialities. (I made a big mistake with my second course, choosing very high mutton, and had to lose it around a pot plant!) A band played during dinner and later there were fireworks; when we went into the casino we saw a spectacular cabaret. After this, many of the guests moved into the gambling rooms and I returned to my hotel room as by now it was after 2 a.m.

Next day, Mrs Edouard Asseilly, a very dear Lebanese lady whom I had met in London, sent her car for me to go to look at the gold market and on to her charming house, Villa Darna, high up on Raseljabely. In the evening came the *pièce de résistance*. It was the first time the Bal des Petits Lits Blancs, which I had been to before and which had been held in various parts of France, had ever been held abroad. The organization was amazingly good.

Around 9 p.m., we left the hotel in about fifty Hertz cars, which had been reserved for the party for the whole weekend, to drive the 40 kilometres in convoy to Bieteddine. My Lebanese driver was an amusing character and drove a large Pontiac at great speed. He had arranged with the other drivers that we would lead the convoy behind three policemen on motorcycles with screaming sirens which cleared our way right up the mountain road. It was a fascinating sight to look back and see the headlights of the other forty-nine cars wending their way up like a golden caterpillar.

On arrival at the Palace of the Emir Bechir at Bieteddine there was first of all a guard of honour of soldiers, then the traditional bodyguard of the Palace in their colourful livery holding lighted flares. Guests went into the immense inner courtyard, which was carpeted and floodlit, to their allotted tables. In the centre was a large lily pond on which yellow and white dahlias floated. The fabulous buffet ran down two sides of the courtyard. There was everything: caviar from Iran, crab from Alaska, fresh lobsters from Turkey, pâté de foie gras galore, reindeer, roast swan, and roast red peacock from New Zealand presented with its fan of feathers as a background.

There were two excellent bands and a star-studded cabaret including Gilbert Becaud and Jacques Charon. There was also a parade of mannequins in couture clothes and jewels from the top Paris houses.

But it was the women guests who really stole the evening. I have never seen so many really beautiful dresses, Lebanese and French, and so many elegant, immaculately coiffed ladies. They wore fabulous jewels, too, including quite a few tiaras. I sat at Charlotte Asseilly's table and she looked extremely chic in a dress of white slipper satin with no jewels except an exquisite pearl and turquoise tiara, and a chinchilla stole. Madame Giscard d'Estaing, accompanied by her husband, looked very attractive and chic in a dress by Maggy Rouff; and Vicomtesse de Ribes looked marvellous with flowers in her hair done by Alexandre. I think she must have arranged to be in the last car of the convoy, so that she was able to make her usual late entry when everyone was seated. At 3.30 a.m., to end the ball, there was a fantastic display of fireworks. Then several hundred of the 850 guests at the ball, including myself, drove sixty kilometres to see the dawn break at the ancient ruins of Baalbeck, where hot coffee and croissants were served. It was an amazing sight to see everyone in their evening dress, still looking soignée walking in the sunshine among these magnificent ruins. I shall never forget that sunrise.

ELEVEN

Racing everywhere
(1965–70)

Ascot is by far my favourite racecourse. To me it is always a joy to race here. You can see the racing so well; everything at Ascot is so well kept and organized; the staff are exceptionally polite, and because the racecourse is owned by The Queen, you get the feeling of private enterprise, which the Clerk of the Course, Captain the Hon. Nicholas Beaumont, carries out so very efficiently. He has the cooperation of The Queen's Representative, Colonel Sir Piers Bengough, who is also most efficient. They make a marvellous team.

One of the biggest improvements in racing in the sixties was the opening of the new Queen Elizabeth II Grandstand at Ascot in 1961, and the rebuilding of the members' stand, including the Royal Box, a little later, around 1964. Royal Ascot took place as usual with all its pageantry each year, though the weather in the form of wet days took its toll. For example, in 1964 the rain on the first day and torrential rain on the second caused racing to be cancelled on the Thursday and Friday as well as the Ascot Heath meeting on the Saturday, when they had planned to run eleven races!

In the early 1960s a very dear friend gave me one of his Jockey Club badges for all four days of Royal Ascot, a privilege he has gallantly kept up ever since. This, besides my Royal Enclosure badge, has been the greatest help as I have always had somewhere to sit and watch the racing in comfort, and I shall always be grateful to that dear friend. Besides the royal meeting I also always enjoy Diamond Day at Ascot, which is usually the last Saturday in July. This is when de Beers sponsor the ladies' race, and the now famous and valuable King George V and Queen Elizabeth Stakes, which always draws the best three-year-olds and upwards in Europe.

The Derby and Oaks have made Epsom famous, and racegoers there, with the exception of box holders, have put up with quite a lot of discomfort for years, in both the Grandstand and the Members. In addition, the paddock is a very long walk from the stands. But big improvements have recently been made. Both stands and the boxes have been rebuilt, but the paddock remains where it was.

At Newmarket, where they frequently seem to rebuild and alter their stands, sometimes for the better, sometimes for the worse!, they always produce good racing. Over the years I have also usually gone up to Newmarket for Tattersalls' special yearling sales at the end of September or first week in October, and again for a day or two of their December Sales. I found it fascinating to watch how the price of good bloodstock rose and rose until it became difficult for anyone except multi-millionaires to compete in buying, as yearlings were changing hands at several million guineas! Those days have passed for the moment as the current recession has hit racing, as it has so many things.

On the National Hunt scene, I usually went to the Grand Military meeting at Sandown, which is always fun, and where you used to meet numerous friends in the three services whom you seldom saw on other occasions. I don't think I missed a National Hunt meeting at Cheltenham during the sixties.

The Grand National meeting at Aintree was flourishing at that time. I always had my seat in the County stand, as well as an open invitation to Mrs Topham's box. Each year other kind friends invited me to luncheon.

The 1965 Grand National particularly impressed me. It was won by Jay Trump, owned by American Mrs Mary Stephensen of Ohio, and ridden by the young American jockey Mr Tommy Smith.

This was a well-deserved win, the culmination of a well-thought-out plan. After Jay Trump had won the very demanding Maryland Hunt Cup twice, the horse was sent to England weeks in advance of the Grand National to get acclimatized with Mr Fred Winter, then in his first season as a trainer. Tommy Smith was there too, for good measure. They could not have given the horse to anyone with more knowledge of Aintree than Fred Winter, who had ridden there on so many occasions, so it was good to see this careful planning work so perfectly.

I personally much prefer flat racing to National Hunt racing. By the sixties, sponsorship was beginning to figure more in racing, and has increased each year, until it is now an essential part of most meetings.

In the mid-sixties, Jocelyn Stevens inaugurated the Oxford and Cambridge Shooting Match each March at the Holland and Holland Shooting School. Six young men from each university come to shoot clay pigeons. The teams first shoot singly in a butt at would-be grouse and one woodcock or snipe, then the teams move to an adjacent field where in teams of three they shoot at would-be driven pheasants that come over high and fast from a high tower in the trees. Then all the points are added up, and the highest wins the Queen Cup. I used to give a Jennifer's Trophy for the best single score.

The young men who compete are always charming. There is tremendous rivalry and happy bantering and they seem to enjoy it all. When it started, it was an afternoon affair, and one year the Oxford team arrived in a helicopter! It was changed after a few years by the very nice Mr Freddie Griffiths Jones, who was in charge of Holland and Holland's wonderful shooting school for many years, as he thought that it would be safer if the shooting took place in the morning! Now the teams lunch extremely well after the shooting and the prize-giving in Holland and Holland's very nice clubhouse.

When Jocelyn Stevens sold *Queen*, I asked that this event should continue, and I have, with the exception of two years, gone there each time to watch the boys shoot and to present the prizes. I am glad to learn that the tradition is continuing now that I have retired.

During the sixties and seventies, I went to quite a few of the annual International Daily Express Powerboat Races from Cowes to Torquay. Quite honestly, I found this race so much more exciting to watch than the sailing yachts during regatta week in Cowes! This year, 1965, was I think the one I enjoyed the most.

I caught a train from Waterloo to Portsmouth on a Thursday evening. Here I took a taxi to the Hovercraft landing beach at Southsea. In a flash, I and my luggage were on board the Hovercraft on our way to Ryde, where we landed six minutes later after a very choppy crossing. I went straight to the Ryde Castle Hotel, where I had booked a room. After a quick bath and change I went down to find Mr Pocock, my invaluable car hire driver for the Isle of Wight, waiting for me. Pocock also drove a very popular local hearse, so by day I sometimes had to fit in with his funeral arrangements, but there were no problems in the evening.

I set off for Cowes for the buffet supper party that Sir Max Aitken and Mr Tommy Sopwith were giving jointly to welcome overseas competitors taking part in the race two days later. The party took place in the original big sail drying room of the Prospect, Max Aitken's fascinating home at Cowes, which is right on the sea with its own landing stage.

Next morning I went over to Cowes, where my first stop was at the Powerboat Race information office to collect a programme. Here I found the honorary secretary Tommy Sopwith, who, on hearing I contemplated trying to see the scrutineering at Clark's Yard, angelically said he would take me himself if I could wait. I knew if Tommy took me I would learn far more than otherwise, so of course I waited. I was very impressed when ten minutes later, standing outside his office, Tommy picked up his walkie-talkie and called his yacht *Philante* to ask them to send a boat to the Squadron steps. At that moment, two Post Office officials spotted Tommy, and suddenly stepped forward in the street and asked him if he had a licence for the walkie-talkie as they were checking up. They were rather overawed when he promptly replied 'Yes', and then with his usual quiet efficiency also gave his code call.

Thirteen-year-old Maxwell Aitken, now the 3rd Lord Beaverbrook, came with us to the beautiful motor yacht *Philante*, which was moored just behind where the boats were being scrutinized, and was being used for testing the radios of the competing boats, which had to pass the rules laid down for the race. The object of the rules was to encourage the building of boats which are suitable for offshore cruising and racing. The race boats had to be between 18ft and 40ft on the waterline, powered by petrol engines of less than 16.4 litres, or diesel engines of under 32.9 litres. They had to have full accommodation appropriate to their size, and, above all, they had to undergo the most stringent scrutineering of all safety equipment.

Young Maxwell Aitken volunteered to take me ashore in a smaller rubber boat which he manoeuvred very efficiently. I went to luncheon with Mrs Dick Fremantle, who had a flat overlooking the sea between the Prospect and Admiral's Walk, where she had a small luncheon party. After lunch, we watched some of the competitors, then I drove back to Ryde to change, and back to Cowes for the very important briefing followed by a cocktail party at the Royal Corinthian Yacht Club. The new Governor of the Isle of Wight, Admiral of the Fleet Earl Mountbatten of Burma, who was to start the race next day from the Royal Yacht Squadron, came to the briefing and party.

Next morning I left the hotel at 8.30 a.m., to allow for extra traffic, to get to the start in good time. On arrival at the Royal Yacht Squadron I was greeted by the dear 5th Marquess Brecky Camden, the Vice Commodore, who had very kindly said I could watch the start from outside the Ladies' Annexe, which was a splendid vantage point. Soon the officials were on the platform in front of the Royal Yacht Squadron, and Earl Mountbatten was just about to take up his position behind the starting gun. After the two warning guns we saw, on the horizon, the starting boat HMS *Brave Borderer* coming along at a terrific speed, then a fleet of around fifty competitors, throttles open, roaring up to the starting line before the final gun went for their gruelling 198-mile race. That was, as always, the most thrilling spectacle to watch. After the starting gun went the brothers Charles and Jimmy Gardner, who had won the race the previous year, quickly flashed into the lead in their new boat *Sunfury*, followed by Dick Bertram in *Brave Moppie*, Tommy Sopwith in *Thunderstruck* and the favourite Jim Wynne in *Maritime*. When they came past the Squadron next time, *Sunfury* and *Brave Moppie* were still leading the way. At this stage we saw Bill Shand Kydd in *Lucytoo*, who was then third, swerve badly and stop! After adjustments and a long delay, he rejoined the race behind all the others and, amazingly, eventually finished eighth, a very fine performance. When the boats came past the Squadron for the third time (I cannot remember how many times they did this before heading for Torquay!) having completed 58 miles of the course, *Sunfury* and *Brave Moppie* were still neck and neck, well ahead of the others. Just before Portland Bill, *Sunfury* had to stop when a nut had worked loose and had to be adjusted, so lost her second place. At the finish it was *Brave Moppie* first, followed by *Thunderbird* driven by Merrick Lewis and Peter Twiss; and *Sunfury*, who had come back into the race to finish third. The Earl of Lucan was among the competitors that year, driving his *Migrant*, and finishing seventh. That year for the first time there was a return race next day direct from Torquay to Cowes, a much shorter route, but I did not stay for that. I returned to London by Hovercraft and train after the boats had set out for Torquay.

In October I was invited by friends in Deauville to join a party flying from Paris to New York in a chartered Air France Boeing 707. The object of the journey was to attend the fourteenth 'April in Paris Ball' that takes place annually in New York in October! This year Mrs Laddie Sandford, wife of the great polo player and a great supporter of charity, whom I knew from Palm Beach, was Chairman of the ball and the theme was 'Deauville, Ville du Cheval', where so many Americans have, like myself, enjoyed very happy times.

We took off from Paris at 2.15 p.m. local time. We had a blissfully comfortable flight with perfect service and landed at 6.30 p.m. New York time. It was quite a slow but at times amusing experience getting through customs with all the luggage. According to New York radio later that evening, we had arrived with over 400 pieces! One French lady I saw had an enormous wardrobe trunk in which I was told was her ballgown and seven pieces of smaller luggage!

The whole trip was most beautifully arranged for us. A fleet of black Cadillacs were at the airport to meet us and take us to the Waldorf Astoria on Park Avenue, where the ball was to take place and where we were all to stay. By the time we all got to our rooms it was 8.30 p.m. I decided to skip dinner, deal with the many telephone messages that were awaiting me, and unpack.

Next morning the telephone began at 8 a.m. and never seemed to stop, which curtailed my shopping, but I managed to have lunch and tea with friends and do a little shopping before the great ball that evening.

The ball, which is run in aid of French charities, occupied not only the Grand Ballroom, which has tiers of boxes all round, but also another five or six large reception rooms. It certainly was a fabulous spectacle. Each side of the wide foyer leading to the ballroom there was an imposing row of prancing white horses about fifteen feet high, with wide sashes round their necks in various French and American racing colours. Two more of these horses had been placed each side of a stage at one end of the ballroom, where a veritable Normandy orchard of apple trees had been arranged. There were also fountains playing in the centre to represent those on the Plage Fleurie in Deauville. Smaller prancing white horses around two foot high were on all the dinner tables. The entire decor had been donated by Mrs Alfred S. Levitt, who brought a big party to the ball. There were two points during the evening that I thought bad. Firstly, they ran out of programmes – I never managed to get one, which I really needed to work from; and secondly, the dinner was badly chosen and inedible, which all the French guests noticed.

Before dinner, when everyone was seated, Mrs Sandford, who had made a wonderful chairman, and the Duc de Fezensac both made short speeches thanking everyone who had helped. Then came an amazing and moving scene – the retiring Mayor of New York Mayor Wagner, Comte Michel d'Ornano, and Monsieur Albert Chavanac paraded round the ballroom with the French and American colours carried by units of the Army, Navy, Air Force, Marines and Coast Guards. They then stood in the centre while both the French and American National Anthems were played. There were over 1,300 guests present, including the Duke and Duchess of Windsor. The ball raised a very large sum for the French charities.

On Saturday Mrs Laddie Sanford invited some of us to go racing at Aquaduct. On Sunday Mr and Mrs Ogden Phipps invited some members of the party including myself to luncheon at their beautiful home, Old Westbury, on Long Island. That evening the French Consul-General and Madame Michel Legendre gave a party at the French Consulate. Next day we flew home.

In January 1966 I went with Mr Robin McAlpine, later Sir Robin McAlpine, and his wife on a house-hunting trip to the south of Spain. This was a new type of venture for me and I found it most enjoyable. The weather was wonderful and Nora McAlpine and I wore cotton frocks, sometimes with a cardigan, in mid-January. We stayed at Los Montoros, a hotel and a few private houses which was then one of Spain's new luxury developments, situated between Marbella and Malaga. The Duke and Duchess of Windsor and the widow of the Duke of Windsor's good friend Biddy Viscountess Monckton of Brenchley were also staying at Los Monteros, the Windsors in one of the cottages.

On our first day we drove over to the Marbella Club for luncheon, and then off into the country as Nora McAlpine wanted a house inland and within easy reach of Malaga airport, as Gibralter was still closed for entering Spain. A friend of Nora's had written to say she had six possible houses for her to see, but the friend had suddenly had to go to Madrid to a sick relative, so had left instructions with her maid Trina. So before we set off for the country we located Trina and arranged to see some of the properties the following day, and then took a drive up to Monda via the picturesque village of Ojen, where a group of women were sitting in a flower-covered recess of the mountain street doing their sewing and crochet, while a little further on their men were sitting talking or dozing in the sun outside the local inn. We drove back to Los Monteros on another route with equally picturesque villages.

Next day, when we collected Trina, we found we also had to take the local hairdresser, Paquita, who owned a lot of property in the country and knew of various houses. These two ladies were no lightweights! We eventually arrived at the first house high on the mountain with a superb view. Both Trina and Paquita clapped their hands to try and attract the farm workers to come and open the house, but without success. Then, being rather embarrassed, and with typical Spanish

charm, they quickly picked some wildflowers and oranges and presented us with them.

At Coin we stopped to get some petrol. By now our hired car was
jogging a bit and it was touch and go whether we would get up the
next mountain. My host nursed the car and we made it, but on arriving
at the second house found the gates locked. Our hearts sank at the
thought of not being able to get in, but happily this time the farm
workers responded to Trina and Paquita's calls and produced keys to
let us in. The car by now was going worse than ever, so we decided
to abandon looking at the third house, which was miles further up the
mountain. Instead we descended towards Malaga, as a lot of the journey was downhill. As we passed through Alhauren El Grande I suddenly saw Mr Robert Belmont, whom I had known since he was a
young boy, working in his orchard. So we stopped and told him of
our car trouble, and Robert at once got hold of his local mechanic.
Meanwhile we went in and spent a happy time with Robert Belmont's
wife Harriette. Eventually, after taking our two escorts to their homes,
we arrived at Los Monteros around 8.30 p.m. and dined around 10.

Next day the Hertz garage sent a man to deal successfully with the
car, so we did a little more house-hunting on our own.

Next day we set off at 10.15 a.m. in the Seat, which was running
well, with a local taxi to carry Trina and Paquita. When we picked
them up we found that Paquita's husband, Antonio, was coming as
well, so the hairdressing business had to be closed for the day. We
drove on up the mountains, and about halfway between Ojen and
Monda there was a signal from the taxi to stop. We turned off the
road down a wobbly cart track which became rougher and rougher
until we could go no further. At this point Antonio took over and said
we would have to walk the rest of the way. He said we would then
find a big house with plenty of water, but no light or telephone. It
transpired later he had never seen it. There was no house in sight, but
we set off, little knowing that we would have to walk for an hour and
a quarter! Eventually, when we arrived, there was the most wonderful
panorama imaginable, but the house was a derelict shell! It was in the
middle of a large estate which the owners, who lived in another part
of Spain, only used for partridge shooting. Happily there were a few
orange trees near the house, so we picked a few oranges to quench our
thirst. We then walked back down, which, though rough going, was
much easier than the climb up. It was another glorious day, so for me,
away from my usual hectic social round, the whole adventure was fun.

As we had brought a picnic we decided to go back to the rather nice-looking house where we had not been able to get in the previous day. While our escorts were getting the keys, we had our picnic lunch sitting on the terrace in glorious sunshine. Our escorts came back with the owner, who, when he put the large key in the door, could not open it. A lot of panting and puffing went on – it really was a hilarious picture – and eventually Antonio managed to turn the key and open the door. Inside it was pretty primitive, with no sanitation or water and prehistoric kitchen arrangements, so we left to see two more houses in Coin, neither of which was possible. While we were here Paquita insisted on us going round her brother's enormous chicken factory. Here we saw thousands of day-old chicks on trays in six-foot containers, a room full of incubators, one full of fattening cockerels and others full of laying hens and pullets. There was a lot of shaking hands and happy banter before we left. After this little diversion we went on to see another house at Chririana. The house was far too near a new building development, so we did not look inside. From here we went back to the hotel.

Next day it was raining hard, so we only went as far as the Los Monteros Golf Club, where there is a fine eighteen-hole golf course. In the afternoon we again went house-hunting, again without any success. On Sunday we drove up to Ronda on what was then a most hazardous and lethal road, with no protection from a sheer drop of hundreds of feet, winding round and round the mountain. Once in Ronda, we went to see the oldest bull ring in Spain and stood in the centre, which was interesting to see at close quarters. I have never been to a bull fight and I never want to go. We then went inside what the locals call their cathedral, where we found a superb silver altar at the far end, opposite the main altar, which was of a magnificent and very decorative gold. We lunched at the Reine Victoria Hotel.

On Monday we set off by car to spend a couple of nights at Puerta de Santa Maria. On our way we stopped for luncheon in the restaurant of the Golf Club at Sotogrande. Sotogrande was then a new luxury development of 3,200 acres, with only the eighteen-hole golf course designed by the famous Robert Trent Jones, the clubhouse, and twelve guest cottages and two or three private houses. Next day we motored into Jerez de la Frontera and went straight to the Gonzalez Byass Bodega, which covers a vast acreage of this town. This firm, most famous perhaps for Tio Pepe, took over a small bodega here in 1835, and by 1966 they had over 500 employees. I was amused to hear that each male employee here was given one bottle of sherry every day to take home, and each woman half a bottle! They are not allowed to drink on the premises. It was nearly 3 p.m. before we left for luncheon at the little fishing port of Sanlucar de Barrameda. Here we lunched outside at a small restaurant right on the beach where they specialize in seafood. The weather suddenly deteriorated and the fishing boats started coming into port. A bell was sounded to announce a fish market on the beach. Donkey carts and barrows quickly arrived to take the fish away. Our restaurant's proprietor was one of the officials, so excused himself to go to the beach where each catch is laid out neatly before the auctioneer comes along. Our luncheon was very simple and fun.

Next day we set off to see a house we had heard about in Jerez. We went up the twisty road through Mijas. The house was charming and we left hoping it would prove the winner, as we were leaving for England the next day. It did prove a winner and Nora McAlpine was happy at getting it redecorated and so on, but sadly she never lived there as she died September the following, very quickly, after cancer had been diagnosed. I felt her death tremendously as she was one of my very dearest friends. In a couple of years her sister-in-law Sheila McAlpine gradually took Nora's place in my heart, and is today my best friend.

At this time Mr James Hanson, now Lord Hanson, whose family transport firm had provided a most successful transport service for business and industry in the UK and North America for over a hundred years, had recently started Air Hanson. That year he had ordered six Hawker-Siddeley 125 jets, which flew at 40,000 feet at a speed of 500 mph, and hoped to have all six in service within twelve months. In August James very sweetly asked me if I would like the use of one of these jets for part of a weekend, which would give publicity to the new air service. The firm had recently been asked to arrange a schedule for a big company, who wanted to fit in meetings at five different European airports. Air Hanson worked out that if they left London airport at 8 a.m. and returned at 9 p.m., they could hold a meeting of one hour at Nice, Milan, Frankfurt, Copenhagen, and Brussels, having lunch in the air between Milan and Frankfurt! It all worked.

James Hanson said he would come as far as Nice with me, joining his wife and sons at the Hôtel du Cap at Antibes, and bringing two friends; but that I could arrange what I liked. It was a most comfortable aeroplane inside with two high-back armchairs, and two sofas seating three and two, so that you could seat seven. We were only four. There was a pilot and co-pilot. On landing at Nice on Friday afternoon there were two cars to meet us, and we went in different directions.

I went to Monte Carlo for a big dinner party that evening. Then, next morning, I went on to La Garoupe to stay with Anne and Antony Norman, who had a party that evening.

On Sunday I was up very early and at 7.40 a.m. I said goodbye to my kind host and hostess, and left for Nice airport. Here I found Captain Burns, one of the HS 125 pilots, already waiting for me with someone to take my bags to the waiting aeroplane. All I had to do was show my passport before walking to a car which took us right up to the HS 125 where Captain Taylor was already on board. As I was the only passenger, I settled into one of the comfy armchairs and fastened my seatbelt, whereupon Captain Burns handed me a wonderful selection of the English Sunday papers and, later, some piping hot coffee. What super service!

We took off at 8.30 a.m. and flew at 25,000 feet, having been allowed to fly the direct route; we landed in exactly one hour at Palma airport in Majorca. Captain Burns took care of me through customs to the waiting car, which had been arranged by Air Hanson. My driver was Matao, a well-known Palma personality, in a Seat from the Hotel Phoenix. First we drove for an hour and a quarter to the Costa de Los Pinos, where I visited the Marquesa de Santa Cruz at her enchanting small summer house built right over the sea.

Around 12.30 I went on to luncheon with Mr and Mrs Gilbert Miller in their luxurious home; here the swimming pool was fitted with jacuzzis all along one side, which was very avant garde in the sixties. I had a bathe before luncheon, when we were joined by Mr Michael Renshaw who was staying at the Millers, and by Mr and Mrs Peter Thorneycroft, later Lord and Lady Thorneycroft, who were staying at the Eurotel. Peter Thorneycroft arrived on a moped, which he was using for getting around to beauty spots in order to paint. We had luncheon at 2 p.m., and during luncheon I discovered Micky Renshaw was having great difficulty getting on a direct flight to Nice next day. So, trying not to appear grand, I was able to offer him a lift in the HS 125 next morning, which he gladly accepted.

After a very happy time talking to dear Gilbert and Kitty Miller, who were neighbours of mine in London and always so kind, I left at 4 p.m. and drove on to Cala Ratjada to see a young friend who was working there that summer. Then on by car via Picafort and Puerto de Pollensa, to Formentor. Here I popped into the Formentor Hotel, where I stayed on my first visit to Formentor years earlier.

Then on up the hill to Mr and Mrs Vane Ivanović's really beautiful house high up above Formentor Bay, with terraces down to the sea, where I was going to spend the night. Vane and June Ivanović have been angelic friends to me for many years, and I have enjoyed many happy times staying with them and their family at Formentor.

That evening I was only greeted by June Ivanović and her dear mother-in-law Madame Milica Banac, as Vane had gone to the weekly Sunday night bullfight in Palma, and was coming back for a supper party around 10.30 p.m. This was arranged at softly lit tables on the lawn, with a nearly full moon and starry sky overhead.

Next morning I was up early and had a breakfast of hot coffee and figs in my room. When I came downstairs at 8.30, I found my dear host there to say goodbye, and Matao outside with the Seat to drive me to Palma airport. On arrival at the airport, I found Captain Burns and Captain Taylor waiting for me, having cleared all papers and formalities for the HS 125 to take off. Michael Renshaw was also ready, so we were quickly taken through customs and we boarded the plane for Nice, taking off as arranged at 10.30 a.m.

Captain Burns again in some miraculous way produced Monday's English morning papers and, later, coffee. We had another blissfully comfy flight to Nice, where I said goodbye to Mickie Renshaw and left my suitcases on the aeroplane, as I was going on to London later. A car and chauffeur were waiting to drive me to Antibes, where I was joining James and Geraldine Hanson for luncheon at Eden Roc, where masses of friends were also lunching.

Later James Hanson and I took off from Nice at around 4 p.m. local time and landed at Heathrow at 5.50 p.m., having had to circle to await our turn to land. I said goodbye to the two fine pilots who had flown the aeroplane so efficiently, and had taken the greatest care of me. I can honestly say that although I had fitted a lot in that weekend and come home with masses of copy, I was not at all tired.

This proved to me how absolutely invaluable a swift, smooth, and efficient air service is for high-powered executives, with a demanding schedule of international meetings and conferences for the ever increasing competitive markets of the world.

There was great interest in the sixties in the young Prince Karim Aga Khan's development on the Costa Smeralda in Italy. The year before, in 1965, I had thought of going there and discussed the matter with Jocelyn Stevens. He thought it was too early for me to go, from what he had heard of the progress of the development out there, so I abandoned the idea. That autumn, while lunching with Captain Kenneth Watt and other directors of Tattersalls at their Newmarket bloodstock sales, I sat next to Karim Aga Khan. I told him how I had changed my mind about visiting the Costa Smeralda that summer and he immediately said 'It will all be ready for you next year, so you must come out.' I went out in August 1966 and I was amazed and thrilled with all I saw.

The development had been beautifully planned and carefully carried out by the original consortium headed by the Aga Khan. They employed three of Europe's top architects, Signor Busirivici and Signor Luigi Vietti, with Frenchman Jacques Couelle, and the result is a lovely dream come true!

There are thirty-five miles of coastline and eighty glorious sandy beaches; the whole of the Costa Smeralda covers 30,000 acres of the province of Gallura. There are no high-rise buildings, no electric pylons, no hoardings or advertising of any kind, and no camping sites; these are all prohibited by the consortium.

On my first visit in 1966 there were four good hotels. I stayed at the very comfortable Cala di Volpe, where I had breakfast on my patio each morning. This hotel has its own private jetty, swimming pool and sandy beach. Inside it has an ancient atmosphere, but all modern comforts and air-conditioning throughout. In my brief stay over a weekend, Mr Rodney Scrase, who was working for the consortium, took me round and I visited the other three hotels, which all had charm.

When I went to lunch at the Hotel Pittrizza I saw Princess Margaret leaving in Karim Aga Khan's beautiful boat *Amaloun*. During my brief stay I visited Karim Aga Khan at his lovely villa, which has picture windows all round, and gives him a wonderful view of all that is going on in the area.

I was most impressed by the harbour, which is large and has every kind of modern equipment for luxury yachts. There was a regatta on that weekend, with over 150 yachts and other boats. The first person I met at the port was Signor Guido Giovanelli, the charming Vice-President of the YCI. Signor and Signora Brianavitch kindly invited me on board their lovely yacht *Susanna II*, which was having a successful season, having already won three major Mediterranean regattas.

Baron Edmond de Rothschild was there in *Gitana IV* and Viscount, Camrose in his fine boat *Idalia*.

On the Sunday evening, there was a prize-giving for the yacht racing. Karim Aga Khan made a very good speech and Princess Margaret presented the prizes. I and several others had to leave the prize-giving before it ended as we had suddenly heard that, owing to an accident in America, all the Nord Aviations 262s were being temporarily grounded and my Monday morning flight was cancelled. BEA from Alghero were already fully booked up. As I had to be in London by Monday evening, I was so grateful when Rodney Scrase, who had an appointment in the morning in Rome, said he would drive me with Sir Geoffrey Crowther, who also had an appointment in Rome next day, to Olbia to catch the night ferry. I had to pack two suitcases in ten minutes (sadly I left out three Pucci shirts that I never saw again!) and we eventually just made the ferry in time and managed to get three first-class cabins. On landing we drove to Rome airport, had breakfast, and I was lucky in getting a seat on the 9.55 a.m. Alitalia Caravelle flight to London and was home by 12.30pm.

At the end of August, Mr and Mrs Robert Sangster very kindly invited me to join them for a week in the Mediterranean on their blissfully comfortable 150-ton motor yacht *Tamarind*. My kind host sent a car to collect me from my flat to take me to London airport, where I met my hostess's teenage son and daughter Carlos and Anna Bianchi, who flew out to Malta with me in a BEA Comet. Jack and Margery Sangster were at the airport to meet us and we drove off to the yacht marina at Lazzaretto Creek in Ta'xbien, where we went on board *Tamarind*.

I unpacked and got settled in my luxurious cabin with masses of drawers and hanging space. At 5.30 p.m. I went with Margery Sangster and Carlos and Anna Bianchi in a car to look round Medina, the ancient capital of Malta. On our return, three other friends of the Sangsters had by now arrived to stay on board *Tamarind*. We dined on board and after dinner some of us went to the new Dragonara Palace Casino.

Next day the sun shone, I had breakfast on deck, and then we went off in *Tamarind* to look around Malta's coastline and anchor off the tiny island of Gozo. The crew lowered the launch and some of the party swam and waterskied before lunch, which we had on board in the very spacious air-conditioned dining saloon. We arrived back in the marina about 7 p.m., soon after which Mr Charles Forte, now

Lord Forte, and his son Rocco Forte came on board for a drink. Later we went with them further along the marina to have a look over Charles Forte's fine boat *Maria Luija*, in which he and his wife and all their family had been spending a holiday. Charles Forte had just recently bought the Phoenicia Hotel in Malta, where Jim and I spent Christmas back in the fifties.

We dined on board and said goodbye to Malta as we were taking off for Lampedusa, a tiny Italian island on the way to Tunisia, at 6 a.m. next morning. On Friday we were travelling nearly all day – it was an eleven-hour journey – and dropped anchor at about 5 p.m. Some of the party had a swim from the boat, then five of us went ashore in the launch to look around Lampedusa. A fleet of colourful local fishing boats, each fitted with a large lamp, were setting out for a night's fishing. We landed at the little fishing harbour, bought some postcards at the local shop, which sold everything from salami to Palmolive soap, and then strolled up the ancient streets, where nearly all the families seemed to be sitting on their doorsteps as the sun set. It was dark as we went back to *Tamarind*, which started off again before dinner for our next stop, Djerba, where Matthews, our excellent skipper, expected us to arrive around 9 a.m. the next day.

I was on deck by 8.30 a.m., by which time we could see Djerba. I soon learnt that on the charts there was only a very narrow channel of any depth to get into the harbour, and that had to be followed very carefully. Very soon this became too shallow and Matthews learnt from a passing fisherman that we would have to wait until the high tide at 2 p.m. After breakfast my host decided we should take the launch, with the skipper, into the port at Houmt Souk and explore the possibilities.

On arrival in the little harbour we found several old-fashioned merchant ships tied up unloading, and we had to climb across two of them to land as there was no other way. Their crew spoke no French or Italian, but by means of signs and smiling faces we landed! By now the skipper realized there was no way of getting *Tamarind* in here. There were no officials to see and stamp our passports, and no sign of transport until a boy on a moped arrived and went off to get us two taxis, which took us first to the very modern Ulysse Palace hotel, where we changed some money and learnt where the police headquarters were so that we could get our passports stamped.

We made a tour around, then lunched and swam at the Ulysse Palace, and some of the party rode camels. We dined on board, and some of the party played bridge or backgammon. I played a little of

the latter and strolled round the deck by moonlight before bed at
11 p.m. I had woken early every morning, so I had been able to get
two hours' writing in and more or less keep up to date.

The engines did not start up until 6 a.m. on Sunday. We were on
route for Gabes, where there is the biggest oasis in the world. I was
on deck around 8.45 a.m., land was in sight, the sky was brilliant blue
and so was the sea. At 10.30 a.m, Margery Sangster, the skipper and
one of the crew went into the harbour in the launch to do a reconnais-
ance and found it was impossible to get up the landing steps as the
tide was going out and we could only land over a wall of huge rough
stones.

It was decided we should lunch ashore. We set off half of us at a
time as it was pretty rough and the launch needed two to handle it.
We landed by the rough stone wall and clambered up. On landing we
were met by an official wanting to see our papers and passports who
was delighted when he saw we had already entered Tunisia the day
before and had them stamped.

My hostess ordered two horse-drawn carriages with canopies, as
there were no taxis. We made our first stop at the fruit and vegetable
market, where we bought very fresh vegetables, melons, lemons,
grapes, peaches, apples and bananas grown locally, and long loaves of
crisp French bread, and sent them back to *Tamarind*. In the middle of
the oasis we saw the old Arab villages of Semassa and Chemini and
the Roman dam called Barrage Romain; we also saw acres of date
palm trees, a banana grove, olive trees, fields of henna and masses of
pomegranate trees laden with fruit. We lunched and bathed in the new
Hôtel de l'Oasis, where we found very modern changing rooms with
showers. We were back on board by 5.45 p.m. after a most enjoyable
and interesting day. Some of the party went for a swim but I decided
to go to my cabin and do some more work.

At 7 p.m. the engines started up and we headed for the gulf of
Gabes, up the coast of Tunisia to Monastir. Around 7.45 p.m. my host
came and said if I wanted to see a satellite there was one in the sky, so
I rushed up on deck and joined the others. We watched this bright
light, which one of the crew had spotted, speeding through the sky at
a terrific pace.

After dinner my host took me and another non-bridge player down
to see the engine room working while we were going along at about
ten or eleven knots, which I enjoyed. We then went forward to the
'pulpit' where you could not hear any sound of the engines. The air

was warm, the moon shining on the sea and there was not another ship in sight. We all stayed up here for some time. I went to bed with my lungs full of good fresh air.

Next morning we were going about the same speed. The skipper did a recce round Monastir but found the water was not very deep, and it was decided that we should go straight on to Sousse, where there is a good harbour and where we could also get fresh water to fill the tanks. We berthed perfectly and landed. We set off in two taxis to see Monastir, and later dined out of doors at the very modern Hotel Esplanade right on the sea. We drove back to Sousse in moonlight with bunches of sweet-smelling jasmine that had been given us. On our way we stopped at a very attractive roadside café where we found no one but male Tunisians, mostly playing cards. (The women are never seen in any public place.) From here we went on to the Boujaffar nightclub in Sousse, where quite a lot of people were dancing to a very good band. Then back to *Tamarind* around midnight. Sadly this was my last night on board.

Next morning we set off to make a tour of Sousse in two open mini-vans driven by motor bicycle engines with striped canopies overhead. We went back to *Tamarind* for luncheon. I finished off my packing then said goodbye to Matthews and to each of his wonderfully efficient crew who had made this trip so comfortable and enjoyable. When the taxi arrived I said a very sincere but, I felt, inadequate thank you to my kind host, who had given me this glorious week on their lovely boat away from the social world and telephones in a part of the globe I had never visited and found so interesting.

Margery Sangster and her son Carlos, who are very keen sightseers, were accompanying me to Tunis by road. On our drive of 100 miles we stopped at Hammamet, another fast-growing resort on the coast. We spent a very comfortable night at the Tunis Hilton and at 7 a.m. next morning I went to say goodbye and thank you to my very dear hostess, who is a very close friend of many, many years.

I arrived back feeling so fit and rested after a super week with plenty of good fresh air. The car was there to meet me with final proof pages of my Jennifer's Diary that had to be read and checked on my way up the M4 so that they could go to press when I got to my office, where I worked until 7 p.m.

Next morning when I was called at 6 a.m., I woke up feeling like death!, very sick, with a terrific headache, which is happily something I almost never get. I had to carry on as I had a busy day ahead, so I struggled to pack my suitcases as I was off again in the afternoon. Then I had a 9 a.m. appointment to get my hair and nails done. From there I went to the office until 1 p.m.

When I got back to the flat I still felt desperately ill and could eat nothing. I did not know what had hit me! I managed to finish off my packing and caught the train at 3.40 p.m. My great worry was that I was going to stay at Burghley House with the Marquess and Marchioness of Exeter, who had, I knew, a very high-powered house party staying for the Burghley Horse Trials World Championships, which had begun that morning with the dressage. David and Diana Exeter had been two very dear friends since before we were all married, and the kindest couple in the world, but the thought of having to cope with rather high-powered people when I felt so ill frightened me.

When I arrived at Burghley, Diana Exeter, who herself had a broken leg in plaster, was angelic and let me retire to bed before dinner. She also sent up a hot water bottle and some very effective anti-sickness medicine to take every three hours. This worked miracles, and with all this cherishing I made a quick recovery and felt fit and well enough to enjoy the next day of the Horse Trials.

The Duke of Edinburgh, who was then President of the FEI, arrived by air soon after I did by air to stay at Burghley. The FEI, or Fédération Equestre Internationale, had decreed that every fourth year, halfway between Olympics, there was to be a World Championship, and Britain had organized one this year at Burghley.

We all lunched in the President's tent near the show jumping arena. Around 1.30 p.m. our beloved Queen arrived, looking very attractive in a soft brown wool dress and jacket. The Queen had broken her journey to see the second day of the World Championships on her way back from London to Balmoral after officially opening the new Severn Bridge the day before. Soon the royal visitors, driven by their host, and accompanied by their hostess and Viscount and Viscountess De L'Isle, set off in an open Land Rover to watch the competitors take part in Phase D of the trials over the cross country course. The Marchioness of Abergavenny, who had come with The Queen, Lord Plunket, the Crown Equerry Lt-Colonel John Miller, later Sir John Miller, Mr James Orr and Lady Victoria Cecil followed the royal party in the second Land Rover, driven by Mr Simon Leatham. I was privileged to have a place in the third Land Rover, which was driven by Diana Exeter's son, Mr Anthony Forbes, so I also had a wonderful close-up view of the obstacles.

After watching the cross country and some show jumping, The Queen returned to Burghley House with her host and hostess, then left with Princess Margaret and her entourage to board the royal train at Peterborough station to travel on overnight to Scotland. The Duke of Edinburgh was to stay on at Burghley until Monday. On Sunday morning the Duke of Edinburgh, our host and hostess and the rest of the house party went to morning service at St Martin's Church in Stamford. Late that afternoon I said goodbye to my dear host and hostess after a truly wonderful and very happy weekend and caught a train from Peterborough back to London.

In 1967 I had an exciting Easter – I flew in a BOAC VC10 to Tel Aviv to spend five days with Mrs Michael Sacher and her daughter Miss Susy Sacher at her enchanting house in Caesarea – the Deauville of Israel!

Audrey Sacher, who was a wonderful hostess, had arranged what was for me an exciting weekend as this was my first (and so far my only) visit to Israel. On my first morning, I walked round the garden, where the most beautiful birds, including jumbo-sized kingfishers and hoopoes with striped plumage and top knots, strutted about the lawns. I was fascinated when I came to the swimming pool, and had to search to find the cleverly hidden dressing rooms, shower and so on built under the rockery.

Audrey took us on a tour of the little old port of Caesarea, then used by underwater swimmers to watch the wonderful variety of fish. In the evening, we had a delicious dinner at the Caesarea Hotel, built and owned by Baron Edmond de Rothschild, whom I had met in Mégève.

Around 10.30 p. m., Mr Jean Bollack, who was among those who joined us for dinner but whom I had never met before, drove me to Tel Aviv to see a *pourim* being given by banker Mr David Shoham and his wife at their home, which was gaily decorated for this Jewish carnival. There were around fifty guests all in fancy dress! I only had a mask which had quickly been made up by Audrey Sacher and myself at the end of dinner. There was dancing and the party went on till 4 a.m., but we left at 1 a.m. to drive back to Caesarea.

On Saturday, Audrey had organized a luncheon party. All the guests were rather special in their own line. I sat next to Dr Eliahu Elath, whom I was delighted to meet again. He was Israel's Ambassador in London for nine years, and was now President of the new Hebrew University in Jerusalem, which he arranged for me to visit. On my other side was the famous General Moshe Dayan, who had just returned from one of his visits to Vietnam during their war. For a time he discussed their modern armaments with Mr Elath. On other subjects he was also most interesting. (Little did I know then that in a few weeks' time a war would have broken out in Israel.)

After lunch on Sunday, I drove with Audrey Sacher and two other houseguests, Sir Norman and Lady Reid (he was then Director of the Tate gallery), through Hadera Afuleh, and on to Kefar Tavor, the famous Horns of Hittin, where the Moslems fought the Crusaders in 1187, then on to Tiberias, the capital of Galilee. We stayed comfortably at the Hotel Galei Kinnereth right on Lake Tiberias – the Sea of Galilee. Before dinner, we went to visit Kibbutz Ein Gev, one of the communal settlements, where their main industry was fishing and farming. I talked to several people living there and found it all tremendously interesting. The kibbutz had a large modern auditorium to take 2,500, and for their annual Festival of Music music-lovers come from all over the world.

Later that night, I saw something I shall never forget as I stepped out on to my balcony: the full beauty of the full moon shining on the Sea of Galilee. Next morning, the same scene left me spellbound. The sky was blue and this time the sun, not the moon, was shining down on the lake. To look across the water at the surrounding hills and the peaceful countryside that were the background to Jesus's life and so much of what took place in the Bible was an unforgettable experience.

At 9.30 a.m., we started our return journey, stopping at the sites of various Biblical scenes, including Capernaeum, where Jesus is said to have healed the centurion's servant, and Tabgha, where Jesus performed the miracle of the loaves and fishes. Further on, we could see the snow-capped Mount Herman in the distance.

I had been warned not to visit Nazareth as I might get a shock, but I felt, as I was near, I had to. It certainly was a painful experience. I have never seen anywhere so totally spoilt and vulgarly commercialized for tourists. It made me sad for a while on a happy day.

Next morning, I left on my own for Jerusalem. The rest of the party were going to meet me later for dinner with friends in Rehovot. I went straight to the new Hebrew university campus on Guvat Ram, which had 12,500 students. Nearly all the University's institutions are housed here. I was met on arrival by Mrs Ruth Burton, who took me on a most informative tour.

After luncheon at the university cafeteria, I met Lt-Colonel Dov

Zion, who was taking me on a quick tour round the city and outskirts of Jerusalem. My escort was a very keen soldier like his father-in-law General Moshe Dayan, and our tour was punctuated by several anecdotes of his activities when very young during the fighting in Jerusalem in 1948. Some were hair-raising! We visited the Notre Dame Hospice, which my escort had helped to capture during previous fighting in Jerusalem. He was in uniform and so enthusiastic I felt we were going round every corner with a gun!

We drove to the Mandelbaum Gate at the frontier to Jordan. The city was then divided; barbed wire fences made it impossible to enter much of the old part. I did see the Wailing Wall and at one point had a glimpse of the Dead Sea. We drove through Mea Shearin quarter, where the ultra-orthodox Jews live, and then out along the road to Bethlehem, and at one point looked down on to Bethlehem and the Church of the Nativity, which was bathed in sunshine. Then we went back to a synagogue to see its famous Chagall windows, which really are superb. It was now 6 p.m., so Dov Zion, who really had been a wonderful guide, drove me to the King David Hotel, where we said goodbye.

I then drove with Professor Alix Keenan and his daughter to their home at Rehovet, where they had a dinner party for eighteen. I was amazed that most of the guests spoke Yiddish all the time – even in front of me, and I don't speak a word! Audrey Sacher and her house guests joined me here and drove me home. I was quite weary when I got to bed!

I had to be up soon after 6 a.m., as I had not done my packing and I had to leave fairly early for Tel Aviv to catch the BOAC flight home. It was with tremendous gratitude that I said goodbye to dear Audrey Sacher, who had given me such a lovely weekend full of interest.

In 1967 in late September, I received a telegram from the Foreign Minister in Tehran, a former Ambassador in London, inviting me to the Coronation of the Shah of Persia on the last Thursday in October, as the guest of the Government. This invitation I refused as I had already planned to fly to Bangkok and Australia and back via America, leaving the following Tuesday. When I told Jocelyn he was horrified and eventually talked me into doing both!

I flew out to Tehran on Tuesday, hoping to arrive at 9 p.m., but as we had to divert to Rome for technical reasons my flight did not get in until 1 a.m. Wednesday. An official from the Ministry of Information met me and I was asked to give a radio interview before I left the airport! A car was waiting and we drove through the decorated streets to the Royal Tehran Hilton, which was the best Hilton I have ever stayed at. Alas, however, my invitation and passes were not there as promised.

Later that morning, I was given a charming 19-year-old student, who spoke perfect English, to look after me. Quite a busy programme for the day ahead had been arranged, but still no invitation or passes. My guide was wonderful: she arranged transport and dealt with everyone from officials to taxi drivers, as so few spoke English and all the street and other signs were in Arabic only.

During that day I chased my official invitation and passes. They were not there at lunch, tea, or dinner time! Having left the Ministry of Information, I walked round to the Golestan Palace where the Coronation was to take place. It had all been redecorated for this great occasion, and the famous Hall of Mirrors, with its superbly worked mirrored walls and ceiling, was beautiful. The jewelled Peacock Throne was under a dust sheet and we were not allowed to see it, but I was able to get a good idea of where I would be sitting.

From here I went on to the Foreign Ministry, which had also been beautifully redecorated. Here I met the Minister for Foreign Affairs Mr Ardeshir Zahedi, who assured me I would get my official passes and told me not to worry. I changed and went to a buffet luncheon in the Hilton given by one of the ministers. Here I met Prince Sadruddin Aga Khan as we selected our lunch, and our Ambassador, Sir Denis Wright, and Lady Wright, who kindly invited me to tea that day at the embassy.

I got back to the hotel rather weary as with my flight being so late I had had less than four hours in bed. After a relaxing hot bath and change, I felt refreshed and ready to enjoy a dinner party at the attractive and beautifully furnished home of a former Iranian Ambassador in London, Mr Mohsen Rais and his charming and very dear wife Marie.

It was quite a problem getting there as the traffic was terrific, with so many people coming into the city, often with their families, to see the marvellous decorations. Every house and shop was lit and so were all the high towers.

Sir Denis and Lady Wright were at the dinner party, as were the Netherlands Ambassador and Madame de Jonquire, whom I had met previously in Hong Kong, also several others, including my hostess's brother-in-law Mr Gharagozlou, who was very close to the Shah, and was one of the masters of the ceremony at court. He very kindly told me that if I got to the ceremony next day in good time he would take me right up to see the Peacock Throne, which he did: I even touched it! He also showed me the fabulous 25-foot-long train that was to be put on the Queen's shoulders. It was very wide, made of dark green velvet bordered with white mink and a colourful embroidered design carried out in real jewels. It was one of the most beautiful garments I have ever seen.

After the Rais party, I went on to the Foreign Minister Mr Ardeshir Zahedi's lovely home, where I found the guests dancing. He had very sweetly invited me to dine too, but I had already accepted the Raises' invitation and was only calling in on my way home, as I had said I would. He showed me all over the house and I met all the guests, who were very chic and extremely friendly. They were not going to be too late as my host and many of the guests were going to the Coronation. As I left, Mr Ardeshir assured me again that my seat and everything would be all right for the next morning.

I had a 4.30 a.m. call as I had to be ready in the foyer at 6 a.m. When my driver arrived he told me we had to collect my official tickets for my seat at the Golestan Palace on the way! At last I had them in my hands: it had been such a desperate worry.

When I arrived at the Golestan Palace, I found I was not seated in a press seat, but in a wonderful seat just behind the diplomatic corps, to the left of the throne. The palace was not a huge building; there were not a vast number of guests and everything was much more compact than for our beloved Queen's Coronation. The sun and the hundred-candle Venetian glass candelabra shone on the fabulous mirrored background, and with everyone in evening dress, except the beautiful French Begum Aga Khan, who wore a short cream and gold dress and beige mink hat, it was a very glamorous scene. All the men were in evening dress, most of the ambassadors in court dress and the courtiers in their colourful household dress, and nearly all the men wore orders and decorations. The Shahanshah had his family, too numerous to mention, around him, and the beautiful Empress on a chair beside him.

This Coronation was very much a family and national affair. No foreign royalty were invited; instead they were represented by their ambassadors. (A year later there were much bigger coronation celebrations attended by many foreign royals, but there was no ceremony then.) This was a most impressive 'jewelled' ceremony, during which

His Majesty girded on the special belt which was fastened with the biggest emerald I have ever seen, and clipped it to a jewelled sword. Then he donned the royal cape before he placed the heavily jewelled crown with an osprey feather in front on his own head and held the sceptre in his right hand. Her Imperial Majesty Queen Farah, with the help of her ladies-in-waiting, put on the long heavily jewelled cape, then knelt in front of the Shahanshah, who then crowned her with the most exquisite crown, recently designed and made for her by van Cleef and Arpels from the crown jewels.

Queen Farah was the first Empress ever to be crowned in Iran, and sadly, probably the last. After that there was quite a long service and Iranian statesmen and other dignitaries went up to the throne to pay homage. Everywhere I went I heard praise for all that the Shah had done for his country.

After the Coronation, and having seen the royal procession go out into the sunshine, I went on to a large reception room where guests had assembled for a glass of champagne. Alas I could not stay for the banquet and reception at the Foreign Office the following evening. I eventually got back to my hotel around 3 p.m.

I did some telephoning to check up on various points, had my dinner upstairs and was just going to bed when the concierge rang to say there was a gentleman downstairs to see me. I was a bit surprised, but went down and saw a complete stranger standing beside the most enormous roll of white linen. He told me that he had brought this from the Foreign Office as a memento for me to take home. For a moment I was horrified, as I could not think how I would cope, or how I would get on at the customs. I even wondered for a moment if there was a corpse inside it!

He obviously saw the look on my face and went on to say that inside was a Persian rug, and that I would have no trouble at the customs as it had all been arranged. (My son has the lovely rug on a polished floor in his dining room in Canada today.) My new-found friend also told me that when I got to the airport there was a little caviar waiting for me. This turned out to be two large tins.

The kindness and generosity of everyone to me had been overwhelming. I got top VIP treatment at the airport and I took off at dawn on a Pan American Boeing 707 round-the-world flight, and wrote copy all the way home.

On Saturday my faithful secretary and Uta Thompson, who was on our executive staff, very sweetly volunteered to come into the office and type my copy and captions so that I was able to take galley proofs to correct with me when I left for Bangkok the following Tuesday.

On Tuesday, having been to the Opening of Parliament in the morning and got my copy written and typed by 2.45 p.m., I then realized I had forty-nine minutes to go before I left the flat and London for eighteen days! I took a Qantas flight to Sydney, stopping off in Bangkok for two nights. I boarded the flight feeling dead tired, the last week having been such a rush, but I got myself comfortable for the night, fastened my seat belt, and did not get out at any of the stops. I arrived at Bangkok feeling very fit and rested, and it was only now that I thought Jocelyn was right to make me fit in Iran as well as this trip!

After two days visiting friends and shopping at Jim Thompson's silk shop, I took off for Sydney again on a Qantas flight and landed at about 8 a.m. next morning. Although it was so early Lady Lloyd Jones, a great personality in Sydney, who had invited me to stay at her lovely home Rosemount, was at the airport to meet me with a fine Rolls and chauffeur – this was her son's as hers was in Melbourne.

I had never been very keen on visiting Australia as I had been told it was a do-it-yourself country, and that no one had any staff, and in hotels you carried your own luggage and could not get your clothes pressed, so you can imagine my surprise when I arrived at Rosemount to find four middle-aged, very well-trained British maids who had been with Hannah Lloyd Jones for years. Katharine, her wonderful housemaid, asked for my keys, said she had a hot water bottle in my bed, and that I was to go and have a sleep and she would call me and have my bath run at 12.30 as Her Ladyship had a luncheon party at 1.30 p.m. For a moment I thought I must have landed in the wrong country!

It was a delightful luncheon party of ten, including Hannah's son Charles Lloyd Jones, whom I had already met in London. I always remember the flowers around the house as there were clumps of arum lilies, cinerarias, azaleas and double stocks all in full bloom as well as three or four hundred flowering cymbidium orchids staged in three rows and making a bank all along one wall, which I could see from my bedroom window. We dined with friends that evening.

On Sunday, when we arrived in Melbourne, Hannah's Rolls and her wonderful English chauffeur Holmes were at the airport to meet us and drive us to the Hotel Windsor.

Here I thought I would see the 'do it yourself' I'd heard about –

but not at all. We were graciously taken up to our rooms, where our luggage arrived in a few moments. My pressing was done beautifully and throughout our stay the service was excellent. I wished I had come to Australia earlier, but I have made up for that by visiting that wonderful country a number of times since, even twice in 1988, which was their Centennial year.

On this my first visit, I thoroughly enjoyed Melbourne Cup Week. I missed Sir Rupert and Lady Clarke's annual Sunday luncheon party for around a hundred guests out at Bolinda Vale, but I went to and enjoyed it in years to follow. They still hold it each year. I went to a wonderful seated and placed dinner party for around a hundred guests given by Sir Norman and Dame Mabel Brookes, when we dined off superb china, and silver or gold plates which Dame Mabel had collected over the years. The Prime Minister, Mr Harold Holt, was there, also his predecessor Sir Robert Menzies and Dame Pattie Menzies. Sir Robert was Prime Minister twice, in 1939–41 and 1949–66; many believe that with his great brain, foresight and tremendous wisdom he was the best Prime Minister Australia ever had.

On Melbourne Cup Day, when the traffic is always chaotic, Hannah had somehow wangled that we join the diplomatic cars and have our numbered place in the convoy with police outriders clearing the way. We had kindly been invited, as I have always been on later visits, to the luncheon given by the Chairman and committee of the Victoria Racing Club, and I had been sent badges for the committee box. Cup Day is a public holiday in Melbourne; there is an attendance of around 85,000 at Flemington racecourse, where bands play, and there are numerous diversions.

In 1968, when I was in the Bahamas staying with Sir Harold and Lady Christie, they very sweetly invited my son, Jim, to fly down from Montreal and join us from Wednesday to Saturday, which was the day I had to leave. On the Wednesday night they took us to dine with Mr Aristotle Onassis on board his famous yacht *Christina*, which I had been on several times in Monte Carlo.

It was a delightful, quiet and gracious evening with an exceptionally good dinner. Madame Maria Callas was staying on board and very unobtrusively acted as hostess, looking extremely chic in a superbly tailored black dinner dress with a slit right up the front, revealing beautifully tailored long white satin trousers.

After dinner, Maria Callas went out of her way to make Jim, who was years younger than anyone else, feel at home. She asked him to come over and sit beside her and tell her all about life in Montreal, and took the keenest interest in all he told her.

Sadly, that was the last visit Maria Callas was to make to the *Christina*, as around ten days later Mrs Jackie Kennedy came to stay on board, and eventually married Ari Onassis, which, as the world knows, broke Maria Callas's heart.

On the last evening of what had been an enjoyable break with my son, I had a severe shock. We were just going to dine with the Eddie Taylors at their house in Lyford Cay, when I received a cable from my employer, Jocelyn Stevens, saying 'Have sold *Queen* to Michael Lewis. Don't worry. All well. See you Monday. Love Jocelyn.' I was absolutely stunned, and so grateful to have Jim with me.

Next morning we left for New York, where my English-born future daughter-in-law Gillian Hewitt flew down from Montreal to meet us. It was the first time I had met Gilly and I went home to England feeling happy about Jim's choice. Gilly has been a wonderful wife, and they celebrate their Silver Wedding in 1993.

I flew on home on Sunday, happily on the same flight as Tommy Sopwith, who is a contemporary and a great friend of Jocelyn Stevens. He was able to tell me more about Jocelyn selling *Queen* magazine, as there had been no sign or sound of such a deal before I left. I learnt that Jocelyn, who by then was doing a lot of work for Sir Max Aitken at Express Newspapers, suddenly got a call from Mr Michael Lewis, who invited him out to lunch and made him such a huge offer for *Queen* magazine that he could not refuse!

The morning I returned, Jocelyn telephoned to say he was bringing Michael Lewis down to my office. I had no time to discuss the sale with him. When I met Michael Lewis, who knew nothing about magazines, he told me that he owned fifty-one companies, one of which I believe was a printing company. I quickly realized the exhilarating days and all the fun of working on *Queen* were over.

I had never had to look for a job since I was sixteen, when I ran away from home, and I decided that at sixty-five I was now too old to start looking! I remembered by dear father saying 'Sometimes it is better to sit tight and see what happens', which is what I did.

There followed for me a very miserable and worrying two and half years as I watched the success of *Queen* reduced. However, I carried on as usual.

In 1969 I made a trip to South Africa. This time I flew to Tenerife for one night, to Las Palmas for the night, and then joined the Union

Castle Line's *Pendennis Castle* at Las Palmas and sailed to Capetown.
I had a lovely airy cabin and a table alone in the dining room at my
request.

This was the only time I have spent Christmas on board ship, which
was an interesting experience for me. We started the day with Holy
Communion, which was celebrated quietly and reverently at 7.30 a.m.
in the Cardroom, converted for the purpose. There was another Christmas carol service in the lounge at 10.30 but I did not go to this as I
had left London with an inflamed sinus, earache, and a hacking cough,
and I still had no voice. I settled down to work until 11.45 a.m. when
The Queen's message was relayed. I received several very welcome
Christmas cables from friends. The Commodore, who never stopped
going round first and tourist class to see everyone was happy, kindly
invited me to an enjoyable luncheon where we kept off Christmas fare.
In the evening, I joined Captain and Mrs Gordon Kirkpatrick in the
ship's private dining room, where they had a dinner party for ten.

We arrived at Capetown on New Year's Day 1969. I went, as always,
to the Mount Nelson Hotel. After a hectic two days during which I
went racing at Kenilworth and visited several friends, I took off for
Kimberley to visit Mr and Mrs Harry Oppenheimer's Mauritzfontein
stud, where I was going to spend the night. I landed around 5 p.m.
and I was met by Doctor Tremayne Toms, who was managing the
stud so efficiently. We drove across barren land until we suddenly came
to a little green oasis in which sat the house and stabling. Harry and
Bridget Oppenheimer sadly at the last moment could not join me here,
but there were three other guests staying. While it was still light, I went
with Doctor Toms to see about twenty yearlings and three stallions,
including Wilwyn, who had won twenty-one races in England, and
the Washington International at Laurel Park.

Next morning I set off at 8 a.m. with Doctor Toms and we drove
round to see around forty mares, and mares and foals, which were so
kindly led out for me to see. Then we drove back to the main stables,
where we sat under the shade of the pepper trees around the grassed
stable yard while more mares and their progeny were led in front of
us. Doctor Toms, who was outstandingly knowledgeable, a qualified
veterinary surgeon, and very interesting about bloodstock and stud
management, was so kind and long-suffering over my endless questions. There were many very promising foals and yearlings at this lovely
stud, which I shall always remember visiting.

Next I flew to Johannesburg to stay at Mr and Mrs Charles Engelhard's Court House. The house was fully staffed, though they and their family were at their home in New Jersey. While I was there I dined with Jane Engelhard and Harry and Bridget Oppenheimer, who had not only lent me their beautiful home, and arranged for my clothes to be pressed and her hairdresser to do my hair, but had also asked Mrs Garth Trace to arrange a buffet luncheon beside their lovely pool on Sunday and invite all my friends. It was a beautifully arranged and gracious party with delicious food, and the greatest fun for me to see so many friends as I was only on a flying visit.

On Monday I was asked to give interviews to four of South Africa's women editors and make a recording, all of which I did very reluctantly as I always find them frightening, but I knew it was good for the magazine!

Then I flew to Nairobi, on to Mombasa, and from there to Tanzania. I was met at the airstrip at Olmolog in West Kilimanjaro by Colonel William Stirling of Keir, who had arrived from England the previous day. He drove me to nearby Nduimet, a charming, comfortable house with a lovely garden, where I met Mrs Charles Pretzlik and Mr Kenneth Childe, both directors with Bill Stirling of the Agricultural Development and Industrial Company of Tanzania, known as ADICT, which had already made vast developments in road making and farming in this part of the world.

After luncheon Bill Stirling and Kenneth Childe left in the Cessna to spend the night at one of the other farms in the Kirm valley. I unpacked and repacked, ready to take off in the Cessna, when it returned with Sue Pretzlik, for Ngoro-Ngoro, to spend the night there and to go round the game reserves in the crater early next morning.

We were at the airstrip when the Cessna returned rather late, as we wanted to get up there around 6 p.m. because of failing light; we only just made it in time. On arrival we flew round the top of the crater to buzz Dhillon's Lodge to signal them as arranged to send their Land Rover to pick us up as, unlike the larger Crater Lodge, they had no radio communication. We then flew down into the crater, where we had to circle twice low over the airstrip to clear it of a herd of zebra grazing there, and landed at 6.15 p.m. On landing our pilot spoke to the radio operator at Crater Lodge, who said they would stand by and send one of their Land Rovers to rescue us in case Dhillon's Lodge had not seen us.

As it was terribly hot in the Cessna we decided to get out and sat on the ground to watch the very swift sunset and wait. It was fascinating to see the wild animals around us carrying on in their natural way, and the zebras playing as darkness fell. It was slightly alarming when one wildebeest came fairly close to the aeroplane and snorted his disapproval!, but he eventually got bored and went off to join his friends. A jackal came and had a look at us but he too went off after the second round.

Eventually, at 6.45 p.m., we saw the lights of the Land Rover coming down the twisting road of the mountain. Our luggage was transferred from the Cessna, the pilot radioed Crater Lodge to say we had at last been picked up, he locked the Cessna and off we went up to the top of the crater, which is about 7,000 feet high. Dhillon's Lodge had only opened that winter. We found it was for the young and hearty who liked roughing it! The bedrooms were unheated, and I woke up around 3 a.m. absolutely freezing. The lights had been cut off, so I had to grope my way round with a torch to find a woolly cardigan.

We were up early and with our guide and our dear pilot we were off in the Land Rover before 8 a.m. as we wanted to take off from the crater at noon. Ngoro-Ngoro measures over ten miles from east to west, a floor area of 103 square miles with no break whatsoever in its 2,000-foot wall. In addition to its abundance of wildlife it is also inhabited by ten thousand Masai, who herd about a hundred thousand cattle. This tribe used to be renowned for their bravery in killing lions, a feat they are now forbidden to perform.

Before we left the rim of the crater we came across around a dozen elephants sunning themselves and were able to drive up close to photograph them. Later we passed some Masai with a herd of cattle. As we drove round in the crater we saw every kind of animal imaginable, except giraffe. I thought the lions were the most fascinating. We nearly ran over one or two sunning themselves, and by a small lake saw lionesses lying hidden in the rushes with the lions further back. Our guide told us they were waiting for a kill. Apparently the lionesses always do the killing and they were waiting for a wildebeest, zebra or some other animal they might fancy to eat to come to water, when they would pounce. Happily we did not witness a kill.

After a welcome hot bath and change once we had returned to Olmolog and comfy Nduimet, the four of us dined quietly and watched very good television from Nairobi. It was quite cool as we were 6,500 feet above sea level. I slipped away at 10 p.m., healthily tired, and slept well. I set my alarm for 6 a.m. as I wanted to get some writing done. At 6.30 a.m. I had the joy of watching the sun rise over the snow-covered Mount Kilimanjaro, a truly beautiful picture. We breakfasted at 9 a.m. outside on the patio beside a lovely rose garden in full bloom. I sat out here writing while the others flew off on other projects and returned for lunch. At 2.30 p.m. I took off in the Cessna having said goodbye with overwhelming gratitude to my dear host and to dear Sue Pretzlik for all they did for me.

When we had landed I rather wistfully watched John and the very chic yellow and white Cessna take off, thinking what fun my brief visit to Tanzania had been and what a godsend the Cessna and John had proved.

Jocelyn Stevens very generously told me after I had been on his staff for around a year that I must use car hire more often, and not, as I had been doing, rely so much on taxis. Accordingly, during the sixties, I organized myself with car-hire firms.

In the Newmarket district it was Chilcotts; in the Newbury district it was Mr Durnford; in the Isle of Wight it was Mr Pocock of Ryde. In Perthshire, it was Duff's Garage, Crieff, and Thomson Taxi, Perth; in York, Streamline Taxis; in Tunbridge Wells, Beeline Car Hire and so on.

In London the Silver Car Hire took care of me. It was then run by a wonderful lady called Mrs Nye whose husband, a National Hunt jockey, had had a bad fall on his head and could never work again. Mrs Nye was especially kind to me – she would keep one chauffeur for me in order that I did not always have strange drivers, and so that the driver learnt the places I went to.

It was at the end of 1969, when my driver was leaving to go else-where, that Mrs Nye said she had a new young driver whom she thought I would like. This was how the wonderful, faithful Peter Haimes came into my life. I owe so much to his exceptionally careful driving. He has driven me thousands of miles in all conditions all hours of the day and night, and always got me to my appointment on time. One of my requests on a Saturday one summer was to be driven to a wedding in Shropshire, where I arrived five minutes before the time I said, and then, after the reception, on to Gleneagles, where I said I must arrive before midnight. We arrived about 11.45pm!

He drove for the Silver Car Hire until Mrs Nye retired and sold the business to very unsatisfactory owners, as far as I was concerned, who sent me other drivers. That was in 1972. So I asked my Managing Director, Mr Marcus Morris, who already had one chauffeur on the staff, if it would be possible to take Peter on, as he could drive other people in the firm when I did not need him (sometimes I had one or two blank days running, and I was often abroad). Marcus very kindly agreed immediately, knowing I often worked an eighteen- or twenty-hour day, and Peter joined the firm.

His car was always immaculate. On one occasion I had been to a late wedding in Wales where it poured with rain and the car park was in a field that got very muddy, as did the car. I was staying at a small country hotel nearby and did not get back there until around midnight. We had to leave at 8 a.m. for an engagement before luncheon on Sunday. Most of the mud had disappeared from the car, but dear Peter was full of apologies that it did not look as clean as it should!

In all the twenty-two years that Peter drove me, I never had one grumble from him, and I must have been so very trying at times. What is more amazing is that I never had one grumble from dear Mrs Peter about Peter's often long hours and his working so many weekends. Mrs Peter has always been the first to help me on the few occasions I have been ill, or in need of help.

The saddest aspect of my retirement was the loss of Peter and the car. Happily, though, in the end I have not entirely lost him: the wonderful firms I eventually worked for – the Hearst Corporation in America and the smaller National Magazine Company in London – very kindly said I could continue to have the use of Peter and the car when the Managing Director, Terry Mansfield, did not need him. The two companies also most generously opened an account for me with a car-hire firm, so that whenever Peter is not available, I always have transport – the greatest kindness anyone could show me. I am so grateful to Frank Bennack and the directors of the Hearst Corporation, and Terry Mansfield of the National Magazine Company.

In August 1970, after two and a half rather miserable years, for me a miracle happened!

I was over in Deauville, and got back to my hotel around 8.45 p.m., very weary as I had been out since 2 p.m., racing, to polo, to see a stud, and to a cocktail party. I was told by the telephone operator that London had been trying to get me on the telephone every half-hour since 3 p.m., and would be ringing again at 9 p.m., but I was given no name or number. When I had rung my office at 1 p.m. all had been well, so I began to worry that Jim or some other member of my family had had an accident.

By the time the telephone rang at about 9.15 p.m., I was a bundle of nerves! It was Michael Lewis, furious that I had not been available earlier. He said 'I have sold *Queen*. They don't want me, but they want you. Will you go?' I asked who he had sold it to, and when he told me that it was the National Magazine Company and its parent company Hearst Corporation, and that they wanted to buy *Queen* to merge it with *Harpers Bazaar*, and that Willie Landels, who had been Jocelyn's very good art editor, would be the editor, I agreed. I learnt later from Dick Berlin, then the head of the Hearst Corporation, who was buying the magazine, that they did not really want it without *me* and my Jennifer's Diary!

So I and my diary moved to what is now *Harpers & Queen*, where the diary still is today. It was a very happy magazine marriage: *Harpers & Queen* was a sensational success. Willie Landels was a truly wonderful editor for seventeen years, and it was a tragedy for the magazine and all of us when he left in 1987. Willie already had a trained staff, including Fiona Macpherson as his deputy editor, who, like several others, had worked on *Queen* when Jocelyn ran it. Robert Johnson, *Queen*'s faithful production manager, also moved to *Harpers & Queen* at the time of the merger and only retired in March 1992.

Financially it was also a happy story, as I was told that, until the merger, *Harpers Bazaar* had always lost money. The first year of the *Harpers & Queen* marriage we broke even, and since then the magazine has always made a profit. Long may it do so.

In October 1970 I left a very nice office in New Fetter Lane for my new, much smaller office in Chestergate House near Victoria station. It was much nearer home, and had a wonderful view nearly as far as Heathrow. I was allowed to bring my special office furniture, which Jocelyn had had made for me. It took a bit of settling down, but I soon found that our parent company, the Hearst Corporation, and the London-based National Magazine Company were both wonderful to work for, and my enthusiasm for my work started to return.

I got along happily with the Managing Director of the National Magazine Company, Mr Marcus Morris, and when he retired I was delighted when Mr Terry Mansfield was appointed. He had worked on *Queen* magazine for Jocelyn and left after Michael Lewis took over, so I knew him quite well, and I thought he would be a good managing director, which he has happily proved to be. I hope for the company's sake that Terry Mansfield will carry on for many years to come.

TWELVE

From South America to the Seychelles, from Le Mans to Mustique

(1970–75)

Early in February 1970 I made my first flight in a Boeing 747 jumbo jet of Pan American Airways. They had only been in service for two or three weeks so it was rather exciting. When I entered the aeroplane, I was amazed at the sense of space inside: the Boeing 747 is nearly eighty feet longer than the Boeing 707, and the cabins seem much higher.

Pan Am were the first airline to put these jumbo jets into service, and the passengers all round me were trying the Boeing 747 out for the first time. My neighbour was a Vice-President of American Airlines, who were putting their first Boeing 747s into service ten days later between New York and Los Angeles, and he was watching everything intently. Another told me he was Colombian, had been in Germany buying steel for his firm in Colombia and had returned via London so that he could try the Boeing 747; another passenger was an American from a pharmaceutical firm who said he travelled between 80,000 and 100,000 miles a year, had just been to Lisbon and also thought he would return via London to try out the 747. They all volunteered this information, which made me realize what interest a new passenger aeroplane creates. I noticed that in first class there was only one other woman passenger.

We had a wonderful flight to New York and in spite of head winds landed fifteen minutes ahead of schedule. I was staying the night with friends overlooking Central Park and my host was at the airport to meet me. Next morning, when I boarded the Pan American Boeing 707 to Eleuthra, it seemed rather small! After my brief stay on Windermere Island, which is so peaceful, I went on to spend a very hectic social week with friends at Lyford Cay.

Shortly after my return to London I went to the annual dinner dance of the Helicopter Club of Great Britain, at which Admiral of the Fleet

Earl Mountbatten was the guest of honour. Tommy Sopwith was then Chairman of the HCGB and presided with his usual charm and efficiency. The ballroom of the Excelsior Hotel at Heathrow airport, where the ball was held, was big enough to accommodate three heli-copters as well as 150 guests at candlelit tables. A gleaming green and white Bell Jet Ranger, one of my favourites, was on the left of top table, a red and white Hughes 500 was on the opposite side of the room, and a smaller Brantly, on which so many helicopter pilots have learnt to fly, was nearby. That was the only time I have ever dined with helicopters as decor! Lord Louis and Tommy Sopwith made very brief and witty speeches, and I had a very jolly evening.

The following week the small sitting room of my tiny flat was covered in lights and television cameras for an interview I had very reluctantly agreed to give for Mr Eamonn Andrews' *Today* programme on Thames Television. This lasted much longer and was far more trying than I had feared. I do not like giving interviews, or being televised, and only ever agree reluctantly. One of the other interviews I can remember was by David Frost on one of his television pro-grammes, when I was led to believe that I was to appear with Sir John Betjeman and one of the Mitford sisters – which was one of the reasons I'd agreed to do it. I found, when I arrived, Miss Barbara Cartland and the then butler to the 6th Earl of Verulam! I was also interviewed by the late Roy Plomley, who was quiet and charming, on his *Desert Island Discs* radio programme, and by Terry Wogan on his programme *Wogan* in 1990. I remember I had a great rush to get there after a Royal Garden Party, but I found him quite relaxing and friendly.

I always enjoy flat racing, but 1970 was one of the most enjoyable years of all. That was because I had the joy of seeing Mr Charles Engelhard's wonderful horse Nijinsky win not only the 2,000 Guineas and the Derby, but also the valuable King George VI and Queen Elizabeth Stakes, and the St Leger, each time ridden by Lester Piggott. Then I went over to Paris, as did thousands of others, to see Nijinsky sadly beaten by a short head in the even more valuable Prix de l'Arc de Triomphe. In spite of this defeat, I still think Nijinsky, who was bred by Eddie Taylor (I saw him as a foal at Eddie's stud) and was by Eddie's famous sire Northern Dancer, was one of the greatest race-horses we have seen this century. Since then, Nijinsky has bred very many good winners.

It was a great joy to me to see Mr Paul Mellon's Mill Reef win the Derby the following year, as, like Nijinsky, I had seen Mill Reef as a yearling before he came to England. I had brought a photograph home – he was then unnamed – and published it in my Jennifer's Diary, so it was rather pleasing that he turned out to be such a winner. He went on to win both the King George VI and Queen Elizabeth Stakes at Ascot, and the Prix de l'Arc de Triomphe at Longchamps.

In September 1970 my first grandchild was born, and I flew out later in the autumn to watch her christened Lucy Katherine. She has now celebrated her twenty-first birthday!

In 1971 when Lord Grey of Naunton was the last Governor of Northern Ireland, he and his wife Esme, both of whom I knew when he was Governor of the Bahamas, invited me to fly over and stay with them for the weekend for the annual garden party held on a Friday at Government House. I arrived just before lunchtime. After luncheon, when changing in my room, I suddenly realized that just below my window there were masses of policemen and sniffer dogs; the security was very tight everywhere the whole weekend.

There were around 800 guests from every walk of life; I met a few friends who were trying to live a normal life in Northern Ireland. Over twenty years on they are still living under stress with terribly sad and worrying problems around them.

On Saturday morning Esme Grey entertained 400 Girl Guides in the garden of Government House and presented around 150 Queen's Awards to Guides who had won these coveted prizes. Esme had only then just come out of hospital with heart trouble. I went over that day to luncheon at Shane's Castle with Lord and Lady O'Neill and their three young sons Shane, Tyrone and Rory, who after lunch took me for a ride on the then new Shane's Castle Light Railway, which runs for about a mile and a half through the grounds with a glimpse of the Lough. I had a blissfully quiet evening with my host and hostess. On Sunday I went with them to Hillsborough Parish Church, again under the tightest security. After luncheon together, I flew home with even more admiration for those people trying to carry on a normal life.

At the end of the year, I somehow managed to be away for over three weeks on quite an ambitious trip, which included New York, Venezuela, Colombia, Peru and Brazil.

In New York, Mr Richard Deems of the Hearst Corporation had booked me in at the Waldorf Towers, where I had a very comfortable suite which was filled with flowers, including a wonderful arrangement from Mr Richard Berlin, then the President of the Hearst Corporation. With the flowers Dick Berlin wrote a very warm welcoming note, in

which he generously said that I was doing a good job on *Harpers &
Queen*.

Dick Berlin was a brilliant businessman: it was he who guided the
Hearst Corporation out of a very bad financial period into profit to
become the immensely successful, huge corporation it is today. In spite
of being such a fine businessman, Dick Berlin was also a very kind and
lovable personality, and, I found, a tremendously interesting man to
be with. He had a beautiful wife called Honey who was a lot of fun
and whom I visited on several occasions in their apartment in New
York.

During this visit, Dick Deems, who was then head of the magazine
sector of the corporation, and his wife Jean, who have become good
friends of mine, gave a dinner party in my honour at the 21 Club for
fifty guests, including quite a few from the Hearst Corporation.

After three or four days in New York, I flew in a Pan American
Boeing 707 on to Venezuela where I stayed with Sir Raymond and
Lady Smith in their lovely home, Quinta San Antonio, near the
Country Club in Caracas. I arrived at Caracas airport around 9.30 p.m.
and found Raymond Smith with a car beside the aeroplane, accompanied by Señor Lopez, a senior executive of Caracas airport, who
took my passport and papers and whisked me through all formalities
in a flash. Dorothy Smith was inside the airport and we soon left on
the forty-minute drive to their home, where a guard with a loaded rifle
unlocked the tall wrought-iron gates.

Next day, a group of friends came to drinks before we all went on
to luncheon at the Jockey Club. We were greeted there by Señor
Reinaldo Herrera Uslar, who had previously been in London with his
wife Mimi. Reinaldo, I remember, very sweetly gave me a ticket in a
sweepstake with which I won the splendid sum of 140 bolivares, about
twelve pounds sterling! There were eleven races, the last two run under
artificial light.

During the few days I was here, Dorothy and Raymond showed me
the sights in and around Caracas. We also had a very busy social life,
visiting a number of beautiful Venezuelan houses.

One day, I had a most interesting experience. I had said I would
love to see an oilfield, so Raymond Smith very kindly arranged it. I
was up on the chosen day at 6.15 a.m., and Chu Chu, the Smiths'
Venezuelan chauffeur, a great character, drove me to the Aero Club,
right in the centre of Caracas, where I met Señor Ricardo Paris and his
attractive American wife Darlene. Ricardo Paris's grandfather started a

business in Venezuela in 1884 called Casa Paris SA, which in 1946 became a chain of supermarkets called Super Victoria, which Ricardo was now running. He very kindly said he would fly me in his Beechcraft twin-engined aeroplane to Cabinas, so he, Darlene and I took off around 8.30 a.m. and flew along the coastline with Ricardo pointing out to me various projects. Before we landed, he flew me low for a long way down Lake Maracaibo to show me the hundreds and hundreds of oil derricks sunk in avenues in the lake for as far as the eye could see: a fantastic sight I shall never forget. They belonged, I gathered, to Shell Venezuela, Creole-Standard and MGO Gulf, who all operated around there.

We landed at Cabinas around 10.30 a.m. and were met by Mr Demetrio Quintero of Shell, with an air-conditioned car and chauffeur. Ricardo then took off in the Beechcraft to do some work at a nearby town.

The temperature was a hundred degrees Fahrenheit. We passed the large pipeline that carries oil to the tankers at Port Miranda, a refinery, and to oil storage vats. Beside each pipeline we saw the pipe that contains hot steam to thin the oil flowing in the larger one. These steam pipes cannot be laid under roads, so every time they come to one, they are raised high over it to form an archway. We saw hundreds of oil-pumping derricks everywhere. They were beside gardens, pumping away beside washing lines, beside schools and children's playgrounds – even on parts of the golf course! Shell Venezuela then had 3,852 derricks working on the land, as well as 534 in the lake. There must be even more today.

Demetrio Quintero, who was one of Shell's senior engineers, was charming and a wonderful guide. He was a bit shaken when, as he was showing us how the derricks worked, I asked if he could undo a screw of a derrick and show us how thick the oil is when it first comes out of the ground. He very kindly did so, however, and we saw a very few drops of terribly thick black oil that had just been pumped from 2,500 feet below ground. The derricks we had seen earlier on the lake, he told us, pump oil from 14,000 feet.

At 3.30 p.m. we were airborne again, flying home via the north coast, coming down to between 500 and 700 feet when we arrived at the coral islands of Las Aves and Los Roques, with lovely sandy beaches set in the very blue Caribbean sea. We flew on over Sarqui, which has fabulous white sand, and other lovely coastal spots. We were not allowed to land in the centre of Caracas after dark and we only just made it! We were the last aeroplane to land that day. As we taxied along, I saw Chu Chu and the Rolls ready to take me home to Raymond and Dorothy, who were worried that we had got lost because we were so late.

On Sunday, I was up again at 5 a.m. as I had to leave for the airport at 6.15 a.m. to catch the only flight to Bogotá. In spite of the early hour, Señor Lopez was at Caracas airport to take care of me. I took off in an Avianca Boeing 727 that had just come from Frankfurt. On arrival at Bogotá airport, I was met by Mr and Mrs Ralph Hanke with the British Ambassador's car, which he had kindly sent to meet me. Mr Thomas Rogers, who was the British Ambassador, and his wife were most awfully kind and gave a delightful luncheon party for me on Monday. The Ralph Hankes were also extremely kind, and invited me to dine on the Sunday night, when I happily met the Ambassador and Mrs Rogers.

I stayed at what was considered the best hotel, but it was absolutely soulless, with ghastly food and service, and a view from my room of shoddily built skyscrapers. I felt so lonely and depressed every time I went back to that room. The city itself I found very sad, too; the streets and the pavements were in terrible disrepair with huge holes and there were beggars everywhere, including masses of children who stood outside the hotel and rushed up every time you went in or out. They would steal anything off you, too! At night, hundreds of people were sleeping on the pavements with children and dogs around them.

On Tuesday I took off at 1 p.m., again in an Avianca Boeing 727, for Lima, Peru, where I landed around 4 p.m. It was a good flight, part of it over the Andes. I was met at the airport by Mr Antony Walter from the British Embassy, and by Señor George Rivera Schreiber, whose father had been Peruvian Ambassador in London. George Rivera Schreiber kindly drove me to the Bolivar Hotel, where I was staying. This I found was a really comfortable hotel, full of charm with wonderful service.

Next morning, the British Ambassador, Mr Hugh Morgan, a very dear quiet man, with an extremely attractive and vivacious wife Alexandra, came to collect me and drove me to the embassy. From here, we all drove up with Señor Ricardo Alvarez Calderon to Los Condores, a country club right up in the mountains where there was glorious sunshine. I was told that the sun only shines in Lima from December to April. For the other months, the city is covered in low cloud;

therefore many people who live there go up to the mountains at weekends.

We came down to have luncheon at 3.30 p.m. at the very exclusive and famous Club Nationale in Lima, which is rather like White's in London, though it allows lady guests, which of course White's does not.

I had meant to keep my last day free to write and do my packing, but it was not to be. Firstly, I was interviewed by two journalists who, to my horror, both arrived with a photographer. Then Mr David Bolger, the then head of the Bank of London and South America in London, who was at the Ambassador's party the previous evening, sent a car to take me and three delightful visiting bankers, Mr Leslie Simpson, Mr Norman Langdon, and Mr Brendan Cooper, to go round the famous Gold Museum of Peru. This is a must if you visit Lima. It has exhibits dating from as early as 800 BC and others made centuries later. That afternoon, George Schreiber and his partner, Señor Pablo Arana, took me sightseeing until it got so dark we could see no more! I had originally hoped to visit the old town of Cuzco and the lost city of the Incas, Machu Picchu, but I found that needed an extra two nights and two days which I could not spare on that visit.

On Saturday, I took off at 8.40 a.m. in a Braniff DC8 for Rio de Janeiro, where the British Ambassador Sir David Hunt and Lady Hunt had so kindly invited me to stay at the embassy. I was given my front window seat as requested. We flew over the beautiful but cruel-looking mountains of the Andes, some snow-capped, some volcanic, then over the vast Lake Titicaca and on to São Paulo, where we landed for thirty minutes. We then flew over some coffee farms, to land at Galeao Airport, Rio de Janeiro, at around 4.15 p.m.

Lady Hunt, accompanied by one of the airport officials, met me, so I was very quickly through all formalities, and on our way to the magnificent British Embassy residence. This was built when Mr Ernest Bevin was Foreign Secretary, and he wanted it to be the best in Rio de Janeiro! Nowadays it is a museum – all the embassies have been moved from Rio de Janeiro to the ultra-modern city of Brasilia.

On arrival at the embassy, I found I had a large and lovely bedroom and bathroom, and a highly trained maid to look after me. When I came downstairs to join my host and hostess before we went out to dinner, I could not believe that they had had a large charity ball in the embassy the previous evening as everything was back in its place.

David and Iro Hunt gave me the most wonderful welcome and a super week in Brazil: they gave parties at the embassy and they took me out to meet interesting friends, to enjoy lovely homes, and to see many other things of interest. On my second morning I went with David and Iro Hunt to visit Dame Margot Fonteyn's aunt, Doña Maria Cecilia Fontes, at Estrada da Gavea Pequeña, her beautiful home high up in the hills, where she was living with a large staff, and in every luxury. I thought at the time what a contrast her lifestyle was to that of her wonderful niece, dear Margot Fonteyn, who was having such a struggle financially, and still having to dance to earn money!

From here, we went to luncheon with the famous and brilliant cosmetic surgeon Senhor Doctor Ivo Pitanguy, who was very 'dishy' to look at!, and his attractive and charming blonde wife Marilu, at their lovely house, also up in the hills. When I sat next to Ivo Pitanguy at dinner later in the week, I saw he was rather staring at my face while talking to me, and I said at once in a jokey way 'I can see you are summing up how long it would take you to fix my wrinkles!' He went rather red, and we both laughed. They were a delightful couple and full of fun.

Next day I lunched with a very dear Brazilian friend I had known in London, Senhora Ricardo Jafet, who always looks so very chic. She had arranged a ladies' luncheon party of twelve very nice friends for me to meet.

That afternoon I went with Iro Hunt to the Fundacao Romao de Matos Duarte, an orphanage for children up to the age of eighteen – there were 500 of them. This is run by nuns with the help of some of the older girls who want to stay on to work here, the only home they know, and to care for the younger children.

We were shown around by the kind and gentle Mother Superior Mother Joana Nobrega, whom the children obviously loved. I think the most moving part of that tour was the tiny baby section. Thirty or more babies from a few days of age to around three months old lay there in rows of cots, oblivious to their difficult future.

I also met several members of *Bem Querer* (To Be Willing), a young voluntary organization formed by teenage girls of leading Brazilian families, who work at the orphanage two days a week. Iro Hunt, who helped so many good causes in Rio, did a lot for that orphanage and was giving a party at the embassy that Christmas for 300 of the older girls. As we were leaving, I saw something that really tore my heart –

a round cupboard on a turntable which up to a few years previously had stood at the gate of the orphanage; this is where mothers used to place their newborn babies for nuns to collect.

During my visit, I flew up to São Paulo for one night, and to Brasilia for the day. Each time, I was driven to the airport by the embassy's head chauffeur Severino, who spoke no English; and of course I spoke no Portuguese. However, on arrival at the airport each time he took care of me like a nanny, carrying my suitcase to where I had to check in, taking my ticket and passport and dealing with all formalities. He then signalled me to go and sit on a seat opposite the booking clerk, who, he indicated, would tell me when to go to the flight. All announcements were made only in Portuguese.

The clerk saw that I was looking worried when by 9 a.m. he had not yet called me for the 8.30 a.m. flight to São Paulo, so he came over and told me, speaking perfect English, that the flight had been delayed for over an hour, and that I was not to worry!

I was met at Viracopos airport by Mr Bernard Hickley from the British Consulate in São Paulo and his wife, who had kindly invited me to stay the night. We drove straight to their house, where I tidied up quickly as I was due at 1 p.m. at the home of Senhor and Senhora Sergio da Cunha Bueno Mellao, in Rua Venezuela, where Renata Mellao had arranged a luncheon party for me. She had kindly invited me earlier than her other guests, so that she and I could have a quiet talk on our own first.

My hostess is a most beautiful and very chic Brazilian lady, and had invited some delightful and very elegant Brazilian friends. When The Queen and the Duke of Edinburgh made their official visit to Brazil in 1968, they stayed with Sergio and Renata Mellao at their country home, Estancia Endorcia Campinal.

We were around twelve for a beautifully arranged luncheon. It was 4 p.m. before I left. Dona Sodre had arranged a cocktail party – all ladies! – from 6 to 8 p.m., so that I could go racing afterwards. As so few husbands could get away from work by 6 p.m., Dona Sodre had had the original idea of only inviting wives!

Dona Sodre was a wonderful hostess and introduced each guest carefully. There were around twenty or more extremely pretty girls and attractive ladies, all beautifully dressed. Many Brazilian women marry young, at sixteen or seventeen, as their mothers and grandmothers have done before them, so the average grandmother is under forty. Before the end of the party, my dear host, Roberto Sodre, whom I had also met previously in London, arrived home and braved all the ladies! I was so delighted to meet him again.

Three days later, I set my alarm for 5.00 a.m. The wonderful Josephine brought my fruit juice and hot coffee at 5.45 a.m. and at 6.15am I left with Severino (Josephine's husband) for Santos Dumont airport, where he checked me in on the 7 a.m. Varig flight to Brasilia for the day. Here I was met by Mr Richard Tallboys, the charming First Secretary in charge of the British Embassy in Brasilia, and his very sweet Australian-born wife, who then drove me round Brasilia to get a view of the city, which is ultra-modern. Not only are the streets one-way, but the pavements are too, so you never meet a friend if you are on foot.

The only really beautiful building I saw was the Palacio dos Arcos, which is the Brazilian Foreign Office; this is most wonderfully designed and is surrounded by a moat in which are set some superb modern sculptures. Inside, there is a vast marble hall with a spiral staircase that has no visible support, and on the ground floor a most attractively designed tropical water garden. We went up to the first-floor reception room, again vast, where the Foreign Minister receives 3,000 guests on the annual Day of the Diplomat Ball. We saw the banqueting hall, a smaller dining room and smaller reception rooms.

Later the same day I flew back to Rio, where Severino and the car were waiting. I had expected, as it was my last night, a quiet evening at the Embassy in the company of my kind host and hostess, but when I got home, I found that after dinner we were going up to the hills to the wonderful new home of Senhor Manoel Bayard Lucas de Lima and his beautiful wife, Beatrizinha, to see how wonderful Rio looks at night.

Because of the kidnapping of four members of the diplomatic corps in the preceding eighteen months, great security precautions had to be taken, not only at the Embassy, where there were armed guards at the entrance, but also every time the Ambassador went out. There was always an armed body guard in a preceding Land-Rover, an armed guard sitting beside the chauffeur, and another one in the car behind. All were fully trained, skilled marksmen. When I was in the Rolls alone going to and from the airport, I was always locked in, and the first day I was shown the alarm button under my feet.

I was very sad to say goodbye to dear David and Ira Hunt, who had given me such a wonderful week. David has now returned to this country, and they have a delightful home in Sussex. David Hunt, who is a very brilliant man, has won the final of *Mastermind* on television on two occasions. Brazil ended my South American tour, which I found most exhilarating.

On my many summer visits to Greece I was as always taken the greatest care of by Mr and Mrs Nico Brissimis, such staunch, loyal friends for many years. During my visit in 1972 we all flew over to stay with Mr Perry Embiricos in his lovely home, Tragonissi, in the Petali group of islands, which have been owned by the Embiricos family for many years. At the airport on the Saturday I met Mr and Mrs Winston Churchill and their enchanting children, who had flown out from England in his Piper Seneca, and had been staying on Spetsia. They were then off to spend the day on Skiathos, famed for its fabulous sandy beach. We took off in an Alouette helicopter and landed on a small clearing in the rock, where we were greeted by our kind host and British ballerina Dame Alicia Markova, who was another house guest.

We had a bathe in the sea before luncheon. I was interested in the beautiful garden with green lawns that had been created in twelve years, and in the kitchen garden where there were long beds of melons and cucumbers growing outdoors, and an apricot, peach and nectarine orchard. After luncheon we went in one of my host's motor boats to visit his elder brother Mr Andy Embiricos and his American-born wife and teenage son Nico on the nearby island of Xeros. This family home I found particularly fascinating as the guest rooms were at one time the harem of a Turkish general who lived there, and the main house was only built during the 1914–18 war. It was ordered by the late Marise Embiricos by post from an American catalogue! The result was a charming comfy home.

A very special party that I well remember going to that summer was one given by the American Ambassador and Mrs Walter Annenberg at the American Embassy residence, Winfield House. It was arranged to perfection. Walter Annenberg's fine collection of Impressionists was a beautiful setting in itself, and the profusion of beautiful flowers everywhere was sensational. Looped garlands of fresh pink roses formed chandeliers right down the high built-out ballroom, and there were swags of these flowers over every window. Lilies, stocks and other sweet-smelling flowers were at the doorways and around every pillar, and the candles on the tables were all in bowls of tightly packed pink rose heads. These glorious flower arrangements had been done by Michael Goulding.

There were also an outdoor canopied dance floor and two bands. One of these was Meyer Davis, who had been flown in from America. Everything was arranged beautifully. After they had stopped receiving, Walter and Lee Annenberg went quietly round seeing everyone was happy: they were always wonderful hosts. The 600 guests varied from the Prince of Wales to Mr Frank Sinatra, and included Princess Margaret and the Duke and Duchess of Kent, and friends from the Government and from all over the world. I dined with Lord and Lady Keith before coming on to the dance, so I had a good start. The evening seemed to fly by and when I looked at my watch it was 2 a.m. What a super party to be able to remember.

The first of the royal weddings of the seventies that I went to was the marriage of Princess Anne to Captain Mark Phillips at Westminster Abbey in 1973. Her Royal Highness made a most attractive bride, wearing a dress of white wild silk, with her silk tulle veil held in place by a sunray diamond tiara, as she walked up the aisle on the arm of the Duke of Edinburgh. Her Royal Highness did not have a long retinue of bridesmaids. She was attended only by her youngest brother Prince Edward, wearing the kilt, and her cousin Lady Sarah Armstrong-Jones, wearing a long white wild silk tunic dress and a little Juliet cap. Both were then nine years old. Sadly the Princess Royal, as she now is, and her husband have recently had a divorce.

In June, the Chairman and directors of Moët et Chandon, who own Dior perfumes, invited me and a party of their friends to stay at their lovely Château de Saran on the Côte des Blancs and to a christening party at Epernay for their new perfume, Diorella.

I was told that I had to fly over to France on the eve of the Epsom Derby, which meant quite a rush. We took off after lunch and landed at Rheims and drove straight to the charming Moët et Chandon Château de Saran, where I changed quickly. Then I drove with Lady Duke, who was then the chatelaine at the château, to the Trianon in Epernay, owned by Moët et Chandon. Here in the courtyard, a picturesque brass band was playing. We entered and went up the marble staircase to the magnificent gold and mirrored suite. Here we were received by the good-looking and most charming Comte Robert-Jean de Vogüé, the Président d'Honneur of Moët et Chandon, and his very elegant wife, and the then Chairman and his wife, Monsieur and Madame Bernard Picot.

Later we all walked across the beautiful formal gardens to the Orangerie, where tables laid with pink tablecloths adorned with pink candles in silver candelabra were arranged around the palms and other plants. In the background, a pyramid of champagne glasses had been built. I sat on the right of my dear and very amusing host Bob de Vogué and had a most enjoyable dinner. Just before the sweet courses, a gigantic iced christening cake in the form of a bottle of Christian Dior's Diorella was wheeled in on a trolley by the chef. Then my host asked me and another godmother to take part in cutting the cake while he stood between us. While we cut the cake, Bob de Vogué took his sword, and with one dramatic sweep he slashed the top off a bottle of vintage champagne to celebrate the occasion. In the meantime, the pyramid of glasses behind us was being filled with champagne and cascaded down like a fountain. Diorella certainly had a good send-off. It was well after midnight before we left for Saran.

I only had a very few hours in bed as I had to be up at 5.30 a.m. to motor to Paris to catch an early flight to London as it was Derby Day. I remember boarding the aeroplane and seeing Mr and Mrs Alec Head – he was then France's leading trainer – and their son Freddie Head, who had a mount in the Derby, sitting there. Alec Head asked me why I was going to the Derby from Paris. They were so surprised to see me on the flight.

On a Sunday in the autumn of 1973 I boarded a Qantas Boeing 747 flight to Sydney for the official opening by The Queen of the Sydney Opera House the following Saturday. I was in my front window seat and settled myself down comfortably for the night. Our flight, originally routed over Damascus, was diverted, owing to the war in the Middle East, so we took a longer route via Tehran. Next morning we flew down the Persian Gulf, over Muscat, out across the Arabian Sea, on to Bombay and the lower part of India; then luncheon was announced. I returned to my seat as I had been working up in the Captain Cook cabin. After luncheon I had an hour's sleep, then I did my patchwork until we landed at Singapore, where we were asked to disembark as we had a two-hour wait. When we reboarded at around 21 hours local time, I opened my copy of David Niven's hilarious book *The Moon's a Balloon*, which was making me laugh. Dinner was to be served quite soon. Suddenly, when about thirty minutes out from Singapore, our captain announced that one of our engines had gone, and that necessitated our landing again at Singapore after using up the required amount of fuel to make it safe to land. I had had this happen in a Boeing 707 on my way to the Bahamas several years before, so I was never in any way worried as I heard later other passengers were.

I went on reading my amusing book and never saw the fire engines and ambulance lined up ready as our pilot made a perfect landing on three engines.

We were told we would have to stay the night. First-class passengers were taken with only their overnight hand luggage to the Singapore Hilton, where I had a large and comfy room. We were supposed to take off in the morning. But, alas, a call came to our rooms to say the other aircraft they hoped to get was not available as there was a strike on in Bangkok where they had spare engines, so we would have to wait until another engine arrived from Sydney. I had the chance of going on Tuesday night economy class on another airline without my luggage, which I declined. The Qantas officials were splendid and did everything they could for us, including on Tuesday afternoon arranging a most interesting coach tour of Singapore, during which I shared a seat for two with Mr Harry Secombe, then a rather large gentleman, which left little room for me! He had joined the flight at Singapore to Sydney for an engagement there, and kept us all in fits of laughter. We at last took off on Wednesday, and landed at 10.45 p.m. at Sydney airport.

I had cleared all formalities, and, arriving days late, believed no one would be there to meet me, so it was to my joy and amazement that I saw Sir John Pagan, the former Agent-General for New South Wales in England, and Lady Pagan in evening dress after an official dinner, there to meet me with their car and chauffeur to drive me to the Wentworth Hotel. I have never been so grateful for such true Australian kindness, just when I really needed it.

I had missed the Wednesday briefing and ticket collection for the royal visit, so I went along to the Sydney Opera House on Thursday morning to try and collect my tickets for the opening and various other functions. As I had not turned up the day before, no one seemed to know what had happened to my tickets. Everyone seemed in a flap and no one seemed to know who had what! Eventually I left with all I needed except the ticket for the Gala Opera on the Monday, which eventually arrived at my hotel.

On Saturday, the moment for the long-awaited official opening by The Queen of the Sydney Opera House had arrived. There was a howling gale blowing all day, otherwise everything was perfect. The setting was fabulous, and the sun shone on the new opera house, which is right on the harbour. It is a fantastic-shaped building made of ceramic tiles, and an acre and a half of glass composed of 2,000 panes in 700 different sizes. It was started in 1957 by a Danish architect, followed by a number of other architects, and had taken sixteen years to complete.

The harbour was filled with nearly two thousand craft of every size, from battleships, pleasure steamers, yachts and motor cruisers to barges, rowing boats and an amphibian car! Most of the boats were dressed overall. Two large fire-fighting floats played their jet sprays in the shape of the opera house, and there were hundreds of balloons in nets on barges which needed constant attention owing to the gale, in case they broke loose before the given time.

The opening ceremony was timed for 3 p.m. I arrived at 1.45 and took up my allotted place on a seat nearly opposite the royal dais, in a wonderful position to see all that was going on. Guests arrived in their hundreds, stands were filled to capacity and by the opening it was estimated there were one million spectators around on sea and land. All the women wore pretty summer dresses but were clutching their hats; I only saw one blow off into the sea.

Trumpeters played a fanfare as the royal Rolls-Royce drew up. The Queen stepped out wearing a neat aquamarine blue silk dress and close-fitting small hat to match, accompanied by the Duke of Edinburgh. They were received by the Governor, Sir Roden Cutler, and Lady Cutler and the Premier and Lady Askin, then proceeded to the royal dais. After 'God Save The Queen' had been played, there was a spectacular fly-past of nine F111s by the RAAF. Then came the most dramatic moment when Aborigine, 'Bennelong' stood in this howling gale on top of the highest point of the opera house and in a clear voice for two minutes delivered a most moving prologue, simulating the Aborigine after whom the point was named. The Premier of NSW, Sir Robert Askin, then made a speech of welcome confirming Australia's loyalty to the Crown. The Queen then made her very sincere opening speech in a clear, resonant voice, and calmly overcame the difficulty of the gale blowing her notes about in her hand.

After The Queen had declared the new Sydney Opera House open, there was a fly-past of helicopters. Then Her Majesty went inside to unveil a plaque and make a short tour of inspection. During this period, guests were entertained by the band of the Australian Navy and on the dais by dancers and actors of the Ma-Wai-Hakona Maori Group, who gave a colourful performance. As The Queen came out of the opera house, the sixty thousand coloured balloons in barges in the harbour were released to make a fabulous spectacle as they rose in the sunlight

over hundreds of craft whose sirens and horns then sounded a tumultuous welcome, and a spirit of excitement pervaded the air. The whole
of this elaborate opening and the other official opening functions to
follow were arranged voluntarily by Sir Asher Joel, who had a fantastic
gift for organization, combined with original ideas which he made sure
were carried out to perfection.

That Saturday evening I dined with Sir John and Lady Pagan, who
had a large dinner party before we all went on to the opening concert
at the newly opened Sydney Opera House, which was attended by The
Queen and the Duke of Edinburgh. Her Majesty, looking superb in a
gold and silver embroidered white satin evening dress with a pearl and
diamond tiara and diamond necklace and earrings, and the Order of
the Garter and the blue riband of the Order of the Garter across her
bodice, arrived punctually. They were received by the Governor General and Lady Hasluck and the Governor and Lady Cutler. One felt so
proud of our dear Queen. She looked magnificent. It was a big occasion
with a number of Australian dignitaries present and everyone wearing
evening dress and their orders and decorations.

After the concert, The Queen and the Duke of Edinburgh went to
a small reception and met the conductor and the artists. I went to a
bigger one in the foyer, and with Mr Charles Lloyd Jones and his
cousin, Mrs John Lewis, I made a short tour of the opera house and
saw the organ, which is the biggest I have ever seen, with 127 stops,
consisting of 10,500 pipes, the largest mechanical-action organ in the
world.

The Queen's final official engagement was at the opera on Monday
evening when Her Majesty and the Duke of Edinburgh attended a
performance of *The Magic Flute*. On this occasion, The Queen wore
an orange silk organza dress embroidered in rhinestones (which went
so well with the orange seats of the opera house), a diamond tiara and
necklace, but no Order of the Garter. It was a much less formal occasion
than Saturday. The Queen and the Duke of Edinburgh sat in the centre
of the front row of the circle with Lady Susan Hussey, the Hon. Sir
Martin Charteris, Mr Ronald Allison and the other members of their
small entourage behind. At the end of the performance, the royal
couple left in an open car for the airport. All along the route, they
were cheered by hundreds of loyal Australian citizens who had been
standing for hours to catch a glimpse of their own Queen of Australia.
The Queen boarded the Qantas Boeing 707 wearing her evening dress
and tiara, and said goodbye to the Duke of Edinburgh who was staying

on in Australia for another two weeks for a tour under the Duke of Edinburgh Award Scheme.

The Hon. Colin Tennant, now the 3rd Lord Glenconner, had several times invited me to visit the Caribbean island of Mustique, which he had bought and carefully developed, so in February 1974 I planned a trip via St Lucia and St Vincent. When I arrived at Mustique Colin Tennant was waiting with a jeep beside the airstrip as the Islander landed. He quickly took me off to see some houses being built, several of them designed by Oliver Messel, before luncheon. I visited Princess Margaret's house, designed by Oliver Messel, which was at the time let to friends; the Earl of Lichfield's house nearby was just being finished, and I saw Lady Honor Svejdar's newly built dream house, also designed by Oliver Messel, high up overlooking Honor's Bay. There was only one hotel on the island, the Cotton House, where I stayed for the night. It only had eight double bedrooms and bathrooms, all beautifully furnished and very comfortable. The only slight setback on my visit was shortage of water; I only managed to get a couple of inches of tepid water to bathe in.

The hotel had a giant, cool living room with wide shady verandahs all round. This was furnished with fascinating ornate and magnificent pieces, which gave the feeling of elegant living in the old plantation days. We lunched beside the swimming pool at the Cotton House and in the afternoon Colin Tennant took me on another tour of the island. In the evening Colin – wearing, I remember, a pale blue satin shirt!– arrived to collect me and took me to the little Humming Bird restaurant on the water's edge, where we joined most of the householders in residence and their guests for a delicious chicken barbecue and dancing to a discotheque, which was very colourful and fun. As I went to bed I reflected on what a unique, simple and gracious little island this was to escape to from the worrying modern world.

Next morning my kind host drove me in the jeep to the airstrip, a few minutes' drive. I said goodbye and lots of thanks. I left full of admiration for his high standard of development and all he was doing for the care and happiness of the islanders of Mustique, who, I could see, as we drove round, had respect and gratitude for what he had already done.

In the autumn of 1974 I flew out on my second visit to Beirut, where I had been invited for a weekend for the finals of the British-Lebanese Backgammon Championships. On arrival, I was met by Mrs Mona Aki of Middle East Airlines, who had a car waiting to take me to the Saint George Hotel. I was killed with kindness as M. George Asseilly, who was away in England, also sent his car and chauffeur and charming secretary to meet me! What a wonderful welcome. On arrival at the hotel I was taken up to a lovely bedroom with an enormous balcony right over the sea.

On Saturday morning I drove with Mr Omar Saab up to see the new facilities for skiing in the mountains behind Beirut. Their saying is 'In Beirut you can ski in the morning and swim in the sea in the afternoon.' We took the road that eventually leads to Turkey via Tripoli and Syria, turned off and climbed 1,800 metres to the village of Faraya-Mzaar. Here a very attractive summer and winter holiday village had sprung up with a large modern hotel where later we had an excellent luncheon. It was near very modern and fast ski lifts and T-bars which take you up to a height of 2,443 metres to numerous ski runs. The chair lifts installed carried 500 skiers an hour. Lebanon may seem a long way to go to ski, but Middle East Airlines were then running very reasonable party flights.

In the evening I went with friends to the casino to dine and see the floor show. This was one of the most spectacular shows of its kind in the world and went on for over two hours. There was never a dull moment, from showgirls riding on elephants between the tables, to white Arab horses galloping towards you on an electric carpet!

On Sunday I lunched with George Asseilly's dear mother, Mrs Edward Asseilly, at the Saint George. In the afternoon I went to the Phoenicia Hotel (where I stayed on my previous visit), where the British-Lebanese Backgammon Championships had just started and were being televised. There were two teams of six players, and play was expected to end at 7.30 p.m., but it went on until 8 p.m. when the two teams had each won the same number of games and, amazingly, points! As the well-known Lebanese banker Mr Henri Pharaon, who was one of the players, had arranged a dinner party at his lovely home, it was decided to adjourn and have the play-off after dinner at Mr Pharaon's home. Earlier, having seen that the match would go on longer than expected, I slipped away just before 6 p.m. to my hotel to change and to visit the British Ambassador Mr Paul Wright and his very dear wife, whom I had not met for fifteen years, now Sir Paul and Lady Wright, at the British Embassy. The Wrights had been living abroad for years while he was fulfilling diplomatic posts, and I was so happy to catch up with news of her and Paul, and of her children, whose father Mr John Rathbone, an MP, had been killed in 1940 in World War II.

As Paul Wright was also dining with Henri Pharaon, he kindly took me on to the house and took me home later. Henri Pharaon had one of the most beautiful homes in the Middle East, full of priceless treasures that he had moved room by room from Syria. It was a formal, perfectly arranged dinner of around twenty-four guests at one long table on which was exquisite silver and glass. At the end of dinner there were short speeches from our host and both captains of the backgammon teams, and from Monsieur Tony Fanjey, son of the then President of the Lebanon, who was a minister in the Lebanese Government. Around 11 p.m. the television cameras arrived and took up position around the solitary table and backgammon board on which the final play-off match was to take place. I learnt that this would take two hours, so I was relieved that Paul Wright and Monsieur Fanjey decided not to stay and watch the end, and I was home before midnight. I learnt next morning that it went on until 4 a.m., Lebanon winning in the end after a very friendly championship, which they hoped to continue annually.

I flew home next morning never thinking that it would be the last time I would see wonderful Beirut as it was then. The wars and destruction of everything, including the Saint George Hotel, started soon after my visit.

Early in 1975 I had the great honour to be invited to attend an evening reception given by The Queen and the Duke of Edinburgh at Buckingham Palace. It was a very unexpected invitation, so doubly exciting. A little while before the evening, the very dear and kind Lord Plunket, who was Deputy Master of The Queen's Household from 1954, rang me to enquire if I had found friends to go with to the Palace on the evening of Her Majesty's party. As I had kept very quiet about my invitation, I had not heard of a soul going. I suddenly had a brainwave and thought of Dick Wilkins, who I had known well for so many years and who was a close friend of the Royal Family, so I enquired if he was going. Patrick Plunket, immediately said 'Yes, and I will ring Dick and ask him to bring you, as it would be much nicer for you to come with him than come alone.' I thought that really was the kindest act, and from a very sick man, who, to the sorrow of all members of the Royal Family and a great number of friends, died a few weeks later aged only fifty-two.

On the evening, Dick Wilkins gave me dinner at the Savoy and off we went to the Palace. Having Dick with me, I was not a bundle of nerves and so I was able to enjoy every moment of the evening. I so well remember going up the Grand Staircase to the Green Drawing Room, where The Queen, wearing a very pretty evening dress, received me with a radiant welcoming smile and kind words. It is a moment I shall never forget! Next to Her Majesty stood the Duke of Edinburgh in jovial mood. He kindly referred to my escort; next was Queen Elizabeth the Queen Mother, who also gave me a warm, kind welcome, and the Prince of Wales, who of course was then unmarried. Walking round the state rooms, which were full of exquisite azaleas and other flowers from the Windsor Castle gardens, were Princess Anne, Mrs Mark Phillips, Princess Alice Duchess of Gloucester, the Duke and Duchess of Gloucester, the Duke and Duchess of Kent, Princess Alexandra, the Hon. Mrs Angus Ogilvy, and the Hon. Angus Ogilvy. The other guests included the Prime Minister and Mrs Harold Wilson and three of his predecessors in that role, government ministers and back benchers from all parties, Trade Union leaders and their wives, leaders in commerce and industry, philanthropists, bishops, historians, editors of newspapers, financial and political writers from some of the provincial as well as London papers, and a number of guests from the film, stage and television worlds. I remember Princess Alexandra asking me if I had seen Jimmy Saville as she wanted to speak to him. Happily I had seen him and could direct her.

I am sure that everyone enjoyed this wonderful evening that our beloved Queen had personally taken so much interest arranging. I enjoyed every moment and have always felt very privileged to have had the honour to be invited.

In June I went to the first of only two wedding receptions I have been to at Arundel Castle. This reception was after the marriage of the Earl of Ancram, son of the Marquess and Marchioness of Lothian, to Lady Jane Fitzalan-Howard, youngest daughter of the late Duke of Norfolk and Lavinia Duchess of Norfolk, that had just taken place in the Cathedral Church of Our Lady and St Philip Howard, Arundel. The bride, who wore a dress of white silk organza embroidered on the bodice and a diamond tiara holding her tulle veil in place, had a retinue of eleven children. The young couple, both looking radiant, received the guests, who numbered around a thousand, alone at the end of the Long Gallery. Their parents moved between the Great Hall and the lawn in the centre of the castle, where the sun was shining, and greeted relations and friends. These included a great many tenants and employees from the Arundel estate, from the Yorkshire, and Scottish estates of the bride's family, and from the bridegroom's family homes in Derbyshire and Scotland. The young couple cut their wedding cake with the sun shining on them in the centre of the lawn in the courtyard with all their friends around them and then the Earl of Perth proposed their health with a charming brief speech. I have always remembered this wedding as such a very happy, beautifully arranged one in this fine setting.

Later the same month, I travelled down in a rush from York, where I had been to a dinner in aid of the National Society for Cancer Relief, on the sleeper to London, so that Peter could meet me at 6.30 a.m. and drive me quickly to the flat to have a bath, change, repack and be ready to leave again at 8.30 a.m. for the Twenty-Four Hours Sports Car Race at Le Mans.

At 8.30 a.m. prompt, Mr Patrick Forbes, then Managing Director of Moët et Chandon England, called with a car to take me to Gatwick. On our way we stopped to collect the Hon. Sir Clive and Lady Barbara Bossom, who were also guests of Moët et Chandon to see the race: Clive Bossom had just been made Chairman of the Royal Automobile Club.

We were due to take off from Gatwick at 10 a.m. in a charter Piper Navajo Chieftain from Thurston Aviation Company at Stapleford, which eventually arrived for us an hour late! I sat out in the sun and managed to get through quite a lot of proof reading, so I did not personally worry at wasting time. After a good flight, we landed at Le Mans beside the course, where two cars came right up to the aircraft to take us into the very attractive Moët-Hennessy Club in the middle of the race circuit. Here Comte Frédéric Chandon de Briailles, the Chairman of Moët et Chandon, and his young son Olivier were waiting to greet us. Very quickly a glass of ice-cold champagne was given to us all and a delicious cold luncheon was served on the lawn of the club under the trees.

Around 3 p.m. we left for the Moët et Chandon-Hennessy stand right beside the track to watch the start of the famous 24 hour Le Mans race. Fifty-five cars were competing. This close-up picture is something I have always remembered. As the cars slowly took up their positions three abreast, the noise became sensational. One saw the last-moment checking, a tremendous roar and they were off!

There were two drivers to each car and they mostly changed places after driving for one or two hours. After watching the cars come round for several laps of the course, which is 13,640 metres each lap, some of us decided to go and watch from another point. So, after walking through the shops, milling crowds and campers with loudspeakers and car exhausts blaring everwhere, we eventually arrived at the two sharp S-bends before the long straight stretch from Tertre Rouge Virage to Mulsanne.

To me this was all a great thrill. It was my first ever Le Mans and I wanted to get the atmosphere and see all I could. So after watching the race here for several laps, we crossed the course by an underground tunnel and walked back on the other side of the track, going through the fairground where there were giant wheels, switchbacks, round-abouts and every imaginable fairground attraction accompanied by the loudest hurdy-gurdy music. It was a glorious afternoon and there were spectators and campers everywhere in every form of dress, most of them preparing to spend the night out around the race track. There were then annually over three hundred and fifty thousand spectators at this race. From here we returned to the Moët-Hennessy Club, where I sank into a chair and enjoyed a long cool soft drink before setting off with Clive Bossom and an escort to the Gulf-Ford pits, where the team's well-known manager, Mr John Wyer, with exceptional kind-ness allowed us to have a close-up of the refilling and change-over of drivers of the Gulf-Ford GR8, driven by Mr Derek Bell and the Belgian Grand Prix driver Monsieur Jackie Ickx, which by then had gone into the lead.

We saw Jacky Ickx step into his fireproof driving suit and put on his crash helmet and visor, and we saw each mechanic ready with petrol hose in hand, another with an oil can, and another with a spanner and so on. The whole servicing and change-over took under a minute. Jack Wyer, who had been manager of the successful Aston Martin team, was at that time considered the greatest and most successful team manager there had ever been. I was introduced to Derek Bell, a real extrovert, who had just come off the track. He had his wife and children there from Sussex to watch the race.

We walked back to the Moët-Hennessy Club, where we were joined by Barbara Bossom, the 3rd Lord Redesdale and Patrick Forbes before setting off again to watch the race. Later we had a tidy-up in the club, then our host Freddie Chandon took a big party off to dine at the Welcome & Co restaurant beside the race track, where we had a super dinner. After dinner, with a new moon overhead, we sat out watching the cars racing in the dark at 100 m.p.h. At midnight the stands

opposite were still full of spectators. We all decided to leave around
1 a.m. On our way to two cars that were waiting to take us to our
various billets, Clive Bossom and Clem Redesdale, such a dear and
amusing man, could not resist one of the crêpes Grand Marnier being
sold freshly made on one of the stalls! I stayed very comfortably with
Monsieur and Madame Gaillard-Bergerall in rue de la Mariette. I was
quite glad to get to bed, only having had a few hours' sleep sitting in
the train the previous night.

At 10 a.m. on Sunday, after a lovely hot bath and delicious breakfast,
I said goodbye to my kind host and hostess and drove back to the race
track and left my hand luggage at the Moët-Hennessy Club. I then
went to watch the racing. I got the impression at this point that
everyone at the course seemed a little weary and there was not as much
sparkle around as the day before. At 11.30 a.m. some of us were taken
in two official cars to see the long straight stretch on the other side of
the course before the slowing-down for Mulsanne. Here we saw
another side of the intense organization, with members of each team
displaying flags with instructions to their drivers. This was a very active
part of proceedings, and, like the pits, barred to the public, as timing
and precision are so vital. We again had a delicious buffet luncheon at
the Moët-Hennessy Club under shady trees. At 3.30 p.m. the Bossoms,
Patrick Forbes, Clem Redesdale and I went along to the Dunlop stand,
where they had kindly invited us as it was much closer to the finishing
line than the Moët et Chandon stand, where we had watched the last
few laps. The race finished at 4 p.m. Happily, we were all able to raise
a great cheer for a British win, the first since 1969. Number 11, the
Gulf-Ford GRS driven by Bell and Ickx with Derek Bell at the wheel,
went over the line nearly two laps ahead of the French Ligier JS2
driven by Jean-Louis Lafosse and Guy Chesseuil, with another Gulf-
Ford driven by Vern Schuppan and Jean Pierrier third. It was a great
triumph for John Wyer and his team. Freddie Chandon invited John
Wyer and his wife and the six leading drivers to the Moët-Hennessy
Club, where magnums of Moët et Chandon were soon opened for the
teams and a number of friends to celebrate with. Around 7.30 p.m.,
we said goodbye to dear kind Freddie Chandon de Briailles who had
been such a wonderful host to us all, and arrived back at Gatwick
around 7.30 p.m. our time. I had enjoyed every moment of my first
Le Mans and I was so grateful for all the kindness, care and hospitality
of all at Moët et Chandon.

I arrived at the flat at 8.45 p.m. to find my dear son, who had been spending two nights in Sussex with his in-laws, waiting for me. It was his last evening in England. I had a quick tidy-up and we walked round to the Dorchester Grill to enjoy our last dinner together for many months.

Next morning I left the flat with Jim at 9.30 a.m. for London airport, where we were joined by my daughter-in-law and her parents and my granddaughter. For me those partings with Jim are always the greatest sadness, so I was grateful for a very busy day in my office.

This year, in November, I made a five-day trip to the Seychelles, flying out with Mr John Houlder and his wife, and a party of his friends, mostly from the gas and oil industries, and mostly accompanied by their wives. The object of our visit was the opening of the Mahé Beach Hotel, a new Houlder hotel, which had just been built on the southwest coast of Mahé Island, the largest of the beautiful Seychelles Islands.

I was amazed to see that trees and lawns and masses of flowers and climbing tropical plants were already established around the hotel. I had a large bedroom and sitting room on the fourth floor, looking out over the sea and the verdant green Thérèse Island, with a large balcony where I enjoyed my breakfast each morning.

One day I flew over to Bird Island in a charter Islander aeroplane with John and Eileen Houlder, and several others. We touched down on the tiny airstrip of this enchanting little island, which at that time had only one large thatched building, a restaurant with a large bar. This was built entirely by Monsieur Guy Savy, who runs both the restaurant and the eight little thatched double and single chalets, with bathrooms, around it. In those days, that was all there was on the island, and it was totally unspoilt. I hope it has remained so. There is the finest pale pink sandy beach which goes on for miles, one of the best I have seen anywhere in the world, blue, blue sea, with lovely fluffy terns and other birds everywhere you look.

Another day, I was flown over to the much bigger Praslin Island, which at that time they were planning to develop quite fast.

We lunched and dined, usually outdoors, at the Mahé Beach Hotel; otherwise we tried some of the many little restaurants, some adjoining smaller hotels, nearly always outdoors. It was so enjoyable being in such a big party, as I always seemed to be doing things with different people.

On our second evening, I drove over with John and Eileen Houlder and two others in the party to dine with Mr James Mancham, soon to be Sir James Mancham, then Prime Minister of the Seychelles, at his house La Maison Blanche. It was a beautifully arranged dinner party of twelve. James Mancham, who is a qualified barrister, I found most interesting and intelligent, with great *joie de vivre*. That night he was full of the expansion of the Seychelles, being determined to make it of a very high standard, with no high-rise buildings. He wanted to make it a haven for tourists while at the same time bringing prosperity to the island and islanders.

He was keen, he told me, on travel and the joys of air travel. I always remember his remarking to me that now, with air travel, the world was his village. He was Chief Minister 1970–75, then Prime Minister of the Seychelles from 1975–76, and President in 1976–77, but he had to leave when there was an uprising and coup about 1976. Since then, he has spent much of his time in England.

On Saturday evening, there was the big 'opening' party. The official opening was performed by the Prime Minister, Mr James Mancham, in the presence of the Governor, Mr Hamilton Allen, and members of the Government, followed by speeches, including one by John Houlder, who paid tribute to the architect, Mr Graham McCullough, and to all those who had taken part in building the Mahé Beach Hotel, which he said was the first of its type in the Indian Ocean. He went on to say that they employed over 300 in the hotel, only fifteen of whom had ever worked in a hotel. The rest had all been trained by the Mahé Beach Hotel management.

During this wonderful six days, I had hopped to so many islands, seen so much, including watching the locals pick tea, seen coffee growing, wonderful tropical flora and birds, and was given such a lovely whirl that I only had time to bathe in the sea once!

I hope to return one day, if my time does not run out!

THIRTEEN

Recession at home, travels abroad

(1976–79)

In 1975 and 1976, as there were far fewer parties owing to the continued recession, I travelled quite a lot so as to fill my pages! Having
made that fascinating trip to the Seychelles in 1975, I took off in
January 1976 for South Africa. But this time I went the leisurely way,
in every comfort, in a large and airy cabin in the Union Castle Mail
Steamship Company's flagship RMS *Windsor Castle*.

Peter drove me to Southampton and right up through the giant
dockside shed beside the ship and to the area for passport controls and
formalities. A porter was beside the car immediately to take my luggage, which he assured me I would next see in my cabin. Peter had
timed my arrival here to be well in advance of the boat train from
Waterloo to avoid a crowd. I said goodbye to him and went up the
gangway.

Once I was on board, a young ship's officer met me, escorted me to
my cabin and introduced me to Joe Lewis, who was to be my efficient
and willing steward for the next thirteen days. My cabin had two
large portholes and masses of hanging and drawer room, pretty chintz
covers, and really comfy furniture, including a large armchair. I decided
to unpack before we left port. Then I went up to the promenade deck,
where Mr Bernard Cayzer, the Deputy Chairman of the UCMSC, and
a very dear man, and Mr John Andreae, one of the directors, had kindly
invited me to the pre-departure cocktail party in the small drawing
room. At the party I met the Captain of the *Windsor Castle*, Captain
Philip St Q Beadon, and his very pretty wife Tracey.

At 1 p.m. prompt, we sailed out of Southampton. I watched the coast
of England fade further and further away before I went down to luncheon. I had caused dear Bernard Cayzer quite a problem by asking if I
could have a table for one instead of sitting at the table of one of the
ship's officers. I had been given a small table for two, right on the side of
the restaurant, which was just what I had hoped for. I could not face the

thought of having to lunch and dine at a certain time for thirteen days, or having to make conversation to the same group of strangers!

The Captain very kindly invited me to dine one evening, which I was delighted to accept, and so did another of the ship's officers; otherwise I was happily alone except when a fellow passenger and friend, Rohays Boyd-Rochfort, had a cold and stayed in her cabin for a couple of days, and her husband, Sir Cecil Boyd-Rochfort, the famous trainer, asked if he could come and join me. As he was a dear man, and no effort, I was delighted to see him.

On the first night at sea there was quite a lot of movement in the ship and both sky and sea looked extremely stormy. Around 6.30 p.m. I changed and joined friends for a drink before dinner, which I decided to have soon after 7.30 p.m. as I wanted to get to bed early, having come on board really tired.

On my way up from the dining room I found the ship was pitching a lot and it was quite difficult to walk; the following day I learnt that we had been in a Force Nine gale. Soon after I reached my cabin, feeling rather odd, it suddenly dawned on me that I was probably feeling seasick for the first time in my life! I at once took an Avomine tablet, which stopped the nausea, and happily I was soon tucked up in my comfy bed with a bottle of Schweppes Malvern water beside me, feeling much better.

The next thing I heard was the 8 a.m. World News on Saturday morning. As the sky looked grey, I decided to stay in bed for another hour and dozed off. The next thing I knew a steward was bringing me a cable at 1 p.m! So, having missed lunch, I returned to bed and quickly fell asleep again until I heard the 6 p.m. World News on a loudspeaker. This time I shot out of bed and into a bath as I had been invited to the Captain's cocktail party at 6.45 p.m. By now the sea was calmer and the ship steady. When I was dressed I suddenly realized I felt better than I had done for weeks.

The party was great fun. I then enjoyed a delicious dinner all on my own without having to make any effort. When I came on this trip I had promised to try and relax and to take life quietly so that I could enjoy and benefit from the comfort and care that the *Windsor Castle* provided. I did this up to a point, as I had brought a lot of work with me which had to be done before I arrived in Cape Town. As I have never been athletic or a swimmer I did not join in the deck games or dive into the swimming pool. I took a good walk each day round and round the deck, and rode miles on a bicycle in the gymnasium. There were heated swimming pools in both first and second class on the *Windsor Castle*. For others more energetic, as well as the gymnasium to exercise in, there were a variety of deck games, two cricket matches, and the Crossing the Line ceremony. There was bridge afternoon and evening, cinemas, a hilarious pantomime, endless cocktail parties before lunch and dinner, dancing to a good band in the lounge, and lastly the Late Night Disco. What I found amazing was that all this activity could be going on without disturbing anyone. If, like myself, you did not wish to compete, you could enjoy perfect peace and quiet. Otherwise something was organized to keep passengers amused every hour throughout the voyage.

On the last night I went with two friends, Sir Anthony and Lady Burney, who had boarded at Las Palmas, to have a look at the Late Night Disco, where the young were dancing enthusiastically and having a really happy time. I soon found myself joining hands and singing 'Auld Lang Syne' on the dance floor in truly British fashion.

At 9.30 a.m. the next morning I said goodbye to my excellent steward Joe Lewis, who had taken the greatest care of me and my cabin. I had thoroughly enjoyed my thirteen days at sea with every comfort. It is so sad that this very fine shipping line no longer exists, and there are no longer luxurious cruise ships like the *Windsor Castle* sailing to and from South Africa.

I had a lovely room at the Mount Nelson Hotel looking out on Table Mountain. This hotel then belonged to the Union Castle line and Bernard Cayzer took a great personal interest in seeing that it was superbly run. Now the hotel is owned by another very dear friend, American Mr James Sherwood of Sea Containers, who also own my beloved Cipriani Hotel in Venice.

During that visit I went racing at both Milnerton and, very comfortably, Kenilworth on 'Met Day', which is the Cape's biggest racing event of the year, when the President and Mrs Diederichs and several Members of Parliament were present.

Mrs Gordon Kirkpatrick, who spends three months of each winter in Cape Town, took me to watch a very good cricket match, and kindly invited me to her birthday party, which she always celebrates out here. I also visited Mr and Mrs Theo de Klerk at the charming house they had just had built to Lavinia de Klerk's design; and I drove out with Mr and Mrs Leonard Shawzin to spend the night at their delightful home at Hermanus, which is famous for its wonderful sea air. I flew home at the end of a glorious trip.

One of the early *Harpers & Queen* annual Oxford *v.* Cambridge clay pigeon shoots at the Holland and Holland shooting school, with some of the competitors and their supporters. *(Bill Bates)*

1977. Mr Forbes Robertson, carrying the BDS flag and pennants, leads the Silver Jubilee Relay Drive sponsored by *Harpers & Queen*, with a foal trotting alongside its mother. I am just visible in a feathered hat in the fourth carriage.

The Queen and the Duke of Edinburgh leaving the final checkpoint of the Silver Jubilee Relay Drive in the grounds of Balmoral Castle, with the Crown Equerry Colonel Sir John Miller carrying the BDS flag and pennants.

In conversation with the former Prime Minister, Mr Harold Macmillan, at a wedding in 1981.

The winners of the 1982 Rolex Jackie Stewart Celebrity Challenge, THE Team –
The Duke of Kent, King Constantine of the Hellenes, Captain Mark Phillips,
the Hon. Angus Ogilvy, and, seated, Jackie Stewart. *(Mel Grundy)*

With Mrs Joseph Lauder and the Princess of Wales, watching a polo match at Smith's Lawn, Windsor Great Park, in the eighties. *(Tim Graham)*

After a polo match at Smith's Lawn with Prince Charles and Major Ronald Ferguson.

Lunching with Sir Raymond and Lady Smith on the terrace of the Kulm Hotel, St Moritz, after a morning at the Cresta Run.

With Mr Anthony Marengo (second from right), then Managing Director of Cartier UK, watching the Cartier polo match on ice in a snowstorm at St Moritz in the eighties.

With Lady Pagan, racing at Randwick, New South Wales, in 1991.

Right: Fleur Tukham, my very able and efficient assistant during my last four years at *Harpers & Queen.*

Below: Peter Haimes and 'Mrs Peter', who has never complained about Peter's long hours, or about anything! Peter has driven me safely since 1969 for thousands of miles, at all hours, without ever a grumble or a cross word.

For the first time ever that year *Harpers & Queen* sponsored a garden at the Chelsea Flower Show in the grounds of Chelsea Hospital. I had quite a lot to do with this venture, as it was on my advice that the directors of *Harpers & Queen* chose Mr Vernon Russell-Smith to design the garden. He in turn chose Waterers, and their subsidiary Sunningdale Nurseries, to carry out the construction and supply the trees and plants and so on, and their splendid senior landscape foreman, Mr Geordie Bolan, to carry out the work. The Managing Director of Waterers at that time was Mr Michael Fane, whom I had known since he was born.

The result was a really beautiful garden named the *Harpers & Queen Moonlight Garden*, of which I was extremely proud. By the time it was complete and ready for judging, I thought that dear Vernon Russell-Smith and all concerned had excelled themselves. To the tremendous joy of all at *Harpers & Queen* and to Vernon Russell-Smith, Michael Fane and all the team who had worked so hard, the *Harpers & Queen Moonlight Garden* was awarded an RHS Gold Medal!

Later, on the Monday evening, when the Royal Family always make their tour of the show accompanied by the President, then Lord Aberconway, my directors had kindly given me the privilege of being in charge of the garden of which I felt so proud with, of course, Vernon Russell-Smith and, I think, Geordie Bolan to answer questions. Sadly our beloved Queen had left that morning with the Duke of Edinburgh on a state visit to Finland, so never saw our garden, but Queen Elizabeth the Queen Mother, accompanied by Lord Aberconway, came into the little garden and walked all round it, with her usual charm taking the greatest interest in the design and plants and all she saw. The Duke and Duchess of Kent had a quick look; Princess Alexandra the Hon. Mrs Angus Ogilvy and Prince Michael of Kent both took the keenest interest in the design, construction and plants, and were so warmhearted and sincere in their admiration. Princess Alice Countess of Athlone stopped to have a look and was very complimentary about the garden.

The advent of Concorde meant that I could sometimes fit in functions that I could not have done with slower flights. In May I was persuaded to take up the opportunity to fly for the night to Caracas for a dinner party. When the time arrived I wondered if I had been mad to agree to accept Sir Raymond Smith's invitation and if I would feel rather ill on my return, which I did not want, as in the meantime I had received a kind and unexpected invitation to a buffet supper on the Sunday night that The Queen was giving for some of the Royal Windsor Horse Show executives, supporters and riders, which I had accepted and was looking forward to.

Friday, Saturday and Sunday were in the end exciting and the greatest fun. On Friday, in spite of being at the Rose Ball until 1 a.m., I was up very early and went to my office and coped with my mail. Then I left London with my luggage and drove to the Royal Windsor Horse Show, where The Queen was already present. I watched some of the judging before lunching with the Chairman of the Show, Mr Geoffrey Cross, in the President's Marquee. At 2.45 p.m. I left the show and drove straight to Heathrow and I caught the 4 p.m. Air France Boeing 727 flight to Paris, arriving at Charles de Gaulle airport at 5.45 p.m. local time. I was met by an Air France hostess and collected my luggage and checked in for the 7 p.m. Air France Concorde flight to Caracas and was then taken to their comfortable Concorde lounge. When I boarded the aeroplane around 6.30 p.m. I was given a front window seat as requested and sat back to relax.

This was my first flight on Concorde and I was impressed on a very hot day how cool and fresh the cabin felt as one entered. My seat was far more comfortable than I had been told to expect. I had plenty of space to read, write and sew. The take-off was exciting: the lovely feeling of power and the smooth ascent were impressive. The Mach indicator was just in front of me and soon registered forty-five. It steadily climbed until at 7.39 p.m. it registered one hundred, which I was told meant we had broken the sound barrier and were now flying at supersonic speed. The indicator went up still further and when it touched 200 I learnt we were flying at 1350 miles an hour. Yet looking out of the window one did not feel one was travelling fast.

We landed on the island of Santa Maria in the Azores to refuel, but I did not get off the aeroplane. I noticed when we took off again over the sea that we were up to supersonic speed in ten minutes.

At Caracas my host, Sir Raymond Smith, was at the aeroplane to meet me with Madame Pouverall of Air France. I was quickly whisked through customs and out with Raymond Smith to find Chu Chu and the Rolls. Then we were quickly on our way. After greeting me, my dear hostess Dorothy Smith took me up to my comfy bedroom, where a housemaid was waiting to see if my evening dress needed pressing. I unpacked and had a lovely refreshing bath and was downstairs before any of the other guests had arrived, so had time to go in and have a word with Dorothy Smith's wonderful cook Emelda, who had been with the family for twenty years. She was all smiles and welcome in spite of cooking a dinner for twenty-four.

We had drinks, as on my last visit, out on the patio. All the ladies, like my dear hostess, wore beautiful dresses and looked very chic. The male guests were all pretty high-powered and intelligent, so I had to concentrate a lot. It was around 10.15 p.m. local time, 3.15 a.m. at home, when we went in to dinner. Happily I did not feel in any way tired and was enjoying every moment of the evening. More friends came in after dinner. After they had gone I sat and talked to my host and hostess for a short while and it was around 2 a.m. before I put my light out.

I was awake and up when I was called at 6.15 a.m. and at 7.15 a.m. I joined Raymond and Dorothy, who both came to the airport to see me off. When Chu Chu put my suitcase in the car, Emelda and all the others of the staff were around the front door to wave goodbye, which I thought was very endearing. On arrival at Caracas airport, I was quickly whisked through formalities and Raymond and Dorothy were allowed through to the departure lounge. I very soon had to say good-bye to these two dear friends of many years, who had made my visit such a happy one.

When I boarded the Concorde I was given a very warm welcome by the same crew as the previous day. We took off sharp at 9am local time, and as we had no land or buildings to fly over and were soon over the sea, the Mach indicator very soon showed we were flying at supersonic speed. I did an hour's writing, then I got out my patchwork and did quite a lot of sewing on the flight. I was very amused when one of the pilots walking down the aisle stopped and said 'You are setting up a record. You must be the first lady ever to sew patchwork while travelling at supersonic speed.'

Thanks to the wonderful pressurization in the Concorde I did not feel in the slightest way tired when I got back to my little flat at around 10.45 p.m., after having had one of the most exciting and enjoyable trips of my life. I had a splendid night's sleep. On Sunday morning I went to church at the Queens Chapel with prayers of gratitude in my heart.

That Sunday evening, I went to Windsor Castle for the most enjoyable supper party at which most of the guests had been connected in some way or other with the Royal Windsor Horse Show. On arrival I met one of the Horse Show committee, who greeted me saying 'Oh, you didn't go to Venezuela after all.' He could hardly believe me when I told him I had been there and back.

Early in July that year, I went to America and Canada for part of the state visits made by The Queen and the Duke of Edinburgh to both countries, and for part of the Equestrian Olympics in Montreal. In New York, Mr John Miller, then President of the Hearst Corporation, very kindly sent a car to meet me at the airport, and put a car and chauffeur at my disposal while I was in New York, which is always for me the greatest kindness anyone can offer.

On Wednesday morning I flew up to Washington, where the royal party were due to arrive later in the day from Philadelphia, where the royal tour had started when Her Majesty and the Duke of Edinburgh arrived in the royal yacht *Britannia*. I collected my accreditation and passes with the greatest ease; Mr Ronald Allison was then in charge of the royal press office. This was a gruelling tour for The Queen as so much had been squeezed into her schedule. On Wednesday afternoon I went to quite a small reception at the British Embassy for the press, radio and television. As it was a very warm day, it mostly took place outdoors. The Queen and the Duke of Edinburgh received their guests on the terrace and then came down on to the embassy lawn and spoke to many of the guests quite informally.

That evening The Queen and the Duke of Edinburgh, who were staying at Blair House, attended a state dinner at the White House given by the then President and Mrs Gerald Ford. Surprisingly, this dinner took place in a marquee in the garden, followed by an entertainment; then there was dancing in the house. The following day The Queen had eleven official engagements!

Among these, I went to the very moving dedication ceremony of the Nave in Washington Cathedral, then to the luncheon at the Capitol that the Vice-President of the United States, Mr Nelson Rockefeller, and the Speaker of the House of Representatives were giving in honour of The Queen and the Duke of Edinburgh in the unique setting of the famous Statuary Hall. In the afternoon I went to the National Gallery, where The Queen was received by the President of the Gallery, Mr Paul Mellon. In the evening The Queen and the Duke of Edinburgh gave a banquet at the British Embassy in honour of the President and Mrs Gerald Ford, at which there were eighty guests. This was followed by a reception to which I was kindly invited. The banquet took place in the embassy's magnificent ballroom, carefully supervised to the smallest detail by Lady Ramsbotham; and the reception took place in the embassy garden. A fanfare from State Trumpeters of the Blues and Royals heralded the arrival of The Queen on the terrace with the

British Ambassador Sir Peter Ramsbotham. In spite of her gruelling schedule on a rather hot and humid day The Queen looked really superb wearing a beautiful crystal-embroidered green silk dress designed by Norman Hartnell, with an exquisite diamond tiara, a diamond necklace and other beautiful jewels. With our Ambassador Her Majesty walked slowly down the garden path to a Henry Moore statue which was on loan for Bicentenary Year. Here a number of presentations were made to The Queen. At this memorable and perfectly arranged reception in this beautiful setting with a full moon overhead I enjoyed every moment. I was introduced to the Vice-President of the US, Mr Nelson Rockefeller, and his attractive wife, who were both charming and so friendly, and to many others. I also met a number of friends I already knew.

The royal party were due in New York later that day. It was now well past midnight. I was staying in the Sheraton Carlton, a most comfortable, rather old-fashioned hotel where the British Embassy had kindly arranged for me to stay. Having paid my bill, I was ready in the lobby, as requested, by 6.30 a.m., to join a party flying in a chartered plane, also arranged by the British Embassy, to New York. Here two buses were waiting with two police motor cycle escorts to take us very swiftly to the Summit Hotel, where again the embassy had arranged accommodation and where the Hearst car and driver were waiting for me.

For The Queen and the Duke of Edinburgh this was another hectic ten-engagement day in a hot, humid atmosphere. At the Federal Hall the Mayor of New York proclaimed The Queen a citizen of New York with a Bicentenary medal, after which The Queen made a delightful short speech, which I arrived just in time to hear. I also did not want to miss The Queen and the Duke of Edinburgh's five-minute memorable walk-about along Wall Street. The crowds here to see The Queen were unbelievable! Everyone was thrilled with her warmth, charm and friendliness. There were no handshakes, but she made cheery remarks to a number of individuals. These were five minutes in which our beloved Queen won the hearts of thousands of New Yorkers. Next, at the Waldorf Astoria Hotel, a luncheon was given by Pilgrims of the US and the English Speaking Union of the US.

After luncheon The Queen did a quick change, this time into a pretty green dress with a small close-fitting hat, as she was off on a tour by motor car, standing up and holding on to a handrail so that the crowds lining the streets could get a good view. This amazed the people of

New York, who were used to VIPs driving around in bulletproof cars!

That evening The Queen and the Duke of Edinburgh gave a dinner party for about a hundred guests, followed by a reception on board the *Britannia*. I had the honour and privilege of going to the reception. This was a delightful uncrowded and beautifully arranged party, at which the dinner guests and members of the royal entourage were all present.

At 11.15 p.m. the band of the Royal Marines from *Britannia* beat the retreat on the jetty. They then played the British and American National Anthems. Suddenly, while the American National Anthem was being played, a superb and powerful voice started singing the words from the Sports Deck above. I saw The Queen look up in surprise and smile. It was the voice of the famous opera singer Miss Leontyne Price, who had been one of the guests at the dinner. It was another wonderful, moving and nostalgic Anglo-American moment, complete with the moon shining overhead.

Instead of going on the next few days of the royal tour I flew up to Montreal to spend five days with my son and daughter-in-law and my granddaughters, and to catch up on my writing. At the end of those happy five days, on the Friday, I moved into the Ritz-Carlton Hotel in readiness for the Montreal Olympics, as I knew I would be working at all hours, and that it would be easier. Two dear friends, the Marquess and Marchioness of Exeter, who were over for the Olympic Games, were also staying here; also the Grand Duke and Grand Duchess of Luxembourg, who are such a charming, kind couple. Princess Anne was riding in the Equestrian Olympic events, so The Queen and the Duke of Edinburgh had an added interest.

On Saturday I went with my son, who had far better seats than mine, to the Olympic Stadium for the Opening Ceremony of the Olympic Games. At 3 p.m. The Queen arrived, accompanied by the Duke of Edinburgh, and received a tremendous ovation from the audience as she appeared in the Royal Box. Later The Queen stood up alone for a very long time while the contingents from the various countries, by tradition led by Greece, then in alphabetical order, entered the arena carrying their national flag and saluted in some form or other as they passed the Royal Box. When The Queen, again standing up, had proclaimed the Games open, there followed the Olympic rituals, including the arrival of the sacred Olympic flame.

That evening The Queen gave a large reception at the Palace des Arts to celebrate the opening of the Games of the XXI Olympiad, at which I had the privilege to be present. Her Majesty arrived from *Britannia* looking very regal in a dress of off-white silk embroidered all over in iridescent beads, a diamond tiara and necklace. She was received by the Governor General of Canada and Madame Leger.

During the evening, accompanied by Mr Pierre Trudeau, The Queen made an informal tour of the guests, who numbered around two hundred. These included the Grand Duke and the Grand Duchess of Luxembourg, Prince Gholam Reza Pahlavi of Iran, Prince François of Liechtenstein, the Marquess and Marchioness of Exeter, Lord and Lady Porritt, Lord and Lady Luke, Jonkeer van Karnebeek of the Netherlands, Mr and Mrs Julian Roosevelt, and others connected with the Olympics from all over the world.

On Sunday morning I went with my son to Christ Church Cathedral for morning prayer, which was attended by The Queen, accompanied by the Duke of Edinburgh and Prince Andrew. I went back with my son to luncheon at his home with his family.

In the evening The Queen gave a delightful, very friendly reception for the International Olympic Press on board *Britannia*, to which I was kindly invited. The Queen and the Duke of Edinburgh received their guests as they came on to the deck.

One of the ship's charming officers came over and asked me if I spoke French as there was rather an important guest who spoke very little English. I went over and was doing my best and having quite a reasonable conversation with this French Canadian gentleman when I saw the Duke of Edinburgh coming across towards us. I thought he was about to take over from me. Not at all. His Royal Highness came up to me with a big smile and said 'Since when are you a sports writer?' I replied 'Well, Sir, I am an all-rounder – I do write about polo, racing, eventing, golf, tennis, Olympics and so on as well as social functions', at which he laughed and said 'Have fun.' I had stayed with David and Diana Exeter at Burghley House one year for the European Championship Horse Trials when the Duke of Edinburgh was also a house guest, and he obviously thought he would pull my leg here!

For the next two days I watched many of the Olympic athletic events, including exciting cycle racing, and of course part of the equestrian events. I had to fly home on Friday before the Olympics ended, and once again there was the agony of saying goodbye to my very dear son.

For some reason, I forget why, I flew home via New York. I went on an Air Canada flight to New York, due to arrive at 5.15 p.m., which allowed me plenty of time before my onward flight at 8.45 p.m. When we arrived over Kennedy airport the pilot announced that we might have to circle for twenty-five minutes, which did not worry me as I knew I had ample time. Then to my dismay he suddenly announced that we were returning to Montreal to refuel. After refuelling we once again set off for New York, where once again we had to circle over Kennedy airport, this time for thirty minutes. By the time we landed it was 9 p.m. I soon learnt that my flight to London had left. I miraculously managed to get the last seat on the last British Airways flight out that night to London. My problem then was that I was now not due to land until 11.15 a.m., instead of my original 8.30 a.m., and I had accepted Sir Philip Oppenheimer's invitation to Diamond Day Luncheon next day at Ascot at 12 for 12.30 p.m. I was not travelling in suitable clothes, so I had to think quickly. Quite forgetting it was then about 3 a.m. in London, I rang my poor chauffeur Peter and asked him to take down a list of the clothes I needed and to take Mrs Peter to my flat in the morning to get them out, and to bring them and my race glasses and badges to the airport, and to telephone my host, all of which they kindly did.

Happily my flight landed ahead of time. We drove straight to the Post House, where I took in my dress and hat to wear racing, made a quick change in the cloakroom, and arrived at the luncheon at Ascot just after the other guests were seated. Philip and Pam Oppenheimer were so kind and understanding. I sat down and relaxed, knowing I could now enjoy a delicious luncheon followed by De Beers' wonderful Diamond Day racing, which I always look forward to.

The following year, on the Saturday after four days of Royal Ascot, I spent a most unusual day. I had a very early call as I had to be at London airport by 7 a.m. to fly to Dyce airport near Aberdeen. At London airport, I joined Mr and Mrs John Houlder and a small party organized by Houlder-Offshore to visit SSV *Uncle John*, a newly built vessel connected with the oil industry, owned jointly by Houlder-Offshore, Ellerman Lines and Ugland UK. Cars met us at Dyce and we drove straight to Peterhead Docks. Here a crane was waiting for us, and, two at a time, guests were asked to step into a small cage and then the crane lifted, swung, and landed us on a spacious deck.

The *Uncle John* is a semi-submersible subsea construction vessel, primarily intended for subsea pipe connections. At that time, a lot had been said and written about platform fires on the North Sea oil rigs, but very little about the consequences of a major pipeline fracture. The

Uncle John is a rapid intervention vessel, designed to pick up survivors and keep a burning platform from collapsing by spray cooling, until the arrival of assistance.

She is capable of pumping cooling spray, which we saw demonstrated, over a burning platform for months on end while relief wells are being drilled, even in the very worst weather. The *Uncle John* was then the only vessel which could insert temporary plugs to prevent a major oil escape, and get the pipeline back into production without delay. We saw all this equipment, the engine room, and the very well-designed cabins, usually for two. What I found most interesting of all was the Diving House and the fine facilities for divers. These were brilliantly explained to us by one of the very efficient diving superintendents, Mr Serge Gerand, himself a deep-sea diver of great experience. He explained about the pressurization of divers, who, he told us, can live under pressure for thirty days at a spell – of course with rest periods – in their special pressurized rest apartments. We saw the 24-hour monitoring equipment, their specially heated suits, their medical supplies, and how their food is supplied to them through double glass doors.

The *Uncle John* was built to have thirty resident divers. We were able to talk to quite a number of the crew, who had only the previous evening come in from a week's further training at sea in the *Uncle John*, and I spoke to several of the divers, whom I salute as very skilled and brave men.

1977 was the Queen's Jubilee year, and *Harpers & Queen* sponsored the Silver Jubilee 1977 Relay Drive organized by the British Driving Society in aid of Driving for the Disabled. This was a relay of horse-drawn carriages driven by members. It started in April, from Cornwall and Kent, and ended in Scotland in October. There were a number of different checkpoints – several of which I went to to support the *Harpers & Queen* sponsorship. Unfortunately for me, after I had promised to go to the Northern Driving Championship show at Holker Hall, Cark-in-Carmel, which coincided with the Relay Drive Checkpoint, where I had promised to be by 11 a.m., I was also invited to the ball that Viscount and Viscountess Cowdray were giving at their Scottish home, Dunecht, in Aberdeenshire to celebrate the coming-of-age of their son the Hon. Charles Pearson, and the coming out of their daughter, the Hon. Rosanna Pearson. I decided I must somehow do both!

I flew up to Aberdeen to spend one night with Major Stanley Cayzer,

who was a very old friend, and his wife, at Cabrach, which is quite
near Dunecht. I went with them to the ball and arranged for a car
from Aberdeen Car Hire to pick me up at Dunecht at 1 a.m.

Dunecht looked magnificent floodlit, and Pipe-Major Jim Coutts in
full regalia was playing Scottish tunes around the courtyard as we
arrived. Dancing took place in the large high ballroom with a gallery
all around. Masses of pretty young girls and young marrieds, all wearing their prettiest dresses, and most men wearing the kilt, were dancing
reels and Scottish country dances with great joyfulness.

Around 1 a.m., when longing to stay another couple of hours at this
party which resounded with enjoyment, I drove back to nearby Cabrach
to change into day clothes, collect my luggage, then set off to drive
through the night to Holker Hall. There was no rail service for this cross
country trip in the morning, no way by air other than charter, and that
was too dicey with the possibility of early morning fog and the current
air control problems, so my only hope was to motor.

I breezily said to my driver, a sensible Aberdonian, that we would
stop a couple of times for him to have a break and cup of tea or coffee,
never dreaming that we would pass nowhere open that could produce
refreshment. So when we arrived at Perth around 3.15 a.m., I said we
would divert a little and go to the Perth Station Hotel, where I had
stayed and always found them most helpful on my travels. I rang the
bell and the night porter, who happily recognized me, said of course
we could have tea or coffee, and to come in. He brought a large pot
of very strong piping hot coffee, which sustained my poor driver for
the next five hours. After Perth, we ran into a heavy thunderstorm and
spectacular lightning and heavy rain. From then on it rained.

We eventually arrived at Holker Hall, the lovely home of Mr and
Mrs Hugh Cavendish, now Lord and Lady Cavendish, at around
8.45 a.m. in torrential rain. As we got there horse boxes were arriving
in every direction. The first person I met was Mr Joseph Braithwaite,
the splendid agent at Holker, who was busy getting things up to the
showground. Once I was inside the house, the butler took me up to
a warm and pretty bedroom and quickly brought up a breakfast tray
with piping hot coffee and hot toast. After enjoying this, and a refreshing hot bath, I went downstairs to meet my young host and hostess,
Hugh and Grania Cavendish, who were running the whole estate quite
brilliantly. I put on everything I had in the way of a Husky and a
mackintosh and strong shoes, and we set off in the torrential rain for
the showground.

Later, still in teeming rain and blustery gales, we found the then Chairman of the British Driving Society, Mr John Richards, boarded his coach and set off with the flag of the BDS Silver Jubilee Drive, sponsored by *Harpers & Queen*, flying. We drove right across the park and around the big show ring, with John's guard, Mr Ronald Ratcliffe, standing on the back of the coach rendering famous tunes on his coaching horn.

When we came to a halt, I was asked to get down to hand over the flag so that it could be given to other representatives who would take it further north for its last lap to Balmoral. Eventually the show packed up at 3 p.m., owing to the bad weather. When I took my little fur hat off my head, I had to wring it out to get the rain out of it, but happily my head was dry. After tea by a huge open fire, I left to catch a train from Lancaster to Euston, where I arrived at 10.30 p.m. I was so grateful to see dear Peter on the platform to cope with my luggage and drive me home.

The last checkpoint of this Jubilee Relay Drive four weeks later also had slight problems. I was staying with very dear friends, Earl and Countess Cadogan, in Perthshire and I drove over on the morning of the drive to Ballater, where I was due to meet my Managing Director, Mr Terry Mansfield, and his wife, and the President of the BDS, Mr Sanders Watney, to drive from Ballater to Balmoral in the Chairman of the BDS Mr John Richards' road coach. There were heavy showers as I arrived. Luckily I had borrowed one of Bunnie Cadogan's very full shooting mackintoshes and had put a plastic clothes cover over my hat.

I soon learnt the sad news that when John Richards's horses were on their way in a trailer horse box the previous evening the vehicle had blown over in the gale. Happily the horses were not as badly injured as at first feared, and all recovered later. It meant, however, we had all lost our transport.

Mrs Candler, then the wonderful secretary of the BDS, went round those driving alone and very sweetly they all volunteered to take a passenger. Mrs Lulham from East Sussex, who was driving her splendid little grey pony Mousie to a Mulliner gig, very sweetly said she would take me. It was a unique and wonderful sight before we started off, to see everyone getting ready in two fields. There were carriages of every shape and size, and ponies and horses of every colour with their drivers, some of them with grooms as well. Some members had come from Northern Ireland, and one Hampshire member had driven all the way from Southampton to Balmoral by road, using two horses in turn. There was a splendid feeling of camaraderie and good fellowship. There were no prizes to be won, no competitive jealousy; everyone was there for the fun and love of driving horses and, above all, to help a good cause. The drive raised enough money to buy two specially equipped carriages for the disabled.

At 11.45 a.m., around sixty horse-drawn vehicles, some quite vintage, lined up for the eight-mile drive to Crathie Church, where The Queen and the Duke of Edinburgh had attended a service that morning. Here, everyone assembled in the car park for a break before we set off again at 2 p.m. for the last lap up the long drive and just past Balmoral Castle. At this moment the rain stopped and the sun came out. The cavalcade from Ballater was led by Mr Forbes Robertson of Fettercairn, who was the BDS Area Commissioner. He was carrying the Relay Flag, and driving his pair to a dogcart with the three-month-old foal of one of them running alongside! I was told that the mare always went better with her offspring beside her! It was quite a turn.

Mrs Lulham and Mousie and I were in fourth place, which was rather nice as it meant we didn't have a whole line in front. Spectators lined the eight-mile route nearly all the way and waved us on.

Around 3 p.m., when the vehicles were all lined up on the lawns of Balmoral Castle, the then Crown Equerry Lt-Colonel Sir John Miller arrived to see that everything was in readiness for the arrival of The Queen and the Duke of Edinburgh. Shortly after, our beloved Queen, wearing a cornflower blue coat and a little hat to match, and the Duke of Edinburgh arrived, not in a car but, to everyone's joy, with His Royal Highness driving a pair of Fell ponies to the Edinburgh dogcart. Mr Sanders Watney made a brief speech thanking Her Majesty for having the final checkpoint at Balmoral and presented her with a silver tray from the BDS to commemorate her Silver Jubilee.

Mr Forbes Robertson then presented the Relay Flag with all its pennants to The Queen, who then made a complete tour of the lines of sixty vehicles, having a word with all the drivers. After she spoke to my driver, Her Majesty also very sweetly expressed her surprise at seeing me there! I felt so grateful and very honoured to be there on such a unique occasion.

I am very grateful to God for giving me good health. During my fifteen and a half years working for the *Tatler*, I only had one day off sick. On that occasion I had a temperature of 104 degrees and, feeling like death, thought I had better spend a day in bed, but I did not call a doctor as I knew he would keep me there! I managed to travel, with my temperature down to 102, to Cheshire for a hunt ball two days later, and I was happily none the worse.

However, in February 1978 I really had to stop. It started in Lyford Cay, where I got conch poisoning and felt desperately ill. I saw the doctor at the Lyford Cay hospital right away but I did not respond to treatment. I kept on with my engagements but after three days and two X-rays I was in even greater pain, so I decided to fly home. I'll never know how I made that journey. British Airways took such care of me, the ever reliable Peter was at the airport and I was soon back in my own little home, where I immediately called Doctor Michael Yates, in whom I have such faith. He, like the Lyford Cay doctor, prescribed a remedy, but as I was no better in ten or twelve hours he said I must go into hospital. Everywhere seemed full, but thanks to the dear, kind Earl of Ranfurly, then Chairman of the London Clinic board, I managed to get a room in the London Clinic right away. My then wonderful secretary Jane Hodges, now Jane Hughes, packed a suitcase with what I needed and took care of my keys, and, feeling desperately ill and worse every hour, I went in straight away.

I remember as I left the flat wondering if I should ever come back. I thought of my dear Uncle Martin Kemp-Welch, who had died in the Clinic, and my beloved brother Peter Kemp-Welch, who had also died there, and thought I would probably make it three. Happily I didn't!

When I had been X-rayed at every angle and still no one could discover what was wrong with me, it was decided I must be opened up. Doctor Yates had got a young surgeon called Mr Harvey White to do the operation. Shortly after my X-rays, when Harvey White came into my room, he suddenly said 'We have met before.' Feeling in great pain, I was struggling to think of some social occasion, when he added 'You took me out to tea when I was fifteen years old and in Furleys at Winchester with your son Jim!' I found it very endearing that he had remembered it all those years. There was also another surgeon at the Clinic who had seen the X-rays, and he came and asked me if I would mind him being at the operation too as he was so curious to see what was wrong. When he had left the room I rather worriedly asked Doctor Yates if I would have to pay two surgeons; he assured me that in no way would I have to do that.

The result was that dear Mr Harvey White saved my life after having me on the operation table for quite a few hours, straightening out my insides. The conch poisoning had given the final twist to my intestines, which had been gradually working their way into a hole left open when I had had a caesarian many years previously. I shall always be so grateful to Mr Harvey White's skill and patience as I have felt so much fitter ever since that operation, which was when I was already the wrong side of seventy! He was also very understanding after the operation, when I asked whether, if I had no visitors, I could have my secretary to see me each day. As I had brought back plenty of copy written and in my head, I was able to keep my Jennifer's Diary going without a break.

There were nothing like as many outstanding parties in the seventies and eighties as there were in the fifties and sixties, but there were three very good ones in 1978.

The first one was given by Viscount and Viscountess Garnock and her sister, the Marchesa d'Ayala Valva, at the sisters' family home, Combermere Abbey in Shropshire. The party was to celebrate, rather late, a number of family birthdays starting with David Garnock's fiftieth birthday which had been in 1976, his son the Master of Garnock's twenty-first birthday, which had also taken place in 1976, and David's daughter the Hon. Caroline Lindesay Bethune's twenty-first birthday that year. Also Pempi Garnock's youngest daughter, Miss Gigi Callander, reaching nineteen years, and Taisa d'Ayala Valva's daughter being just eighteen. As you arrived at the house, the lake, the undulating lawns and trees looked super floodlit, and inside, the host and hostesses stood with the four young people beside them. There were two bands, one especially for Scottish reels, and a discotheque well away from the main dance floor, and the breakfast was the really old-fashioned type with grilled kidneys and bacon, scrambled eggs and kedgeree. The guests were of all ages and quite a few came from overseas. So many of them knew each other, and the whole ball went with a tremendous swing from the start.

I stayed with Earl and Countess Cadogan and went with them to the second dance. This was given by the Earl and Countess of Mansfield and Mansfield to celebrate the twenty-first birthday of their son and heir, Viscount Stormont, at their famous home, Scone Palace. Here a marquee had been built beside the palace for dancing, but all the reception rooms, which, like the marquee, were filled with sweet-scented lilies and other flowers, were used for sitting out, and breakfast was served in what were originally the huge kitchens with the original copper saucepans on the walls. These kitchens are now used as a canteen when the house is open to the public. This being a dance in

Scotland there were programmes, and the ball opened with the Dashing White Sergeant, for which the floor was packed. It was a colourful scene with all the men wearing the kilt, including Alexander Stormont's godfathers, the Duke of Atholl, the Duke of Fife and Mr John Richardson. Members of all the old Scottish families were present and I met masses of Scottish friends. It was a really happy occasion with a lovely, truly Scottish atmosphere. It was also a joy for me going with Bill and Bunny Cadogan, who for a great many years have been two of my dearest friends, and one could have all the fun of reliving the ball the next day. Usually I have no one to do this with!

The third ball was one given by Mr Joseph and the Hon. Mrs Czernin for their two eldest daughters, Miss Charlotte and Miss Henrietta Czernin, at Seaford House. This was foremost very much a family party as, although there were several hundred guests, some of these from overseas, there was also a very strong family element.

Joseph and Hazel Czernin had their three youngest daughters Alexandra, Philippa and Isabelle Czernin at the ball, as well as their only son, Peter Czernin, then only twelve years old. Also Hazel Czernin's dear father, Lord Howard de Walden, and his attractive new wife (his first very dear wife, Nucci, having died of cancer, far too young, three years before). Also her three sisters and their husbands and some of their teenage children, aunts and uncles, and cousins galore. But it was the setting that was so interesting. Seaford House, which stands on its own at the southeast corner of Belgrave Square, was for nearly forty years the London family home of the Howard de Walden family, but is now the home of the Royal College of Defence Studies. It was bought by Hazel Czernin's grandfather, the 8th Lord Howard de Walden, from the executors of the 5th Earl of Sefton in 1902 for his mother, and then on his marriage in 1912 he went to live there himself until it was requisitioned in 1940. Soon after the Government had requisitioned the house, it suffered serious bomb damage. The Air Ministry used it as offices from 1943 to 1946, when it was assigned to its present role. A feature of the house is the fabulous onyx staircase, which the 8th Baron had made from onyx found in a mine he bought in South Africa. It is very wide until it divides halfway up. The present Lord Howard de Walden and his twin sister were born in this house, and with their other sisters were brought up here.

For the ball Michael Goulding had done enormous and superb flower arrangements in the large entrance hall and in all the fine reception rooms with their ornate ceilings. Dancing took place in the ballroom and sitting out in another room that was the original ballroom. A good band played for dancing, and everything was arranged to perfection. It was a really good dance that everyone enjoyed.

First thing in 1979, the Stewards of the Hong Kong Jockey Club very kindly invited me out for a week, at the same time as members of the Jockey Club and their wives and others connected with racing in the UK and France, for the official opening of their wonderful newly built Sha Tin Racecourse.

I stayed, as always, at the Mandarin, which Mr Peter Stafford made famous for the perfectly trained staff, and where they take the greatest care of me. On arrival in my room I enjoyed the traditional ritual of the housekeeper (a man) bringing me a Chinese porcelain teapot of China tea and pouring it out for me. Then, as usual, I was asked if I would like my unpacking done. I always refuse as, wherever I am, I like to unpack for myself. Arriving at a private house, I always hang on to my suitcase keys so that no one can unpack for me. If they do, it takes so much time finding where everything is. I do not mind being packed for to return home!

An excellent non-stop programme had been arranged for us all by Major General Bernard Penfold, who had held the responsible appointment of General Manager of the Royal Hong Kong Jockey Club since 1972. A fleet of luxury buses waited outside the Mandarin Hotel, and other hotels where guests were staying, to take us to each event. On Thursday, my first afternoon, we all drove over to Sha Tin in the New Territories to make a complete tour of the stands, stables and racecourse.

On arrival, we were divided into groups. I went with the Deputy Clerk of the Course, Mr Jim McCaffrey's group. I was amazed at all I saw. The horses are all stabled at Sha Tin or the old racecourse, Happy Valley. Resident trainers at both Sha Tin and Happy Valley are provided with a very nice flat at the racecourse, paid a good salary, and receive a good percentage of the winnings. They have no worries about unpaid bills from bad owners! The RHK Jockey Club also pay the wages of the lads who look after the horses and those who ride out (in those days in Hong Kong the lads did not do both), and for all the fodder, shoeing and veterinary bills. The Hong Kong trainer has no stable expenses, only his own food and upkeep. This is of course totally different from the UK system.

Then we went to the Jockey Club and other stands, some with spacious boxes, which were fabulous and the last word in comfort, as was the course, with very modern equipment, including a computer system, audio-visual apparatus and a giant closed-circuit television facing the stands.

After that most interesting tour, we arrived back at the hotel at 6 p.m. I did a quick change and joined quite a few others to go to Happy Valley racecourse for a cocktail party given by the Chairman of the RHK Jockey Club, Mr Peter Williams, and the stewards to meet the Invitation Race jockeys, who included our many times champion jockey Lester Piggott, the current champion Willie Carson, then champion for the fourth time, and Pat Eddery, our current champion.

We raced at Sha Tin on both Saturday and Sunday. Sunday was the big day, and the highlight of the afternoon was the Hong Kong Gold Cup, which was won by Mr Lock Shiv-Cheung's Observatory, ridden by Pat Eddery. It was a fantastic weekend for Pat Eddery, who has been champion jockey in the UK nine times, as he not only won both the Jockeys' Invitation Races, but he brought off a treble on Sunday.

I left the Mandarin the next morning at 8 a.m. with two officers from the Ministry of Development, and the executive officer from the Ministry of the Community, who were taking me over to the New Territories to see the tremendous developments there. We travelled over in a former Governor's yacht now used by the Government for the New Territories. On our short voyage we had a splendid view of the coastline and the enormous developments of high-rise housing and factories; also an enormous container terminal where ships were loading up their cargo. We landed in fifteen minutes, then took a small green bus that was waiting for us. We proceeded to the new highway, already the scene of many fatal accidents, in spite of the notices saying 'Arrive Alive'. On arrival at Tuen Mun New Town, I was taken up to the roof of Top Court to see the work forging ahead on housing developments, schools and a recreation park. They were expecting a population of half a million to be living in high-rise flats, all built on reclaimed land.

After luncheon, I was taken to see Sha Tin New Town, in the same district as the new racecourse. Here we made a tour of two new developments of modern high-rise flats that were housing those who were previously squatting in shanty towns. I seemed to climb up and down miles of concrete steps on that project!

I also saw the first two Housing Authority estates to be built here. They were twin tower blocks containing 2,170 flats. Further phases were planned to bring that project up to 6,000 flats. I went round two of them. All the tenants I spoke to were smiling and seemed happy with their new homes. I was so pleased to see the tremendous change in the situation from my first visit to Hong Kong in the fifties, when they had over one million refugees from China. In 1978, the Housing Authority had about two million people housed in 372,000 Housing Authority flats in Hong Kong.

From Hong Kong I flew on to the Philippines to stay with two very dear friends, Mr and Mrs Jaime Zobel de Ayala, in their lovely home in the Forbes Park area. Jaime Zobel de Ayala was Philippines Ambassador in London for four years in the early seventies, when his Spanish-born wife Bea Zobel was one of the most beautiful and elegant ambassadresses at the Court of St James's. I had already stayed one summer with Jaime and Bea Zobel and their seven beautifully behaved children at their home in Sotogrande.

As we drove up to the front door in Manila I saw there was a security guard, which apparently they have at many private houses. I was taken by my hostess to a very large air-conditioned bedroom and bathroom, where a sweet-looking Filipino maid called Felia in a crisp pink cotton frock and white apron (like all the other maids) was waiting to take care of me during my visit. I was delighted to find that everyone spoke English.

My hostess took me to see many things of interest. One morning Bea Zobel and I went to the top of Jaime Zobel's office building where his Bell Jet Ranger helicopter and pilot were waiting on the flat roof to fly us off to the country on a sightseeing tour. Mrs Joe McMicking met us here and the three of us took off. It was the first time I had taken off from the top of a skyscraper in the middle of a city. We flew over part of the city, then over the fishing area, which is divided into sections by bamboo poles. We also flew over the farming district, where some people were wading in at least a foot of water behind their Indo Brazil Caratou bullocks drawing their ploughs. We also saw men and women working in the rice fields and cutting the canes in sugar plantations, and saw banana plantations and maize fields. The land, where not under water, shows a rich red soil.

We landed at the National Arts Centre of the Philippines at Mount Makiling, Leguna. The NAC is built on seven hills, in seven clusters. It consists of a very modern theatre open on all sides, a clubhouse, a guest house, class rooms, practice rooms, a library, offices and 104 cottages, and a cafeteria/conference hall to seat 200. The youths who are taught in this fairytale setting often come from the poorest families in the Philippines. They have the most fantastic opportunity to learn. When they join they sign an oath of dedication to their art.

Next morning I took off again in Jaime's helicopter, this time with both my host and hostess, to fly to a new development resort, Puerto Azul, about sixty kilometres from Manila, which took us over different and fascinating country. We landed at the attractively designed Golf Hut and went off in golf buggies for a tour of the new championship golf course designed by Mr Gary Player and Mr Ron Kirby. We lunched at the picturesque Nayong Caysubic right on Caysubic Beach, and then took off for Calatagan, Batangas. Here Jaime and Bea Zobel had a lovely country home right on the sea, approached by a long drive bordered by a bougainvillea hedge that was in full bloom. I found that Felia and Johnnie, the butler, had driven down to help the resident staff look after us; when I arrived in my room there was Felia waiting to take care of me.

Jaime's stepfather and mother, Joe and Mercedes McMicking, and two young friends came to dine informally. After dinner, sitting comfortably on chaises longues under a starry sky, we watched a very good colour film on a large screeen erected in the garden and went to bed around 11 p.m. after another interesting and enjoyable day.

On Sunday we boarded the helicopter around 11 a.m. and flew across the sea to Puerto Galena, on Musidora Island, where we landed on a firm sandy beach near a very attractive little thatched wooden cabin which my host and hostess had built on this so far totally unspoilt little island. Jaime and Bea had a bathe before the three of us had luncheon. I thought how blissful it would be to stay here. The peace and simplicity would be heaven! Alas, that was not to be. At 2.30 p.m. we boarded the helicopter and took off for Manila.

When we arrived home we changed, and drove round to the Manila Polo Club at Forbes Park Polo Ground for the opening match of their season. Lt-General and Mrs James Dyce Alger had very kindly kept seats for us and invited us to join their table for the cocktail buffet that followed the polo. The low-goal match was finished, and we watched a very fast high-goal match. During the afternoon I met the President's son and younger daughter, Mr Bong Bong Marcos, who was just about to join the Philippines navy, and Miss Irene Marcos, who had just left St Mary's Convent at Ascot. There was a wonderful buffet and a dance band.

One evening Jaime and Bea gave the most beautifully arranged and gracious dinner of twenty-eight guests in my honour at their lovely home. All the ladies wore the very becoming and exquisite Maria Clara Filipina costume, with a strong Spanish influence, which dates back to the eighteenth century. The men wore the long and beautifully embroidered Filipino shirts. We dined outdoors at two round tables with white tablecloths and all-white flowers. Above each table were circular white canopies lit from high up by real Victorian lamps.

After a delicious dinner and plenty of intelligent and amusing conversation, we moved to the swimming pool, where comfy chairs had been arranged along one side. From here we watched the Bayaniham Philippines Dance Company sing and dance in national costume on the other side of the pool. The programme included *Manton de Manila*, which is danced with Spanish silk shawls and enlivened by the rhythmic use of pandecetas and tambourines. They gave an excellent performance. The company, which had then toured the world eight times, is always composed of students from the local university. I went over to meet the dancers, who were all charming and refreshingly young and enthusiastic.

After five blissful days with dear Jaime and Bea, who had made my visit such a happy and fun one, I had to sadly say goodbye. Also goodbye to little Felia, who had taken such care of me and my clothes.

From Manila I went on to Bangkok for one night and stayed at the Oriental. Next morning I went along to Jim Thompson's wonderful silk shop, which I never fail to visit when I am in Bangkok, and in the afternoon I flew home.

Soon after I got back, on an exceptionally cold February evening, I drove down to West Wycombe Park in Buckinghamshire, where Sir Francis Dashwood and his Italian-born second wife Marcella had kindly invited me to a party. This was to celebrate the restoration of his beautiful eighteenth-century Palladian home after fifteen years of really hard work. Francis Dashwood and his very sweet first wife Victoria, who tragically died very young of cancer in 1976, had worked indefatigably with the help of experts, including the late Mr John Fowler. The decor and furnishing throughout had been done with impeccable taste and such loving care over every detail. It is so sad that Victoria did not live to enjoy the completed result.

On the night of the party we had a delicious dinner. Guests then went into the music room, where they were entertained by former members of the famous Kings College Cambridge Choir.

When I left to go I found my faithful chauffeur Peter hatless at the front door to tell me that the car had been stolen! He and another chauffeur had gone to have a meal in High Wycombe, had parked the car in a council car park, and on their return found it had gone. Dear Maria Carmela Viscountess Hambleden, who had driven herself from London in her mini, quickly came to my rescue. She drove me and Peter, who stands six foot four and somehow squeezed into the back of the car, for the thirty miles up to London, for which I was truly grateful. The car was recovered a few days later covered in mud as though youths had been driving it through a ploughed field!

FOURTEEN

Enter the eighties

(1980–84)

1980 was the year our beloved Queen Elizabeth the Queen Mother was celebrating her 80th birthday. I was privileged to be at two of the most important events of that year.

The first was Queen Elizabeth the Queen Mother's 80th Birthday Thanksgiving Service in St Paul's Cathedral. I remember I had a wonderful seat in the front row in the southeast aisle. It was, I think, the most moving and nostalgic service I have ever been to, even taking into account the Service of Thanksgiving, also in St Paul's, after World War II, which was referred to during the service.

At this 80th Birthday Thanksgiving Service dignitaries of the Church of England, of Scotland and of the Roman Catholic Church were taking part. The royal party was received by the then Lord Mayor of London, Sir Peter Gadsden, carrying the Pearl Sword. The steps of St Paul's were lined with representatives of the Regular Armed Forces, of whom Queen Elizabeth the Queen Mother is Commandant-in-Chief, and there was a Guard of Honour from the Irish Guards. Inside St Paul's, The Queen's Body Guard of the Honourable Corps of Gentlemen at Arms and The Queen's Body Guard of the Yeoman of the Guard added colour to the impressive scene.

It was also very much a family affair. Our beloved Queen, who did everything to make it her mother's day, and the Duke of Edinburgh sat on two chairs beside Queen Elizabeth. Just behind sat many members of Queen Elizabeth's family, young and old, including Princess Margaret and the Prince of Wales. The latter had driven to St Paul's with his beloved grandmother in an open carriage. The Prime Minister, Mrs Margaret Thatcher, and members of the Cabinet were also present.

The Cathedral was packed. The service began with the hymn 'Praise My Soul, the King of Heaven'. The Archbishop of Canterbury gave a very fine address, paying tribute to a great lady. The Moderator of the Church of Scotland, the Right Reverend William Johns, and the Cardinal Archbishop of Westminster, Cardinal Basil Hume, both said some prayers. Then the National Anthem was sung. I noticed that The Queen sang both the hymns without once looking at her service sheet. As Queen Elizabeth left with her daughters and son-in-law, she gave a radiant smile to members of her family and to others as she walked down the centre aisle to the waiting carriage. Then, with the Prince of Wales beside her, and a Queen's escort of the Household Cavalry, Queen Elizabeth the beloved Queen Mother drove to Buckingham Palace through streets lined with cheering crowds.

The second big 80th birthday celebration I went to was the brilliant Royal Gala at the Royal Opera House, Covent Garden, on the actual evening of Her Majesty's birthday, 4th August. The house was absolutely packed; everyone in the stalls, the boxes and the first two circles was in evening dress. Those in the upper parts of the house were in their best clothes. The audience was in a truly happy mood: I saw nothing but smiling faces.

The Royal Box was beautifully decorated. Queen Elizabeth arrived looking radiant, wearing a crystal-embroidered white crinoline, a diamond tiara and necklace, and other jewellery, with The Queen Mother, who was in pink with a diamond tiara, and the Duke of Edinburgh. Queen Elizabeth got a tremendous welcome as she took her seat between her son-in-law and daughter. Also in the Royal Box with Her Majesty were the Prince of Wales, Princess Margaret, Princess Anne, Mrs Mark Phillips, and Captain Mark Phillips, Prince Andrew and Prince Edward. Nearby in the Royal Circle were a number of Queen Elizabeth the Queen Mother's relations and friends.

The programme included *Mam'zelle Angot*, *A Month in the Country*, then the fine new ballet by Sir Frederick Ashton called *Rhapsody*, with music by Sergei Rachmaninov and beautifully danced by Lesley Collier and Mikhail Baryshnikov. The setting as well as the choreography was by Sir Frederick Ashton, who with Queen Elizabeth the Queen Mother's permission dedicated the ballet to her. There was tremendous applause. Then the casts of the three ballets, and I think the whole staff of the Royal Opera House, came on to the stage, and finally a huge pink iced birthday cake was wheeled on, when everyone sang 'Happy Birthday' and looked up at the old Royal Box beside the stage, where Queen Elizabeth the Queen Mother stood alone. It was a very moving scene. After that, Queen Elizabeth went backstage, where she cut her birthday cake and met the artists and many of those who had helped to make the evening such a success.

In 1980 I went to a rather unique dance given by Major and Mrs Nigel Chamberlayne-Macdonald at their lovely home, Cranbury Park, near Southampton. The reason for the dance being unique was that it was to celebrate the 21st birthday of their son, Mr Alexander Chamberlayne-Macdonald, the ninetieth birthday of Alexander's grandmother Mrs Tankerville Chamberlayne, who happily danced quite a few dances during the evening, the nineteenth birthday of their daughter Diana Chamberlayne-Macdonald and the two-hundredth birthday of the house, Cranbury. I don't think I have ever been to a party to celebrate so many various birthdays! I was at Cranbury for Penelope Chamberlayne's coming-out ball, and then again later for her daughter Diana Chamberlayne-Macdonald's coming-out ball, and Diana's wedding to Viscount Garnock, now the 11th Earl of Lindsay, in 1982. Likewise I was at Jamie Lindsay's father David Lindsay's first wedding, and at the coming-out balls and weddings of both Jamie Lindsay's aunts Lady Elizabeth Greenacre and Lady Mary Varney!

Twice I have visited Texas for a weekend. The first time, in 1980, I flew from Paris to Houston with a party of French guests for the opening of the Meridien Houston. During this visit I was one of the lucky ones to be taken to see round the National Aeronautics and Space Administration at the Lyndon B. Johnson Space Centre. We saw some of the rock taken from the Moon, astronaut Gordon Cooper's Mercury capsule, the Apollo 17 spacecraft, and the Skylab trainers where astronauts study complex tasks in preparation for scientific missions. We went up to the Mission Control Centre, and then through to see the full-scale Space Shuttle trainers. I found this visit tremendously inspiring.

My second visit to Texas, a few years later, was for two dazzling nights in Dallas for the opening of a fabulous project: the Hotel Crescent Court, a magnificent and gracious 218-room hotel, which also has a beautifully designed shopping centre alongside it, as well as an eighteen-storey office block. The prime mover behind this truly fine development, which has proved a tremendous success, was Mrs Caroline Hunt Schvellkopf, whose father left a fortune to her and her two brothers. It is Caroline Hunt and her company who manage the new Lanesborough Hotel, built on the site of the old St George's Hospital at Hyde Park Corner, a splendid new asset for London.

I always enjoy going to the Farnborough Air Show in September, but I always dread the terrible traffic jams and the hours it takes getting there. In 1980 I was very fortunate, as Sir Raymond and Lady Smith invited me to join a party of around twenty friends they were taking to the Farnborough Air Show by helicopter from Battersea Heliport, returning by car. The Heliport was buzzing that morning. I saw King Husain of Jordan and his wife take off, and I looked around to see eight other helicopters from various firms.

We flew in a six-seater August 109AS from Allan Mann Helicopters of Cobham. It took just over five minutes! On arrival we went to one of the Aerospace luncheon chalets that are raised in tiers with a glazed front so that everyone gets an uninterrupted view of the aircraft and of the flying display. In spite of bad weather, I remember being riveted to my window watching a display by an old Lancaster bomber accompanied by a Spitfire and a Hurricane, all three of which contributed to our winning World War II. It also brought back nostalgic memories for me of when I worked in an aircraft factory milling boosts for the Rolls-Royce engines in Spitfires.

The Red Arrows gave a superb display flying nine British Aerospace Hawks. Later I met their very intelligent commander, Squadron Leader Brian Hoskins, who told me they were delighted with their new Hawks. I also watched many other modern aircraft, including the French Dessault, a Brazilian Bandierantes, Italian Machis, a prototype Dormer that needed a very short take-off and carried nineteen passengers, an Aerospace BA 748 troop carrier which also took off in amazingly short space, and the Aerospace super-jets, the Hawks, the Jaguar and the Tornado with its swing-back wings.

My visit to Farnborough ended rather abruptly when I realized I had been so enthralled that I had missed the time of departure and the rest of my party had gone back to London in three limousines without me!, each thinking I was in one of the other cars. Happily for me, I soon found friends who were leaving and gave me a lift home, and I rang dear Dorothy Smith, who was sitting in a panic at Claridge's.

Christmas is not my favourite time of year, especially since Jim has been living in Canada. I used to go over and spend some Christmases with him and Gilly and the children, but since they moved from Montreal to Ottawa about fifteen years ago, I have been over less frequently. Ottawa is even colder than Montreal in the winter, and during the last Christmas I spent there with my beloved family I nearly died of cold.

Mr and Mrs Antony Norman have, on several occasions, very kindly invited me to spend Christmas with them at their lovely home, Château de la Garoupe, near Antibes. On each occasion they took me, and anyone else in their house party, to the Christmas Eve party that the immensely rich American widow Mrs Frank Jay Gould, whose late husband was one of America's multi-millionaires, used to give each year at her amazing home, El Patio, at Cannes, right up until her death.

At these parties, Florence Gould, who was a very colourful character, always greeted her guests wearing a lovely dress, but it was her jewels that were really stunning. One year she would wear a truly magnificent ruby and diamond necklace, with a large corsage ornament, earrings and bracelets to match. Another year, it would be the turn of the sapphires, which were sensational; or her famous emeralds. This show of exquisite jewellery encouraged the other lady guests to wear their best jewels.

One year at this party, I remember Mrs Eric Loder, a very elegant and gracious lady, wearing the most beautiful rubies and diamonds with a white chiffon dress. On the way home, as her chauffeur turned into the drive of her beautiful villa at Cannes, they were ambushed by jewel thieves. What the thieves did not know was that Elinor Loder, after every big party, always stopped at the casino and put all her jewellery in the safe there – with the exception of one big ring she always wore. Her assailants got away with the ring and rough-handled her and the chauffeur. She was still very shaken by the experience when I met her two days later, but luckily not seriously hurt.

When Florence Gould died in the early eighties her jewellery was sold by Christie's in New York. It filled a special 45-page hardback catalogue and fetched a fabulous sum.

At her Christmas Eve parties, Florence Gould always seated over eighty guests for dinner in her dining room, which had huge picture windows overlooking a lawned roof garden surrounded by thickly bedded white cyclamen with a cleverly lit Christmas tree at the far end. When they sat down to dinner, each guest found a very attractive gift in their place, perhaps a Christian Dior silver photo frame for each lady, and beautiful leather wallet-notebooks for the men.

After dinner, guests would stroll round the house admiring Florence Gould's wonderful collection of pictures, which were thick on the walls. Sometimes you saw a new purchase, possibly a priceless Impressionist, lying about waiting for a space to be found to hang it!

Staying with Antony and Anne at Christmas was always very social. Besides going out to friends or to a restaurant for dinner each evening, Anne had a luncheon party for twenty at La Garoupe on both Christmas Day and Boxing Day. Her staff were wonderful: her cook, Céleste, was one of the best in the world; Georges, their butler, was trained to perfection and a great character (he sadly died in the early eighties); and there were the housemaids, Julienne and Marie. Julienne had been with Anne and Antony in their other homes on La Garoupe estate and once reminded me of how many years she had looked after me! They always gave me the warmest welcome, and I hope they will again on my next visit.

I have been privileged to be an old friend of the famous Hennessy family on both sides of the Channel for many years. So I was truly delighted when an invitation came from Comte Alain de Pracomtal, whose mother was a Hennessy, and the directors of Jas Hennessy & Co of Cognac to a dinner at the Mansion House at the end of January in 1981.

This was a delightful occasion attended by the Lord Mayor and Lady Mayoress, Colonel Sir Ronald and Lady Gardner Thorpe, and the Sheriffs, and guests were received by the Comte and Comtesse Alain de Pracomtal and Monsieur and Madame Kilian Hennessy. There were glorious flowers everywhere and the band of the Irish Guards played during the reception and dinner, which was a most carefully chosen and delicious meal, served, as you can imagine, with superb wines. The Apostolic Delegate, Cardinal Bruno Heim, said Grace before dinner. The band played 'God Save The Queen' and 'La Marseillaise' when before the coffee we all rose to toast The Queen, and then the President of the French Republic.

With coffee at the end of dinner the three hundred guests were introduced to Hennessy's new prestige cognac, Paradis, which is truly superb. It is blended only from brandies that have grown old for fifty years or more in oak casks in the Hennessy cellars in Cognac. The firm was founded in 1765 and eight generations of Hennessys and seven generations of the Fillioux family, whom I do not know, have built up this wonderful collection of old brandies, which are unique. Paradis is most elegantly bottled, and we were each sent home with one as a gift.

In 1981 I went to my next royal wedding, when our beloved Prince of Wales married Lady Diana Spencer in St Paul's Cathedral.

As at The Queen's wedding, there were a number of royal guests and friends from all over the world at the ceremony. It was a fairytale romance and the bride had already won the hearts of the nation. On my way to St Paul's I went through streets crowded with well-wishers. I thought I had never seen happier smiling crowds, many of whom had been waiting all night to see this beautiful young bride and her handsome bridegroom.

I got to St Paul's before the doors opened at 9 a.m. The sun was shining through the windows on the scarlet carpet which had been laid everywhere. I had visited St Paul's a couple of days earlier to get an idea of how it would be on the day. I knew roughly where I would be sitting, and on the day I found I had been given a lovely seat in the slightly raised press stand in the southeast aisle with a truly wonderful view right across and down the Cathedral. There were beautiful yellow and white flower arrangements.

The Prince of Wales had taken a personal interest in the music for the service, and I think it was more beautiful than at any wedding I have attended. Taking part were the Bach Choir, the orchestra of the Royal Opera House, the English Chamber Orchestra, the Philharmonia Orchestra, Trumpeters of the Royal Military School of Music and of course the organist of St Paul's, Dr Christopher Dearnley, with the Gentlemen, the Choristers and the Children of Her Majesty's Chapels Royal. In addition to all this talent, during the signing of the registers Miss Kiri Te Kanawa, later Dame Kiri Te Kanawa, sang superbly a beautiful aria from Handel's *Samson*.

Everyone was seated by the time the Prince of Wales arrived wearing the full dress naval uniform of a Commander and also wearing the riband and order of the Garter and the star of the Order of the Thistle. He was accompanied by Prince Andrew, his best man.

There was a fanfare of trumpets as Lady Diana Spencer arrived at the West Door to walk slowly up the nave with her father, Earl Spencer. Her beautiful wedding dress is well known worldwide. Its exceptionally long and very wide train looked wonderful in the wide nave of St Paul's, and her very full tulle veil was held in place by a magnificent Spencer family tiara. She really was the most beautiful bride you could imagine.

After the service, the bride and bridegroom drove back to Buckingham Palace in an open landau drawn by the famous Windsor Greys, with a Prince of Wales escort of Household Cavalry. When they arrived at the Palace, they came out on the balcony in the traditional manner to wave to the cheering crowds in the Mall.

This was such a colourful wedding, with the sun shining everywhere. It is one that, like The Queen's wedding, I shall always remember.

One of the very best parties of the eighties was the one given by Lady Elizabeth Shakerley that evening to celebrate twenty-one years of Liz Anson's Party Planners and her own fortieth birthday. She cleverly gave the party on the night of the royal wedding when everyone felt rather flat.

It took place in the ballroom and all the adjoining reception rooms of Claridge's, where the flower arrangements in every room were out of this world. In each corner of the reception room before you entered the ballroom were blue birch trees, in which were perched white doves, and in the middle of this room was a circular seat with superb flowers in the centre.

The green and yellow ribbons, flowers and whole decor in the ballroom were superbly simple and elegant. As Liz quite rightly said, no one wanted to sit down to a large formal dinner after the wedding festivities, so instead there were a number of piping hot breakfast dishes, being replaced all the time. Also bowls of raspberries and strawberries and baskets of other luscious summer fruits on three buffets for everyone to help themselves from and then go back and join their friends at one of the many candlelit dinner tables. I found I was helping myself between two royal guests, who were very chatty!

Lester Lanin and his band were over from America and kept the dance floor packed. For those who did not want to dance, there were large screens on some of the walls showing a truly wonderful video of the royal wedding which you could watch over and over again. I saw The Queen looking at it several times with great enjoyment, and I found myself sitting with friends still watching it all at midnight. The Queen and the Duke of Edinburgh, who both enjoyed the good dance band, had all their children except the bridegroom with them at this lovely party.

We all missed Queen Elizabeth the Queen Mother, who had decided after the wedding to have a quiet evening at home. Nearly all the other members of the Royal Family were at the party, and a number of the royal guests from overseas, and of course many members of the bride's family. Some of the older guests left between midnight and 1 a.m., but the large majority, including the younger royals, danced until 3 a.m. Claridge's excelled themselves. The chef produced really superb hot dishes and the service throughout was impeccable.

In May 1982, Mr James Sherwood, the President of Sea Containers Group, very kindly invited me to go on the inaugural run of the *Orient Express* from London to Venice. This was a most amusing experience.

My host and his very intelligent and dear wife Shirley Sherwood had done a brilliant job getting this luxury train together. As many readers will know, James Sherwood's involvement in the *Orient Express* began by chance when, on the spur of the moment, he bought two *Orient Express* sleeper coaches built in the 1920s at a sale at Sotheby's in Monte Carlo in 1977! Shirley Sherwood helped a great deal throughout the project by overseeing all the designs and authentic top-quality 1920s furnishings, including beautiful china, glass and linen.

When I arrived at Victoria station, I found a long red carpet laid on the platform beside the Pullman-coached *Orient Express*, and the band of the Coldstream Guards was playing popular tunes of the 1920s. Our invitations had said 'Dress – 1920s'. As I hate dressing up, I had come in my ordinary clothes, and so did quite a few others, but the majority of the guests were wearing clothes of the 1920s. Some of them looked decidedly odd: waistlines were around the hips, and there were cloche hats, feather boas, brow bands, long strings of pearls and long cigarette holders. The men had risen to the occasion with bow ties, striped trousers and striped waistcoats with blazers, and 1920s boaters and panamas.

The send-off had a great feeling of fun and celebration and I was so glad I was actually travelling and not just seeing the passengers off. Inside, everyone was seated, I, happily, with the Hon. William and Mrs McAlpine, now the Hon. Sir William and Lady McAlpine. Bill McAlpine is a tremendous enthusiast and collector of vintage trains and had helped Jim Sherwood get the revised VSOE going. Much of the restoration work, including the beautiful inlaid panelling, had been done by his skilled craftsmen at his Steamtown, Carnforth workshops. Soon after the VSOE left Victoria, an excellent luncheon was served.

On arrival at Folkestone, the cross-Channel ferry was waiting, and on landing at Boulogne we had no luggage problems, but just went straight to the magnificent *wagons-lits* of the VSOE that were lined up on two platforms. Here, another band was playing French tunes of the 1920s. It was now 5 p.m.; I settled in to my luxurious sleeper.

Later I changed for dinner, for which Jim and Shirley had sweetly invited me to their table. I remember noticing as I left my sleeper that the corridors were all carpeted, which gave an added feeling of comfort. On arrival in the dining car, I found the most gracious scene on a train that I can remember. I can also remember two lovely sisters, both in the prettiest 1920s evening dresses, bubbling with fun; they were the Duchess of Westminster and her sister Miss Marita Phillips. Everyone was in evening dress, much of the 1920s period. We had a suberb four-course dinner and during the meal, as we approached Paris, there was a heavenly red sunset. After dinner, I went along to the bar-parlour, where everyone was sitting around in easy chairs or sofas listening to tunes of the 1920s played on a grand piano. Everyone was in a relaxed, happy mood, and some were singing some of the old songs.

I left around midnight, and, remembering that I had had a little difficulty before dinner with the lock on my sleeper, which the sleeping car attendant quickly sorted out, I was wondering if all would be well on my return. When I went into my sleeper, I found my bed turned down, a huge luxurious square pillow and super bed linen, mineral water safely in a special place and, on my bed, a bottle of toilet water – a gift from the management.

I slept soundly and woke as usual at 6 a.m. When I opened my eyes, I saw that we were travelling through beautiful scenery. I was brought some fruit juice, coffee and a croissant in bed at 7.30 a.m., and then dressed and got some writing done before I went along to the dining car, where the most wonderful buffet luncheon had been laid out. I met the young head chef called Michel Ranvier, who had produced the super dinner and buffet luncheon.

During the morning, one of the attendants came to my cabin and asked me which hotel I was staying at, then put a Cipriani label on my cases, so on arrival I did not have to worry about luggage.

My only criticism of this lovely trip was the excess of press and television people everywhere. Once out of your sleeper, you fell over television wires, or a microphone was put in front of your face for a quote. Once when I was talking to a friend, one of these men came up and wanted us to repeat our conversation to the microphone! I am afraid we refused.

There was a tremendous welcome at Santa Lucia station in Venice: miles of red carpet, tremendous happy, cheering crowds behind barriers, and a gondoliers' band playing haunting water music. A red rose was presented to every woman passenger, and Shirley Sherwood, who came off the train looking very chic in a 1920s suit, received a bouquet. This trip really was a fun experience that I shall always remember, and I shall always be grateful to dear Jim and Shirley Sherwood for including me.

On arrival at Venice station, concierges for all the top hotels were waiting to escort guests to the various waiting launches. I was going to stay at my very favourite resort hotel in the world – the Cipriani –

where I have stayed since it was originally started by the Guinness family. On arrival, the guests were met by Dottore Natale Rusconi, a perfectionist, and one of the very best hoteliers in the world.

In the evening, Natale Rusconi had arranged for the *Orient Express* passengers a delicious buffet dinner at tables under the floodlit trees in the new garden, with a group called The Straw Hats playing far away in the corner, and a newish moon shining overhead. This gracious yet informal party in this beautiful and romantic setting provided a nostalgic finish to a memorable journey. Sadly, I could not spend more than one night here. I popped across in the Cipriani launch to San Marco in the morning and later to the airport to catch an afternoon flight home.

Later that year I was invited to the Rolex-Jackie Stewart Celebrity Challenge in North Wales.

I had watched Mr Jackie Stewart driving to victory in motor races. I had also met him and his wonderful wife Helen Stewart on the eve of the Monaco Grand Prix party that Prince Rainier and Princess Grace of Monaco used to give at their palace in Monaco, and I had travelled on the same flight once or twice to various parts of the world. But I never thought I would see Jackie running charity weekends quite brilliantly, at the same time raising worthwhile sums for charity, and giving everyone present enormous enjoyment and fun.

In the late seventies, Jackie Stewart teamed up with Rolex of Switzerland Watches, and the event was called the Rolex-Jackie Stewart Celebrity Challenge. The weekend was centred round a truly wonderful clay pigeon shooting competition on the Sunday. This was held at the North Wales Shooting School at Sealand Manor, Clwyd, North Wales, which is run most efficiently by Mr Noel Jones and his brother Mr Allen Jones, whose family have farmed there for many generations.

The first of these events was held in 1978 and was attended by twenty-four celebrities from every sphere. This one, in 1982, was the second. I arrived to stay, as most of the others did, at the very comfortable Grosvenor Hotel, Chester, where a number of rooms had been reserved. Here I was greeted by Mr Iain Nelson, the Managing Director of Rolex in London, who were the main, very generous sponsors. Jackie Stewart always managed to find a number of other smaller sponsors.

After unpacking, bathing and changing, I came down for the official dinner, where I was then warmly greeted by Jackie and Helen Stewart. The guests of honour at the dinner that evening were the Duke of

Kent, his sister Princess Alexandra, the Hon. Mrs Ogilvy, and the Hon. Angus Ogilvy, the Duke and Duchess of Westminster, and the Duke and Duchess of Roxburghe. The men were all competing next day. There were over a hundred other guests. The celebrities besides the royal guests included personalities from the theatrical and film world, broadcasters, riders and golfers, and all sorts of others. At the end of the dinner, there were three speeches, all very brief.

On Sunday, most of the competitors went up to the shooting school to practise before luncheon. I went up to watch the practice, and was amused to see how some of the best shots missed their targets at first, making a practice well worthwhile.

The competitors took part in teams of four. In 1982, 'THE Team' comprised the Duke of Kent, King Constantine of the Hellenes, the Hon. Angus Ogilvy and Captain Mark Phillips, who was the captain. The Lords Team, sponsored by Mappin & Webb, were the Duke of Westminster, the Duke of Roxburghe (who is a beautiful shot), the Earl of Lichfield, and their captain, Lord Montagu of Beaulieu. There was a Ladies' Team, too, sponsored by the famous Barbour country clothes. It comprised the Duchess of Roxburghe, the Marchioness of Northampton (now Rosie Marchioness of Northampton), Lady Charlotte Curzon (now Lady Charlotte Dinan), and Lady Cecil Cameron of Lochiel (the latter's very jokey husband, Mr Donald Cameron, said he was the team's manager!). Though the Ladies' Team never won, they usually ended with quite a good score. There was also a Riders' Team that included the young American jockey Steve Cauthen, who shot quite beautifully and won the prize for the best single score, for which the Duke of Roxburghe was the runner-up. There were numerous other teams, including The Sportsmen and Jackie's Team. When it came to the pheasant flush, the wives acted as loaders.

The winners that year were THE Team. Jackie Stewart and Allen Jones carried out the prize-giving most efficiently and Princess Anne, who had only arrived on Sunday morning, presented the prizes, assisted by Queen Anne-Marie of the Hellenes and Princess Alexandra, who were both on the prize-giving platform. The prizes, all generously donated, were magnificent. Just before the prize-giving, we all saw what the money raised from this event had bought: a very specially equipped ambulance to be presented to the Friends of Dorincourt – a home for physically disabled people in the Chester area. Jackie Stewart is a great believer in always giving something in kind that is needed by a deserving cause, rather than the money, and I think he is right. That way you know the money has reached the need for which it was raised!

During the summer of 1983, Lord and Lady Howard de Walden gave a dance at their lovely home near Hungerford, with the most wonderful collection of circus amusements. The ladies looked so graceful riding side-saddle on the merry-go-round horses with long evening dresses flowing. The hurdy gurdy music was well away from the very good dance band that kept the floor packed the whole evening. John Howard de Walden, his late mother and all his family give the best parties you can think of.

Two other good party givers who were present that evening were Mr and Mrs John H. Heinz II. As they walked on to the lawn their faces fell a little, as they were giving a party two weeks later at their lovely Ascot home – with the theme 'All the Fun of the Fair'!

At the Heinz's 'Fun Fair' party, I was persuaded, much against my will, to go on the big wheel by a strong young man who accompanied me. This was an experience I had avoided for over eighty years. I must say that when I was on it, I did not find it as frightening as I had imagined it would be. But I am sure that for me it will be a 'once and only'.

Drue and Jack Heinz gave a variety of parties, usually attended by one or more members of the Royal Family, from the quite simple but very enjoyable summer dances in the courtyard of their London mews home to a masked ball at the London Zoo, to a Fancy Dress Boat Party down the Thames, when to my mind the best fancy dress was Lady Adeane, who came as a traffic warden, wearing a black wig and spectacles, with a warden's cap and navy blue suit. No one recognized her as she went about in a very bossy manner directing guests.

Jack and Drue also gave several very good parties at their Ascot home as well as the 'Fun Fair' evening. Sometimes they insisted the guests arrive in boats across the lake. I can remember a party that they gave for Mrs Ronald Reagan, who had come over for the Prince of Wales's wedding. It was a rather damp, misty evening and Mrs Reagan said she was freezing! I took her at once to a lovely warm fire that, in spite of its being July, was burning in the library, and we both warmed up very quickly.

I think the Heinz party that I enjoyed most was the 'Fun Fair' one to celebrate Jack's seventieth birthday, when the invitation said 'presents under 57 pence'. That evening they had screens on the lawns with blown-up pictures of Jack throughout his seventy years. He was such a dear kind man. I think, if I remember rightly, that The Queen came to that party. I am grateful to both dear Jack, who has sadly left us, and dear Drue for asking me to so many of their good parties over the years.

In September 1983, Baron Thyssen-Bornemisza kindly invited me to a dinner and dance he gave for his second son, Baron Lorne Thyssen-Bornemisza, at his lovely Oxfordshire home, Daylesford, which he had bought from the late Viscount Rothermere. The dance took place in a large marquee which Lady Elizabeth Shakerley and her Party Planners had decorated quite beautifully in Heini Thyssen's colours of blue and red with a gypsy encampment mural all round. There was a profusion of flowers, including hundreds of red roses and blue delphiniums. Invitations had said 'Dress Romantically' and guests certainly had done so. The belle of the ball was Heinie Thyssen's daughter Baroness Francesca Thyssen-Bornemisza, who looked radiant in an exquisite black Edwardian dress with long white kid gloves. Her mother, Fiona Baroness Thyssen-Bornemisza, also looked lovely wearing an Edwardian evening dress.

It was a wonderful party, but only held in the marquee. I longed to go into the house to see how the new owners had furnished and arranged it, as I had stayed there with the late Viscount Rothermere and Mary Viscountess Rothermere, when Esmond Rothermere had it filled with the most beautiful furniture and pictures and graceful furnishings. I did a recce on my own, and could find nowhere I could enter. Later I found the present Viscount Rothermere also longing to see inside his father's old home, so Vere Rothermere and I set off together and he, of course, knew the back ways in, but we found everything locked and we never managed to see inside!

The reason was that Heini Thyssen and his fourth or fifth wife, a young and very attractive Brazilian, had just parted. She was living at Daylesford and had barricaded herself in the house with their young son and her reputedly rather tough brother. No one could enter that evening; nor did it seem there was any sign of life in the house. Even Heini Thyssen could not get in his own home and told me himself that he had to go back to London and stay at Claridge's! Anyhow, he gave a very good party, which everyone, old and young, thoroughly enjoyed.

On a Monday at the very end of July in 1984, I took off at 11.55 a.m. in a British Airways Boeing 747 to Los Angeles for the Olympic

Equestrian Sports. Having been to a morning wedding and reception near Colchester, and on by helicopter to De Beers Diamond Day racing at Ascot on Saturday, with a dance in the country that evening, and to the Cartier International Polo day at Smiths Lawn all day Sunday, I boarded the flight feeling full of end-of-the-season fatigue. I went to my front window seat and settled down for the ten-and-a-half-hour flight. After luncheon, at which I only ate a starter and some fruit, I settled down comfortably with my legrest extended and slept peacefully for nearly five hours. I awoke feeling really rested.

At Los Angeles airport a car and chauffeur called Clyde were waiting to take me to the Olympic Press Centre in Los Angeles, where I picked up my accreditation card and my invaluable car park label that I had previously applied for. From here Clyde drove me the 110 miles to the Rancha Santa Fe Inn near San Diego.

It was around 8.15 p.m. local time (4.15 a.m. next morning London time) when I arrived. I went straight to unpack in my bungalow room, where I had a cup of cold soup before I retired at 10 p.m. Stupidly I did not ask how to turn off the air-conditioning, and after fiddling for a while I had to give up. I woke up in the middle of the night freezing! I took the blankets off the second bed but I still could not get warm, and was too frightened at that hour in that strange inn to ring for someone to come and turn the air-conditioning off. When I rang next morning they found I had turned it down to below fifty degrees Fahrenheit!

The reason for my driving a hundred miles to near San Diego to stay was the very unusual arrangements of these Equestrian Olympics. The dressage phase had taken place on Sunday and Monday at Santa Anita racecourse, Los Angeles. Tuesday was a travel day. Wednesday was the speed, endurance and cross country phase, which took place over the golf course of the Fairbanks Ranch Country Club, once the home of Douglas Fairbanks and Mary Pickford, five miles from the Santa Fe Inn. Thursday was another travel day. The final eventing phase, the show jumping, took place back in the centre of Santa Anita racecourse.

On Tuesday, kitted out in my most comfortable non-slip rubber-soled golf shoes, I went over to the Fairbanks club to walk the cross country course, accompanied by one of the officials. I was quite tired by the time I had looked at the thirty-three obstacles, some very frightening, as the temperature was well up in the eighties. The Duke of Edinburgh and Princess Anne also made a tour of the course that day.

Next morning I was up before 6 a.m. as 50,000 spectators were expected and I knew there would be traffic jams. The five-mile drive took over one hour! On arrival I went straight to the start as I wanted to watch one of our riders, Virginia Holgate, take off. In a short while the Duke of Edinburgh, then President of the FEI, arrived, and I saw him later in the day at the Waterfalls. In contrast to the previous day, when I had met quite a few English friends connected with equestrian eventing, this day, with the exception of the Duke of Edinburgh and the British riders, I never set eyes on anyone I had ever seen before! Many friendly Americans came up and spoke to me. I probably looked a little lonely.

As Thursday was described on the Olympic programme as leisure day, when the horses would be travelling back to Santa Anita, I had decided to visit the Getty Museum on the Pacific Highway at Malibu. Unlike most of our museums, where you can walk straight in, at the Getty Museum you have to book your time well in advance. Fortunately I knew the very talented young assistant to the curator, Mr Adrian Sassoon, and he worked miracles in gettng me a 10 a.m. appointment. Adrian Sassoon also very gallantly came round the museum with me, and could answer my various queries and tell me interesting facts about some of the exhibits.

I drove on from here to the Baltimore Hotel in Los Angeles, where many of the Equestrian Olympic officials and others were staying. On entering my room I nearly fainted! It was large and airy, but the decor was unbelievable! There was a green carpet, deep purple bedspread and purple-covered sofa with bright orange cushions and long bright orange curtains. I have never seen anything so ugly. Such a contrast to my elegant room at the Beverly Wilshire hotel on previous visits to Los Angeles.

Thanks to the Hearst Corporation of America I had a splendid seat at Santa Anita to watch the show jumping phase of the Equestrian Eventing Olympics, quite near all the Olympic VIPs. I also enjoyed the comfort of Mrs Mark Barlow's wonderful British Event Supporters' Club, for which she raises funds to run a tent at Badminton and something at the various Olympics. You could go along to the club room and sit down to rest if you needed, or buy a wonderful sandwich or salad luncheon and cool drink and sit down and have it in comfort without any queuing. I noticed that Princess Anne came in to have a light luncheon here on both the days that I was at Santa Anita.

There were ten teams competing in the final jumping phase of the eventing, and two individual Mexicans and one Swiss. Our team, Lucinda Green, Ian Stark and Virginia Holgate, were lying fourth at the start of the jumping phase, with America in the lead. The American rider Karen Stives was leading for the Individual Gold Medal with the very popular New Zealander Mark Todd second. After very exciting jumping, during which the British team caught up, there were only two jumps between an American and a British victory when Karen Stives, the last American rider, came in to jump. She had one jump down. British hopes rose, but then she went on to jump a clear round, so America won the Gold Medal for the first time ever, with Britain winning the Silver and Germany the Bronze. That one jump down cost Karen Stives the Individual Gold Medal, which went to Mark Todd. This was the first equestrian gold medal ever to be won by New Zealand and was a very popular victory. I looked across at New Zealand-born Lord Porritt, who was Governor General of New Zealand from 1967 to 1972, and the pride on his face was good to see.

I had always wanted to cross the Rockies by train in the famous 'Canadian', which is fitted with observation domes. So when I heard that my son Jim was going to be in Edmonton, Alberta, for a convention in August, I asked him to try and get leave to go with me across the Rockies, which he did. I then asked Jim to book us the most comfortable hotel and train accommodation for the trip at my personal expense.

It was a wonderful few days (with the exception of one big disappointment).

I flew out to Edmonton two days before Jim's convention ended, so that I could see something of Edmonton with Mr and Mrs Herbert Pickering, who had been my neighbours in London when he was Agent General for Alberta. They very sweetly showed me so much in a very short while.

On Thursday, when Jim's convention ended, we set off in the afternoon in a little hired Pontiac on the four-hour drive to Jasper Park Lodge, set near the Jasper National Park Game Reserve. Here, arriving around 7.30 p.m., we were given a warm welcome and taken to one of the enchanting log cabins facing Lake Beauvert. Our cabin was extremely comfortable, with two well-furnished bedrooms with adjoining bathrooms, a spacious sitting room, colour television and three telephones. After settling in we walked along to the main hotel building, where we had a delicious dinner in the Moose's Nook restaurant, one of four different restaurants here. Later we strolled back to our cabin for the first of two very comfortable and happy nights here. Jasper is right in the mountains, 3,480 feet up, with an eighteen-hole golf course, tennis courts, a heated swimming pool, boating on the lake, horse riding, and facilities for fishing. Quite a few visitors had hired bicycles to ride around this fascinating estate. There are endless beautiful walks and numerous sightseeing tours.

In the afternoon my son went on a trip in the cable car Trambay, which took him eight thousand feet up the Whistlers Mountain where you get a spectacular view of the valley. I did not go as the public relations officer had heard I was staying at Jasper and wanted to take me round and show me everything. In the evening Jim and I went for one of the beautiful walks before dinner. Guests staying here sometimes see little black bears who come to see what they can find left on any of the breakfast trays or other trays. Sadly we never saw one.

Jim discovered at Jasper that in the local village we could hire a 'guided auto tape tour', a cassette which you could plug into the car cigarette lighter socket. On Saturday, with our little cassette installed, we set off at about 9.30 a.m. for Chateau Lake Louise, where we had booked for luncheon. The drive, on a fine sunny day, was far more interesting and spectacular than I ever dreamt it could be. The cassette was a super idea. You had the benefit of the knowledge of a very informative guide, who told you as you went along where to stop, what to look for at a specific point you were passing, what you were coming to, even when to turn off for five minutes while you passed nothing of interest, and facts about local trees, flowers and animals – without the bore of having a person in the car!

From Lake Louise we drove on quite a short distance to stay the night at the Banff Springs Hotel. From Banff station before luncheon the next day we caught 'The Canadian' to Vancouver, hoping to spend the afternoon and evening seeing the wonderful scenery of the famous Rockies. Here came the big disappointment of an otherwise blissful trip. As we left Banff it was grey and drizzling. We just saw Mount Temple, but not many more of over 140 mountains that can be seen on this trip. Soon heavy rain set in with a thick mist, and visibility was reduced to virtually nil! We looked out of the windows of our luxurious compartments, and went up for spells of an hour in the observation car until dusk, but we could see very little of anything except mist and rain even up there. So I never saw the full beauty of the Rockies, which was sad. However, I felt I was lucky to have had that lovely drive the previous day, and this was only a small setback on a very happy trip with my dear son.

I was very kindly invited for four or five years by Mr James E. Bassett III, the President of Keeneland racecourse and Keeneland Bloodstock Sales, to go and stay in Lexington for the Keeneland July Selected Yearling Sales. There I watched yearlings sold, some of them for millions of dollars each. In 1984 Ted Bassett invited me out later in the year, in October, for the first running of the Queen Elizabeth II Challenge Cup, at which The Queen was going to be present, and to go round some of the Kentucky studs.

I accepted his kind invitation with great pleasure, but I said quite firmly that I did not wish to go round any of the studs at the same time as The Queen, as Her Majesty's visit was a purely private one. The only official part of Her Majesty's visit was to attend the races.

The Queen made history when she arrived at Keeneland racecourse. It was the first time that The Queen – or indeed any reigning King or Queen of England – had been racing in America, and the people of Kentucky were overjoyed that Keeneland should have this honour. The Union Jack was flying beside the Stars and Stripes, everyone wore their best dresses, and the racing was of a high standard.

On arrival at the racecourse, looking very relaxed wearing a brown and white silk dress and a white hat, Her Majesty was received by the President of Keeneland and Mrs James E. Bassett III. They then went through the club lounge up to the large Lexington Room, where there are long windows overlooking the racecourse and a luncheon area at one end. Here several presentations were made by Ted Bassett before luncheon. The Queen sat on Ted Bassett's right at luncheon, with Mr Charles Nickols, Jr, who is very knowledgeable on bloodstock, on her right. I was very kindly seated near the royal table with Sir Philip Moore and leading personalities of American racing.

When the 'off' for the first race was announced, The Queen asked her host if she could go to the window and watch the race, much to the joy of several others like myself, who also wanted to see the race run. Later The Queen, accompanied by her host and hostess, went down to the paddock to see the horses before the big race. This was won by the favourite, Sintra, owned by Mr Set W. Handcock and Mrs William C. Sickle, to whom The Queen presented her beautiful Georgian designer cup made by Aspreys.

After this the royal party and around fifty others, including myself, walked across to the famous Keeneland sale ring, where so many international classic winners have been sold. Here the President put on a mock auction of six yearlings, describing them as six of the top yearlings that had been sold there over the last ten years. Those of us sitting in the auditorium were asked to bid. I really enjoyed myself bidding for two lots, one going up to 10.2 million dollars! After the sale, which goes much faster than the French or English bloodstock sales, the two auctioneers, the three Keeneland handlers and the tellers were presented to Her Majesty, who then went to see the 'barns' and one or two famous Keeneland sales rendezvous. For all of us present, this had been such a truly memorable, relaxed and happy day.

In 1984 my beloved Mrs Mott, who was my wonderful and faithful daily for thirty-four years from 1944 until she retired in 1978, celebrated her eightieth birthday. Mottie, who was one of the best friends I have ever known, took the greatest care of me, and of my flat, and never uttered a grumble or cross word in all those years, and at times I must have been maddening! For years, really until her husband died, Mottie did not have an easy home life as he was very thirsty and a great problem over jobs. Happily she had a very good son, Johnny, who has looked after his mother well, and a daughter who married a good husband, but she died in 1971, aged forty-four years, leaving four young children.

On Mottie's birthday I took most of the day off, and collected her and brought her to the flat, where we were joined by Rita and a widowed friend, Mrs Pollington, who had both worked with her.

We all had luncheon with a little glass of champagne, then we went to the matinée of Tommy Steele's very bright and enjoyable musical *Singing in the Rain*, which they all loved. I managed to get seats in the centre of the second row of the stalls, so that they could hear easily. Rita, who was Spanish, sadly died in 1990. She was originally with my brother Peter and his wife as cook, but when he died she asked to come to me once a week to do my mending and clean the silver, so that she could keep in touch with the family!

Mottie, now eighty-eight years old, has now lived for many years in a comfortable council flat in a building for old people with a warden, and I see her when I can. But she still rings me, as she has done since she retired, every other Thursday at 8 a.m. to know I am all right!

FIFTEEN

The last few years

(1985–91)

Early in 1985, I flew out to St Moritz two weekends running. The first trip was for a very original project – the Cartier Winter Polo Tournament. This made history as it was the first time the game had ever been played on ice. There were two matches: one on Saturday for the Doctor Berry Memorial Cup and another on Sunday for the Cartier Cup.

On Saturday it snowed really hard all day and conditions were truly appalling, but courageously the players and committee went ahead with the match. Cartier had a big luncheon marquee beside the lake and while we were lunching the groundsmen were busy rolling the fast-falling snow on the polo ground, and jeeps with snow-clearing shields were rushing about clearing snow off various parts of the lake.

Many of Cartier's guests stayed in the lovely warm marquee all the afternoon, but I felt I had come here to write about this match and I must watch it. So at 2 p.m., with the President of Cartier, Monsieur Alain Dominique-Perrin, and the then Managing Director of Cartier in England, Mr Anthony Marengo, and a very few others, I ventured out well wrapped up against the icy wind and driving snow to watch the match sitting on a snow-covered *open* stand! With great fore-thought, the organizers had provided large blankets, to wrap around one's legs and waist, which were an absolute godsend.

In spite of the weather, this extraordinary idea of polo on ice drew 2,500 of the paying public to watch the match. The ponies were stabled in a well-heated marquee and returned there between chukkas. I was very worried that ponies or players might get hurt, but happily there were no casualties. The only fall I saw was when a rider went over his pony's head into a pile of soft snow when the pony stopped suddenly!

The ponies were very specially shod with the Huf-Grip, invented by

Mr Peppino Cattaneo of St Moritz, which prevents the snow balling in their shoes, and which of course had special non-skid screws. The ball they played with was bright orange.

A St Moritz team were playing against a German team, the former all wearing burgundy shirts with Cartier across the front. The German team, who had brought their own ponies from West Germany, won convincingly by six goals to two.

By the end of the match, I had about two inches of snow lying on my hat and I was shivering cold. Someone rather cheekily said I looked as if I had a large white pancake on my head!

On Sunday we had blue skies and sunshine. The same teams played, and, surprise, surprise, St Moritz won by five goals to one. We had several diversions. Before the match started we had a parade of traditional horse-drawn sleighs dressed overall. Then we saw three parascenders, launched from a light aeroplane, land perfectly on the polo ground. During the half-time interval we had a show by a dare-devil trick-riding Cossack. Then two hang-gliders, who had taken off from a nearby peak, landed perfectly with very effective orange flares following in their wake.

Cartier were wonderful hosts to a very big party. In the three nights we stayed at the Palace Hotel, there was never a dull moment!

The following weekend was not so original but it was equally enjoyable. It was the Cresta Centenary celebrations. On the Friday I flew out with British Airways, and Mr Colin Cooper greeted me at Zurich. The celebrations were for a week, but I was only staying for a long weekend. Princess Alexandra, the Hon. Mrs Angus Ogilvy, was the guest of honour and flew out with the Hon. Angus Ogilvy to spend from Friday to Monday in St Moritz, then they went on to stay with friends somewhere else for a brief skiing holiday.

Quite a busy week was planned, with racing each morning on the Cresta starting at 8.30 a.m. for the big trophies, including the Morgan Cup, the Nigel Moores Memorial Race, the Gunther Sachs Cup, the Bolt Cup, the Centenary Cup and the Grand National on the final Saturday. There was also Cresta motor racing on the frozen lake, and an ice hockey match. Next there was the arrival of the Centenary train, when all the cars that had taken part in the Sotheby's-Cresta London-to-St Moritz motoring event lined up at the station to meet it. Pipers of the Scots Guards, resplendent in their scarlet tunics and kilts, were also there playing beside the platform as the train drew in. There were also Centenary cocktail parties and dinner parties, an official luncheon party, and on Sunday evening a commemorative service.

On Sunday morning, I was up early and at the Cresta by 8.30 a.m. to watch the Nigel Moores Memorial Race, for which there were 115 starters! This is always a very friendly race full of bonhomie.

This year the race was run on old-fashioned well-padded wooden toboggans, with most of the riders in old-fashioned costumes in contrast to the go-fast wetsuits. Of course all riders wore the official crash helmets, also hand, elbow and knee shields. There were many plus-four suits, one dinner jacket complete with white shirt and black bow tie, and Tony Emerson from Lincolnshire went down wearing his pink hunting coat, the tails flying as he rounded Shuttlecock! Bill Shand Kydd, who was then, and may still be, the only rider to have ridden in the Aintree Grand National and the Cresta Grand National, went down in a funny array of borrowed clothes, as he had lost his on his way out. James Sunley won the race.

After the race, I slipped away before the prize-giving to tidy up to go and watch the unveiling by Princess Alexandra of a truly beautiful bronze in the form of a life-size Cresta rider with his skeleton (toboggan) ready to start down the run, which the St Moritz Tobogganing Club, who run the Cresta, decided to give the people of St Moritz to celebrate the Centenary.

In the many years of going to St Moritz and very kindly being included in a number of wonderful, exotic parties, and meeting some very interesting international personalities, and some much-publicized ones, I think I have enjoyed my mornings up at the Cresta run with the young sporting world, and the après-Cresta mornings in the bar or on the terrace of the Kulm Hotel, as much as anything. Long may the Cresta flourish!

The next and last royal wedding of the eighties was the marriage of the Duke of York and Miss Sarah Ferguson in Westminster Abbey with the Archbishop of Canterbury officiating with a number of other clergy.

The bride, who wore her auburn hair loose and looked radiant, was given in marriage by her father Major Ronald Ferguson, and wore a beautiful dress of cream duchess satin with a heavily beaded bodice; her tulle veil was held in place by a diamond tiara, over which, going up the aisle, she wore a rather heavy headdress of cream roses. She was attended by eight children – Lady Rosanagh Innes-Ker, Prince William, Peter and Zara Phillips, Andrew and Alice Ferguson, Laura Fellowes and Seamus Makim – the bridesmaids wearing peach silk taffeta dresses with floral headdresses, and the two older pages in mid-shipmen's full dress uniform of 1782–97, with the two younger boys in sailor suits. The Queen, Queen Elizabeth the Queen Mother, the Princess of Wales and Princess Margaret all wore blue. The bride and bridegroom drove in an open state landau, drawn by the Windsor Greys, back to Buckingham Palace for the wedding luncheon.

Sadly, as I write, an official announcement has been made that this bride and bridegroom are to separate after less than six years of marriage.

Early in 1987, I was invited, not for the first time, to an International Symposium on Anterior Segment Micro-Surgery.

The first time was back in 1977, when I was invited by Mr Eric Arnott, one of our most brilliant eye surgeons, whom I had known since he was a boy, to attend an international congress on cataracts at the Inter-Continental, which was to be attended by nearly 400 of the leading eye surgeons from all over America, Russia, Japan, Canada, Australia, South Africa, Saudi Arabia, Hong Kong, New Mexico, Hawaii, France, Germany, and many other countries in Europe and from Britain.

During three morning sessions the world's finest eye specialists demonstrated to fellow ophthalmic surgeons the great advances being made in cataract surgery. They carried out twenty operations in two of the very well-equipped operating theatres of the Charing Cross Hospital. Television cameras were attached to the surgeons' microscopes, and live pictures of the intricate operations were beamed to the Inter-Continental's Conference Room, where delegates could see them very clearly on one large screen and on a number of television monitors arranged around the room.

When I arrived, Eric Arnott's charming secretary took me to my seat, which she said they had arranged at the end of a row in case I felt queasy watching the operations and wanted to leave quickly. Straightaway, however, I was far too gripped by what I saw to think of anything else.

I watched nine operations. It was amazing how the techniques of each surgeon differed, and how tidily or untidily they appeared to knot their stitches. I wore some sort of badge on my chest like all the surgeons, and I was rather pleased that when my two neighbours came back from having a cup of coffee in the middle of an operation and asked me which of two fluids or jellies was being used, I found I was able to answer promptly, which showed I had been concentrating and taking it in. I began to think my neighbours took me for a female eye surgeon!

I came away from here with the greatest feeling of confidence that, in future, I need have no fear if I have to have a cataract operation, so perfectly can an operation be performed today. But it also taught me that I would always want to go to a really good and proven eye surgeon.

In 1987 the symposium I was invited to was to be held at the then nearly new Regent Hotel in Kowloon, Hong Kong. I decided I would rather stay at the Mandarin Hotel in Hong Kong, where I was known, and take the ferry across each day.

I left the Mandarin at 8 a.m. on the Wednesday and took the Star ferry across; I was in the Regent Hotel before 8.30. I picked up my necessary badges and papers and was ready for the start at 9 a.m.

Again, several hundred top eye surgeons of the world, with the exception of the Russians, had assembled here for the symposium, which was held in the vast conference hall of this modern hotel. On arrival I met Mr and Mrs Huw Thomas – Anne Thomas had organized the symposium. When I went into the conference hall I saw the big television screens and smaller ones round the room as before. But I was most disappointed to find that, owing to lack of facilities at the Hong Kong hospitals, nothing was being televised live. Each surgeon, when speaking, had his talk visually explained by a video. A few exceptions used slides. This, I felt, lost a lot of the feeling of the operation really being performed. Sadly I missed the opening day, Tuesday, when much more time had been devoted to the modern role of lasers in refractive surgery.

Wednesday's session on 'Pathological aspects of lens implant surgery' went on with the exception of a coffee break until lunchtime, when, as before, I hoped to lunch with the Eric Arnotts and Huw Thomases and all the eye surgeons, but instead I was whisked off by the hotel's PRO to lunch with her in the restaurant and hear all about the hotel! I was hopping mad, but it happened so quickly there was nothing I could do. I was back in my seat by the start of the afternoon session, which went on until quite late with a break for tea.

The Thursday session was a morning one, when we heard fourteen speakers who were limited to ten or fifteen minutes. The symposium ended with a talk entitled 'What is the future of the anterior segment micro-surgeons? Where do we go from here?'

I came away feeling, from the little I had heard about lasers, that I personally would rather stick to the surgeon's knife.

Next day I went to China for the first time! I had to be up very early to be over at the Regent Hotel by 8 a.m. to join about forty of the eye surgeons, some accompanied by their wives, to go in two buses on a day trip to China. We drove through miles of the New Territories which have been miraculously reclaimed from the sea and on to the frontier, which was then defined by barbed wire fences. I had been warned that there might be a long delay at the immigration and customs point, but thanks to the Huw Thomases good organization, we went through very quickly. They had typed out a list with our names and numbers, and we were asked to line up in numbered rotation, which worked well.

After the border, our Hong Kong guide handed us over to a charming young and very cheery Chinese guide who spoke perfect English. He was excellent, and welcomed the new freedom the Chinese were then enjoying. From now on the road was not as good as the Hong Kong side until we approached the new town of Shenzhen, where there were modern motorways. We drove through their well-planned industrial area, where we saw acres and acres of modern-looking factories on one side of the road and a similar acreage of high-rise modern blocks of flats for the workers and a large shopping centre on the other.

Our first stop was at Wong Bai Ling in the old and rather slummy part of the town, where we were shown an old and, I thought, rather smelly house! I and one or two others quietly went off to look at another cleaner, occupied, house where we noticed all the hallways were full of bicycles. Quite near there were better-looking streets and typical suburban houses.

We stopped at a flower show and an exhibition of art and at Lake Shenzhen before we arrived at what we were told was the best restaurant, then called the Spring Garden Hotel. We had a number of tables reserved for us in a far room. We had to go through the restaurant where around 200 locals were already lunching, 98 per cent of whom I noticed were men! The restaurant produced a very good lunch, which included many really crisp dishes. I am not keen on Chinese food, but I enjoyed this meal.

After luncheon we went to a local market, then to a shopping arcade where the rest of the party bought Chinese satin-embroidered shawls, embroidered table mats, jade and porcelain. One charming American couple bought two large *famille rose*-style vases which must have been a problem to get home safely. I only bought one small real fur panda as a memento of my day in China, and he is still in my sitting room today.

After I had gone to bed that evening, my very dear nephew John Kemp-Welch and his wife Diana arrived at the Mandarin from Japan on the last lap of a business trip. By coincidence, they had the suite above mine and we were able to meet several times in forty-eight hours.

Another evening I dined with one of my former secretaries, Mrs Geoffrey Shutt, and her husband, who is a brilliant construction engineer and had been helping with much of the development in Hong Kong for some years. He first came out to build Hong Kong's underground railway, which goes from the island to the New Territories. We dined at the Royal Hong Kong Yacht Club, which has a wonderful view over the harbour and was a new venue for me. It was a very happy evening.

I had never been to Vienna, and I longed to go. Twice, kind British Ambassadors and their wives had invited me to stay when they were posted there, but I was never able to fit a visit in. So in the autumn of 1987 I decided to give myself a present, and to see if my very dear niece, Mrs Mervyn Bourdillon, could come with me for a weekend. As her husband is Lord Lieutenant of Powis, Epony Bourdillon has a number of commitments during the year, but I was lucky and she found a free weekend. We did quite a lot of homework before we left and were grateful for the help and advice of Lt-Colonel and Mrs Blair Stewart-Wilson, who had lived in the city for a year when Blair was Defence Attaché. I have given the whole itinerary of our weekend, as any reader following this programme is bound to enjoy themselves.

I booked a car and an English-speaking driver to meet us at the airport and drive us for the whole weekend. He was a splendid man called Helmut, who even took us sightseeing on our way in to the hotel.

I booked us in at the Bristol Hotel on Karnther Ring, which I had been told was a good and central hotel. We had two pleasant rooms and were very comfortable there. I had rung the concierge in advance to get us seats for various functions, which he did most efficiently. Charming Viennese friends of Mary Stewart-Wilson did the rest and were very gallant in looking after us.

After checking in, we went off on a tour of the city, then to Vienna's famous and fashionable tea shop Demmels, in the Kohlmarkt, which produces fabulous patisserie and iced cakes. We went back to the hotel to unpack. Then a kind Austrian friend of Mary's collected us and took us over to the wine district to dine at Oppolzen, one of the most attractive of the Henrigen wine gardens. We had an excellent Austrian meal in a really local setting. It was all very informal, colourful and jolly. The other guests were all Austrians in attractive leisure clothes quietly radiating a lot of happy laughter.

On the Saturday morning, we walked to the famous Kunsthistorisches Museum, to see their magnificent collection of European art. From here, we walked across to the Hofburg Palace, the winter home of the Habsburgs until 1916. This palace is enormous, with a chapel in one end and the famous Spanish Riding School housed in another wing. We lunched in the very gracious restaurant in the Schwarzenburg Palace at a table overlooking the gardens with a most attractive couple, Doktor and Frau Peter Kurtz; he is a Harvard graduate and is Director-General of Estée Lauder for the whole of south-eastern Europe. They had angelically given up a day's shooting and a day at their country home to take us to luncheon. We had *Tafelspitz*, an Austrian boiled beef speciality.

In the late afternoon, we went to the famous gilded Musikverein to hear the Vienna Philharmonic Orchestra with the brilliant violinist Rainer Kuchl, conducted by André Previn, who is one of my favourite conductors. It was the most glorious music to listen to in this fabulously beautiful concert hall. From here, we went back to our hotel, where friends of Epony, Mr and Mrs David Baird Murray, were waiting to very kindly take us to dinner in the restaurant at the Sacher Hotel, where we had another delicious dinner, including a slice of their famous *Sachertorte*.

On Sunday, we were up in good time to go to church at the Bungkapelle, the Baroque chapel of the Hofburg Palace, where the Wiener Sängerknaben (Vienna Boys' Choir) sing Mass at 9.30 a.m., all dressed in sailor suits. It was a moving and reverent service with superb singing (you have to get seats in advance for this).

From here, we walked round to another wing of the Hofburg Palace to the fantastic Spanish Riding School, which dates back to the sixteenth century. Thanks to the splendid concierge, Herr Johan Kratschmer, we had super seats in the front row below the Imperial Box. We were so near to the horses that I thought that if I held my hand out with a Polo in it, I might stop the show!

We saw a brilliant performance by these magnificent, perfectly trained Lippizaner horses in their own fine setting. I never dreamt that the school, with its Baroque architecture, would be so beautiful. In the afternoon we set off for the Schönbrunn Palace, driving through the beautiful Vienna woods. On arrival, Helmut got us a private guide so that we did not have to join a large group and could see more. I cannot begin to describe the beauty of the rooms and the furnishing; they just have to be seen.

On our way home, we stopped at the Belvedere Palace, which, in the time of the Emperor Franz Josef, was the summer home of Prince Eugène of Savoy. Today it houses a fine collection of modern art. We then stopped and went inside Stephansdon Cathedral, to see the beauty of the high altar and the Gothic pulpit. Then Helmut insisted on us stopping and going in the Griechenbeisl Inn, used in the film *The Third Man*, to see the wall with signatures of so many famous people, including Mozart, Beethoven, Mark Twain and Orson Welles.

We arrived back at the hotel in time to change comfortably into evening dress. Then, as it was a fine evening, we walked across the street to the Staatoper, or the State Opera House. Here we saw a lavish production of *Turandot*, superbly produced and sung. It really was a glorious dream come true!

After the opera, we walked back across the street to our Bristol Hotel to have dinner quietly together in the candlelit restaurant, where violins played Viennese music softly.

On Monday morning, before we left for the airport, Epony went off with Helmut to do some quick shopping, including a return visit to Demmels to buy some of their patisserie to take home for her family. On our way to the airport, we diverted a little to get a glimpse of the Blue Danube River. We said goodbye to Helmut, who had taken such care of us, and caught the British Airways flight to London airport. Epony had been the most wonderful companion, and for me, my visit to Vienna had been all I hoped it would be, and more!

The last two royal trips of my career were both to Madrid. In 1987, I flew out there for the state visit of the Prince and Princess of Wales, who were in Madrid for the first time. A very busy itinerary had been arranged by the Spanish authorities in conjunction with the British Ambassador, Lord Nicholas Gordon Lennox.

I flew over late on a Monday, the night before the arrival of the royal couple, having only landed from Canada that morning! (I had been to Ottawa for a few days to attend the confirmation of both my grand-daughters.)

I stayed in Madrid, as I have always done, at the Hotel Ritz, which was being so well run by Mr John Macedo. On Tuesday morning early, I went over to the Palace Hotel to collect my accreditation pass and to listen to briefings given by Mr Victor Chapman, the very capable Assistant Press Secretary at Buckingham Palace, and by Mr Bill Henderson, the charming Information Officer at the British Embassy in Madrid. Thanks to Victor Chapman and his capable assistant Miss Kiloran McGrigor, I received all the various passes I asked for with speed and courtesy.

The Prince and Princess of Wales landed at 4.30 p.m. at Barajas airport, and then flew by helicopter to El Pardo Palace, where they were staying. Here they were greeted by the Infanta Doña Elena and the Infanta Doña Cristina.

By 6 p.m., the Prince and Princess of Wales had changed and were downstairs ready to preside at a media reception. They dined privately that night with the King and Queen of Spain.

Next morning, the Prince of Wales attended a seminar of the British Invisible Exports Council, and made a very constructive speech. The day after, both the Prince and Princess of Wales attended a fashion show at the Hotel Ritz, of clothes all made by the top British designers; this was attended by members of the Spanish Government and their wives, a great number of Spain's smartest ladies, some escorted by their husbands, and members of the diplomatic corps. Happily, it was a very good show and one could feel proud of British fashion. At the end of the show, to everyone's delight, the Prince and Princess of Wales stood near the ballroom and shook hands with everyone who had been at the show and reception.

One of the two highlights was when, on their first day, the King and Queen of Spain gave a luncheon of 150 guests in their honour at the Royal Palace. The guest list was wonderfully varied, headed by the King's father, the Conde de Barcelona, the Prime Minister, Señor Felipe Gonzalez, and members of the Government, the Director of the Prado Museum, Señor Alfonso Perez Sanchez, golfer Señor Severiano Ballesteros, opera singer Señor Placido Domingo and so on.

The second highlight was on the Thursday evening when the British Ambassador and Lady Nicholas Gordon Lennox gave a wonderful party at the British Embassy, which took a lot of planning as the embassy residence is not very large and they had to seat a hundred and twenty guests. They had a marquee built out over the garden for dinner, and a dance floor which was cleverly laid between two French windows of the house. There were glorious flower arrangements both in the marquee and in the house. The suite of reception rooms was also very much in use. We all had drinks here before dinner, and guests circulated through the rooms meeting friends; we then came back here for coffee after dinner. Mary Gordon Lennox is a wonderful organizer. Earlier, I had felt very worried for my dear hostess, as there was a tremendous thunderstorm with torrential tropical rain about an hour before guests were due to arrive. Happily, it did no damage.

Guests were received by the Prince and Princess of Wales and Lord and Lady Gordon-Lennox. The Princess of Wales, as always, looked beautiful, wearing a very pretty dress with a black strapless top and a very full red taffeta skirt. When I was received by the Prince of Wales, he very kindly enquired whether I was bearing up all right, having seen me at functions for three days. This was the royal couple's last evening in Madrid, but not in Spain.

The two Infantas looked enchanting. Doña Elena, who sat on the Prince of Wales's right at dinner, wore a beautiful red dress with a sequinned bodice. Mary Gordon Lennox sat on His Royal Highness's left. The British Ambassador sat between the Princess of Wales and the Doña Cristina, who wore a beautiful white dress. After dinner, six young Spanish ladies, friends of the two Infantas, wearing attractive Spanish dresses, performed several flamenco dances with partners. Some of the guests, including the Prince and Princess of Wales and the two Infantas, were invited to join in.

Altogether, it was a very happy party enjoyed by everyone. The Prince and Princess of Wales left soon after 1 a.m. and so did some of the older guests; the young guests went on dancing much longer!

I felt this royal visit was a very relaxed and happy one. The people of Madrid gave the Prince and Princess of Wales a tremendous welcome wherever they went, and the fact that the King and Queen of Spain and the two Infantas were all close friends of their royal visitors made it a little less formal.

Towards the end of the following year, 1988, I returned to Madrid (never a hardship!) for the state visit of our beloved Queen and the Duke of Edinburgh. Although this was a more formal visit than that of the Prince and Princess of Wales, it was also a very happy one, and

The Queen looked so relaxed, as if she was enjoying herself throughout.

I once again arrived a day early. I was met at the airport by the same English-speaking driver, called Pepe, who had driven me on the previous royal visit. There was a press meeting at the same Palace Hotel that evening, but nothing like as efficiently handled as it was the previous year. This time, the Buckingham Palace Press Secretary, Mr Robin Janvrin, was in charge. I found him very uncaring and unhelpful, and I was on the verge of tears with frustration and worry, when I recalled the very charming and efficient Information Officer at the British Embassy, Mr Bill Henderson – who happily remembered me from the previous year – and his very capable and kind assistant, Miss Eileen Ascroft, who had been Assistant Information Officer at our embassy in Madrid for many years. I told them of my plight, and they immediately said they would do what they could. Eileen Ascroft rang me as promised, and thankfully I eventually received passes for all that I had asked for. Once that had been sorted out, I thoroughly enjoyed this royal visit.

Her Majesty was the first reigning monarch of the United Kingdom ever to make a state visit to Spain. There was an extremely warm welcome for The Queen everywhere she went, and Spanish and British flags flew everywhere. The Queen and the Duke of Edinburgh were met at the airport by the heir to the Spanish throne, the Principe de Asturias, who had been abroad during the previous royal visit, and by a large welcoming group of VIPs. They then drove to El Pardo Palace, where King Juan Carlos and Queen Sofia of Spain were waiting to greet them. Then the Queen, accompanied by King Juan Carlos, inspected the Guard of Honour, and watched a march past of the Guard of Honour, and finally a ride past of the Spanish Household Cavalry, all mounted on white Arab horses.

That evening I had the privilege to be in the Throne Room of the Royal Palace, which, I was told, has two thousand eight hundred rooms, to watch the guests arriving for the magnificent royal banquet that the King and Queen of Spain gave there in honour of The Queen and the Duke of Edinburgh. The Throne Room is a very large and impressive room with red silk brocaded walls, a lot of gilt-framed mirrors, superb chandeliers, and a ceiling painted by Tiepolo, and in the centre of one wall at the top of four red-carpeted steps are two gilded and red brocaded state thrones.

The guests included many friends, among them the Duke and

Duchess of Wellington (he is, of course, a grandee of Spain, where they are known as the Duque and Duquesa de Ciudad Rodrigo); the Marquesa de Santa Cruz, now sadly a widow, looking very chic in a beautiful black dress on which she wore one large, deep purple rose, and a magnificent diamond necklace; Señor and Señora Puig de la Bellacasa, Lord and Lady Nicholas Gordon Lennox, and the British Foreign Secretary, Sir Geoffrey Howe, and Lady Howe, now Lord and Lady Howe of Aberavon, all of whom came over to talk to me before they had taken up their official positions.

When guests were assembled, a gentleman of the Spanish royal household went round very courteously asking them to take their places in the right order of protocol to be received. Members of the Spanish Royal Family were received first, then the Government, the diplomatic corps, the Grandees, and others. The Queen came into the room with King Juan Carlos, and the Duke of Edinburgh with Queen Sofia. With her white chiffon evening dress the Queen wore an exquisite diamond tiara and emerald and diamond necklace and earrings. Queen Sofia also wore a magnificent diamond tiara and a diamond necklace and earrings; her dress was in black faille, with an underskirt of white taffeta spotted in black. Both the Infantas, I noticed, wore tiaras and, like their mother, the Queen, the blue riband of an order across their very pretty evening dresses. All the men wore orders and decorations. The Countess of Airlie and Lady Elton, who were in attendance on The Queen, also wore diamond tiaras with their evening dresses.

It was a magnificent occasion. Before they went into dinner, I was amused and amazed when Mr Robin Janvrin saw me, and stopped and said 'Oh, you managed to get here.'

The following evening, I was kindly invited to the reception after the banquet given by The Queen and the Duke of Edinburgh in honour of King Juan Carlos and Queen Sofia. This took place in the state rooms of the magnificent El Pardo Palace, where they were staying. On arrival at the reception, I found the wide staircase lined with troopers from our Household Cavalry looking absolutely splendid in their uniforms and plumed helmets. After all the guests had assembled in the grand first-floor reception rooms, the Queen and the Duke of Edinburgh arrived accompanied by King Juan Carlos, Queen Sofia, the Prince of Asturias, who is a very handsome young man, the Infanta Elena and the Infanta Cristina. The Queen, looking radiant, wore a champagne-coloured evening dress with an embroidered chiffon jacket, and in her hair, instead of a tiara, she wore two very pretty diamond wings, which looked most attractive. This was the only time I have seen Her Majesty wearing these diamond wings. Queen Sofia and many of the ladies present wore tiaras and there were some superb dresses.

Next morning, I was at the Municipal Museum by 9.45 a.m., as the Queen and the Duke of Edinburgh were due at 10.45 for the inauguration of the 'Wellington in Spain' exhibition. The Duke of Wellington, who had lent many of his treasures from Apsley House and Stratfield Saye, had flown over several times to monitor the setting-up of the exhibition. Valerian and Diana Wellington were the first people I met on arrival and they introduced me to Mr Roger Fry, who had headed the committee that arranged the exhibition. This was a fascinating and cleverly hung exhibition with many exhibits never shown in public before, at which I could have spent hours.

The Queen and the Duke of Edinburgh arrived punctually, accompanied by King Juan Carlos and Queen Sofia, who had made their visit such fun. There was a large attendance on the royal party, all longing to see this exhibition. From here, they went to Madrid University, then drove out to El Escurial. In the evening, there was a reception at El Pardo Palace for the British community in Madrid. On Thursday morning, The Queen and the Duke of Edinburgh flew to Seville for the day for official engagements, and on to Barcelona, where they stayed on board the royal yacht *Britannia* to fulfil more official engagements. I, however, ended my visit after the 'Wellington in Spain' exhibition.

As I was leaving for Australia the following Wednesday, I wanted to get home to get the Spanish royal visit written and to press. I was so happy to have been in Madrid for this memorable historic event – my last royal visit. It was wonderful to see the very warm welcome The Queen received from the people of Spain wherever she went.

In 1988, I seemed to travel more than ever. In January and February I went to Paris, to California to stay with dear friends, to New York to stay at the Pierre, to Jamaica to stay with Mr and Mrs Anthony Watson at their well-run and comfortable Plantation Inn, Ocho Rios, and on to Palm Beach to stay with Mrs Arthur Little, Jr.

In March, I made the first of two visits to Australia, for Bicentenary Year, the first to Sydney for the Sydney Easter Show, the biggest agricultural show I have ever been to, and the Randwick Racing Festival.

From the moment I landed in Sydney, I was, as always, killed with kindness. Mr Charles Lloyd Jones had very kindly sent his red Bentley and Holmes, the wonderful Yorkshire-born chauffeur who for many years, drove his mother, the late Lady Lloyd Jones, to meet me, and we drove to the Sheraton-Wentworth, where I always stay. As it was by now around 8 p.m., I was able to see the Bicentennial illuminations in Sydney, which were beautiful.

Next day at 1.30 p.m., Holmes and the Bentley were waiting to take me and a very dear Australian friend, Lady Pagan, up to the Sydney Easter Show Showground. The Princess Royal was to open the show officially at 2.30 p.m. On arrival, Her Royal Highness, who wore a champagne-coloured silk suit and a jaunty hat, drove round the vast arena in an open carriage with Captain Mark Phillips beside her. It was a most impressive opening, which included the fabulous parade of many categories of livestock.

The other event I had come out for on this trip was the Randwick Easter Carnival, which each year comprises racing on four days over Easter and the following week. Like Royal Ascot, this meeting has some of the best racing of the year in Australia. Mr Jim Bell, the Chairman of the Australian Jockey Club, had very kindly sent me badges for the Committee Stand and the Members' Stand, and invitations to luncheon each day in the Vice-Regal Room. On the opening Saturday, it is the Australian Jockey Club Derby; on the Wednesday, it is Ladies' Day – and the ladies really do dress up!, in their very best silks and satins, feathers and flowers. That day the AJC Oaks is run, and on the final Saturday it is the turn of the Sydney Cup.

Mrs Richard Gibb, who gave a delightful cocktail party during the Bicentennial Show week, also very kindly took me to the annual NSW Easter International Polo Tournament at Mr and Mrs Kerry Packer's Warwick Farm, about an hour's drive from Sydney, on the Sunday. Mari Gibb had borrowed her son-in-law John Lewis's very luxurious minibus fitted with large sliding windows each side and five comfortable armchairs! It was the first time I had ever been in a minibus and I had no idea that one could be so comfortable. Besides myself, Mari Gibb had invited Marge Pagan and Lady Packer to join us in this comfortable conveyance.

One of the first people we met on arrival was the famous polo player Mr Sinclair Hill, one of the Vice-Presidents of the NSW Polo Association, who has played polo in England. When he saw us, he at once guided our minibus to a front-row position. Mari Gibb had brought the most wonderful picnic luncheon, which the driver laid out on tables under a large tent umbrella that seemed to come out from the side of the minibus. There was enough for a feast, and many other friends came to enjoy Mari Gibbs's good luncheon. The weather was not, alas, too kind, and at times it poured, but they played on, and we watched some first-class polo.

After my return from Sydney, and visits to Paris, Deauville, Venice and Athens, I caught the British Airways Shuttle to Edinburgh one afternoon, where I stayed the night very comfortably at the Caledonian Hotel for a dance. At 6.45 p.m., a car was waiting to drive me to Alyth, near Blairgowrie, where I was going to dine with the Hon. Malcolm and Lady Mariota Napier (she was one of the debutantes I took to Barcelona some twenty years earlier). After a lovely party of fifty-five guests, and a delicious dinner at their charming home, Bardmony, where they also had a houseful of young guests, we all drove over to Kinnettles House by Forfar, the home of Mr Hugh Walker-Munro. Here, the three joint hosts, Mr Hugh Walker-Munro, Lady Mariota Napier and Mrs Timothy Llewellen Palmer, were giving a dance for their sons and daughter, Mr Geordie Walker-Munro, Miss Eloise Napier, and Mr Charlie Llewellen Palmer. Kinnettles House is a typical grey stone Scottish mansion.

For the dance, a very large marquee had been built on to the house – it had to be big as a number of reels and Scottish dances were included in the programme. Outside, there was also a Bouncy Castle, which gave a lot of joy. Here I watched many young people taking off their shoes and bouncing about with lots of happy laughter! I was told later that there were four pairs of grandparents enjoying the Bouncy Castle at the same time! It was a great attraction and good fun. This dance went with a swing from the start and the hosts had to stop the band at 5 a.m., although the discotheque went on! It was such a good dance that I did not leave until after 1 a.m. and it was after 3 a.m. before I put my light out.

At the end of September, on a Friday afternoon, I flew to Dublin for the Cartier Million, being run at Phoenix Park for the first time on the Saturday. Some of the Cartier party were staying at Luttrellstown Castle, some at the Shelbourne. I chose the latter. That evening, I joined a party at a charity ball held at the fifteenth-century Royal Hospital, at Kilmainham, now used for special events.

During the evening, there was a £10 raffle for a Cartier watch, which raised £22,000 by the sale of tickets. It was won by Mrs Norma Smurfit, who had, with Mrs Andrew Heffner, organized the evening.

Mrs Smurfit generously gave the watch back to be auctioned, when it made another £5,000, and was again given back to be auctioned, when the auctioneer said 'The first bid of £3,000 gets the watch'. It was quickly snapped up.

On Saturday, the President of Cartier worldwide, Monsieur Alain Perrin, and his attractive wife flew in from Paris in time for the pre-Million Race luncheon for two hundred guests that Cartier were giving at Luttrellstown Castle. Several members of the racing world arrived by helicopter and landed on the lawns of the castle. After luncheon, I was kindly given a lift in one of these 'choppers' to the racecourse, thus avoiding traffic jams.

The winner of the race that year received £500,000, the second £200,000, and the third £100,000, and the rest of the prize money went to the other horses, including £10,000 to the horse finishing tenth in the race! All the runners had to have been purchased at Goff's bloodstock sales. Most of the runners were owned by syndicates, sometimes split up into quite small shares. The winner was Corwyn Bay, which cost a syndicate £60,000, and ran in the name of Mr Albert M. Stall. Corwyn Bay was trained in Ireland by Mr Tommy Stack, who was a very popular leading Irish National Hunt jockey who won our Grand National.

I watched the race beside Sir Ian and Lady Trethowan, Colonel and Mrs Tommy Wallis, and Mrs Dick Hern, three of whom had a quarter of one share in the Kennet Valley Thoroughbred Syndicate. This syndicate was formed by Mr Nicholas Robinson and the Hon. Harry Herbert, whose brother-in-law Mr John Warren, who is a bloodstock agent, chose and bought four yearlings quite reasonably at Goffs for the syndicate. Three of those four yearlings had already won in England. Now the syndicate owned the second in the Cartier Million, Miss Demure, who cost £58,000, and was ridden by Willie Carson; also the third, French Pretender, ridden by John Reid. These two had that afternoon won £300,000 in prize money!, so it was no wonder my neighbours were cheering as the horses came past the post. To add to the excitement, John Warren's very pretty wife, Lady Carolyn Warren, looking beautiful dressed in blue, won the first prize for the Best Turned-Out Lady racing!

A few weeks later, I took off on the Wednesday on a Cathay Pacific Boeing 747 flight to Hong Kong and Melbourne on my second Australian visit this Bicentenary Year, for the Bicentenary Melbourne Cup Week.

My friends in Melbourne always get very hurt if I go to Sydney and not to Melbourne, and vice-versa. So having been to Sydney for their big Easter week, I promised to come to Melbourne for Cup Week.

I arrived at around 11 a.m. At the baggage claim area, I met the Hon. William and Mrs McAlpine, now the Hon. Sir William and Lady McAlpine, who had come on another flight direct from London. They had come out to see the exhibition of his famous steam engine, *The Scotsman*, that was touring Australia. I also met Mr Peter Stanley, who had come out for Cup Week; he very kindly immediately helped me with my suitcases.

We were all staying at the Regency Club at the Hyatt on Collins. Coming from a cold November England, it was wonderful to see sunshine and feel the temperature up in the eighties. On arrival at the hotel, I was taken to a lovely double room on the thirtieth floor, but it was very short of drawer and cupboard space for even one person. So I rang to have another chest of drawers and a hanging rail, of the kind you have for coats for a party, put in my room, so that I could get on with my unpacking.

At 5.45 p.m., two of my dearest Australian friends, Sir Rupert and Lady Clarke, came to collect me and take me to a very large and delightful cocktail party given by Sir Donald and Lady Trescowthick at their attractive home in Toorak. Sir Donald is, like Rupert Clarke, one of Australia's leading financiers. On our way to the party, we collected Sir Edward Dunlop, one of Australia's brilliant surgeons, and also an author.

After the cocktail party, we four went on to the Derby Eve Ball. Here we were joined by Rupert and Kath's youngest son, Mr Peter Clarke, and his wife, and their only daughter, Mrs David Cutler, and her husband. Vanessa Cutler, who before she married worked for Colefax & Fowler in London, now had three young sons and a baby daughter. During the ball, for the first time I watched the crowning of a beauty queen. To my surprise, this was carried out by the Clerk of the Course at Ascot, Captain the Hon. Nicholas Beaumont! Nicky Beaumont and his dear wife Ginny were the guests of honour of the Victorian Racing Club for Cup week, and in the party of Mr Peter Armytage, Chairman of the VRC, and Mrs Armytage.

Next day was Derby Day. Although the racing is of a higher standard than on Cup Day, it never draws such a big crowd. Mr Peter Armytage had very kindly sent to my hotel my badges for the Directors' Box on both Derby and Cup Days, and invitations to luncheon and tea both days in the Committee Room at Flemington racecourse. Rupert and Kath Clarke angelically took me racing both days, so I had no transport problems.

On Derby Day, I was very happily seated for luncheon with Sir Henry Bolte, a most interesting and entertaining personality, who was Premier of Victoria from 1955 to 1972, and whom I had known for many years. I met many other charming Australian friends that day.

That evening, I went to a private dance given by Mr and Mrs John Coote at their South Yarra home in honour of their house guests, the 29th Knight of Glin and Madame FitzGerald, and the Hon. Desmond and Mrs Guinness. Having reconstructed and redecorated their Australian home, it was at that point for sale, as John Coote had just bought Coote Castle in County Cavan, where he and his family now live. I met a number of friends here and after an enjoyable party I left around midnight. On my way home, I had a funny experience. I suddenly realized when I got to the elevator to go up to my room that the friends who had kindly given me a lift had taken me to the wrong hotel, and that I didn't know at which hotel they had left me! I asked where I was and got the concierge to get me a taxi to take me to the Hyatt.

On Sunday I drove out to Rupert and Kath Clarke's annual luncheon party at Bolinda Vale, Clarkfield.

On Monday, there were more Cup Week celebrations. I went to the enormous Celebration Stakes buffet luncheon at the Melbourne Hilton. In the evening, I went to Parliament, where the Premier and Mrs John Cain were giving a reception, during which guests could go and see both chambers. The guests here included Members of Parliament, leading citizens and quite a few from the racing world. From here, I went with Rupert and Kath Clarke to a much smaller party given in an enchanting little garden by friends of the Clarkes. While at this party, I suddenly remembered I had invited Mr and Mrs Slip Mitchell, who had come to Melbourne for Cup Week from their stud at Scone, NSW, where I had stayed on a previous visit, to have drinks with me at the Hyatt! There was nothing I could do, and sadly when I got back to my hotel they had just gone, after waiting quite a long while.

On Tuesday, the Great Day had arrived. All banks, shops, schools, everything you can imagine closes on Cup Day! There is a holiday for everyone in or around Melbourne.

As on Derby Day, everywhere at Flemington racecourse was in

perfect order, with gorgeous flowers bedded out everywhere. That year, Queen Beatrix of the Netherlands and Prince Claus were the guests of honour, and drove up the course and alighted in front of the Directors' Box, where they were met by the Governor General and Lady Stephen, with the Chairman of the VRC, Mr Peter Armytage, and Mrs Armytage.

The winner of the Bicentenary Year Melbourne Cup was a fabulous mare called Empire Rose, who is nearly seventeen hands high. She was owned by New Zealanders Mr and Mrs Fred Bodle and Mr T. Bodle, and trained in New Zealand by Mr Laurie Laxon. Empire Rose had romped home an easy winner of a big race on Derby Day, then came out four days later to win the Cup! It was a great triumph for her trainer and for her owners, who have a stud in New Zealand; this was their biggest win so far.

Queen Beatrix, who has such a jolly nature and was so friendly to everyone in the Directors' Box, went down with Mr Armytage to present the cup to the winning owners. Queen Beatrix left just before the seventh and last race, having received a very warm welcome from the Australian people, and having, I am sure, enjoyed her day. We stayed until after the last race, when Rupert and Kath Clarke kindly took me back to my hotel, where I said goodbye.

I had firmly refused all invitations for that evening, as I was leaving for England next morning. I had been going non-stop since I arrived five days previously, and I wanted to pack and sort out my papers ready to write.

Next day, I was rather worried when I got a call from Cathay Pacific to say my flight was delayed from a 12.45 check-in to a 2 p.m. check-in, as I was running to a tight schedule. On arrival at Melbourne airport, I was told not to worry, that we would take off at 4 p.m., and that I would catch the 11 p.m. connection in Hong Kong. We did not in the end take off until 5.30 p.m., but having been assured about the connection, I settled down and enjoyed a blissfully comfortable and carefree flight with wonderful care from a super cabin crew.

When we landed at Hong Kong at 11.10 p.m., still thinking all was well, I strode off as quickly as I could, expecting the London flight to be waiting for us. It had, however, taken off as scheduled ten minutes earlier! I soon realized there was nothing I could do – there was no other Cathay Pacific flight until 11 p.m. next day. The airline issued a voucher for a room at the Regal Airport Hotel, where I put my bedside light out at 3.20 a.m. Australian time.

Fortunately, I always travel with my work in my hand luggage, so next day, instead of contacting friends in Hong Kong, I settled down to writing my Melbourne Cup story, and caught the 11 p.m. flight to London that night and slept well on the way home. Happily we landed at Gatwick ahead of the 8.50 a.m. we were due. I was grateful for this, as I knew I had to get up to London and change at the flat before attending a memorial service at 11 a.m. Once through customs, which I cleared quickly, Peter drove me as fast as morning rush-hour traffic would allow, to arrive at the flat at 10.30 a.m. No time for a bath! But after a quick change, I was at the Guards Chapel by 11.05 a.m.

This was for the memorial service for the late Mr Patrick Forbes, Managing Director of Moët et Chandon in London for many years, who had died far too young; I had known him as a boy when he was in the Brigade of Guards. The Guards Chapel was packed. Many friends had come from France, including Comte Ghislain de Vogüé, the Chairman of Moët et Chandon, who gave the address. Later I went to my office. From there at 6 p.m., I went home to have a bath and change before going on to a charity ball at the Dorchester. By the time I got to bed around 2 a.m. next morning, I admit I was quite tired!

I received an invitation for this autumn saying 'David Lindsay and Les Callander Girls, Sarah, Tori, and Gigi, invite you to an Explosion of Fun at Combermere in celebration of Pempe's first 60 years'. This was from the Earl of Lindsay and his three step-daughters, all four good organizers.

Over the years, I have been to family weddings and to several dances at Combermere, but I honestly think this was the very best. The decor was absolutely fabulous, the dinner delicious, the band excellent, and there were 250 really special friends of all ages. What was so clever was that it really was a surprise party, as although Pempe Lindsay had an idea something was going on, she did not see the decor in the marquee until she was in her evening dress ready to receive the guests, when David Lindsay took her in to see it. She never saw a guest list, so as she received us all it was the first moment she knew we were coming.

Their lovely family home, Combermere Abbey, was used for sitting out. Dinner took place in the marquee at tables arranged around the dance floor. The band had strict instructions from David Lindsay only to play tunes from the thirties, forties and fifties, and not too loud, which they carried out, so one was still able to enjoy a conversation once the dancing started. Around midnight, there was the most wonderful display of fireworks across the lake, in which it was reflected. These were cleverly accompanied by music, which made it all very romantic.

I have known both David and Pempe's families for so many years that this was a wonderful evening for me, seeing so many members of both families, and seeing many young friends whom I knew as debutantes, now married with teenage or older daughters of their own. I enjoyed every moment of this lovely party.

To add rather a sad note, little did I think then that September night that this would possibly be the last time I would see my dear host, whom I had known since he was a small boy, and who seemed so hale and hearty and was in such tremendous form. The following March, it was suddenly diagnosed that David Lindsay had cancer, and, to the sorrow of his very dear wife and family and a multitude of friends, David died later that year, aged only sixty-four years.

The outstanding ball of 1989 was the lovely one given by the Duke and Duchess of Argyll at Inveraray Castle to celebrate the coming of age of their only son, the Marquess of Lorne. I stayed for this dance with Iona Argyll's very dear parents, Sir Ivar and Lady Colquhoun, at Luss, their comfortable family home about thirty miles from Inverary.

We all dined at Inveraray before the dance. I had previously stayed quietly at Inveraray Castle with Ian and Iona Argyll for no special event, so I knew the setting. This time, there were the most exquisite floral decorations all over the castle. As we went up the steps, the Inveraray piper was playing. As we entered the Great Hall with its balcony all round, and an imposing array of ancient firearms and spears arranged so meticulously on the walls, Ian and Iona Argyll, the latter looking so beautiful in red, were there ready to greet us. Dinner was arranged in a large room in the castle at round, candlelit tables. I sat at Iona Argyll's table with friends all round me. We had a scrumptious dinner.

After the sweet course, we watched a charming traditional ceremony. The Inveraray piper came in and played traditional tunes. He then left the room and returned without his pipes, to receive, with great ceremony, a dram of whisky in a special silver quaich from the Duke of Argyll. Toasting His Grace and present company, he drank the dram down in one go, then saluted His Grace, and marched out.

Ian and Iona Argyll soon left us to take up their positions in the large drawing room leading to the marquee to receive the other guests arriving for the dance. Standing with them were the Marquess of

Lorne, very handsome wearing the kilt, and their only daughter, Lady Louise Campbell, looking very pretty in blue. As is still the custom at many dances in Scotland, there were dance programmes, mostly of reels and Scottish country dances, a lovely old-fashioned idea, which the young were enjoying, going round their friends, filling up their programmes. Although Inveraray has a lot of space, Ian and Iona Argyll had a very large marquee built out with a vast dance floor so that it was really comfortable for dancing, and I noticed that even at that size the dance floor was full all the evening. I have never seen so many people, old and young, with smiles on their faces! Everyone present that evening enjoyed themselves.

In 1990, having heard how good the climate was and how the Maktoum brothers had developed Dubai into an up-and-coming resort, I decided that I would like to see it and booked in a week in February. Little was I to know that the following February the Gulf War would be underway.

I was very fortunate as Mr and Mrs Maurice Flanagan, whom I had only met once at a Dubai-sponsored raceday at Longchamps, having heard of my proposed visit, invited me to stay. I stayed with them for the first four nights, but stuck to my original plan of staying at the Hyatt Regency Hotel for the last three nights, so that I could know what an ordinary visitor would find.

When I eventually arrived at the Hyatt Regency Hotel I found it first rate. I had a large comfortable bedroom and the service was excellent. There was also a large ice-skating rink adjoining the shopping area on the ground floor, and a splendid outdoor swimming pool on the top floor, beside which I lunched one day with friends.

Maurice Flanagan is head of Emirates Airlines, and he and his wife had lived in Dubai for fifteen years. They had a charming house and I was given a pretty bedroom and sitting room with my own patio for breakfast, bordering a very green lawn with an old mulberry tree in the centre and the sea just beyond. Audrey Flanagan was angelic and gave up all her time to take me round and show me everything.

I was absolutely amazed how well everything had been developed. One of the first things the Maktoum brothers did was to instal the biggest desalination plant in the world so that there was always masses of water, and instead of the rather arid, desert-like look I expected, there was a great deal of well-landscaped green grass and trees.

When we motored out on a very good modern road through the desert to luncheon at the Hatta Fort Hotel, set among the Hajan

Mountains, I noticed the verdant oases in the valley being cultivated with vegetables and other crops. There were other more sandy stretches where camels and goats roamed. On arrival at the hotel, I went for a stroll around, and found the swimming pool had piped underwater music, which did not disturb anyone sitting around the pool, but I was told was fascinating for swimmers! This was new to me.

On our way home we went camel racing at one of the two camel race tracks. This was a fascinating experience. We went into a very comfortable red-carpet-covered stand, adjacent to which was an even more luxurious stand, for men only. There were several closed-circuit television sets in both stands so that you had two good views of the racing, which seemed to go on non-stop. As soon as one race was over, the runners for the next race were lining up at the start. I walked round to the paddock, where I found all the camels sitting down with their owners and their families sitting around them. I was told that there was no prize money, but the winning owners received something in kind, such as a car or a truck. Horse racing has not yet become an established sport there.

I lunched one day at the Jebel Ali Hotel, which is right on the sea, but also has a fine pool, and a lot of attractive landscaping around it; the latter reminded me of Gleneagles. I was recommended to stay here, but as it was forty minutes out of the city, and as I was alone, I thought I would be better staying right in the city, where I was told it was perfectly safe to walk around.

I went with Mrs Michael Willis all round the Emirates Golf Club and its fabulous eighteen-hole championship golf course, and to watch the polo played on a ground of well-rolled sand. The ponies mostly came from the Argentine and looked very fit and well cared for. At the polo, I met Irishman Mr Paddy Crolty, who looks after Sheikh Mohammed bin Rashid Maktoum's riding horses, and he very kindly invited me to go round the stables the following day, which I did. There were over a hundred riding horses and ponies, some of which had been in training in England, but were not fast enough. Sheikh Mohammed's very young son came through one of the stable blocks riding his Shetland pony, and very politely passed the time of day and rode on.

One evening, Maurice and Audrey Flanagan gave a lovely buffet dinner, with over thirty guests, for me. Here I met leading personalities in the worlds of industry, banking and administration. Every English family I met were enjoying every moment of living here, and told me that quite a few English had retired out here. There is no government in Dubai, which is the best-run country I have ever visited. The country is run entirely by the Maktoum family. While I was there, I met Sheikh Ahmed bin Saeed Al Maktoum, who is a very young uncle of the Maktoum brothers who race in England. His part in running the country was then as Chairman of Emirates Airlines, which that year had won four prestigious awards.

I was so grateful to the dear Flanagans for having me to stay and for all they did for me, and I was so glad that I had the whim to visit Dubai. I hope to return one day to a country so well run, where you can walk about safely and where if you are a resident you pay no income tax!

In 1990, I went to another very well-planned 'surprise' birthday party. This was the party arranged by the Marchioness of Tavistock and her two elder sons, Lord Howland and Lord Robin Russell, to celebrate the fiftieth birthday of the Marquess of Tavistock, who two years previously had nearly died when he had a very bad stroke. Robin Tavistock survived, thanks to the prompt action of his butler, the skill of a brilliant surgeon, good nursing and the untiring care and encouragement twenty-four hours a day from his devoted wife Henrietta, helped by their two older sons, Andrew Howland and Robbie Russell.

The party took place in the Sculpture Gallery at Woburn Abbey, which is very near to but not adjoining the abbey; and guests were asked to arrive by a special route so that they did not drive past the house itself. It was a luncheon for over a hundred friends, arranged rather like a children's party. As you arrived, there was a barrel organ playing merrily, and a man on stilts. Inside was a young man riding a unicycle, with balloons and decorations everywhere. A minibus had been sent to Eton to collect Robin and Henrietta's youngest son, Lord James Russell, who brought several friends with him, including Viscount Lumley, whose parents, the Earl and Countess of Scarborough, were house guests.

When we had all gathered in one area, the house guests being the last to arrive, then Andrew Howland asked us all to keep absolutely quiet when given a sign. The moment came. Complete silence, and in walked Robin and Henrietta Tavistock. His face was one of sheer amazement; then, when he saw his father, the Duke of Bedford, who he thought was at his home in Switzerland, tears of emotion flooded his eyes for a moment. Ian Bedford had stayed at Claridge's the previous night to keep the secret. Robin told me later that he thought he was coming down to the gallery before luncheon to join the rest of the house party to see a new sculpture that had just arrived, so his amazement on walking in and seeing over a hundred faces of friends he knew well, and his father, was a most moving moment.

I had the honour of sitting at Robin's table for luncheon, between Ian Bedford, who I had also known since he was a boy, and the Hon. David Sieff, so never a dull moment! Also seated at Robin's table was the brilliant surgeon Mr Alan Crockard, who operated on Robin in 1988 to save his life. In front of us on the table was a super birthday cake, iced in Robin's racing colours, with fifty little candles in minature gold candelabra. At the end of luncheon, when Robin cut his birthday cake, David Sieff rose and asked us all to join in drinking Robin's health, to which Robin replied in two sentences, welcoming everyone and saying he hoped we would all come to his hundredth birthday party!

For Easter I once again went to Forest Mere, that wonderful health hydro near Liphook which has done me so much good for years. Way back one summer, in the fifties, when I was working on the *Tatler*, I had been through a very heavy season with one or more dances nearly every night for three months, as well as other functions and my office work by day, and was just hanging on until a three-week holiday I had planned when, to my dismay and distress, my editor came to my office to see me and told me that Gordon Beckles, who did an excellent weekly article for the magazine, had died suddenly, and could I please cancel my holiday as he could not have two regular articles out of the magazine. My heart sank, as I knew I had to cancel, but I felt so tired and ill myself that I wondered how long I could go on!

I suddenly thought of Enton Hall, a health hydro which I had heard was well run, so I booked myself in there for a long weekend. It worked miracles, and after even those few days I came out feeling better than I had done for months. I went there without fail twice a year after that visit – I must have been the only client who ever went to a ball one evening in evening dress! – until Doctor Sandieson, who was in charge at Enton, was asked if he would go and take charge at Forest Mere when it opened. So from then on, I have been to Forest Mere, where the treatments and exercising and peace and quiet really work miracles for me. Sadly, Dr Sandieson has retired.

Mrs Hughes, who runs Forest Mere so well, has always been so kind in fitting me in, and the staff are marvellous. I of course seldom went there without work and, on a weekday, I was always in touch with my office, but even so I benefited from the good treatment, comfort and fresh air. I have not had a proper two- or three-week holiday since 1962, and I am sure that if it had not been for the few days at a time that I have spent each year at Forest Mere, I could not have carried on my work until I was eighty-five!

A very original twenty-fifth wedding anniversary party that summer was the one given by Mr and Mrs Nigel Elwes in a big top circus tent beside their home, near Alton in Hampshire. The very large big top circus tent, lined in blue, was originally used by a circus and had all the correct circus lights, trapeze ladders, poles, and trimmings. Around the perimeter of the tent were colourful circus-type stalls. The waiters and waitresses wore circus costumes and there were jugglers and jesters moving around before and during dinner for around a hundred guests, to which I had kindly been invited. I had also been at their wedding.

Nigel and Carolyn Elwes had their son, Mr Andrew Elwes, and their daughters, Miss Serena and Miss Melisa Elwes, with them, and many of their young friends were at the dance. At the end of dinner, Andrew Elwes said a few words and asked everyone to rise and drink the health of his parents. Nigel Elwes then rose and made a charming speech thanking everyone for coming, and then said he had a few awards to make. First, he said he had prizes for the two young guests who had written the worst replies to their invitations. After those presentations had been made amid much laughter, Nigel said he had family presentations to make. They were cufflinks for his son, bracelets for his daughters, and a beautiful ruby and diamond ring for his dear wife as mementoes of the anniversary. So typical of Nigel Elwes, who has such a kind heart.

After that, Nigel and Carolyn took up their place near the entrance to welcome another 150 guests coming to the dance. At midnight, a fire-eater and a real circus clown in a child-size car came on to the dance floor, and gave a brief and hilarious cabaret. William Bartholomew's discotheque then returned to play magnificently, and the dance floor was, I heard, packed until dawn. After the cabaret, I walked completely round the tent, stopping continuously to talk to friends at their tables, which took me nearly an hour. Then I said goodbye, as it was long after 1 a.m., and I was motoring back to London, and I had to start off again at 11.30 a.m. (and so did my poor chauffeur, Peter) for a big pre-polo luncheon at Windsor.

Another very happy party in 1990 was the dinner and dance given by Mr and Mrs Nicholas Oppenheimer to celebrate the twenty-first birthday of their son, Mr Jonathan Oppenheimer, who is a very special, unspoilt young man, with a very kind nature, a good brain, and perfect manners. The theme of the party was to keep it simple, like a children's party. At the end of dinner, a large birthday cake with twenty-one candles was wheeled in, and on it was a miniature helicopter with the blades rotating quite fast. Jonathan had already learnt to fly a helicopter. Later there was dancing to Peter Duchin's super orchestra from New York in the large drawing room. There was also a disco in a nightclub which I never discovered. For me, this was a very nostalgic party, as I was also present at Nicky Oppenheimer's twenty-first birthday party in the same house, when he stood with his dear parents, Mr and Mrs Harry Oppenheimer, receiving the guests, just as Jonathan had done with his parents this evening. Harry and Bridget Oppenheimer were happily over from South Africa and at their splendid grandson's coming-of-age party.

It was only at midnight that Jonathan was actually twenty-one. Soon after midnight, he was quietly asked to come to the front door. Here, with only a very few close friends and a few of the family around, he looked out and there stood a gleaming black Porsche car, a surprise present from his very dear grandfather, Harry Oppenheimer.

I have such happy memories of staying with Harry and Bridget Oppenheimer in Johannesburg, and flying up with Bridget (Harry was too busy working) to their wonderful game reserve with the most comfortable house, where you can watch a wonderful selection of wild animals from their terrace in every comfort.

So many couples simply celebrate a silver, gold or diamond wedding by a party. I find it a much happier occasion if the party has been preceded by a service of thanksgiving in a church, even if it is not the church where they were married. A very happy but rather unusual silver wedding service I went to in 1990 was the very beautiful Service of Thanksgiving at the Chapel of St Mary Undercroft, Palace of Westminster, for Mr and Mrs Michael Grylls', now Sir Michael and Lady Grylls, twenty-five years of happy marriage. The reason I say unusual is that for Michael and Sarah Grylls, it was their first marriage service in a church. When they were young and all plans for their wedding had been made, they broke off their engagement. They met again, and decided to elope and to marry at a registry office. Theirs has been a very happy marriage and they have a son, Edward, who was given leave from Eton for the service and reception, and a most attractive daughter, Miss Lara Grylls, who, during the service, read or rather recited quite perfectly 'Footprints in the Sand'. After the service Michael and Sarah Grylls held a reception on the Terrace of the House of Commons.

In the spring of 1991, I went to a delightful dinner party given by the former American Ambassador, Mr Walter Annenberg, and Mrs Annenberg, at their lovely home, Sunnylands, at Rancho Mirage in California. This, like all Lee Annenberg's parties, was a gracious and beautifully arranged, most enjoyable evening. The guests included the former President of America and Mrs Ronald Reagan, whom I had met previously in London, and had found both so friendly and easy to get on with; also the President of the University of Pennsylvania; Dr Seldon Hackney and Mrs Hackney; Lord and Lady Hanson; the President of the Metropolitan Museum of Art in New York, Mr William Luers and Mrs Luers (he was formerly in the diplomatic corps and America's Ambassador in both Venezuela and Czechoslovakia); and Mrs Alfred S. Bloomingdale, widow of the Beverly Hills philanthropist.

In 1991 I also went to several parties in Sydney, Australia, during a very brief visit. Then, back in England, to a delightful Guards Polo Club Luncheon at the charming country house of the former Crown Equerry Lt-Colonel Sir John Miller. Also the 14th/20th Hussars Regimental Association's Cavalry Remembrance Parade luncheon at the Inter-Continental, at which 300 were present, including quite a few officers and men who had recently served in the Gulf War, where the regiment acted as a spearhead when the Armoured Brigade advanced into Iraq. A short while later, I went to the Hon. Robin and Mrs Denison-Pender's silver wedding party in the River Room at the Savoy Hotel, which was an exceptionally happy occasion; a Sunday luncheon for around fifty guests given by Mr and Mrs Eric Arnott at their country house in Hampshire, which was also most enjoyable; and a dinner party given at Claridge's by Lord and Lady Hanson in honour of the recently elevated Lord White of Hull. The floral decorations that evening were sensational in their beauty, transforming the rooms into an exquisite English country garden. Geraldine Hanson had arranged the whole evening to perfection.

My last big evening in 1991 started with a charity dance at Highclere Castle in Berkshire, which was exceptionally well organized by Mrs Thomas Loyd and Lady Carolyn Warren. They had found generous sponsors and persuaded their friends from miles around, even as far as

Newmarket, to come and support them, so it felt just like a private dance. I did not leave here until around 11.30 p.m.

I then motored on beyond Winchester to Cranbury Park for the ball that Major and Mrs Nigel Chamberlayne-Macdonald were giving to celebrate their son Mr Thomas Chamberlayne-Macdonald's twenty-first birthday. I arrived to find the party in full swing, with beautiful flowers everywhere, and the, today, unusual scene of nearly all the men wearing white ties and tails! The ladies were all wearing their prettiest dresses and some beautiful jewels. After finding my dear host and hostess, I met their daughter Diana Lindsay taking her two little daughters up to bed. Their baby brother, Viscount Garnock, was already in bed. Sadly, Jamie Lindsay was missing this lovely party, as he had been struck with a virus.

It was a really lovely old-fashioned ball, with one modern exception. After I had met all the family and several friends, Freddie Meynell, a director of Seary's, who I had also known since he was a boy, said I must come and see the very exciting roller skating disco, which was creating a lot of merriment. It was the first time a roller skating disco had been installed at a private party. I went through to watch the skaters, some good, some beginners who were hilariously trying to keep up. It was obviously a huge success, as I was told they were still skating at 5.30 a.m., when Nigel and Penelope Chamberlayne-Macdonald thought the ball should end.

I would like to end this chapter by mentioning four farewell parties that I was so generously given, three of which were luncheons.

The first was given to me by the Life President, the Chairman, and the Managing Director, Sir Hugh Wontner, and Sir Anthony Tuke, and Mr Giles Shepard and the other directors of the Savoy Group. This took place in a private room at the Savoy Hotel, which was a lovely surprise for me. It was a delicious, well-chosen luncheon, with a lot of reminiscing and happy laughter; an exceptionally joyful occasion for me.

The second luncheon was a smaller but equally enjoyable one, in the Directors' Room of Garrard the Crown Jewellers. It was so kindly given for me by the Chairman, Mr Edward Green, and the other directors of Garrard. Here, we also had an excellent luncheon, and it was the greatest fun.

It was only when I was on my way to the third luncheon and

read the guest list that I realized I would be the only woman among twenty-five high-powered businessmen! This was the delightful luncheon that Lord Forte and his son, the Hon. Rocco Forte, so kindly gave for me in a private room at Grosvenor House. Here again, we had a very good luncheon. Charles Forte made a very endearing speech, in which he also included the new Portuguese Ambassador, who was present. I also thoroughly enjoyed this very kind farewell party. At each of these parties, I was so very kindly presented with charming mementoes, which I shall treasure.

My very last farewell party took place after my retirement, in October. This was a very carefully planned dinner at Claridge's, given for me by the Hearst Corporation of America, and the National Magazine Company in England, for whom I had worked very happily for twenty-one years, plus another eleven years on *Queen* magazine, which they had bought, with me, in 1970. My joint kind hosts were the President of the Hearst Corporation, Mr Frank Bennack, the Executive Vice-President, Mr Gil Maurer, the Chairman, Mr Randolph Hearst, Mr Richard Deems, who was in charge of the magazine side of the Corporation when we were taken over, and the Managing Director of the National Magazine Company, Mr Terence Mansfield, who also worked on *Queen* magazine, but joined the National Magazine Company before *Queen* magazine was taken over. There were around two hundred guests, many of whom were kind and true friends who had helped me so much in my work for my 'Jennifer's Diary' over the years. Also, my beloved son Jim, who had come from Canada, my dear nephew John Kemp-Welch and his sweet wife Diana, and my dear niece Penelope Bourdillon and her super husband Mervyn Bourdillon.

At the end of the dinner Jocelyn Stevens made a speech, and so did Randolph Hearst, Terry Mansfield and the President, Frank Bennack, who also gave me the most wonderful and original farewell presents from the two companies. They were two beautiful Tiffany silver photograph frames, and 50,000 first-class flying miles! Also ground transport for life, but not always driven by Peter. Nothing in the world could give me more joy or have been kinder than to give me ground and air transport.

When I have got this book finally finished, I am going to carefully plan my first trip abroad that I don't have to write about!

SIXTEEN

Looking back

These memoirs may give the impression that my life was non-stop 'fun and functions' – but I can assure readers that there is also a great deal of very hard work behind the scenes when writing a social diary. Firstly, there is endless checking. The golden rule is 'Check, check, and check again'. I have, through all the years, never failed to read and correct my galley proofs and my page proofs, and wherever I have been travelling in the world, proofs have always reached me to check. That alone entails many hours of concentration and hard work, particularly if you have not got the right reference books with you.

I travelled the world with the current *Debrett*, which the publishers most kindly bound for me without any advertisements, to lessen the weight. There is one angle of my work of which I am really proud, and that is that I have never cost the *Tatler*, *Queen* magazine or *Harpers & Queen* one penny in litigation fees. This is something that none of my predecessors on the *Tatler* achieved! Everyone who wrote the diary before my days cost Illustrated Newspapers quite a lot of money in lawyers' fees and damages.

I have seen a great number of changes during my long life, not least the changes in the Royal Family. I don't remember much about King Edward VII, but I do well remember the reign of King George V and Queen Mary. They were both greatly respected and beloved by the people of this country, but they were also very remote. There was always a bevy of courtiers around them who kept everyone except their close friends and relations at bay. The courts and royal functions were all much more formal than in King George VI's reign. Queen Mary, when she lived in the West Country as a widow during the war, lived a very simple life, but everyone was still in awe of her.

King George V and Queen Mary's eldest son, the Prince of Wales, later Duke of Windsor, was quite different. He was a good-looking and dashing young man who fulfilled his official duties well; and by the twenties he was very popular everywhere. He was also keen on hunting, point-to-pointing and golf, and as he grew up he had quite a busy social life, but not always in a very suitable social world. His abdication, after having succeeded but not been crowned King, rocked the country.

For England, the abdication proved a stroke of good fortune. The Duke of York, who with the Duchess of York and their two young daughters had up to then lived a very balanced and normal life with a group of sound friends, a house in London, and the use of a medium-sized country house, suddenly had to take over as King. What a splendid King he made with his wonderful Queen, now Queen Elizabeth the Queen Mother, to help him. During the worrying war days, as I have written earlier in these memoirs, they set such a fine example to their people and did all they could to comfort the suffering. They were never aloof.

They were also close to and always had the confidence of their children. They brought up their elder daughter, Princess Elizabeth, now our beloved Queen, to have the tremendous sense of duty to her country that she has shown all through her life; with the wisdom she learnt from her parents, she has made us a wonderful Queen. Their younger daughter, Princess Margaret, was not so strictly brought up, and I was always told that, as she grew older, she was spoilt by her father, who adored her. I wonder if the late King, had he still been alive, he might even have allowed his beloved younger daughter to marry her first great love, a divorcee.

The Queen has set us all the finest example of a really superb monarch, dedicated to her country, her husband and her children. But Her Majesty has also not remained aloof, like her grandparents. She is frequently seen at unofficial as well as official functions. Like Queen Elizabeth the Queen Mother, who has set such a fine example, The Queen takes the keenest interest in those she meets and the keenest concern in those in need. She also has a great sense of fun. Her Majesty has never put a foot wrong.

The Prince of Wales has inherited so much of his mother's sense of duty and caring, and of the Duke of Edinburgh's quick eye and ready repartee. Having watched him grow up, I consider him a splendid Prince of Wales who fully realizes the gigantic problems of the world that lie ahead. In my very humble opinion it would be good for the country if The Queen soon appointed her eldest son her deputy, to work like the deputy chairman of a company, so that he could share her responsibilities, see the day-to-day State Papers sent to The Queen and gain knowledge and wisdom from Her Majesty. The Prince of Wales chose a beautiful and caring wife who has produced two fine young sons, Prince William and Prince Harry, who are being brought up in a most sensible manner. Her Royal Highness, who has become the world's most popular younger woman, has also carried out her official duties devotedly, with dignity and great caring for those who are suffering.

The Princess Royal has certainly added a new dimension to the life traditionally led by the monarch's daughter, in the area of her work for charity, and her Presidency of the Save the Children Fund, in all the travelling she has done on the Fund's behalf, and in her other work, aiding industry, fashion, and in her regimental commitments, as well as her sporting activities. It must be the first time that a reigning monarch's daughter has competed as an eventer, including representing England in the Olympic Games. She has also ridden both under National Hunt rules and on the flat!

I have also see tremendous changes in transport and communications. When I was young, horses not motor vans or lorries, were used for delivery. Coal was delivered in both town and country on horse-drawn carts. In the towns it was in bags, and the coalman driving the horse often wore what looked like a folded coal bag on his head. If they were not on a specific delivery, they would drive round the then comparatively quiet streets shouting out 'coal'.

Before the First World War, cars were a luxury, aeroplanes were in their infancy, and there were round hot air balloons and long sausage-like ones. The German long sausage ones in World War I were called zeppelins and sent on bombing expeditions. The hansom cab was still on the London streets; then the very old-fashioned taxis started to take over, and motor buses started to supersede horse-drawn buses, which were always drawn by a pair. The first motor buses I can remember were very old-fashioned: all the tops were open, with a sort of waterproof apron hanging from the back of the seat in front which you held over your chest if it rained. I remember these buses frequently used to boil, and the driver had to stop and take the cap off the radiator to let it cool down.

As teenagers, one played all sorts of games from the top of a bus, including Beaver, in which you shouted if you saw a man with a beard – the first person to shout scored. If you saw a red beard, you shouted

'King Beaver' and scored double points. There were far fewer bearded men in those days!

Another game we played was when passing a bus going in the other direction. You smiled broadly at any unknown passenger, and if they acknowledged you, thinking they knew you, you scored a point. We always rushed to sit on top and get an offside rail seat, sometimes sitting one behind the other so that we were close up for these games. My father would have had a fit if he'd known about our harmless fun.

Hyde Park was full of nannies with children, the small ones in large, wonderful-looking prams; the nannies vied with one another to have the biggest and the best of these vehicles. The prams were often crested on the side, just as a lot of private cars were for many years. I think this rather died out when the English followed the Americans in changing their cars more often.

On pre-war Sundays in London, the ladies wore their best clothes, always with a hat and gloves, to walk down Rotten Row, in Hyde Park, always with an escort, who was often wearing a top hat and morning coat. I remember being dressed up to walk there with my father, who always seemed to stop to greet friends every few yards.

In those days, Tattersalls held their auction sales of horses, more hunters and hacks than racehorses, at their repository beside Knightsbridge Green on Mondays. The horses for sale came into the stables there on the Friday, and would-be buyers could go and see them over the weekend. As I grew older, this was a favourite place to go. Sometimes I also went to watch the sales on Monday.

It was fashionable in the twenties to drive out of London for Sunday luncheon, usually to somewhere like Dorking, Maidenhead, or Bray.

In the hunting field, ladies who rode astride became more numerous during and after World War I. It was not until long after World War II that velvet hunting caps were worn by anyone but the Master of the Foxhounds and hunt servants; men and women followers wore top hats or a bowler hat. Today, you see dozens of velvet caps at any meet.

The telephone service was in its infancy while I was growing up – it was unusual more than usual to find a telephone in a private house in 1912. There were no fridges or deep freezes; ice cream was made in a wooden bucket with a freezing mixture. Nor were there electric carpet sweepers – a stiff broom and dustpan and brush was all the poor housemaids had to use – and very few people had electric light. It was oil lamps or gas, which was considered a luxury. I can remember gas mantles suddenly going up in a flame; then all was black and they had to be changed.

Wireless I never remember in any household until the twenties. I well remember my first crystal set, which my father gave me and which I treasured. The quality of reception improved amazingly quickly and so did programmes. There were not the incessant interviews we have today. Ministers and other VIPs were able to go home and have a good night's rest after an important conference or business trip, instead of being waylaid as they are today by reporters putting words into their mouths when they are desperately tired.

Television was rare in the home until after World War II, but I think I remember one or two in wealthy houses in the late thirties. There was not the terrible publicity we have today; newspapers were more controlled and not nearly so sensational. Today the media run the world – or try to! I have lived to see Sputniks flying round the world, and a satellite launched, and to see, on the screen, Man land on the Moon. It was, I thought, a very moving moment. My great-grandchildren will probably go and spend holidays on the Moon or Mars!

At dances between the wars, there were still chaperones sitting round the edge of the ballroom. After the Second World War, a girl usually went to a dance in a party, in which an older couple were the so-called chaperones, but they seldom sat round on gilded chairs at the dance.

Travelling, though slower, was much more comfortable than nowadays. The seats in the railway carriages were much better upholstered. Above everything, there were always plenty of porters, whether you were arriving in London or the country, to look after your luggage. This was the same at airports. In those days, Croydon and Northolt were the main airports for London, and here there were always masses of willing porters. When Croydon finally closed down, many of the porters moved to Heathrow, and I often got a porter there who recognized me from the old days, so for a while I got very special service.

Nowhere was as noisy as the world is today. The traffic in the streets of the city is so heavy now, and although we no longer have the clanking of trams, we have noisy exhausts, especially from young gentlemen in Porsches, the motorbike messengers, the screeching sirens of security cars, the never-ending electric drills digging up the streets, the demolitions, the mechanized garbage collectors, and so it goes on. Also, indoors, and sometimes outdoors, we have the much noisier pop concerts and dance bands that deafen you. But I think the saddest change worldwide is the terrible pushing of drugs and the addiction of so many young people all over the world. That is, I think, the world's greatest tragedy. It leads to crime and it must be overcome.

Going to church or to a wedding up to, I think, the fifties, you never saw a lady at morning service or at a wedding not wearing a hat, or with at least a piece of black lace covering her head. Now I can count on one hand the ladies at church on Sunday, besides myself, wearing a hat, and often at weddings, and sometimes even at memorial services, half of those present are hatless and gloveless.

What amazes me most, and I find it very odd, is that so many brides who have been living with the bridegroom, often for ages before their wedding, still walk up the aisle in virgin white with a veil, and sometimes they even wear the veil covering their faces!

I have not mentioned much of my private life since 1944 because my son, until he went to Canada in 1959, and my work have really taken up all my time and thoughts. I have never remarried, partly for that reason, although three kind gentlemen have asked me to marry them. One I nearly did marry, and then he died, to my great sorrow, as the result of cancer.

Besides having had a wonderful chauffeur in Peter Haimes, I have had some very sweet and efficient young ladies who have helped me tremendously in my work, as working on Jennifer's Diary you have to work hard! It is also vital to be very accurate, as well as show all-round efficiency. I have only, as far as I know, had one disloyal secretary. She was exceedingly inefficient, towards which I am afraid I am not very tolerant! After I fired her, she told the press that I was cruel to my secretaries. For the good fortune of other employers, she gave up being a secretary and took up freelance writing.

So many of the really super secretaries I had left to get married, or if they stayed on then left to have their babies. Happily, most of them have kept in touch with me, and from those I don't talk to during the year I always get Christmas cards, which I find very endearing. I haven't got space to mention them all, but two of the special ones were Jane Hodges, who became Mrs John Hughes, and Fleur Tukham. Jane, who came to me in her mid-twenties, stayed on after her marriage and did not leave me until she was having her first baby and was with me for over four years. Jane was one of the kindest people I ever knew; to her everything was possible! She carried on so well when I was

away, was tremendously respected in the office, where she coped so
well with numerous queries, and I could leave much of the office work
to her.

Fleur came to me in 1987 as a junior straight from St Godric's
Secretarial College at the age of nineteen years, so she had not learnt
any bad ways in other offices! Fleur, who is very bright and learns
quickly, had been well trained. She had also been exceptionally well
brought up by her parents to care for others and never to be late, and
was always in my office early. Fleur was very well educated at Priors
Field girls' school, and quickly picked up my office routine; she is
respected by everyone at *Harpers & Queen* and has the warmest, kindest
nature and will help anyone and work any hours!

When my senior secretary left, I made Fleur head secretary, which
she coped with very well. Then when the recession came, and I was
asked to try and manage with one secretary, Fleur did all the work
alone quite brilliantly until the day I retired. Latterly I could also send
her to functions, which she wrote about well, and I had glowing
reports each time from the hostess.

Through life, I have been fortunate in having so many true friends
to whom I could turn for advice and who I have been able to stay with
all over the world for functions, or who have invited me on trips or
to various functions, most of which I have been able to write about
for my diary. Some I have just stayed with quietly for a badly needed
break, others have been there to lean on when I have had problems or
sorrow in my life. Deep in my heart, I am so grateful to them all, and
they all come to my mind frequently, whether or not they are still alive.

Among those I miss now who are no longer alive are my ancient
cousin Mrs Richard Morten, who gave me a job and took care of me
when I ran away from home at sixteen; Mr and Mrs Alan Butler, two
generations of Lord and Lady Willoughby de Brokes, Sir Malcolm and
Lady McAlpine, Canadian Mrs Robert Holt of Nassau, Sir Harold
and Lady Mitchell, Sir Adrian Jarvis, who always included me in his
parties going to Le Touquet and Deauville and very frequently took
me racing, to theatres, and was always around when I needed him;
also Major and Mrs Charles Mills at Hilborough, Sir Arthur Pilkington, who was such a dear kind man of whom I was very fond; Mrs
Robin McAlpine, who was a very dear close friend and died so young
of cancer; Sir Noel and Lady Charles – Grace Charles, who was always
very chic, helped me over clothes by lending me her French 'toiles' to
have copied; the late Lord Cornwallis, Mr Dick Wilkins, who always

included me in his Cheltenham National Hunt Festival parties; and many, many more.

Among my dearest friends I happily still have around to enjoy are Mr and Mrs Malcolm McAlpine, who have both been truly wonderful friends to whom I can always turn for sound advice, or for a rest at their comfortable home in Sussex; the Marquess and Marchioness of Abergavenny – the latter, on one occasion, arrived at dawn, after a long drive, to help me when I had been with a very dear mutual friend and he had died. I shall never forget what a staunch comfort Patricia was then; they have both been such wise and dear friends for many years, as have Earl and Countess Cadogan, whom I have also known for so many years, and from whom I have an open invitation to stay in Scotland at any time; also Mr and Mrs Antony Norman, whom I have mentioned before in these memoirs; Mr and Mrs Vane Ivanović, with whom I have stayed so often in Formentor; his sister, Mrs Neil Maclean; Mrs Bud McDougald in Toronto; the Hon. Mrs Julian Berry, and her husband when he was alive; Greek-born Mrs Nico Brissimis, who has taken such care of me in Greece; Lord and Lady Howard de Walden and his family, with whom I have spent very happy times; Lord and Lady Killearn; Mrs Margery Sangster, whom I have mentioned; Mr and Mrs Terence Mansfield; the Reverend Charles and Mrs Roderick, who I can always turn to for advice; Lord and Lady Hanson who are both so kind; and many, many, more dear friends. The ones I have mentioned here are very special to me.

My very special younger relations and friends include my nephew and his dear wife, Mr and Mrs John Kemp-Welch, and my niece and her husband, Mr and Mrs Mervyn Bourdillon; also Sir Thomas and Lady Pilkington – they are particularly special to me – and their young son Richard Pilkington; Mr Adrian and the Hon. Mrs White (Jessie White always gives me a birthday luncheon! and keeps in touch to know I am well); the Marquess and Marchioness of Tavistock who are so caring and kind; Mr Simon and Lady Victoria Leatham; Mr and Mrs Nigel Elwes, the Marquess and Marchioness of Zetland and Mrs Terence Mansfield.

In my old age the friendship and caring of these dear younger people means so much to me.

I look back on eighty-six interesting years in a life which has, like most others, had ups and downs. I have for many years had to work very hard, which I do not regret. God gave me the strength to do so. I know that I have been far happier working hard, with good health and plenty of friends, than many women I have known who have been endowed with such great worldly goods, but who have lived lives of perpetual discontent.

I would not have written these memoirs if it had not been for so many people of all ages asking me to do so. If I had known what hard work it would be writing against the clock, I would never have started! However, here they are, not, I am afraid, nearly as well done as I would like them to have been. With only eight months to write about eighty-five years, it has been like trying to pour a gallon into a pint pot – a lot has not gone in. I know I must have left out so much of what I meant to put in, and left out so many people I wanted to include, which causes me distress. I hope they will understand. I also hope what I have written will be of interest to readers all over the world, many of whom, I anticipate, will be the loyal and dear readers of my Jennifer's Diary in *Harpers & Queen*.

I truly miss my Jennifer's Diary readers, to whom I have really dedicated the last forty-seven years of my life. So many readers of my diary that I do not know have sweetly come up to me in the street or while shopping and told me how much they miss me, which is very endearing. I have tried to keep a high standard in my life, and in my Jennifer's Diary. It will break my heart if I live to see the standard of Jennifer's Diary drop.

Now that my memoirs are finished, I feel at my age I may very soon go to the departure lounge for yet another exciting flight – this time to the unknown!

INDEX